Beyond Cleveland On Foot

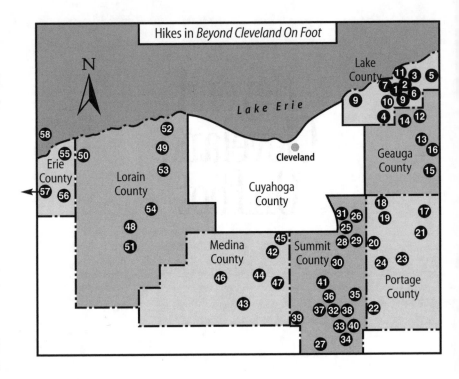

Hikes in *Beyond Cleveland On Foot*

Beyond Cleveland On Foot

2nd Edition

Patience Cameron Hoskins
Rob and Peg Bobel

GRAY & COMPANY, PUBLISHERS
CLEVELAND

Photo credits are listed on page 340.

Gray & Company, Publishers
1588 E. 40th St.
Cleveland, OH 44103-2302
info@grayco.com

Library of Congress Cataloging-in-Publication Data:
Hoskins, Patience Cameron.
Beyond Cleveland on Foot / Patience Cameron Hoskins, Robert
and Peggy Bobel.—2nd ed.
Includes bibliographical references and index.
1. Hiking—Ohio—Guidebooks.
2. Walking—Ohio—Guidebooks.
3. Ohio—Guidebooks. I. Bobel, Robert. II. Bobel, Peggy. III. Title.
GV199.42.O3H67 2003   796.5'1'09771—dc21
2003002486

This guide was prepared on the basis of the most accurate information available to the authors at the time of publication. However, because of constantly changing trail conditions due to natural and other causes, the authors disclaim any liability whatsoever
for the condition of the trails described herein, for occurrences
happening on them, or for the accuracy of descriptions. Users of
this guide are cautioned not to place undue reliance upon the
continuing validity of the information contained herein and to
use this guide at their own risk.

ISBN 1-886228-40-X
Printed in the United States of America

First printing

Contents

Preface to the Second Edition

We were very pleased to be asked to help update Patience Hoskins's excellent first edition of *Beyond Cleveland On Foot*. After having completely reviewed that edition line by line, we take our hats off to Patience. She did a wonderful job and deserves the gratitude of the entire Northeast Ohio hiking community.

Since the first edition of *Beyond Cleveland On Foot*, there have been significant changes and additions to the trails of Northeast Ohio. Metropolitan park districts in particular have added new trails and whole new park units. Some parks that were just getting under way in 1996 now have well-developed trail systems, and a number have new visitor or nature centers. In this completely revised second edition we have updated all the hikes and added six entirely new hikes, including four new town hikes.

Northeast Ohio hikers can look forward to even more additions to local trail systems, since significant countywide, and even regional, open-space plans are currently under way. For instance, in 2001 Summit County unveiled its Trail & Greenway Plan, the result of two years of planning with local communities and citizens, and the Cuyahoga County Planning Commission presented its greenspace plan early in 2002. Of particular interest, an eight-county plan covering much of the region presented in this guidebook is emerging from the work of the Northeast Ohio Regional Park Consortium.

Underlying the political lines on maps are natural regions connected by rivers and separated by watershed divides. The hikes in this guide will take you to two distinct physiographic regions—the narrow band of Lake Plains along Lake Erie and the Glaciated Appalachian Plateau. Through these hikes you can explore the watersheds of nine rivers: the Grand, Chagrin, Cuyahoga, Rocky, Black, Vermilion, Huron, Tuscarawas, and Mahoning. You will cross a continental divide separating streams flowing to Lake Erie from those flowing toward the Ohio River; and you will see some of the most beautiful places in Northeast Ohio.

As Barry Lopez reminds us in his small, eloquent book, *The Rediscovery of North America*, our American way of life has tended to alienate us from the land, leading to a disconnection from place. He explores what we need to do to reconnect to these places we call home. We hope this book encourages you to do as he suggests: "[look] upon the land not as its possessor but as a companion," and in so doing "begin . . . to find a home, to sense how to fit a place." Lopez recommends that to do that, we should walk the land, visit it frequently, listen to it, and pay attention to it.

People seek parks for many different reasons ranging from an interest in plants and animals to a desire for good, healthy exercise. And whether the parks are called reservations, preserves, or rail-trails, they are all, in essence, refuges—for all of nature, for ourselves. Whatever you seek, whether solace or companionship or greater understanding of the place we live in, we hope this guide helps you find it.

—Rob and Peg Bobel

Preface to the First Edition

Beyond Cleveland On Foot is a companion volume to *Cleveland On Foot: A Guide to Walking and Hiking in Cleveland and Vicinity.* That book, first published in 1992 by H & P Publishing Co., contained 33 walks and hikes in urban and suburban Cleveland, including Cleveland Metroparks, Cuyahoga Valley National Park, and selected state parks and nature preserves, all primarily in Cuyahoga County. It is now out of print. The current third edition of *Cleveland On Foot*, revised, updated, and expanded to 45 walks and hikes, with all-new maps, was published by Gray & Company in 2001.

Beyond Cleveland On Foot follows the same format as our previous books but describes 58 new walks and hikes in seven counties surrounding Cleveland: Lake, Geauga, Portage, Summit, Medina, Lorain, and Erie. While no attempt has been made to include all the possible walks and hikes in the parks and communities of these counties, those described in this book are a thorough sampling of the rich resources we have in our corner of the state.

The walks and hikes are listed by county and organized by degree of difficulty, i.e., easy, moderate, or strenuous. Although my ratings are arbitrary, I have suggested these categories based on the experience of the average walker or hiker. Walks are generally in urban or suburban communities and hikes are on wooded trails in parks or forests. If a trail is also suitable for bicycling or cross-country skiing, that is mentioned in the text. Information about hiking preparation and area resources (included in *Cleveland On Foot*) has been updated and reprinted as a useful aid for both the novice and experienced hiker.

Included in each chapter of *Beyond Cleveland On Foot* are hike distance and approximate hiking time, a description of terrain and special features, directions from the nearest interstate highway, and information about parking and restrooms at the trailhead.

Historical walks in three of northeast Ohio's small towns are included here because of the popularity of urban and suburban walking tours. These are Vermilion in Erie County, Oberlin in Lorain County, and Hudson Village in Summit County. I have provided architectural information, when available, and have consulted with experts to ensure the accuracy of historical information. Geological data has been included to enhance the hiking experience in many of the parks where rock formations are of unusual interest. This information has been verified by the Cleveland Museum of Natural History's Curator of Invertebrate Paleontology, Joseph T. Hannibal, who also supplied the information in Appendix A.

To those who have found *Cleveland On Foot* a valuable resource for the enjoyment of our great outdoors, I hope *Beyond Cleveland On Foot* will enlarge the scope of your hiking adventures and bring many hours of further enjoyment of nature's beauty.

—Patience Cameron Hoskins

Beyond Cleveland On Foot

Introduction

This book is for people who enjoy the outdoors, or want to, and who want to find new ways to explore the world beyond their own front door. *Beyond Cleveland On Foot* is for newcomers to hiking as well as experienced walkers and hikers who wish to expand the territory with which they are already familiar and comfortable.

Beyond Cleveland On Foot is for newcomers to Northeast Ohio, too, as it introduces the region's great variety of natural resources. And it is for people who have lived in metropolitan Cleveland and surrounding counties for many years—possibly all their lives—but who may not yet have discovered the wonderful hiking opportunities that abound in these areas. These hikes are for walkers with varied abilities and interests. They can be enjoyed in as little as an hour or two or as long as a full day.

We have checked our descriptions carefully and hope there are no errors or omissions, but if some have crept in please send a note in care of the publisher so that we can continue improve this guide for the next edition. Even if the descriptions are satisfactory, we'd like to know that, too.

We encourage you to share the special joy that comes from walking and hiking, and the sharpening of the senses that makes one feel more alive. We hope you have as much pleasure taking these walks and hikes as we have had in researching and describing them, and that this guide will be only a start for you on a lifelong hiking adventure.

What is in this guide?

The walks and hikes described here are categorized by county, and within county by degree of difficulty (easy, moderate, or strenuous) for average walkers or hikers. Several chapters contain several walks or hikes that may be taken singly or combined for a longer excursion.

Easy Walks usually involve little exertion; just the pace and distance you set for yourself. Most of the easy walks in this book are in small parks, usually on trails under 5 miles long, and on terrain that is mostly flat. Others are in towns and entail walking primarily on sidewalks. Easy walks or hikes often have something of historic, scenic, architectural, geological, or other unusual interest to enjoy. They are also generally suitable for children.

Moderate Hikes are usually 5 miles or more in length and entail ascending and descending moderate or even steep hills for short distances. They may have uneven footing or present obstacles such as stream crossings, but they are generally suitable for average and more experienced hikers in good health.

Strenuous Hikes are usually between 5 and 10 miles and over hilly or rough terrain. Some of these hikes are in remote areas and require carrying a day pack with food and liquid and wearing sturdy boots. On these longer hikes there may be steep ascents and descents and stream crossings without the aid of bridges.

For all hikes described in *Beyond Cleveland On Foot* a note of CAUTION is inserted in the trail descriptions to warn hikers of hazards they need to be especially aware of, i.e., a steep cliff, dangerous erosion on the trail, a swift stream crossing, a bridle trail, an active railroad or road crossing, and any other potential threat to safety or enjoyment.

For any of the walks and hikes described, the prudent hiker, of course, may turn around at any point and return to the car earlier than anticipated. It is especially important to leave the woods when thunder is heard, no matter how distant, as a lightning storm can be very dangerous to the hiker.

Why walk?

Years ago everyone walked out of necessity—to work, to school, to the store. Taking a stroll was a common pastime. Nowadays, having grown up with all sorts of motorized transportation available, we seem to have far less need to walk. But there is value in taking to the woodland trails or even to the neighborhood sidewalks to get away from a frenetic modern lifestyle. Many have learned to love the peacefulness and rhythm of walking and hiking. They appreciate the benefits of physical exercise and the mental relaxation that ensues from participating in this sport. This guide will introduce some of the treasures and pleasures of Northeast Ohio that you can easily observe on foot.

When out walking, slow down and observe. Look for wild animals and their footprints, many kinds of birds in all their splendor, a wide variety of ferns, mushrooms, trees, and wildflowers, cloud formations, and stunning views.

How do you get started? The most important element is your attitude. The hardest part is making a determined effort to get out, perhaps alone or with a friend or an organized group. Once you get past all the excuses you can invent for not walking, you will soon find yourself anxious to go outdoors and begin exploring. There are beautiful days for outdoor exploring in Northeast Ohio in every season.

Hiking Preparation

Advance planning for a hike is the key to a successful and enjoyable trip. *Be prepared before you leave home.* The most basic item to take with you on a hike or walk is a map of the area. Review the chapter in this book for the specific hike you wish to take and study its accompanying map. Sources for trail maps for other areas are listed in the next section, "Hiking Resources."

Next in importance is determining how much time to allow for the walk, what the degree of difficulty is, and how to reach the hiking area. These pointers are enclosed in the box at the beginning of each chapter's hike.

It is also good practice to carry a compass with you. Inexpensive models are available at any outdoor store. Most of the trail descriptions in this book refer to points of the compass and often direct you to head north, east, south, or west rather than make a left or right turn. It is helpful to learn the rudiments of reading a compass. At a minimum, the compass needle, which always points approximately north, will keep you from walking in circles should you lose your way. When you follow the direction in which you wish to go, or another one in consistent relation to it, you will eventually reach a road or other major landmark. You need to know in which direction you are heading when you start out on your hike, so that upon returning you can head in the opposite direction. In the woods, prominent landmarks, such as a stream or rock formation, will help orient you. (Not many trees are unusual enough to serve as a guide or landmark.)

When hiking, comfort is of utmost importance. Most hikers find it helpful to wear clothing in layers that can either be removed or added to as the temperature changes. Cotton keeps the body cooler in hot weather than cotton/polyester blends. Wool in cool weather provides warmth even when wet. Synthetic fabrics such as pile and fleece are an excellent choice for outdoor use, and are lighter than wool. Proper socks provide insulation, padding, and skin comfort. Socks made for hiking come in a variety of weights and blends, and can alleviate the need to wear two pair. Waterproof rain gear can provide protection from an unexpected shower. Rain protection comes "built in" in many of the newer coats and jackets through the use of breathable waterproof fabrics such as Gore-tex.

Boots are the single most important piece of equipment you will acquire and the most difficult to choose. On some easy walks, tennis or walking shoes will be adequate, but on rough terrain and hills, boots with ankle support and a good tread will serve you better.

A beltpack or backpack is necessary for carrying snacks, lunch, water or juice, and extra clothing that you will put on or take off. Try to strike a balance between taking too much and taking too little. Generally, the lighter you go, the better. It is especially important to carry liquids in the pack in all seasons. One can get dehydrated easily without realizing it, even on a winter hike. Basic items to include in the pack are:

- Map
- Compass
- Adhesive strips, tissues
- Moleskin (to apply to sore spots on the feet)
- Insect repellent
- Canteen of water or juice
- Fruit, trail snacks, sandwich
- Pedometer (optional, to determine mileage)
- Small field guides for identifying flowers, trees, or birds.

Safety should be a concern but not a worry. All the hikes in this book are in public places, though sometimes not in heavily populated areas. If you have any doubts about an area, don't continue. This holds true for dangerous weather conditions such as a sudden thunderstorm. Because there is safety in numbers, it is better to hike with a companion or in a group, so that help will be available in the event of an accident or injury.

On road hikes, make a habit of facing traffic as you walk, and walk in single file if traffic is heavy. On bridle trails when a horse and rider approach, trail safety requires that you stop immediately, step off to the side of the bridle path, and remain quiet and still until they are well beyond you. This behavior prevents a fearful horse from rearing up and injuring you or the rider. On paved all-purpose trails, keep to the right so that faster-moving bicyclists and joggers may pass you.

Many dog owners enjoy including their pets on the hikes. Dogs can be great hiking companions and are welcome in most parks. Some areas, such as state nature preserves and beaches, do not allow dogs and are posted accordingly. Parks allowing dogs usually require they be leashed and under control at all times. Hiking courtesy calls for cleaning up after your pet, and more and more parks offer disposable clean-up bags for this purpose.

Your own capacity and endurance should guide your pace and the distance, and length of time you hike. The time suggested in these descriptions is based upon an average pace of 2½ miles per hour or upon particular features of the hike. On steep hills the going will be somewhat slower. Walking uphill is harder on your heart and lungs, but walking downhill is harder on your knees. Adjust the pace according to your comfort. A hiking stick is most helpful on hills, both going up and going down. Rest when your body tells you to, but not longer than a few minutes so as not to break your hiking rhythm.

As in every enterprise, using common sense is basic. You will develop trail sense, too. Watch the path for footprints and disturbed vegetation or leaves, especially in the fall when leaves nearly obscure the trail. You will gradually learn to recognize the trail (when there are no trail blazes or markings) by an opening with noticeable clearing and lack of vegetation, or with wildlife tracks or human bootprints. If you feel you have lost the trail, turn around and retrace your steps to the last intersection. Observation is the key, not only for trail safety but for enjoyment, too.

A last reminder—use the carry in/carry out policy. Part of our responsibility in hiking, walking, and enjoying our great outdoors is to carry *out* whatever you carry *in*. Many dedicated hikers take along a small trash bag and routinely pick up litter as they walk. Some hiking clubs and other outdoor organizations regularly schedule trail cleanup hikes. The carry in/carry out philosophy includes carrying out *more* than you carry in. If everyone did this, consider how much we would enhance the walking experience for all.

Blazes

Trails are often marked by a special symbol repeated frequently on trees or posts indicating the trail's route. Sometimes it is the picture of a hiker, jogger, or cross-country skier on a metal marker nailed to the tree. More often, it is a colored patch painted on a tree six to eight feet above the path.

Illustrated below are typical Buckeye Trail blazes encountered on some of the trails described in this book. A single light-blue 2-by-6-inch blaze indicates the hiking trail is straight ahead. Two blazes, one above the other, indicate a turn in the trail: the lower blaze is always fixed and the *upper* blaze indicates the direction of the turn. A variation used for the turn sign is an arrow pointing toward the trail continuation.

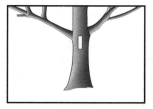 

Hiking Resources

There are many more walks available in this area than could possibly be included even in two books. After trying the hikes in *Beyond Cleveland On Foot* and *Cleveland On Foot*, you may want to pursue some of these other hiking opportunities on your own and obtain information from the organizations listed below.

LAKE COUNTY

General information about Lake County is available from:

Lake County Visitors Bureau, 440-354-2424

Lake County History Center, 440-255-8979; www.lakevisit.com.

Lake Metroparks

Lake Metroparks consists of 25 parks and recreation areas encompassing more than 5,000 acres of land throughout Lake County. Among these facilities are Lake Farmpark, Children's Schoolhouse Nature Park, Concord Woods (park headquarters), Erie Shores Golf Course, Fairport Harbor Lakefront Park, Lakefront Lodge Park, Lakeshore Reservation, and Pine Ridge Country Club. Penitentiary Glen Reservation features a large nature center and wildlife rehabilitation center. A seasonal program guide called *Parks Plus!* lists daily activities and programs of all kinds for all ages.

Lake Metroparks: 800-227-7275; www.lakemetroparks.com.

Headlands Beach State Park

Headlands Beach State Park (Ch. 7) and Headlands Dunes State Nature Preserve are located in Painesville Township in Lake County, just west of Fairport Harbor. These parks on Lake Erie offer pleasant beach walking. Walking on the sand is permitted, but visitors are asked not to walk on any plants.

Ohio's statewide Buckeye Trail begins (or ends) in Headlands Beach State Park and is marked with 2-by-6-inch blue rectangles painted on trees or posts. Information about the park can be obtained from:

Headlands Beach State Park: 216-881-8141.

Headlands Dunes State Nature Preserve is located at the east end of Headlands Beach (440-563-9344).

Mentor Marsh State Nature Preserve

Mentor Marsh State Nature Preserve (Ch. 7) consists of 644 acres adjacent to Headlands Beach State Park owned by the Ohio Department of Natural Resources and the Cleveland Museum of Natural History. The blue-blazed Buckeye Trail is identified here as the Zimmerman Trail. There are other short hiking trails accessible from local roads.

Mentor Marsh Nature Center: 440-257-0777.

Holden Arboretum

The Holden Arboretum (Ch. 10) is a unique 2,800-acre preserve of natural woodlands, horticultural collections, display gardens, ponds, fields, and ravines. A daily admission fee is charged to non-members who wish to use the many resources and trails available at Holden.

Holden Arboretum: 440-946-4400; www.holdenarb.com.

Hach-Otis Sanctuary State Nature Preserve

Hach-Otis Sanctuary State Nature Preserve is in Willoughby Township, one mile east of Willoughby Hills. Managed by the Ohio Department of Natural Resources (ODNR), Hach-Otis has short boardwalks and trails that provide spectacular views of the Chagrin River 150 feet below. Information can be obtained by calling 440-632-3010, or by writing to:

ODNR, Div. of Natural Areas and Preserves: 614-265-6453; www.odnr.com/dnap.

GEAUGA COUNTY

General information about Geauga County is available from:

Geauga County Tourism Council: 800-775-8687

Geauga County Historical Society, Century Village: 440-834-1492.

Geauga Park District

The Geauga Park District consists of 11 parks and nature preserves open to the public and additional preserves not available for recreational use. District headquarters is at the Donald W. Meyer Nature Center in Big Creek Park, Chardon. Geauga Park District publishes a free newsletter listing guided nature walks, canoe trips, and astronomy and other programs for all ages. Chapters 12–16 describe hikes in the Geauga Park District.

Geauga Park District: 440-285-2222; www.geaugalink.com.

Punderson State Park

Punderson State Park is located about 30 miles east of Cleveland in Geauga County, near the junctions of SR 87 and SR 44. The main entrance to the park is on SR 87, one mile west of this junction. A stately tudor manor house provides guest rooms, dining rooms, and meeting rooms. The 996-acre park also has housekeeping cabins, a camping area, an outdoor swimming pool, and Punderson Lake for boating, swimming, and fishing. Fourteen miles of hiking trails go through the wooded hills and open fields to scenic areas of the park.

Punderson State Park: 440-564-2279;

www.dnr.state.oh.us/parks/parks/punderson.htm.

PORTAGE COUNTY

General information about Portage County is available from:

Portage County Visitors and Convention Bureau: 800-648-6342

Portage County Historical Society: 330-296-3523.

The Portage County Park District is a relatively new park district in Ohio. The district manages Towner's Woods Park, Portage County's first county park, and the newer Headwaters Trail and Towner's Woods Rail Trail. The Headwaters Trail is a 7-mile rail-trail crossing the divide of the Great Lakes Watershed and the Ohio River Watershed, connecting the historic towns of Mantua and Garrettsville. Two miles of the multipurpose Towner's Woods Rail Trail are open to the public. Plans call for eventually completing the trail from Kent to Ravenna. Watch for more additions to the Portage County Park District parklands as the young district grows.

Portage County Park District, 449 S. Meridian St., Ravenna, OH 44266;
     330-673-9404.

The Ohio Department of Natural Resources manages several areas in Portage County, including the following state parks and nature preserves.

Nelson Ledges State Park

Nelson Ledges State Park (Ch. 17) is located northeast of Garretsville on SR 282 in the northeast corner of Portage County. This small 167-acre park has interesting hiking trails that wind through ancient ledges that were formed millions of years ago.

Punderson State Park: 440-564-2279.

Tinker's Creek State Nature Preserve

Tinker's Creek State Nature Preserve (Ch. 20) is in both Portage and Summit counties and has several short hiking trails surrounding seven ponds. Adjacent to it is Tinker's Creek State Park, containing a 10-acre manmade lake for water recreation and hiking trails.

Tinker's Creek State Park: 330-296-3239.

A directory of all the state nature preserves can be obtained from:

Ohio Dept. of Natural Resources, Natural Areas and Preserves: 614-265-6453;
     www.odnr.com/dnap.

Eagle Creek State Nature Preserve

Eagle Creek State Nature Preserve (Ch. 21) in Nelson Township is a 441-acre preserve in Portage County with a bird observation blind, a boardwalk, and a system of trails.

Ohio Department of Natural Resources, District Manager: 330-527-5118.

West Branch State Park

West Branch State Park (Ch. 23) is near the town of Campbellsport on SR 14, east of Ravenna. It offers 5,352 land acres and 2,650 water acres for recreational enjoyment. The Buckeye Trail follows the perimeter of Kirwan Reservoir over rolling terrain with ever-changing views for a challenging nine-mile hike.

West Branch State Park: 330-296-3239.

SUMMIT COUNTY

General information about Summit County is available from:

Akron/Summit County Convention and Visitors Bureau: 330-374-7560

Summit County Historical Society: 330-535-1120.

Cuyahoga Valley National Park

Cuyahoga Valley National Park (CVNP), created in 1974, encompasses 33,000 acres of river valley and is administered by the National Park Service of the U.S. Department of the Interior. Located primarily in Summit County but with a small section in Cuyahoga County, it preserves a beautiful 22-mile corridor of pastoral green space between Cleveland and Akron. It is easily accessible to residents of both cities for active recreation, education, study of nature and history, and for that refreshment of body and spirit so needed by those of us who are city dwellers.

The Cuyahoga River, remnants of the Ohio & Erie Canal and its towpath, and the historic Cuyahoga Valley Scenic Railroad extend down the center of CVNP. Miles of trails are found throughout the park, the most popular being the 19.5-mile Ohio & Erie Canal Towpath Trail. This multi-use trail is the spine of the trail systems, which go from Rockside Rd. in Independence to Bath Rd. in Akron.

Park systems and communities outside CVNP are extending the Towpath Trail north to Cleveland and south to Dover/New Philadelphia.

Hikes in CVNP vary in difficulty. Those described in this guide are: Peninsula and Deep Lock Quarry Metro Park (Ch. 28); Brandywine Gorge and Stanford Trails (Ch. 29); Lake and Cross Country Trails (Ch. 30); and the Buckeye Trail from Boston Mills to Peninsula (Ch. 31).

The National Park Service (NPS) maintains headquarters in the small historic town of Jaite, on Vaughn Rd. at Riverview Rd. The restored yellow buildings in Jaite originally served as housing and the company store for the employees of Jaite Mill.

Cuyahoga Valley National Park: 440-526-5256.

Park rangers at visitor centers provide scheduled programs, visitor assistance, trail maps, and information about CVNP. Canal Visitor Center is located in a restored house near Hillside Rd., at 7104 Canal Rd., Valley View, OH 44147; 800-445-9667. Just outside the center, visitors can see a restored, working canal lock. Happy Days Visitor Center is on SR 303, east of Peninsula and west of SR 8; 800-257-9477. The Boston Store is on Boston Mills Rd. near Riverview Rd. Two smaller, seasonally operated visitor information centers are Hunt Farm on Bolanz Rd. and the Peninsula Depot in Peninsula. For a comprehensive listing of activities see www.dayinthevalley.com.

Metro Parks, Serving Summit County

Created in 1921, Metro Parks consists of more than 6,600 acres of land with 11 parks, the 23-mile Bike & Hike Trail, a nature center and arboretum, and several large conservation areas. Metro Parks naturalists conduct a full schedule of guided walks, nature classes, and programs for all ages. The program and events guide lists all the activities offered by Metro Parks.

Beyond Cleveland On Foot includes easy, moderate, and strenuous hikes in the following Metro Parks: Cascade Valley (including Cascade Locks), Firestone, Munroe Falls, Seiberling Naturealm, Gorge, Silver Creek, Goodyear Heights, and O'Neil Woods (Chapters 32–41).

Metro Parks Serving Summit County:330-867-5511;
www.summitmetroparks.org.

Portage Lakes State Park

Portage Lakes State Park (Ch. 27) is near SR 93 and SR 619, south of Akron. It consists of 1,000 land acres with hiking trails and 2,520 water acres.

Portage Lakes State Park: 330-644-2220; www.dnr.state.oh.us/parks/.

Bath Nature Preserve

A notable new park in the county is Bath Nature Preserve, a 404-acre preserve that was part of the Raymond Firestone estate. Bath Township owns and manages the preserve, which has several miles of trails through forests and grassland. The preserve is located on Ira Rd. west of Cleveland-Massillon Rd.

Bath Township Parks Dept.:; 330-666-4007

MEDINA COUNTY

General information about Medina County is available from:

Medina County Convention and Visitors Bureau: 800-860-2943;
www.travelmedinacountyohio.org.

Hinckley Reservation

Hinckley Reservation is the only one of the 14 Cleveland Metroparks reservations not in Cuyahoga County. Hinckley is the site of an annual event focused on the springtime return of the buzzards (actually turkey vultures), and is dominated by 90-acre Hinckley Lake. Whipp's Ledges (Ch. 45) and the smaller Worden's Ledges (Ch. 42) are composed of ancient rock formations deposited millions of years ago. Information is available from:

Cleveland Metroparks: 216-351-6300.

Medina County Park District

Medina County Park District (330-722-9364) consists of 13 park units including rail trails and special-use areas.

The parks with hiking trails include: Hubbard Valley Park (Ch. 43), Buckeye Woods Park, Letha House Park, Plum Creek Park (Ch. 44), River Styx Park, Allardale (Ch. 47), Chippewa Nature Preserve, and York and Chippewa Rail Trails. Wolf Creek Environmental Center at Alderfer-Oenslager Wildlife Sanctuary opened in October 2000.

Medina County Park District: 330-722-9364; www.medinacountyparks.com.

LORAIN COUNTY

General information about Lorain County is available from:

Lorain County Visitors Bureau: 800-334-1673; www.lcvb.org.

Lorain County Metro Parks

Lorain County Metro Parks, formed in 1957, currently consists of 16 locations (10 of which are reservations with trails) totaling more than 6,500 acres. A free bimonthly publication, called *Arrowhead*, lists guided hikes, walks, and nature programs in the parks and at the nature and visitor centers. *Beyond Cleveland On Foot* includes hikes in Black River Reservation (Ch. 49), Vermilion River Reservation (Ch. 50), Carlisle Reservation (Ch. 51), French Creek Reservation (Ch. 53), and Schoepfle Garden (Ch. 56), which is in Erie County but is a Lorain County Metro Park.

Lorain County Metro Parks: 800-526-7275; www.loraincountymetroparks.com.

Findley State Park

Findley State Park (Ch. 52), on SR 58 near Wellington, offers hiking trails and recreational swimming and boating on Findley Lake.

Findley State Park; 440-647-4490; www.dnr.state.oh.us/parks/.

ERIE COUNTY

General information about Erie County is available from:

Erie County Visitors: 800-255-3743; www.buckeyenorth.com.

Erie MetroParks

Erie MetroParks, organized in 1968, includes 10 recreation areas: Osborn Park, Castalia Quarry Reserve, Pelton Park, Edison Woods Reserve, the Coupling Reserve, James H. McBride Arboretum, Birmingham School Park, Hoffman Forest Reserve, Huron River Greenway, and DuPont Marsh State Nature Preserve. Nature education programs and interpretive events are listed in a quarterly publication called *The Leaflet*.

Erie MetroParks: 419-625-7783; www.eriemetroparks.org.

Kelleys Island State Park

Kelleys Island (Ch. 58), the largest U.S. island in Lake Erie, is the location of 661-acre Kelleys Island State Park. The Glacial Grooves of Kelleys Island are internationally famous among geologists. When the Wisconsinan glacier entered Ohio from northern Canada about 25,000 years ago, it deeply gouged the island's limestone bedrock. The mile-thick sheet of ice sculpted deep, dramatic grooves in the rock. Exposed are a set of grooves 396 feet long, 25–30 feet wide, and 15 feet deep.

Kelleys Island State Park: 419-746-2546; www.dnr.state.oh.us/ parks/.

There are two nature preserves on Kelleys Island—North Pond State Nature Preserve and North Shore Alvar State Nature Preserve—and a total of six nature preserves in Erie County.

CUYAHOGA COUNTY

Cleveland Metroparks

Cleveland Metroparks, established in 1917, celebrated its 75th anniversary in 1992. The park district includes 14 reservations and the Cleveland Metroparks Zoo. Because the reserves encircle the city of Cleveland and are connected by parkways, the system is often referred to as "the Emerald Necklace." Hinckley Reservation in Medina County is the pendant of the necklace.

Hiking trails in Cleveland Metroparks, except for Hinckley Reservation, are not included here. Many, however, are described in the companion volume to this book, *Cleveland On Foot.*

Cleveland Metroparks:; 216-351-6300; www.clemetparks.com.

HIKING CLUBS

Sierra Club

The Sierra Club Northeast Ohio Group can be reached by calling 440-843-7272. This group holds regular meetings and offers hiking, canoeing, and other outings for its members. Monthly meetings include programs about environmental issues and enjoyment of the outdoors. Visit the Sierra Club website at www.ohio.sierraclub.org/northeast.

The Portage Trail Group holds monthly program meetings, usually at Shady Hollow Pavilion in Sand Run Metro Park in Akron. For more information, call 330-666-4246, or visit their website at www.ohio.sierraclub.org/portagetrail.

Buckeye Trail Association

The Buckeye Trail (BT) is a blue-blazed 1,200-mile-long trail winding around the state of Ohio, reaching into every corner of the state from Lake Erie in the north to Cincinnati in the south and to Toledo in the west. The BT winds down country roads, through parks, trails and towpaths, towns and countryside.

This Ohio footpath was put together by volunteers of the Buckeye Trail Association (BTA), who conceived the idea, planned, laid out, and blazed the routes, and today take care of maintaining the trail. The BTA sells maps and guides for all portions of the trail, holds meetings, work parties, hikes, and other activities, and publishes a bimonthly newsletter called *The Trailblazer*.

> Buckeye Trail Association, Inc., Box 254, Worthington, OH 43085;
> www.buckeyetrail.org.

Cleveland Hiking Club

The Cleveland Hiking Club (CHC), founded in 1919, celebrated its 83rd Anniversary in 2002 and is one of the largest and oldest continuously operating hiking clubs in the country. The CHC offers many opportunities for large-group hiking. Selected club hikes are listed in *The Emerald Necklace*, published by Cleveland Metroparks. The club also publishes a bimonthly schedule of activities and *NewSteps*, the club's newsletter. To qualify for membership, one must complete six club hikes within one year.

> Cleveland Hiking Club, Box 347097, Cleveland, OH 44134;
> www.community.cleveland.com/oc/chclub.

OTHER LOCAL AND NATIONAL RESOURCES

After getting started with walking and hiking in Northeast Ohio, you may wish to consider joining a hiking organization as you get more involved in the sport. The previous sections list many local organizations to write to for information and maps. In addition, the organizations listed below may offer you an opportunity to do more walking, enhance your knowledge and enjoyment of nature, participate in volunteer trail maintenance work, and, of course, enjoy the friendship and fellowship of others who love walking and hiking and the out of doors.

> **Akron Metro Parks Hiking Club**: 220-628-3031
> **American Hiking Society**: Silver Spring, MD: 301-565-6704;
> www.americanhiking.org
> **Appalachian Mountain Club**: Boston, MA: 617-523-0636; www.outdoors.org
> **Appalachian Trail Conference**, Harpers Ferry, WV: www.atconf.org
> **Cleveland Museum of Natural History**: 216-231-4600; www.cmnh.org
> **Cuyahoga Valley Trails Council, Inc.**, 4621 E. 131 St., Garfield Hts., OH 44105;
> www.nps.gov/cuva/friends/cvtc.htm
> **Keystone Trails Association**, Cogan Station, PA: www.kta-hike.org
> **The Nature Conservancy Ohio Chapter**, Dublin, OH: 614-717-2770;
> www.tnc.org
> **North Country Trail Association**, Lowell, MI: www.northcountytrail.org

Ottawa National Wildlife Refuge, Oak Harbor, OH:; 419-898-0014;
www.fws.gov

Rails-to-Trails Conservancy Ohio Field Office, Gahanna, OH:; 614-428-4320;
www.railtrails.org/oh

Wilderness Center, Wilmot, OH: 877-359-5235; www.wildernesscenter.org

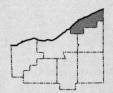

LAKE COUNTY

Lake County, bordering on Lake Erie, is one of Northeast Ohio's prime water recreation areas, with plenty of opportunities for fishing, boating, and swimming. The county's proximity to the lake also makes it a very favorable location for nurseries, orchards, and vineyards because the large lake helps moderate temperature extremes. Grape growing is especially successful along Lake Erie thanks to this tempering effect. The Vintage Ohio wine festival is held annually at Lake Farmpark, and one of the county's vineyards, Chalet Debonne in Madison, has won national awards.

Painesville became the county seat in 1840 and was a major port of entry to the Western Reserve by way of Fairport Harbor and the Grand River. The village was an important stop on the road between Buffalo and Cleveland during the 19th century and continued to prosper when the Cleveland, Painesville, and Ashtabula Railroad came through.

Ohio's largest natural sand beach, one mile long, is in Headlands Beach State Park. Adjacent to the state park are Mentor Marsh and Headlands Dunes state nature preserves, unique natural areas in Lake County. Headlands Dunes is one of the last dune ecosystems along Lake Erie, and Mentor Marsh harbors a wide variety of plant and animal life (Ch. 7).

Other major attractions of Lake County include Fairport Harbor Marine and Lighthouse Museum, Holden Arboretum (largest arboretum in the nation), Kirtland Temple, the James A. Garfield National Historic Site, and Lake County History Center.

Lake Metroparks provides many recreational and educational opportunities in its 25 public parks and other facilities. Information is available from Lake Metroparks: 800-227-7275; www.lakemetroparks.com.

Additional information about Lake County is available from Lake County Visitors Bureau: 800-368-5253; www.lakevisit.com.

1 Indian Point Park

Leroy Township

Distance: 1 mile

Easy

Hiking time: 1 hour

Description: The ridgetop trail slopes downhill somewhat from east to west but is wide and easy to follow, although there are no trail blazes. Use CAUTION on any of the side trails that lead over to the cliff edge, where there are long sweeping views of the Grand River and Paine Creek below.

Directions: From I-90 take Exit 205 for Vrooman Rd.; North on Vrooman about 1 mile, watch for right turn at bottom of hill; right (east) on Seeley Rd. to lower park entrance on left; continue on Seeley to upper entrance; cross two bridges; continue uphill to upper parking and picnic area on left.

Parking & restrooms: Parking areas and restrooms are available at both the lower and upper entrances.

Indian Point Park, listed in the National Register of Historic Places because of its 500-year-old Indian mounds, is one of Lake Metroparks' most geologically and historically interesting reservations. Located on Seeley Rd. in Leroy Township at the confluence of Paine Creek and the Grand River, this small park is high on a ridge overlooking both the creek and the river. The Grand River watershed drains about 40 percent of Lake County land.

A central hogback ridge of Chagrin Shale, steeply sloped and formed by erosion, separates Paine Creek from the Grand River. In 1974 the Grand River received a State Wild and Scenic River designation because of its pristine water quality and its steeply incised, 360-million-year-old Chagrin Shale walls. Multiple layers of this soft gray shale (fossilized mud) are interspersed with harder, light-colored siltstone overlaid with vertical erosion marks. Because of the high cliffs in this small park, hikers enjoy rewarding views of the river and valleys below, particularly in early spring and late autumn, when the trees are bare.

Two parallel mounds on top of the ridge and the ditches alongside it provide an interesting record of native settlement in the late prehistoric period called the Whittlesey Tradition. Farming people who lived along the Grand River from about 1250 to 1650 A.D. built villages high on isolated plateaus overlooking this and other river valleys.

Also on the ridge is a sheltered totem stone engraved in 1910 with the names of high school boys staying at Camp Wissalohichan, a boys' military camp.

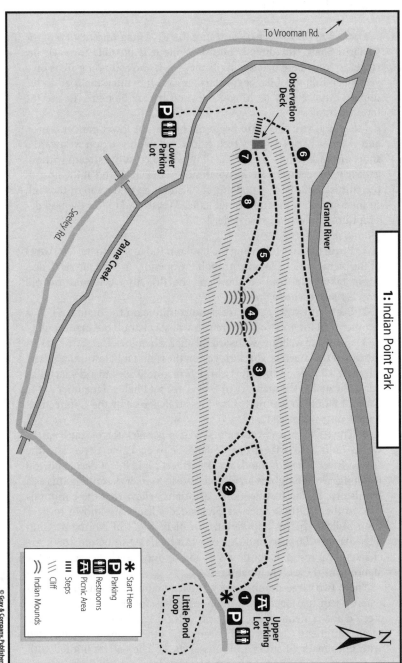

1: Indian Point Park

To Vrooman Rd.

Observation Deck

Lower Parking Lot

Grand River

Seeley Rd.

Paine Creek

Upper Parking Lot

Little Pond Loop

* Start Here
P Parking
Restrooms
Picnic Area
||| Steps
\\\ Cliff
))) Indian Mounds

N

Picnic areas, restrooms, drinking water, fishing, and hiking are available in Indian Point Park.

Option: At the lower park entrance there is a magnificent view of the Chagrin Shale cliff directly ahead. While it is possible to reach the ridgetop from here by crossing Paine Creek and ascending steps on a very steep hill, this hike begins farther east. In winter, the road to the upper entrance may be impassable, and it may be better to use the lower entrance.

[NOTE: If you choose to begin the hike at the lower park entrance, and if the water of Paine Creek is low, follow the stream westward a short distance to find rocks that allow you to cross the stream without getting your feet wet. On the north side of the creek and at the nose of the cliff is a set of 145 wooden steps leading up to the top of the cliff. At the top, follow the trail straight ahead (east) and follow the trail descriptions below in reverse order.]

1 Begin the hike following the Lookout Ridge Trail to the left (west) of the picnic tables, passing through the opening in the split-rail fence. Avoid taking the trail on the right (north). After 0.1 mile this old woods road reaches a fork.

2 Bear left (west) at this fork and continue on the main trail. Pass another trail intersection, where you will stay left on the main trail.

3 Continue walking westward through a hemlock forest that graces the top of this steep hogback ridge. On the right far below is the Grand River. At 0.3 mile on the left is a bronze plaque affixed to a glacial boulder dedicated to the memory of Edna Crofoot Phelps, a member of the Crofoot family to whom this land was transferred by the Connecticut Land Company in 1802.

4 The trail crosses over the first of two parallel north–south earthworks built across the ridge of land between Paine Creek and the Grand River. These mounds are 3 to 5 feet high, 8 feet deep, and 150 feet long. On the right is an Ohio Historic Marker describing this as a prehistoric Indian fortification. Historians believe that these mounds date to the Whittlesey period. Stockaded villages are known to have been built by native populations on high ridges in Northeast Ohio after about 1200 A.D., and this one can be dated to before 1650. Archaeological research continues to add to our knowledge and understanding of these early inhabitants.

These two large mounds are all that remain of north-south walls where earth had been piled high at the base of posts. The naturally steep embankments of the ridge provided a safe location for a village or encampment. Corn, squash, beans, and other crops were cultivated with hoes made of sticks and mussel shells. The natives hunted with bows and arrows and fished with bone hooks and nets.

5 Just beyond the historic marker, take the side trail on the right that leads along the top of the cliff for views of the Grand River below.

CAUTION: Stay behind the fence that has been erected to protect hikers from a steep drop over the severely eroded shale cliff edges.

Pause here for an outstanding view of the Grand River in both directions. Here also is a shelter for a boulder carved by George E. Stevens (1899–1918). To the northwest is a view of the confluence of Paine Creek and the Grand River.

Continue west along this side trail until it meets the main trail and the 145-step wooden stairs ahead.

6 OPTION: From this point you may descend the steps to the bottom then turn right (north) and right again (east) on a small fishing trail that parallels the Grand River. If you do this, look up at the fine Chagrin Shale cliff on the right. You will see interspersed layers of harder, fine-grained siltstone and vertical erosion marks made in the gray shale (see Appendix A). The trail soon peters out. Retrace your steps to the stairs and ascend them to the top.

7 Take the main trail going east. (Avoid the parallel side trail that you came on curving toward the northeast.) On the right at the top is a wooden observation deck from which to enjoy a view of Paine Creek on the south. Continue along the main trail (east).

8 Reach a granite boulder protected under a small shelter, the Camp Wissalohichan totem stone (1910). Barely visible are a carved symbol and the names of campers who attended this military camp for high school boys in the early 1900s.

Continue on the main trail over the two prehistoric earthworks and past the trail junctures on the left to return to the parking area. ■

2 Paine Falls Park

Leroy Township

Distance: 0.1 mile

Easy

Hiking time: ¼ hour

Description: Close to Indian Point Park is Paine Falls Park, a very small scenic area along Paine Creek with a picnic shelter, restrooms, and a short loop trail to the 30-foot falls.

Directions: From Indian Point Park, continue east on Seeley Rd. about ¾ mile to Paine Rd.; right (south) on Paine for 200 feet to park entrance on the right, where there is ample parking.

From I-90, take Exit 205 (Vrooman Rd.); south on Vrooman; left (east) on Carter Rd.; left (north) on Paine Rd.; cross the bridge; park entrance on left.

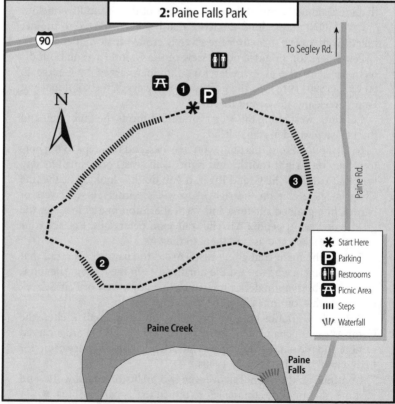

2: Paine Falls Park

To Segley Rd.

N

Paine Rd.

* Start Here
P Parking
Restrooms
Picnic Area
IIII Steps
Waterfall

Paine Creek

Paine Falls

© Gray & Company, Publishers

1 Enter the trail west of the picnic shelter. A historic marker at the head of the trail commemorates Hendrick E. Paine, nephew of Edward Paine, the founder of Painesville. Hendrick Paine, born in 1789, was an early settler from East Windsor, Connecticut, and at the age of 29 built a log cabin and settled here in what was called Paine's Hollow. He built a sawmill at the brow of the falls, and soon an ashery where potash was made. A blacksmith shop, iron forge and furnace, and wagon shop followed. In 1828, Parkman Baker built a tannery nearby, and by 1840 this was a thriving industrial center of Leroy Township with many log homes and a school. Over harvesting of trees and subsequent flooding caused the demise of Paine's Hollow by 1850.

2 Take the steps to descend to a gravel trail and boardwalk for a view of Paine Falls cascading over many layers of Chagrin Shale. This grayish shale was deposited as mud and silt under an inland sea that covered Ohio about 360 million years ago. There are several tiers of very picturesque falls coursing over fossilized mud layers. Chagrin Shale is the lowermost and oldest rock unit exposed in this area (see Appendix A).

3 The loop trail continues up 61 steps to the parking area. ■

3 Hidden Valley Park
Madison

Easy

Distance: 1 mile

Hiking time: ³/₄ hour

Description: The one main trail in this park begins at the south entrance parking area and follows the edge of the Grand River below high Chagrin Shale cliffs. This short, pleasant walk is on a flat, well-delineated trail. Beaver may sometimes be seen swimming in the river, and there is evidence of their chisel work on trees alongside the river.

Directions: From I-90 take Exit 212 (SR 528); south on SR 528 (Madison Rd.) past River Rd.; right on Klasen Rd. downhill to park entrance.

Parking & restrooms: The parking area is off Klasen Rd.; restrooms are located near the picnic area.

Hidden Valley Park, situated in Lake County's Madison Township, is a small, scenic park on the Grand River offering fishing, hiking, canoeing, picnicking, a playground, and sledding hill. The park also has a reservable cabin called the Resource Center, accessed from the park's north entrance off River Rd. The park borders the beautiful Grand River below a spectacular Chagrin Shale cliff, one of the best examples in the county of exposed outcrop of this shale. Most of this grayish shale is beneath the surface of the great lake plain to the east. Interspersed in the shale is fine-grained, harder siltstone that juts out from the surface of the softer shale. Vertical erosion marks are also a feature of this exposed, 360-million-year-old cliff. (See Appendix A.)

Views of the wide, scenic river are visible from a riverside trail. The Grand River, considered by some to be among the finest natural streams in Ohio, was designated a State Wild and Scenic River in 1974. After rainfalls in the spring and summer, numerous waterfalls cascade over the steep Chagrin Shale cliff walls. Nearby Hogback Ridge is close enough for both parks to be easily visited on the same day.

1 The paved trail begins at the parking lot. Follow it westward between the sledding hill and the restroom building to the split-rail fence. Follow the unpaved trail westward and across a wooden bridge over a small stream.

2 About 50 feet past the bridge, pass stands of hemlock, sycamore, and maple trees. Sweeping views of the Grand River appear on the right.

Here, find visible evidence of busy beavers at work. The beaver's

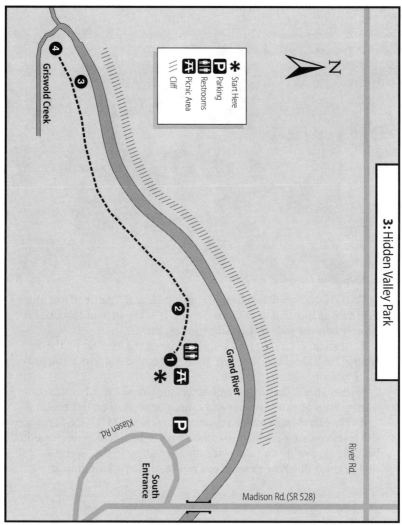

© Gray & Company, Publishers

ever-growing incisor teeth are covered with a hard enamel on the front and a softer dentine on the back. As the beaver gnaws, the back wears faster than the front, thus providing an ingenious self-sharpening system. Beavers usually favor aspen, willow, and birch trees for food and whatever else they can cut down for construction of dams and lodges.

The beaver, an aquatic rodent with a glossy brown fur coat and paddle-shaped tail, can remain submerged for up to 15 minutes. Ordinarily, beavers build lodges, but here they may burrow into the mud alongside the river to create their living quarters. Sometimes you may see evidence of a beaver dam that these animals have built beside the river, but they are frequently washed away by the river's current.

CAUTION: Avoid touching the many stinging nettle plants that thrive along this trail in the summer and fall. The stem of this plant is densely covered with stiff, bristly, stinging hairs.

3 At about 0.4 mile, pass a soft shale rise on the left. Stay on the designated trail; avoid any "bootleg" trails that can be dangerous and promote erosion.

Farther ahead, Griswold Creek enters the Grand River, but this confluence is on private property and cannot be reached on this trail.

4 The gravel trail ends at a couple of benches. CAUTION: Some of the vines covering the trees are poison ivy. ("Leaves of three, leave it be!") Retrace your steps alongside the river, going in the reverse direction to enjoy different views as you return to the parking area. ■

4 Penitentiary Glen Reservation
Kirtland

Distance: 4 miles

Easy

Hiking time: 2 hours

Description: The trails on this hike are generally flat and include both paved walkways and gravel paths. The gravel Bobolink Loop provides views of the Stoney Brook gorge, and the Gorge Rim Loop affords close-up views of this natural feature. An optional walk down a 141-step stairway allows a view of a small waterfall and close-up observation of the gorge.

Directions: From I-90 take Exit 193 (SR 306); south on SR 306; left on SR 615 for one block to traffic signal; right on Kirtland-Chardon Rd. for 2 miles; entrance on the right.

Parking & restrooms: At Penitentiary Glen Nature Center.

Originally established in 1980, Penitentiary Glen Reservation is a 422-acre park named in part for the deep gorge that cuts through it. Early settlers referred to the steep, narrow gorge as "Penitentiary Gully" because it was so difficult to get out of. The gorge itself is not a part of this hike because of its ecologically sensitive flora and rocky steepness. It may be seen only on a guided hike led by a park naturalist. For more information call 440-256-1404.

In 1992, Lake Metroparks opened a new and greatly expanded Penitentiary Glen Nature Center. The center, open 9 A.M. to 5 P.M. daily, houses a large nature display room, the Nature Store, classrooms, the award-winning "Window on Wildlife," and a 150-seat auditorium. The older portion of this building was the horse barn for the Halle family (owners of the Halle Bros. Co. in Cleveland), who owned this land and maintained a summer home and working farm here. Well-marked trails, wetlands, a butterfly garden, a picnic shelter, a handicapped-accessible observation deck, and an outdoor amphitheater are among other improvements made to Penitentiary Glen Reservation.

The Kevin P. Clinton Wildlife Center, a wildlife rehabilitation facility, is located near the nature center. The center's staff aids nearly 2,000 injured or orphaned wild animals every year, with the goal of returning them to the wild. Animals that cannot be released become "ambassadors" and are featured in educational programs.

The Penitentiary Glen Railroad, located west of the center, is operated by the Lake Shore Live Steamers Club and offers free rides on the miniature steam railroad on designated Sunday afternoons during the summer months.

An annual Ohio wine festival is held in early August at nearby Lake Farmpark, another unit of Lake Metroparks. This 235-acre science and cultural center with over 50 breeds of livestock is located on Chardon Rd. (US 6) in Kirtland. To reach Lake Farmpark from Penitentiary Glen, continue southeast on Kirtland-Chardon Rd. to Sperry Rd. Turn right (south) on Sperry Rd. to Chardon Rd. (US 6), then right (west) on US 6 to Lake Farmpark on the left (8800 Chardon Rd., Kirtland). Open 9 A.M. to 5 P.M. year round, the park charges a small admission fee (800-366-3276).

1 Start the walk with a visit to the nature center and the Wildlife Center. Take the path between the two centers and walk past the amphitheater on the right. Turn right on the paved Glen Meadow Loop then bear right again to reach the Observation Deck for a view of the gorge. Stoney Brook below is responsible for carving this deep valley through bedrock and thus exposing layers of sedimentary shale and sandstone that were formed 360 million years ago, when this area was covered by an inland sea.

On the railing of the deck is a thoughtful quotation that reads: "Within ourselves there is a deep place at whose edge we may sit and dream."

2 Follow Halle Home Loop past the Halle family's original rose garden, now a wildflower and rhododendron garden, and descend the steps ahead. Here on the embankment is the porch foundation—all that remains of the summer house that this wealthy Cleveland family enjoyed from the 1920s to 1940s. As you walk along the lower part of the Halle Home Loop, you will notice on your right the broken dam across the brook. This concrete wall once held back water to form a swimming pool for the family to enjoy on hot summer days.

3 At the end of the short Halle Home Loop, bear right onto the paved path and continue to the Bobolink Loop sign. Bear right onto the Bobolink Loop, cross the bridge, and ascend the small rise to a trail intersection.

4 Turn right, following the 1-mile gravel Bobolink Loop in a counterclockwise direction.

5 A path to the right leads to the gorge rim on a side trail for a scenic view. Retrace steps to the Bobolink Loop.

6 Continue on the Bobolink Loop through a meadow with tall prairie grass; the land formerly was a plowed field on the Halle farm. Bluebirds and field sparrows sing from perches in the meadow; groundhogs burrow in holes in the field. A large variety of wildflowers thrives in this sunny meadow in the spring, summer, and fall.

The gravel trail shortly leads into and out of the woods and loops around the field past a side trail that goes to Booth Rd. Turn right to return to the bridge, completing the loop.

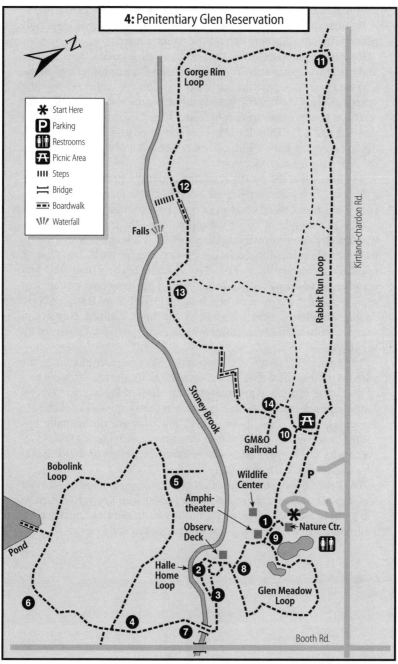

© Gray & Company, Publishers

7 Follow the trail back across the bridge over Stoney Brook, go up the hill and bear left past the wildflower garden and observation deck.

8 Turn right onto the paved Glen Meadow Loop; this loop ends near the marsh and pond behind the nature center.

9 You can see waterfowl at the pond, as well as turtles, frogs, snakes, and many kinds of plants. Turn right to pass the amphitheater (on the left) and continue past the nature center (on the right). Follow the paved trail past the bulletin board and miniature railroad on the left.

10 At the trail intersection in front of the picnic shelter, turn right then left to reach Rabbit Run Loop, which becomes a wide gravel road. Avoid taking the Rabbit Run cut-off on the left and continue ahead to the sign marking a service road.

11 Bear left at the service road sign and just ahead enter the Gorge Rim Loop. This trail goes through a beech, maple, and oak forest to the rim of the gorge, then bends around to the southeast.

12 On the right at about the midpoint of the trail is a set of 141 wooden steps going down into the gorge. This side trip is worth the effort. At the bottom of the stairs is a viewing area from which to observe small, scenic Stoney Brook Falls. Tiny cascades fall over many thin layers of shale to create a picturesque view. The many layers of ancient rock exposed here in sequence from youngest to oldest are: Berea Sandstone, viewed near the start of the hike; Bedford Formation; Cleveland Shale; and here, Chagrin Shale (see Appendix A). Return up the stairs.

13 Turn right (south) at the top of the stairs and continue along the path, bypassing the Gorge Rim shortcut trail on the left. This portion of the Gorge Rim Loop provides the best views of Penitentiary Gorge. Large hemlock trees have been growing in this hospitably cool climate for many, many years. These giants, however, are occasionally uprooted by soil erosion and fall over into the gorge. Stunning moss-covered rocks and feathery ferns also enhance the beauty of this wonderfully cool, moist environment.

14 Reach the next trail junction after crossing a boardwalk over a wet area. Continue straight, rejoining Rabbit Run Loop, to return to the parking area. Children may enjoy a visit to the Penitentiary Glen Railroad for free rides, if it is open on the day of your visit. ■

5 Hogback Ridge
Madison

Distance: 1 mile

Moderate

Hiking time: 1 hour

Description: The ¹/₂-mile Hemlock Ridge Loop begins on a wooden boardwalk and continues on a wide gravel trail high above the cliffs. The hike also includes a descent upon a set of 138 steps to continue the walk on the Bluebell Valley Trail to a waterfall on Mill Creek. The hike continues on the north and west sides of the Hemlock Ridge Loop. (An optional extension to this hike descends to Mill Creek on the Old Emerson Road Trail.)

Directions: From I-90 take Exit 212 (SR 528); south on SR 528 (Madison Rd.); left (east) on Griswold Rd.; north on Emerson Rd. into park.

Parking & restrooms: At the park entrance.

Lake County's Hogback Ridge, located off Madison Rd. in Madison Township, is a small park containing a 100-foot-high, semicircular hogback, or narrow ridge, between Mill Creek and the Grand River. This prominent ridge with steep valleys on either side is so named because it resembles the bony spine of a hog. It is thought to have been used by prehistoric Indians, although excavations in 1929 revealed few artifacts. The hiking trails are south of Mill Creek; there are no hiking trails on the hogback itself.

In the 1800s the Emerson family, for whom the park entrance road is named, operated a mill near the confluence of Mill Creek and Grand River. Old Emerson Road Trail is a park path that follows this old road downhill to Mill Creek. Local residents used to ford the stream to reach a continuation of the road on the opposite side. Old Emerson Road Trail is now used by people fishing the stream for bass, bluegill, and steelhead salmon.

The period from late March through the end of May is the best time to see and identify abundant spring wildflowers in Hogback Ridge. Be sure to bring along a wildflower book to enjoy this activity to its fullest.

Picnic facilities, restrooms, and drinking water are all available here. Nearby, Chalet Debonne Winery and Vineyards (7743 Doty Rd., just east of Emerson Rd.) is open year round (800-424-9463).

1 Enter the Hemlock Ridge Loop at the southeast corner of the picnic area at the fence gates opening onto a wooden boardwalk. This path winds through a maple/beech forest to a bench that invites a pause to view the valley below. Spring wildflowers grow in abundance here, especially trillium, squirrel corn, trout lily, spring beauty, hepatica, and several kinds of violets.

2 At 0.2 mile reach a trail junction and some steps on the right, the intersection with the 0.7-mile Bluebell Valley Trail. Descend the ridge on the 138 sloping timber steps to the floodplain. At the foot of the steps, the Bluebell Valley Trail leads directly to Mill Creek. Trillium and Virginia bluebells carpet the area in late April and early May.

3 When you reach the bank of Mill Creek, note this point carefully, because it is here that you will make a sharp left turn to get back to the wooden steps on the return portion of the hike.

At the creek, turn right (southeast) and follow the path closely, hugging the bank of the stream.

4 At about 0.4 mile, and just before a hill, you will see a very pretty waterfall on Mill Creek cascading over many layers of shale. It is interesting to contemplate the power of this small stream that, over millions of years, has cut through to form the ridge.

CAUTION: Do not approach closer to the falls, because the bank is undercut.

Return along the same path. At the turn described in Note #3, you have the option to continue straight ahead and walk the short loop of the Bluebell Valley Trail, or turn left (west) and follow the path to the steps to rejoin the Hemlock Ridge Loop.

5 At the top, turn right (north) and continue on the boardwalk to the observation deck.

6 At the end of the boardwalk, descend several timber steps on the gravel path to continue the Hemlock Ridge Loop. When the trees are bare, Mill Creek can be seen below on the right. Continue to follow the gravel trail through the forest.

White, black, and chestnut oaks dominate the forest above this river valley. The understory is home to other wildflowers that you might spot in the spring: pipsissewa, Canada mayflower, solomon's seal, foxglove, or wild indigo.

7 At 0.9 mile meet a juncture with the Old Emerson Road Trail. Turn left (south) here to return on the path to a picnic shelter and the parking area. ■

OPTION: You may wish to turn right (north) on the 0.5-mile Old Emerson Road Trail, following the badly eroded path and steps downhill to Mill Creek and back.

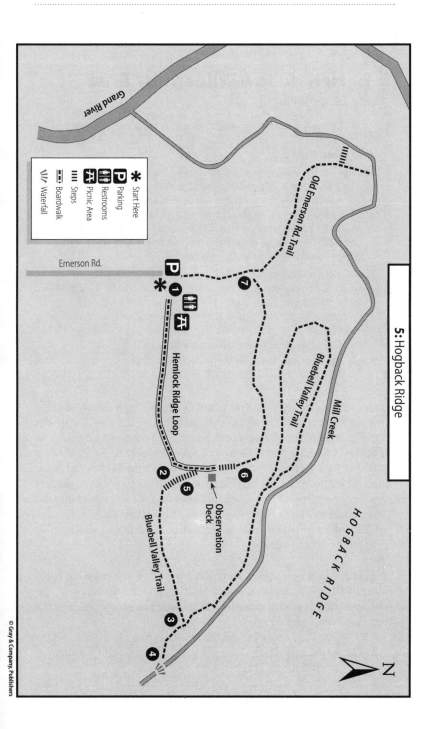

5: Hogback Ridge

Legend
* Start Here
P Parking
Restrooms
Picnic Area
Steps
Boardwalk
Waterfall

Emerson Rd.

Grand River

Old Emerson Rd. Trail

Hemlock Ridge Loop

Bluebell Valley Trail

Mill Creek

HOGBACK RIDGE

Observation Deck

Bluebell Valley Trail

N

© Gray & Company, Publishers

6 Hell Hollow Wilderness Area
Leroy Township

Distance: 1.1 miles

Moderate

Hiking time: 1 hour

Description: The trail leads from the picnic area along a ridge and down a set of 262 timber steps to Paine Creek. CAUTION: There are no marked trails in the valley, and those that are visible are not maintained by Lake Metroparks. Therefore it is advisable to return via the steps to the upper level of the park and complete the main loop trail. The views from the top of the cliff, the ambiance of the quiet woods, and the view of Paine Creek all make a visit to Hell Hollow well worthwhile.

Directions: (Because Leroy Center Rd. is closed west of the park, a rather roundabout route is necessary to reach Hell Hollow.) From I-90 take Exit 205 for Vrooman Rd.; south on Vrooman for 0.5 mile; left (east) on Carter Rd. for 1.7 miles; left (north) on Paine Rd. for 1 mile; right (east) on Ford Rd.; right (south) on Trask Rd. for 0.8 mile; south on Brockway Rd. for 1.6 miles; right (west) on Leroy Center Rd. to the park entrance on right.

Parking & restrooms: Just inside the park entrance.

Hell Hollow Wilderness Area is notable for its high clifftop and for the steps that provide a dramatic descent to the creek valley. Located in Leroy Township, this 609-acre park is similar to others in Lake County in that it includes a 360-million-year-old Chagrin Shale cliff above a deep river valley. The more than 100-foot-deep ravine was carved thousands of years ago by the cutting action of Paine Creek after glaciers retreated from Ohio. Paine Creek flows northwest and empties into the Grand River at Indian Point Park, north of I-90 (Ch. 1).

Hell Hollow offers a picnic shelter, restrooms, drinking water, a play area, and baseball diamond.

1 The gravel Beechridge Loop Trail begins at the split-rail fence north of the picnic area. Views of Paine Creek open up below on the left. Take the leftmost trail, nearest the fence. The return route of the loop is to your right.

CAUTION: Please stay behind the fence to enjoy these views safely.

2 The west-facing cliff provides a good vantage point for sunsets, especially around the time of the winter solstice.

3 Where the Beechridge Loop Trail turns to the right, continue straight ahead onto Wildcat Trail. Descend the steps to the bottom,

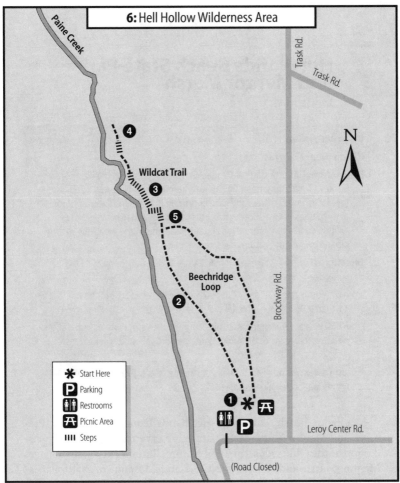

6: Hell Hollow Wilderness Area

Paine Creek

Trask Rd.

Trask Rd.

④

Wildcat Trail

③

⑤

Beechridge Loop

②

Brockway Rd.

✳ Start Here

🅿 Parking

🚻 Restrooms

⛱ Picnic Area

‖‖‖ Steps

① ✳ ⛱

🚻

🅿

Leroy Center Rd.

(Road Closed)

© Gray & Company, Publishers

continue a short way through hemlocks, then descend the last steps to the creek.

4 Reach the creek for a pleasant view of the stream flowing over ancient shale.

Return along the creek to the timber steps, and ascend to the top. On the way up the steps you get another chance to see the shale cliff at close range. The blue-gray rock erodes easily and very little vegetation can get a foothold on the friable, steep slope.

5 At the top of the climb, retrace your steps to the intersection with the Beechridge Loop Trail. Turn left to follow the path through a mature beech woods, back to the picnic area and parking. ■

7 Headlands Beach State Park and Mentor Marsh

Mentor

Distance: 6 miles

Moderate

Hiking time: 2¼ hours

Description: This hike starts at Headlands Beach and follows the blue-blazed Buckeye Trail/Zimmerman Trail along a hummock on the west side of Mentor Marsh. Tall reed grass and cattails grow in the marsh alongside stumps of dead trees from a once-lush forest. Many birds and other varieties of wildlife thrive in Mentor Marsh and the Headland Dunes area. Pets are prohibited in the state nature preserves.

Directions: From SR 2 take exit for SR 44 (north); left (north) on SR44 to Headlands Beach State Park.

From the south, take I-71 or I-77 to I-90/SR 2 east; stay on SR 2 to the exit for SR 44, then follow above directions.

From I-90, exit at SR 44; north 4.2 miles; stay on SR 44 as it joins SR 2 for a short distance, then exits to the north. Continue north about 2 miles to reach Headlands Beach State Park.

Parking & restrooms: Park in the lot farthest to the east (P-1). Several restrooms are located along the beach.

Headlands Beach State Park, Headlands Dunes State Nature Preserve, and Mentor Marsh State Nature Preserve are all under the jurisdiction of the Ohio Department of Natural Resources (which manages Mentor Marsh jointly with the Cleveland Museum of Natural History). Naturalists at Mentor Marsh Nature Center offer many activities, guided hikes, and programs. The center is located at 5185 Corduroy Rd., Mentor (440-257-0777.

The four-mile-long, 644-acre Mentor Marsh, a National Natural Landmark, features a diversity of plants and animals and is the largest coastal wetland along Lake Erie between Sandusky Bay and Presque Isle in Pennsylvania. Although the preserve has become dominated by the tall reed grass *Phragmites australis*, it still retains remnants of a swamp forest and herbaceous wetlands, and is rich in wildlife.

The wetland lies in an abandoned channel and floodplain of the Grand River. During the 800 to 1,000 years the Grand River took to find its present outlet at Fairport Harbor, the old river channel area gradually changed from swamp forest to marsh. The trail goes through part of the beech/sugar maple forest bordering the marsh.

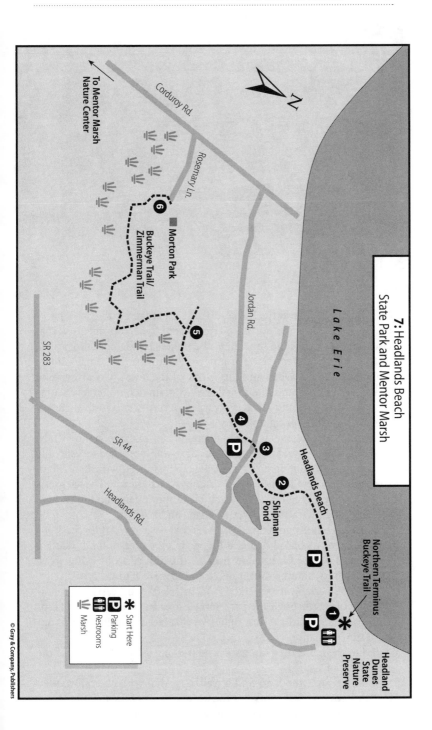

7: Headlands Beach
State Park and Mentor Marsh

Lake Erie

To Mentor Marsh
Nature Center

Corduroy Rd.

Rosemary Ln.

Jordan Rd.

SR 283

SR 44

Headlands Rd.

Headlands Beach

Morton Park
Buckeye Trail/
Zimmerman Trail

Shipman
Pond

Northern Terminus
Buckeye Trail

Headland
Dunes
State
Nature
Preserve

* Start Here
P Parking
Restrooms
Marsh

© Gray & Company, Publishers

1 Begin the hike at the Buckeye Trail sign at the north end of parking lot P-1. This is the northern terminus of the 1,200-mile trail that circles the state. Beyond the sign to the right is Headlands Dunes State Nature Preserve. Very few natural beach dune areas remain intact along Lake Erie in Ohio, and this is one of the finest. The preserve of beach, sand dunes, and interdunal areas contains a number of uncommon plant species and attracts a variety of birds (and birdwatchers), especially during spring migration.

This nature preserve is open to the public for research, nature study, bird watching, art, and photography, but visitors are asked to walk only on the sand and not disturb any of the rare plants growing here. Plant species found here include dune-making switchgrass and beach grass, sea rocket, and beach pea. Monarch butterflies often stop to rest here on their long migration between Canada and Mexico.

Start this hike by going west on the paved walkway/service road, enjoying the views of Lake Erie, different in every season and weather. There are few blue blazes here, because the trail passes parking areas, picnic shelters, and the ranger office and first aid station.

2 At the parking area marked P-16, turn left (southeast) and follow the blue blazes through the park service area to Headlands Rd. Shipman Pond is on the left. Turn right (west) at Headlands Rd. and go uphill a short distance.

3 On the left is the Shipman Pond parking lot and the start of the Zimmerman Trail.

4 Enter cool woods to find a well-used trail with several wooden foot bridges over wet spots. On the left are views of the marsh.

This area used to be swamp forest with naturally occurring vernal ponds, excellent habitat for frogs and salamanders. Researchers from the Cleveland Museum of Natural History discovered that once the marsh became dominant, there was no longer suitable habitat for amphibians, and their populations dropped steeply. The museum therefore undertook a restoration project, excavating areas to re-create vernal ponds for amphibian breeding. The restoration has proved to be very successful, with both salamanders and green frogs taking well to these new breeding ponds. The museum has also reintroduced leopard frogs, which had completely disappeared from the marsh, and is hopeful that their numbers will also recover.

5 Bear left at a trail intersection (1.6 miles). In the autumn and winter you can see the marshlands on the left. Continue to follow the gently rolling trail another 1.5 miles.

6 The trail bears right and comes out at Morton Park, a City of Mentor recreation area with a playground, pool, and restrooms.

The Buckeye Trail continues west along Rosemary Ln., but this hike returns back along the original route to Headlands Beach. ■

8 Chapin Forest Reservation
Kirtland

Distance: 4.5 miles

Moderate

Hiking time: 2¹/₂ hours

Description: This moderate hike on various well-marked, wide gravel trails includes a portion of the blue-blazed Buckeye Trail. There is a moderate hill to climb in order to reach 1,160-foot-high Gildersleeve Knob, from which there is a splendid view of Lake Erie 10 miles to the north.

Directions: From I-90, take Exit 193 (SR 306); south on SR 306; west on US 6 (Chardon Rd.) for 1 mile; right (north) on Hobart Rd. for about a quarter mile; park entrance on right.

Parking & restrooms: Just inside the entrance road there is ample parking; restrooms are adjacent to Pine Lodge Visitor Center.

This 390-acre park is noted for its tall trees and ancient sandstone ledges. Chapin Forest's trees are typical northern species: oak, maple, tulip, beech, and hemlock. Chestnut trees once predominated here, but only stumps remain since the blight of the 1920s. Spectacular Sharon Conglomerate sandstone ledges, similar to others found in Northeast Ohio, are an outstanding feature of the park. These rock ledges were formed about 300 million years ago during the Pennsylvanian Age. They are composed of sandstone embedded with white quartz pebbles locally called "lucky stones." The probable source of these pebbles is far north, in Canada, whose streams brought them to the sandy shore of the inland ocean that once covered Ohio. On some parts of the trails the quartz pebbles are so numerous, they are like ball bearings underfoot.

In the early 1800s, Berea Sandstone was found at what is now Quarry Pond and used to construct foundations for many local buildings, including the 1836 Kirtland Temple, a National Historic Landmark. Berea Sandstone was formed of sand deposited along an ancient continent's shoreline during the Devonian Age, about 360 million years ago. This sand accumulated as river deposits, delta lobes, or offshore bodies of sand.

In 1949 Frederic H. Chapin purchased the land on which this reservation is located and donated it to the state of Ohio to protect the beautiful forest from logging. During the 1950s the Ohio Division of Forestry and Reclamation used this property for experimental research to determine growth and survival rates of various kinds of trees. Some of the trees near the parking area stand in straight rows, just as

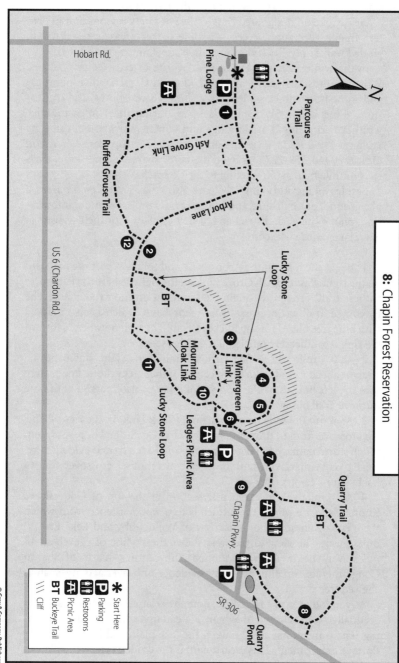

8: Chapin Forest Reservation

Hobart Rd.

Pine Lodge

Parcourse Trail

Ruffed Grouse Trail

Ash Grove Link

Arbor Lane

US 6 (Chardon Rd.)

Lucky Stone Loop

BT

Mourning Cloak Link

Wintergreen Link

Lucky Stone Loop

Ledges Picnic Area

Chapin Pkwy.

Quarry Trail

BT

SR 306

Quarry Pond

N

* Start Here
P Parking
Restrooms
Picnic Area
\\\ Cliff
BT Buckeye Trail

© Gray & Company, Publishers

they were planted by the Division. Under a lease agreement with the state, Lake Metroparks now manages the reservation.

Please hike on designated trails only. For safety reasons and to protect fragile vegetation, access to some ledges areas is restricted to guided walks only. Rock climbing and rappelling are prohibited.

In the winter, Chapin Forest is a favorite of cross-country skiers. Winter enthusiasts gather at Pine Lodge Ski Center, which offers ski and snowshoe rentals, ski lessons, a fireplace, restrooms, and concessions. Pine Lodge Ski Center is open during the winter months, weather permitting. For ski lodge and winter information, call Pine Lodge at 440-256-3810 (winter only) or Lake Metroparks Registration Offices at 440-358-7275. Trail etiquette for shared hiking/skiing trails calls for hikers to avoid walking in the ski tracks.

Besides hiking and skiing, the park also offers several picnic areas, a playground, pond fishing, and limited bridle trails. For more information, phone the park district at 440-639-7275 or visit their website at www.lakemetroparks.com.

1 Begin the hike on the Arbor Lane and follow it past the ball field on the right. Pass the Ash Grove Link on the right. Where the Parcourse (fitness trail) crosses the main trail, remain on the Arbor Lane. The Parcourse Trail again crosses the Arbor Lane, which is also marked with blue tree blazes for the Buckeye Trail. The trail now bends toward the right (southeast) and begins a gentle ascent.

2 At 0.3 mile the Ruffed Grouse Trail turns right, but continue straight ahead uphill to an intersection of the Lucky Stone Loop. Here take the left branch of the Lucky Stone Loop, also marked with blue Buckeye Trail blazes.

3 At about 0.7 mile pass Mourning Cloak Link on the right. (This is a crossover trail to the south branch of Lucky Stone Loop.) Stay left. Much storm damage to tall oak, maple, and beech trees is evident here. Next pass Wintergreen Link on the right (another crossover trail to Lucky Stone Loop). Stay left.

4 At 1 mile reach a trail intersection at the top of Gildersleeve Knob. A short path on the left leads to a wooden fence from which there is a splendid panoramic view of Willoughby and Lake Erie 10 miles away. The view to the west shows the skyline of Cleveland 18 miles away. Below is an abandoned 20th-century quarry of Sharon Conglomerate. Small ponds show evidence of beaver activity, such as chewed trees.

As you look toward Lake Erie, note the relatively flat lake plain that gradually ascends to the Allegheny Plateau upon which you are standing. The transitional area between the lake plain and high area is the Portage Escarpment. This escarpment is the eroded face of the plateau overlaid with glacial deposits.

5 Return to the main trail and continue ahead (east). Avoid taking a side trail on the left marked Scenic Overlook since tall trees obscure the view from this point and there is no protective fence constructed here.

6 Continue on Lucky Stone Loop as it gradually descends. Take the next left turn where the trail goes steeply downhill to Ledges Picnic Area (1.3 miles). Restrooms are available at the picnic area.

7 Following Buckeye Trail blazes, bear left onto Turkey Trail, which parallels Chapin Pkwy. Head eastward to a trail entrance just before Forest Picnic Shelter (1.7 miles). Follow the blue blazes left on this wide gravel Quarry Trail as it winds through a beautiful forest.

8 Just past a house on the left the Buckeye Trail leaves the main trail to go out to SR 306. Continue on the Quarry Trail until it reaches Quarry Pond Picnic Shelter and restroom building. This is the site of the abandoned 19th-century Berea Sandstone quarry that supplied stones for Kirtland Temple.

9 Follow Chapin Pkwy. westward past Forest Picnic Shelter to Ledges Picnic Shelter (3.3 miles).

10 Ascend the hill above the picnic area; at the top turn left to follow the south branch of Lucky Stone Loop. Here you are on the top of the massive ledges of Sharon Conglomerate sandstone. The 320-million-year-old rock ledges were eroded by glaciers that crept in and out of here about 1.6 million years ago until retreating completely around 12,000 years ago (see Appendix A).

CAUTION: Please do not deviate from the trail or climb on any of the ledges.

11 Continue on Lucky Stone Loop past Wintergreen Link and Mourning Cloak Link as the trail descends (3.8 miles).

12 Continue ahead to meet the Ruffed Grouse Trail on the left. Bear left here (southwest) and follow this trail through mature woods past Ash Grove Link trail to reach Twin Ponds Picnic Shelter and the parking area. ■

9 Girdled Road Reservation
Concord Township

Distance: 5.2 miles

Strenuous

Hiking time: 2 hours

Description: This mostly north–south hike goes from Radcliffe Rd. Picnic Area north to Girdled Rd. Picnic Area and returns along the same path. It begins through farm fields, descends to the Big Creek valley, goes through deep woods, and finally ascends two steep ridges to Girdled Rd. The route uses part of the reservation's Big Woods Loop Trail as well as the blue-blazed Buckeye Trail. Horseback riders also use some of these trails. Trail etiquette calls for hikers to step to the side of the trail and remain quiet until the horses and riders pass.

Directions: South entrance: From I-90 take exit for SR 44; south on SR 44; left (east) on Girdled Rd. for 2.5 miles; right (south) on SR 608 for about 2 miles; left on Radcliffe Rd.; park entrance on the left.
North entrance: After turning left on Girdled Rd., continue east (past SR 608) a total of 3.5 miles. The entrance is on the right side of the road.

Parking & restrooms: At the park entrance.

Girdled Road Reservation, located in Concord Township at the Lake–Geauga county line, is a 643-acre unit of Lake Metroparks offering a picnic shelter, grills, a playground, baseball diamond, fishing pond, and trails for hiking, horseback riding, and cross-country skiing. When snow conditions are good, Lake Metroparks grooms the trails for skiing.

The blue-blazed Buckeye Trail is the main trail in this park, running north–south between Girdled Rd. and Radcliffe Rd., just east of SR 608. A section of Big Creek runs through the park and is accessible from the Buckeye Trail. The primary entrance to Girdled Road Reservation is on Radcliffe Rd., on the border between Lake and Geauga Counties. Access is also available from a parking and picnic area on Girdled Rd.

The road for which the park is named was the first road settlers built from the Pennsylvania line to the new city of Cleveland. The name is derived from the method used to clear the road. First a narrow path was cut. To widen the road, settlers then "girdled" the trees on either side of the clearing. Girdling consisted of cutting around the big trunks, through the bark of the tree, disrupting the tree's flow of nutrients and causing it to die. The dead trees were then easier to remove for the road widening.

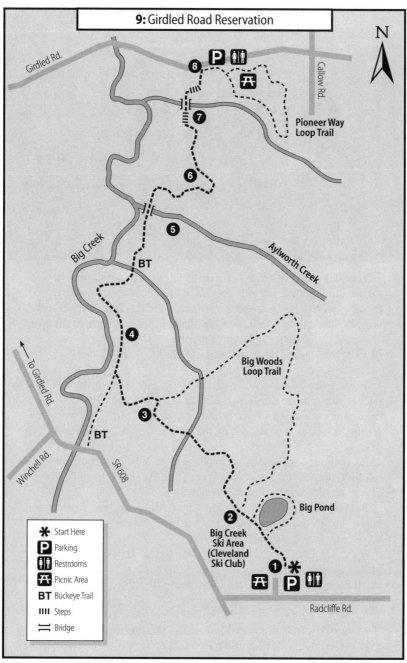

9: Girdled Road Reservation

N

Girdled Rd.

Callow Rd.

8

P 🚻

🏕

7

Pioneer Way
Loop Trail

6

Big Creek

5

BT

Aylworth Creek

To Girdled Rd.

4

Big Woods
Loop Trail

3

BT

Winchell Rd.

SR 608

Big Pond

2

Big Creek
Ski Area
(Cleveland
Ski Club)

1 ✳

🏕 P 🚻

Radcliffe Rd.

✳	Start Here
P	Parking
🚻	Restrooms
🏕	Picnic Area
BT	Buckeye Trail
IIII	Steps
⊨	Bridge

© Gray & Company, Publishers

The walk here can be very pleasant and relaxing, with many views of the streams and the soothing sounds of cascading water. You may wish to allow time to hike around the wetlands at either end of the reservation. Benches allow leisurely observation of interesting natural areas along the trails. Eastern bluebirds use the nest boxes near the wetland. Most of the route is on gravel-surfaced trails.

1 Start the hike at the far end of the grassy area northeast of the parking lot. The trail entrance is behind a pair of split-rail fence sections. The path cuts a swath through a grassy old farm field before entering the woods. A wetland is on the right, encircled by Big Pond Loop Trail.

2 At about 0.4 mile the trail splits into a "Y" intersection. Take the left fork, part of the Big Woods Loop Trail. Follow the trail northwest as it gradually descends to the creek valley.

3 Pass through fields and soon meet the loop trail intersection coming from the right. Stay to the left (west) as the path finishes descending the ridge to Big Creek valley.

4 At the next intersection (1.2 miles) this trail meets the blue-blazed Buckeye Trail going north and south. Here bear right (north), staying on the Buckeye Trail. Cross a muddy spot on logs. Pleasant views of Big Creek open up on the left.

Growing alongside the embankment is a common streamside plant, the scouring rush (also called horsetail). This unusual plant has hollow, jointed stems that are rough and gritty due to silica taken up from the soil and crystallized in its tissues. Horsetails were used by early settlers to scour pots and pans and for sanding and polishing.

Unusually large glacial boulders lie in the stream. These were left behind by a retreating glacier that covered this part of Ohio around 12,000 years ago.

The path crosses a creek bed that is often dry.

5 At 1.9 miles cross wide Aylworth Creek on a bridge and continue on the Buckeye Trail as the trail now begins to go uphill.

6 The Buckeye Trail continues to ascend to the top of the ridge.

7 Descend the hill and reach a set of wooden steps that continue downward to a bridge across a small stream in a deep ravine. The path then ascends three sections of wooden steps and continues up the next hill. Stay on the Buckeye Trail until it reaches the picnic area and road.

8 At 2.6 miles reach Girdled Road Picnic Area. Here are picnic tables, restrooms, and a short circular nature trail.

Return on the Buckeye Trail, descending and ascending the wooden steps, and reach Aylworth Creek again. Continue following the Buckeye Trail until it intersects with the Big Woods Loop Trail. Stay left here.

Continue on the trail as it ascends the hill, taking right turns as you follow the path back to the picnic area at Radcliffe Rd. ■

The method of nature: who could analyze it?
That rushing stream will not stop to be observed. We can never surprise nature in a corner.
    —Ralph Waldo Emerson, *The Method of Nature*

10 Holden Arboretum
Kirtland

Distance: 5.5 miles

Strenuous

Hiking time: 3 hours

Description: This long walk will take you to a variety of Holden's treasures: the deep ravine of Pierson Creek, the rolling Woodland Trail high above the creek, Buttonbush and Owl Bogs, Lotus and Corning Lakes, and Bole Woods. This exceptional area is a National Natural Landmark.

Directions: From I-90 take Exit 193 for Mentor/Kirtland and SR 306; south on SR 306 for about 0.5 miles; left on SR 615 for one long block to traffic signal; right (east) on Kirtland-Chardon Rd. for about 3 miles, past Penitentiary Glen (Lake Metroparks); left on Sperry Rd.

Parking & restrooms: At the visitor center.

The Holden Arboretum is an uncommon preserve of 3,500 acres of natural woodlands, horticultural collections, display gardens, ponds, fields, and ravines, and has 15 miles of trails. With its large collection of 5,400 plants, an exceptional land base, a library, education department, and research division, Holden is among the nation's leading horticultural institutions. Its collections serve several functions: public enjoyment and education, horticultural research, and plant conservation.

Ideal growing conditions at Holden are provided by Lake Erie's moderating effect on daily temperature fluctuations. An extended growing season is provided by winds that blow off a relatively warmer Lake Erie to postpone the first fall freeze. In the spring, crop development is delayed by cool winds blowing over a cold lake that slows fruit blossoming until after the chance of a frost.

Many classes, tours, hikes, bird walks, and other nature activities are offered year round at the arboretum. The preserve was originally provided for through a trust of Albert Fairchild Holden, a noted mining engineer, who died in 1913. The park was initially established in 1931 on just 100 acres of land donated by Holden's sister and brother-in-law, Roberta Holden Bole and Benjamin Bole. Others followed their example, donating both land and operating funds.

Because the arboretum is privately supported, it depends upon memberships and admission fees for maintenance. Non-members who wish to use the many resources available at Holden are charged $4 a day for adults, $3 for seniors, and $2 for children 6–15 years. Admission for members is free.

The Warren H. Corning Visitor Center is named for a major bene-

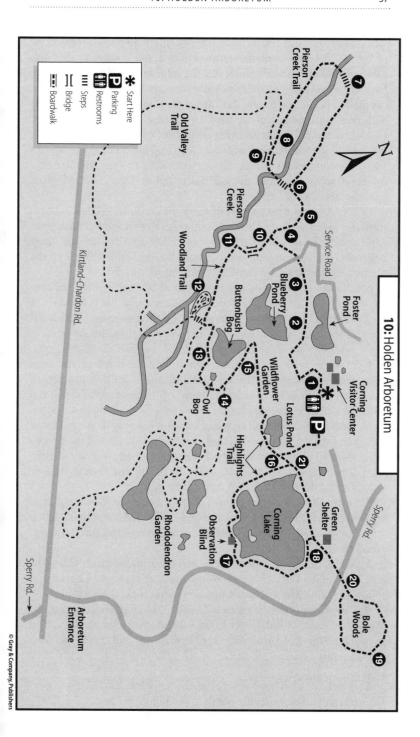

10: Holden Arboretum

Start Here
P Parking
Restrooms
Steps
Bridge
Boardwalk

Pierson Creek Trail

Old Valley Trail

Pierson Creek

Woodland Trail

Kirtland-Chardon Rd.

Service Road

Blueberry Pond

Buttonbush Bog

Foster Pond

Wildflower Garden

Owl Bog

Lotus Pond

Corning Visitor Center

Highlights Trail

Rhododendron Garden

Observation Blind

Corning Lake

Green Shelter

Sperry Rd.

Bole Woods

Arboretum Entrance

Sperry Rd.

© Gray & Company, Publishers

factor through whose generosity Holden Arboretum has the Corning Library of Horticulture Classics, Lantern Court, and major acquisitions of land. The center contains nature exhibits, the library, a rare book room, the Treehouse Gift Shop, and the information desk. Naturalists frequently lead hikes to Stebbins Gulch and Little Mountain, areas not normally open to the public. An annual plant sale is held in the spring with free admission on those days. One of the highlights of a visit to Holden is seeing its magnificent collection of flowering crabapple, lilacs, rhododendrons, and azaleas in May and June. Fishing privileges and cross-country ski touring are open to members only. Membership information is available from Holden Arboretum: 440-946-4400; www.holdenarb.org.

NOTE: Allow the better part of a day for a visit to Holden Arboretum and bring a picnic lunch along, as there is no food service here. After your hike, it is wonderful to soak in the ambiance of the many cultivated gardens, ponds, and natural areas at Holden. Most of the plants and trees are fully identified for your benefit.

In addition to this walk, you may wish to take self-guided walks to the Wildflower Garden, Rhododendron Garden, or the Boardwalk at the bottom of Pierson Ravine using free interpretive maps provided at the visitor center. All trails are well marked with attractive signs.

1 Start this walk at the visitor center. Exit the building and turn right, walking toward the Thayer Building (the original visitor center, now used for classes and other gatherings), then left onto the gravel path. This path leads past picnic tables and a Coast Redwood display. Turn right at the map trail sign and walk a short way to the next trail sign, naming Old Valley, Woodland, and Pierson Trails and the Boardwalk. Proceed ahead, between the Pat Bole Kiosk and a picnic shelter, then down steps and to the left. Cross the bridge and turn right. Follow signs for the Old Valley/Woodland/Pierson Trails.

2 Foster Pond is on the right. This portion of the Woodland Trail leads to both the Pierson Creek and Old Valley trails. Stay to the left at a fork in the trail. (Please respect all fence barriers and stay on designated trails.)

3 At 0.3 mile, you will reach a trail/road intersection. Cross the road and follow the Old Valley/Woodland/Pierson signs. Continue to follow the same Pierson Creek signs, enjoying these quiet woods.

4 Turn right onto the Pierson Creek/Old Valley Trail, leaving the Woodland Trail behind. (Later in the hike you will return to this point to take the Woodland Trail.) The trail here is wide and gravel-surfaced. On the left is a narrow slit of ravine, with hemlocks hugging the steep slopes.

5 Watch for a left bend just before the fence barrier (0.6 mile). Bear left here, still going generally north toward Pierson Creek.

6 Reach the junction for the Pierson Trail Loop. Turn right to follow the loop counterclockwise. The trail narrows and winds through a beech and hemlock forest interspersed with oaks.

7 (1.1 mile) Reach a long flight of steep wooden stairs to Pierson Creek. Here is an enchantingly cool, moist environment that changes its appearance with each season. It can be a welcome oasis on a hot summer day. Turn left at the foot of the steps, following the well-trodden path.

There are many interesting wildflowers, ferns, and clubmosses that thrive here under moist conditions. This valley was once much deeper and wider than it is now. It was filled in by glacial till left by this area's last retreating glacier about 12,000 years ago. Pierson Creek, flowing northward, is slowly cutting through the remaining till.

(1.2 miles) You will reach a small set of steps that go down to the stream, which you will cross on stones. Go up a few steps, turn left and continue along the creek. The next set of steps go back down to creek level, and a small bridge crosses a side drainage.

8 At 1.6 miles a trail intersects from the right. (This is the Old Valley Trail loop, which, if taken, will add another 1.5 miles to the hike, ending near Buttonbush Bog.) Continue ahead.

9 Cross a wooden bridge over a side brook; just beyond is Pierson Creek. Cross the creek on stones. The trail leads up another steep wooden stairway.

The loop trail ends at the top of the steps. Turn right on the Pierson/Old Valley Trail (2 miles).

10 Turn right onto the Woodland Trail (Boardwalk). (This is the same point reached in Note #4.)

11 Cross a ravine on a long wooden bridge. Here the tops of many tall trees were snapped off by a fierce storm, opening up the woods to more light and new plant growth. Avoid taking any side trails.

An interpretive sign on the left explains the American beech bark disease that has marred these woods.

12 On the right is a set of wooden steps that descend to the Boardwalk. If there is time, it is worthwhile to take another walk down to Pierson Creek to learn about the flora of the valley by following several boardwalk loops. This side trip will add only another quarter mile to the hike. The Boardwalk provides access to 58 labeled native wildflowers, ferns, and fern allies. Peak bloom for the flowers is usually during the last week in April and the first week of May.

13 Continue on the Woodland/Old Valley Trail. Benches placed along the trail invite you to sit and absorb the peacefulness of the woods and call to mind the words of Henry David Thoreau:

> You cannot perceive beauty
> but with a serene mind.

The path gently winds southeastward. At about 2.6 miles pass the Old Valley/Highlights Trail on the right and the continuation of Highlights Trail on the left, and continue ahead to Buttonbush Bog, still on the Woodland Trail. Turn right to pass Buttonbush Bog, keeping it on the left. At the north end of this bog is a two-level observation tower overlooking the plant-filled pond. The natural process of succession is at work here slowly transforming this pond to a bog.

14 At the end of tiny Owl Bog, turn left to pass the east sides of both bogs on the Woodland/Old Valley Trail. Owl Bog has become almost entirely filled with organic material (3 miles).

15 At the north end of Buttonbush Bog, turn right onto the gravel road. Blueberry Pond is located to the left of the trail. Alongside Blueberry Pond is a path that goes back to the visitor center. Continue on the road going east, passing the sign to the Rhododendron Garden, which, when it is in bloom in late April and May to early July, is a magnificent sight. The fully labeled Wildflower Garden is on the left and also worth a visit. Straight ahead is Lotus Pond.

16 Stay on the road (Highlights Trail) to the right. Cross a small footbridge and bear right, then turn right to cross another footbridge over the spillway outlet for Corning Lake.

17 Follow a trail counterclockwise around Corning Lake, home to many waterfowl and fish. The small screened building on the edge of the lake is the Observation Blind. Private property is on the right. Continue on the grassy trail along the rim of the lake. In the spring, large yellow pond lilies thrive at this end of the lake.

18 Follow the shore of Corning Lake on the Highlights Trail until you reach the trail sign for Green Shelter and Bole Woods Trail. Turn right and take the path to the Green Shelter (4 miles). This small wooden shelter was placed here by the Green family in memory of their two sons who died in a 1966 boating accident. A sign inside reads: "Dedicated to the wondrous beauty of nature, God's great gift to mankind," and a plaque outside commemorates the two boys. You may wish to stop and sit in the shelter to enjoy a glorious view of the hills to the west. Many bluebird nesting boxes have been placed throughout the fields here.

19 Cross Sperry Rd. to reach the Bole Woods Trail, a one-mile forest loop through an upland beech/maple forest. These tall trees were part of a vast wilderness that extended over much of postglacial Ohio and posed a formidable barrier to early pioneers who tried to penetrate it. The maple trees were left to stand in these woods as a sugar bush to collect sap for maple syrup. Bole Woods has been designated a National Natural Landmark.

The path (occasionally wet in the spring) gently loops to the north through the heart of the woodland. Many of the oaks and beeches tower 60 feet or more. The forest floor supports abundant wildflowers

in the spring: trout lilies, Dutchman's breeches, squirrel corn, toothworts, trilliums, violets, and many others. Some large beech trees here were felled in a storm.

20 When you emerge from the trail, continue toward the Arbor Vitae Collection; go through the Arbor Vitae on the gravel road, or around it if protective fencing is up. Near the Arbor Vitae a large sugar maple shades a bench. The maple's low and spreading branches indicate that it grew in the open, without competition from neighboring trees. Cross Sperry Rd. and walk back to the Green Shelter, then continue alongside Corning Lake. Pass a storage building and turn right on the walkway (Highlights Trail) that borders Lotus Pond (on the left).

21 Follow this walkway back to the parking area. On the way you will pass some of Holden's magnificent horticultural collections and a small reflecting pool. ■

To the attentive eye each moment of the year has its own beauty, and in the same field, it beholds, every hour, a picture which was never seen before, and which shall never be seen again.

—Ralph Waldo Emerson, *Essay on Nature*

11 Painesville

Distance: 2 miles

Walking time: 2 hours

Description: This is an easy walk on sidewalks through Painesville's historic district and through part of the campus of Lake Erie College.

Directions: From I-90 take Exit 200 for SR 44 (Chardon/Painesville); north on SR 44 for 1.5 miles; right on SR 84 (Johnny Cake Ridge Rd.); north on SR 86 (State St.) into downtown Painesville; left on Main St. for two blocks to town square.

Parking & restrooms: Park at any of the public parking spaces around the public square. There are public restrooms at Painesville's Recreation Park just east of downtown. To reach the park, continue north on SR 86 one block to Latimore St.; right on Latimore to enter the park.

The city of Painesville is in Lake County alongside the Grand River and not far from Lake Erie. While it is only 2.5 miles from the lake as the crow flies, it is almost 7 river miles upstream of the river's mouth, since the Grand River takes a wide arcing loop around Painesville before reaching Lake Erie. It was not the river so much as it was an ancient form of Lake Erie that influenced Painesville's location. Over geologic time Lake Erie has fluctuated widely in size, and as the lake grew and shrank, it repeatedly deposited low ridges of sand parallel to today's shoreline. These sand ridges or old lakeshores proved to be favored routes for early settlers, and it is along one of these east–west ridges that Painesville developed. Today US 20, also called N. Ridge Rd., largely follows one of the old ridges through the center of town, and Johnny Cake Ridge Rd. and S. Ridge Rd. follow similar ridges south of town.

Painesville is one of the handful of towns that can boast of being the earliest settlements in the Connecticut Western Reserve. Within two years of the time that Moses Cleaveland began surveying the Western Reserve, this part of the reserve had been platted out in anticipation of pioneers making their way west. In 1800 the first pioneer settlers arrived, a group of 66 led by General Edward Paine and John Walworth. In that same year Connecticut gave up its claim on the reserve; it became part of the Northwest Territory and was named Trumbull County. The first settlement at Painesville's present location was on about 80 acres just north of the present downtown and was named after a geologic feature. Some of the sand ridges and isolated dunes

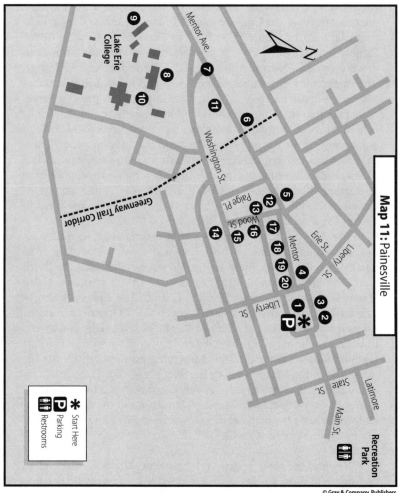

© Gray & Company, Publishers

were covered with oaks that could tolerate the infertile, sandy soil. These areas were known as Oak Openings, and it was that name that was applied to the early settlement. Later, in 1805, General Henry Champion mapped out a village at the site of the Oak Openings settlement and named it Champion, after himself. In 1832 that section of the township was incorporated and took the name of Painesville, after Edward Paine. In 1840, when a separate Lake County was established, Painesville became the county seat.

Painesville flourished throughout its early history, becoming a center for both manufacturing and agriculture. It was on a major east–west route through the state, and by 1851 an east–west railroad also came through town. It was also an important stop on another route—several prominent citizens of Painesville were active in assisting slaves traveling the Underground Railroad en route to ships at Fairport Harbor that would take them to freedom in Canada. Today Painesville is a city of over 15,000 people, with an attractive, revitalized downtown and a historic district, and it is home to Lake Erie College. The Painesville Department of Recreation and Public Lands provides 100 acres of park and public lands, including the very popular Recreation Park that sits alongside the Grand River. In the spring and fall fly fishermen space themselves out along the river's ripples and pools to enjoy some of the region's finest steelhead trout fishing. The 75-acre park also has ball diamonds, playgrounds, a youth fishing pond, ball courts, and three rentable picnic shelters. For information, phone the Recreation Office at 440-639-4898. Recreation Park, although not included in this hike, is only a few blocks from downtown and is worth visiting for access to the Grand River.

Painesville is close to several beautiful natural areas, so if time allows, you could combine this town walk with a visit to one of the areas nearby. Mentor Marsh State Nature Preserve and Headlands Beach State Park are within a short drive, as is the Lake Metroparks Helen Hazen Wyman Park, located on the Grand River just upstream of Painesville. Lake Metroparks has also opened the Greenway Corridor Bikeway that follows an abandoned B & O Railroad right-of-way and links Painesville to rural Painesville and Concord townships. Fairport Harbor and the Fairport Marine Museum are also worth a visit. The museum was founded in 1945 by the Fairport Harbor Historical Society, making it the first Great Lakes lighthouse museum in the country. It is open on Wednesdays, Saturdays, Sundays, and holidays, Memorial Day weekend through Labor Day weekend. For more information phone the museum at 440-354-4825.

1 Begin at the town square, Veterans Park. Plenty of shade trees, benches, and picnic tables make Veterans Park an attractive destination for downtown explorers as well as county office workers on their lunch hour. This downtown green space anchors Painesville's historic district and offers a quiet counterpoint to the imposing county buildings and commercial district surrounding it. There are several places to get a bite to eat nearby. In the summertime the octagonal gazebo in the square is surrounded by flower gardens and is a popular site for weddings. The annual Party in the Park is held in Veterans Park in the summer, and in December Santa Claus arrives during the Spirit of the Season event.

A monument to Civil War veterans is at the east end of the park. Here a small plaque, difficult to read due to age and weathering, describes how Abraham Lincoln's train, bound for his inauguration in Washington, D.C., paused in Painesville for the president-elect to speak to a crowd of well-wishers, and four years later another train bearing the president came through town, but this time it was his funeral train, solemnly passing his many mourners.

2 Leaving Veterans Park from the northeast corner, cross the street at the crosswalk near the Lake County administration building. Bear left to cross a service lane and walk along the north side of North Park Place. The Methodist Episcopal Church dates to 1873 and is listed in the National Register of Historic Places. Its architectural design is Gothic Revival, a style popular with church designers of the time.

3 Continue walking westward. The Lake County Courthouse is next, an imposing structure that was constructed in 1909. To its west is the courthouse annex, originally built as the town's post office.

4 Cross Liberty St. to reach the Painesville city hall. The city hall sits at the corner of Richmond St., Mentor Ave., and Liberty St. and overlooks Veterans Park and the city square. On a sunny day its copper dome is especially dramatic against the blue sky. Here at the city hall you enter the Mentor Avenue Historic District, a National Register of Historic Places district comprised of several blocks of historic homes and buildings. The district stretches along Mentor Ave. from the downtown square to Lake Erie College and along both sides of Wood St.

The architect of the city hall was Jonathan Goldsmith, well known to historians as the leading Greek Revival master builder of the Western Reserve. Goldsmith lived from 1783 to 1847 and was most active as a designer and builder in Northeast Ohio between 1819 and 1843. Much of his building design took place in Painesville, where he designed the city hall, the Shepard House, and the Denton-Powers House, all in the historic district, as well as many other houses and public buildings, including the Rider Tavern, located at 792 Mentor Ave., west of the historic district. Goldsmith died in Painesville and is buried in the township cemetery.

As is typical of Greek Revival public buildings, Doric columns support the portico of the Painesville city hall. The hall has a central dome and cupola, six-over-six lighted windows, and stone lintels and sills. The building was constructed in 1840 and originally served as the Lake County courthouse until the newer courthouse was built on North Park Place.

A historic marker in front of the city hall introduces visitors to the Mentor Avenue Historic District. The district is significant architecturally for its rich variety of well-preserved historic buildings and homes, and historically because it was home to citizens of local and national importance. The district is also remarkable for being relatively intact despite its closeness to the center of town. House styles range from Greek Revival to Italianate and Queen Anne, and date from 1820 to the early 1900s.

5 Continue down Mentor Ave., passing the city hall addition, historic homes, and a modern office building. At a five-way intersection, cross Erie St. and continue on Mentor Ave., passing more historic

homes. Cross Jefferson St., pass three more historic homes, and reach
the Shepard House at 234 Mentor Ave. The Shepard House, built in the
Greek Revival style, is the second of three buildings in the historic district attributed to Jonathan Goldsmith. The house sits back from the
street on a rise and is shaded by a very large tulip tree. Levi Shepard arrived in Painesville with his family in 1820 and moved into this house
in 1833. He was farmer, real estate agent, and county trustee.

6 Cross the Greenway Trail Corridor and continue west on Mentor
Ave. Pass several more historic homes. The brick Steele House at 332
Mentor Ave. marks the western boundary of the historic district and is
another fine example of the district's 19th-century architecture.

7 Cross Mentor Ave. to enter Charter Oak Park, a tiny triangular
park commemorating Painesville's founder, General Edward Paine. A
small statue of Paine is central to the park. Paine was a captain in the
Revolutionary War and achieved the rank of brigadier general in the
New York State Militia. Near the statue is a more recent addition to the
park, a young oak tree planted here by the New Connecticut Chapter
of the National Society of the Daughters of the American Revolution
to commemorate the bicentennial of the United States Constitution.

8 Cross Washington St. and enter the Lake Erie College campus.
The sidewalk leads directly to the main building on campus, College
Hall. This handsome administration building is listed in the National
Register of Historic Places. The four-story brick building has a central
tower above the entrance and four-over-four windows; its style is
known as Italian Villa. This building dates back to the founding of the
college and continues to play a central role on campus.

Lake Erie College has roots that reach as far as South Hadley, Mass-
achusetts, and Mount Holyoke Female Seminary (now Mount Holyoke College). In 1847 a graduate of Mount Holyoke, Roxena B. Tenney,
was asked by the trustees of the Willoughby Medical College to come
to Willoughby and start a seminary for young women. Ms. Tenney accepted the invitation and established the Willoughby Female Seminary
in a building that had been vacated by the medical college.

In the mid-1800s very few women received a formal education beyond the elementary level. This began to change with the development
of "female seminaries," schools that provided a higher level of education for young women with emphasis on their becoming more capable
managers of their households, better mothers, and missionaries of
Christianity. The curriculum was certainly not on a par with that of
men's colleges, but nonetheless the seminaries were the first institutions to provide women an education beyond the basics, and some
grew to become degree-granting colleges.

The Willoughby Female Seminary was the only women's college in
the Western Reserve at the time of its founding, and it operated until
1856, when a fire destroyed the school's only building. The trustees
quickly reorganized and moved the school to Painesville, renaming it

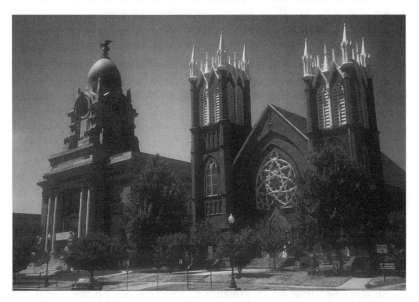

Lake Erie Female Seminary. The cornerstone for the new school was laid on July 4, 1857, and in the fall of 1859 Lake Erie Female Seminary accepted its first 127 students. The curriculum and operation of the school were patterned after Mount Holyoke's, and Mount Holyoke graduates were sought out as teachers. As Gladys Haddad tells us in *Ohio's Western Reserve: A Regional Reader*, the male trustees of the seminary hired female teachers who were expected to "possess a missionary spirit that moved them to 'labor faithfully and cheerfully, receiving only a moderate salary.'" Haddad also reports that a *Painesville Telegraph* editorial at the time commemorated the advent of the school, commenting, "It is quite a modern idea, this, that Girls are capable of any considerable intellectual improvement." The editorial went on to commend the seminary's goal of educating women, since "the great interests of civilization will be safe when in the hands of the sons of educated mothers."

By 1898 Lake Erie Female Seminary had expanded its course offerings, and it began to offer college degrees. The name was changed to Lake Erie College and Seminary, and later shortened to Lake Erie College. Today the college admits 815 men and women each year, offering a core liberal arts education and career-oriented majors in 21 fields of study, including education, environmental science, equine facility management, international business, medicine, and veterinary medicine.

9 Proceed to the right of College Hall and turn left to walk alongside its west side. The Austin Science Center is on your right. Bear right onto a diagonal path through the campus to reach Kilcawley Hall. In the basement of Kilcawley Hall is the Indian Museum of Lake County, Ohio, well worth a visit if you have the time. Tucked into a small room down a hall and around a corner, the museum is a bit of a surprise, with its fine collection of Native American artifacts and art. The museum houses exhibits on the earliest inhabitants of the region (and the state) from 10,000 B.C. to 1650 A.D., as well as Native American art and crafts from all of North America, from 1800 to the present.

The Indian Museum was established in 1980 by the Lake County chapter of the Archaeological Society of Ohio. The museum owes its existence largely to the volunteer amateur archaeologists who labored during the 1970s to save hundreds of artifacts from a construction site in Eastlake. The Reeve Village Site yielded much information about the prehistoric Indians of the area and is well documented at the museum. Many of the amateur collectors donated their own artifacts to form the basis of the museum's collection. Lake Erie College provides space for the museum, and the museum in turn hires students for its staff. The museum includes a library open to anyone conducting research. The Indian Museum of Lake County is open May 1–September 1, 10 A.M. to 4 P.M. weekdays, 1 P.M. to 4 P.M. Saturdays and Sundays; and September 1–April 30, 9 A.M. to 4 P.M. weekdays and 1 P.M. to 4 P.M. Saturdays and Sundays. The museum is closed on major holiday weekends and during Lake Erie College's winter and spring breaks. Groups visiting must call ahead to make reservations at 440-352-1911. Admission is charged: adults $2; seniors $1.50; students K–12 $1; and preschoolers free.

10 From Kilcawley Hall turn back toward College Hall and walk past the Arthur S. Holden Center, home to the college bookstore and dining hall as well as classrooms and offices. Continue behind College Hall toward the Fine and Performing Arts Center. To your right and down a slope is the Lincoln Library. At the Fine and Performing Arts Center bear left, working your way back to Washington St.

11 Cross Washington St. near Charter Oak Park to reach Mentor Ave. Turn right on Mentor Ave. to go back toward the town square. The first two houses on Mentor Ave. are two of the finer and more elaborate Queen Anne–style homes in the historic district. These Queen Annes show the typical irregular form of the style: both have corner octagonal towers, steep gable roofs, bay windows with stained-glass transoms, and shingled siding.

12 Continue down Mentor Ave. and again cross the Greenway Trail Corridor. Historic homes, many with flower gardens, line this entire block of Mentor Ave. Cross Paige Place and continue to the end of the block, where you'll reach the Harvey House. An Ohio Historical Society plaque is in front of the house. This was the home of Thomas Harvey, an educator who was at various times a professor at Bowling Green University, trustee of Lake Erie College, superintendent of Painesville schools, founder of the Northeast Ohio Teachers College, and state superintendent of schools under Governor Rutherford

Hayes. He is best known to some as the author of the *Harvey's Grammar* and *Harvey's Readers* books, successors to the McGuffey Eclectic Readers series of reading-instruction books.

13 Turn right on Wood St., also part of the Mentor Avenue Historic District. Wood St. is a pleasant side street lined with houses in a mixture of different styles, including some handsome Italianate homes. At the end of the block is a modern single-story nursing home.

14 Cross Washington St. and turn right. Painesville's Harvey High School, named after Thomas Harvey, is on your left. Just beyond the high school is an Ohio Historical Society bicentennial plaque commemorating another notable gentleman who spent his early years in Painesville—Daniel Carter Beard. Beard was a nationally recognized illustrator who is perhaps best known for *The American Boy's Handy Book*, a volume of woodcraft and nature lore very popular around the turn of the 20th century. Beard founded the Sons of Daniel Boone in 1906 and later helped establish the Boy Scouts of America (BSA). His contributions include designing the BSA uniform and emblem.

15 Return to Wood St. and cross to the northeast corner of Wood and Washington streets. On the corner to your right is the large Perkins House, partly hidden by tall maples and evergreens. This was the home of William Perkins, one of the first Lake County representatives to the Ohio Congress.

16 Continue northward on Wood St. back toward Mentor Ave. There are several more historic homes along the way, including one with a wrought-iron fence, and what appears to be a stepping-stone for mounting a horse or carriage.

17 Turn right on Mentor Ave. and walk east toward downtown. The Wilder House at 85 Mentor Ave. is a fine example of an early Western Reserve/Greek Revival house. This was the home of Grandison Wilder, who owned a successful Painesville plow factory.

18 Two doors down from the Wilder House is the Denton-Powers House, built in 1820, the third building in the district designed by Jonathan Goldsmith. Doctor Denton, one of Painesville's early physicians, commissioned Goldsmith to build the home for Denton's wife; however, she died before the house was completed. Denton himself was killed in 1830, and a succession of other doctors and professionals occupied the house in the following years. The Denton-Powers house is of the same Greek Revival style as the Painesville city hall. Mimicking the city hall, the home has four Doric pilasters that act as columns and support the triangular, low-pitched gable, or pediment. Note the elliptical sunburst in the center of the pediment. The home also has windows with six-over-six panes, as does the city hall. Only one of two original side wings remains.

19 Next to the Denton-Powers House is one of Painesville's more picturesque 20th-century homes (now a bed-and-breakfast), a small house designed in the Cotswold style, which is recognizable by its steep hip roof, brick and half-timbered surfaces, narrow casement windows, and low eaves, all reminiscent of English countryside cottages.

20 The First Congregational Church, United Church of Christ, at the corner of Mentor Ave. and Liberty St., was the first church in Painesville and in Lake County. The congregation was organized in 1810, moved into its first building in 1829, then built the present church in 1862. A modern addition faces Mentor Ave. If you step around the corner you can see that the original structure's design is Early Romanesque Revival. It is built of brick and sandstone, has round-arched windows, buttressed towers, and projecting brick moldings, or cornices, along the tops of the walls.

Cross Liberty St. and return to Veterans Park to end the hike. ■

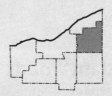

GEAUGA COUNTY

Geauga County, the second county to be founded in Connecticut's Western Reserve (1805), is home to Ohio's second-largest Amish settlement (after Holmes County), centered at Middlefield. Geauga County's farms are rich in soil, water, and woodlands. Dairy farming, cheese making, and maple syrup production are among the county's main agricultural activities. Several of the towns in Geauga County resemble New England villages because they were founded by eastern pioneers who were attracted to the area's beautiful rolling farmland and sugar maple forests. Chardon, the county seat—neatly laid out high on a central green—is listed in the National Register of Historic Places. With an average of 106 inches of snow annually, Geauga County is a great destination for winter enthusiasts.

Century Village in Burton, operated by the Geauga County Historical Society, is a complex of 20 restored buildings furnished with antiques preserving the Reserve's early history. The outdoor museum is open from May through October for guided tours (440-834-1492).

One of the earliest buildings in the county is Welshfield Inn, at the junction of US 422 and SR 700. Built in the 1840s as a hotel, it later served as a post office and, during the Civil War, became a stop on the Underground Railroad. It is now a restaurant (440-834-4164).

Punderson State Park offers boating, swimming, fishing, hiking, and lodging. It is especially popular with cross-country skiers.

The Geauga Park District protects thousands of acres of wildlife habitat and provides outstanding natural areas for public recreation in 11 parks and preserves. The Rookery, a 446-acre park in Munson Township along the Chagrin River southwest of Chardon, opened in 1997 and features one of the largest great blue heron nesting colonies in Northeast Ohio. West Woods, a 900-acre preserve in Russell and Newbury Townships includes pristine Silver Creek and outstanding rock ledges. Other preserves are not open to the public because of the sensitive nature of their rare foliage.

Information is available from Geauga Park District: 440-285-2222.

Information about Geauga County is available from the Geauga County Chamber of Commerce and Tourism Council: 800-775-8687.

12 Whitlam Woods
Hambden Township

Distance: 2 miles

Easy

Hiking time: 1 hour

Description: The main ravine is ascended and descended on steps, but the rest of the trails here are primarily flat. Some of the paths in Whitlam Woods are wet at times, but a fine footbridge crosses the main stream. The ruins of an old sugarhouse can be seen on the Sugarbush Trail, a reminder of the maple sugaring activity for which Geauga County is well known. Tall hardwood trees in the park provide ideal rest stops for birds when they flock here during migration season; birds also frequent the meadow adjacent to the parking area.

Directions: From I-90 take Exit 200 to SR 44; south on SR 44 for 3.5 miles; left (east) on Clark Rd.; right (south) on Robinson; left (east) on Pearl Rd. to the park entrance, on left.

From the town of Chardon, take North St. at the north end of the town square for 1.3 miles; right on Woodin Rd. for 0.75 mile; left on Robinson Rd.; pass Big Creek Park on the left; right (east) on Pearl Rd. for 0.75 mile; sign for Geauga Park District and Whitlam Woods on left.

Parking & restrooms: Near the park entrance.

Whitlam Woods is a 110-acre park in Geauga County near Chardon that is administered by the Geauga Park District. In 1959 Fred Whitlam made a generous gift to Geauga County to be used to buy a parcel of land that would be a memorial to his parents and other pioneers, and be a place where "the children [could] roam ." His gift not only created Whitlam Woods, it also led to the establishment of the Geauga County Park District in 1961. Whitlam Woods is located near Big Creek Park and is bisected by two of Big Creek's tributaries and their ravines. The memorial forest consists primarily of mature beeches, maples, and hemlocks. Because it is so small, Whitlam Woods can be enjoyed as a second hike after visiting Big Creek Park (Ch. 14).

1 Enter the Overlook Trail straight ahead (north) of the parking area and follow it to its end. This 0.1-mile dead-end trail overlooks ravines on either side and offers a view of the forest from a sheltered bench. Return the same way and turn left (east) onto the Bridge Trail to descend on a switchback path and steps to the streambed.

2 Cross the stream, a tributary of Big Creek, on the footbridge and hike up a set of steps. An inviting bench is at the top on the left.

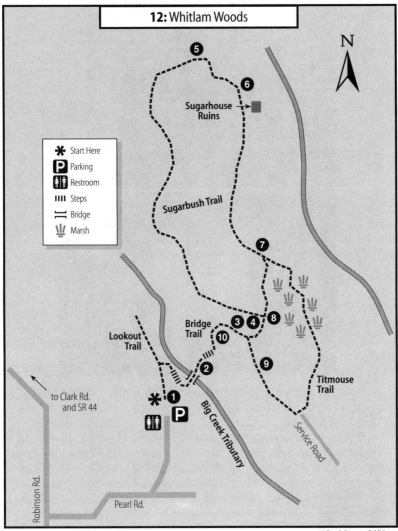

12: Whitlam Woods

N

* Start Here
P Parking
Restroom
IIII Steps
Bridge
Marsh

Sugarhouse → Ruins

Sugarbush Trail

Bridge Trail

Lookout Trail

Titmouse Trail

to Clark Rd. and SR 44

Big Creek Tributary

Service Road

Robinson Rd.

Pearl Rd.

© Gray & Company, Publishers

3 Bear left at the intersection of the Sugarbush Trail with the Titmouse Trail.

4 Stay left at the next intersection to continue on the Sugarbush Trail loop. Another bench invites contemplation of the woods high above the ravine on the left (west) and calls to mind John Muir's words:

> I care to live only to entice people to look at
> nature's loveliness. My own special self is nothing.

5 The trail winds through a splendid upland hardwood forest with

tall maples and oaks. After about a half-mile, it bends around to the east where, in the fall and winter seasons, there is a clear view of the ravine and stream.

6 On your left, watch for a brick chimney and hearth ruin and the remains of a sugarhouse. All that is left of a large maple sugaring operation in this forest are the foundation, a few scraps of metal from buckets. Take a brief detour to view the ruins, if you wish.

7 Once back on the main trail, continue south until you reach an intersection with a bench and signs for both the Sugarbush and Titmouse Trails. Stay right on the Sugarbush Trail.

8 At the next Sugarbush Trail and Bridge Trail signs, bear left on the Bridge Trail, then turn left again at the sign for the Titmouse Trail.

9 Enter the Titmouse Trail, pass a service road on the right, and continue through a red maple forest. Here the trail may be marshy at times. When you reach the Sugarbush Trail, turn left and follow it southwest.

10 Continue west on the Bridge Trail. Descend the stairs, cross the footbridge, and ascend the steps and switchback path to the top of the ravine. Turn left at the top onto the Overlook Trail to return to the parking area. ■

13 Headwaters Park
Claridon Township

Distance: 5 miles

Moderate

Hiking time: 2 ¾ hours

Description: This hike follows the Buckeye Trail on a foot path and then a dirt and gravel road over gently rolling terrain. The way is marked for most of its length by Buckeye Trail blazes, 2-by-6-inch blue rectangles painted on trees in both directions. In some spots the blazes may be hard to find, especially in the wooded portion. The hike proceeds about 2½ miles to US 322 and returns by the same route. Different views of the forest and lake are always a pleasant surprise when hiking the same trail in the opposite direction.

Directions: From I-271 take Exit 34 (Mayfield Rd./US 322); east on Mayfield/US 322; right (south) on SR 608 (Old State Rd.) for 2 miles; left into park.

Parking & restrooms: At the parking area. NOTE: There is also a small parking area on US 322 before it crosses the reservoir. A second car can be dropped here in order to eliminate the return hike.

Headwaters Park is a 926-acre reservation surrounding East Branch Reservoir near East Claridon in Geauga County. The Geauga Park District manages the reservation through a lease agreement with the city of Akron, which owns the land. Akron created the drinking water reservoir in 1932 by damming the East Branch of the Cuyahoga River. The Cuyahoga rises not far from here in the woods of a dairy farm near US 6 and SR 86.

Near the south end of this reservoir is a public boat launch area. Information about fishing and boating can be obtained from the Geauga Park District: 440-285-2222.

This hike is a pleasant walk on the west side of the reservoir. Waterfowl are plentiful in the reservation, especially during spring and fall migration. Hikers might see bald eagles, osprey, tundra swans, and many species of ducks. Wildflowers grow in abundance in the beech/maple forests bordering the reservoir.

1 Begin the walk on the park entry drive marked with blue Buckeye Trail blazes. On the left (west), the BT turns into the woods going northeast. Although its blue blazes may not be easy to see, the trail's entry is alongside a log railing used for tying up horses. Follow the path through a pine forest. At 0.2 mile cross a stream and continue up the side of a small hill through a tall maple and oak forest.

2 At 0.3 mile there is a fork in the trail. Bear to the right and emerge

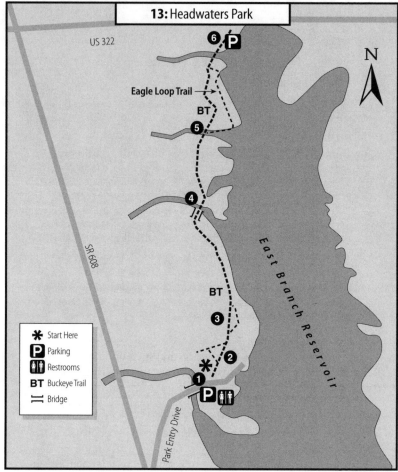

© Gray & Company, Publishers

onto a wider, more heavily used trail marked with blue blazes.

3 Follow the blue-blazed trail past several intersecting trails. Continue until the path drops down to the road. Turn left here (0.5 mile). Continue to follow the blue blazes of the Buckeye Trail along the road.

4 Cross a wooden bridge and note the unusually deep rust color of the water, an indication of the high level of iron that leaches from the rocks in the stream.

5 After crossing through a large, open meadow and reentering the woods, you may wish to turn right onto the Eagle Loop Trail, a scenic 0.8-mile trail that wanders along the shore of the reservoir and returns to the main trail. At the main trail (Buckeye Trail), turn right.

6 After 2.5 miles, the trail emerges onto the other parking area at US 322. Retrace your steps by turning south and following the Buckeye Trail in the reverse direction. ■

14 Big Creek Park
Chardon Township

Distance: 4 miles (2 mile option) | Moderate

Hiking time: About 2 hours (option for 1 hour)

Description: The easy individual trails in this park are short, only a mile or less, but together they cover an expanse of gently rolling terrain with views of ponds and streams. Bird-watching in Big Creek Park is especially rewarding during spring and fall migrations. Wildflowers are abundant in the spring. Tall maple, beech, and oak trees provide brilliant color in the fall.

Directions: From I-90 take exit for SR 44 (Exit 200); south on SR 44 for 3.5 miles; left (east) on Clark Rd.; right on Robinson Rd.; park entrance on right.

From Chardon, take North St. at north end of village square 1.3 miles; right (east) on Woodin Rd.; left (north) on Robinson Rd. for about 1.5 miles; park entrance on left; at entrance take left turn to the Aspen Grove parking area.

Parking & restrooms: At the Meyer Center and adjacent Aspen Grove.

Big Creek Park is located just north of Chardon. It contains 642 acres of mature woodland through which Big Creek and its tributaries flow. It is very near Whitlam Woods and can be hiked in conjunction with a visit to that park (Ch. 12).

Samuel Livingston Mather's gift of 505 acres of land to the state of Ohio was the genesis of this park. Geauga Park District acquired additional acres to bring it to its current size and now owns the entire 642 acres. The forest is especially important as a nesting habitat for neotropical songbirds.

A nature center, named for the district's first park director, Donald W. Meyer, contains nature exhibits, classrooms, a small library, and a bird feeding area. Park personnel are available to assist the visitor with information, maps, and literature about the district's natural areas (440-286-9516). The center is open weekdays 8 A.M. to 4:30 P.M. and on weekends 10 A.M. to 6 P.M. (winter weekends, noon to 4 P.M.) Fishing, primitive camping, picnic shelters, and a system of trails for hiking, cross-country skiing, and horseback riding are among the resources offered in Big Creek Park. A section of the Buckeye Trail passes through the area and is identified by 2-by-6-inch blue rectangular markings placed at intervals on trees.

1 Start the hike on the blue-blazed Buckeye Trail to the right of the small shelter, sundial, and flagpole at the west end of the Aspen Grove parking area. This trail is also identified as the Trillium Trail. Enter the trail to the right going north and very soon pass Chestnut Pond.

2 At the pond the trail, still the Buckeye/Trillium Trail, bears left and overlooks a stream on the left.

3 At a park bench, bear right and continue to follow the Buckeye/Trillium Trail. Pass restrooms and the Maple Grove parking area. At 0.4 mile, reach a set of wooden steps going down to a ravine. Bypass these steps and leave the Trillium Trail here. Continue on the Buckeye Trail to the right. Pass the picnic shelter and picnic grove and turn right to exit at the Maple Grove Picnic Area and parking area.

4 Just off the parking lot is a sign for the White Oak Trail, identified with an oak leaf. This 0.3-mile loop trail is a favorite cross-country skiing trail, as it follows gently undulating land at the far north end of the park.

At the first trail intersection, stay left to remain on the White Oak Trail. Continue on the White Oak Trail through a beautiful stand of white oak and other hardwood trees.

5 At the next trail junction, the White Oak Trail turns sharply to the right. Cross a small wooden bridge, pass a spur of the Buckeye Trail that goes east out of the park. Pass picnic tables and shelters to reach the campground parking area.

6 At the campground, follow the gravel road south to an asphalt-paved road, which leads back to the Maple Grove Picnic Area and parking.

7 At the west end of the parking area, pass the White Oak Trail entrance again. At the blue Buckeye Trail blaze, turn right to go past the Maple Grove shelter. Behind the shelter enter the Trillium Trail again and descend the wooden steps that were bypassed earlier in Note #3. The steps lead down to a boardwalk and bridge over a tributary of Big Creek, and up the opposite side of a broad ravine.

8 Soon there will be a sign for the Boreal Trail on the right. The 0.1-mile Boreal Trail loops to the top of a ridge and affords a fine view northwest across the valley as well as a view of Big Creek below. At an intersection where an illegitimate trail goes downhill to the creek, stay to the left to continue on the Boreal Trail until it intersects with the Trillium Trail again.

9 Turn right to follow the Trillium Trail south until you reach the Meyer Center. The Donald W. Meyer Center, opened in 1991, is the administrative center for Geauga Park District. It is also used for nature classes and programs, and there is a small wildlife viewing area.

NOTE: This marks the 2-mile or midpoint on this hike; the hike may be ended here or continued for another 2 miles.

10 On the southwest side of the parking area is a sign for the paved Cascade Trail. Enter the trail here and continue south. This is also the Buckeye Trail and is another fine cross-country skiing trail. At a sign for Beechwoods Trail, turn left to reach the park entry road.

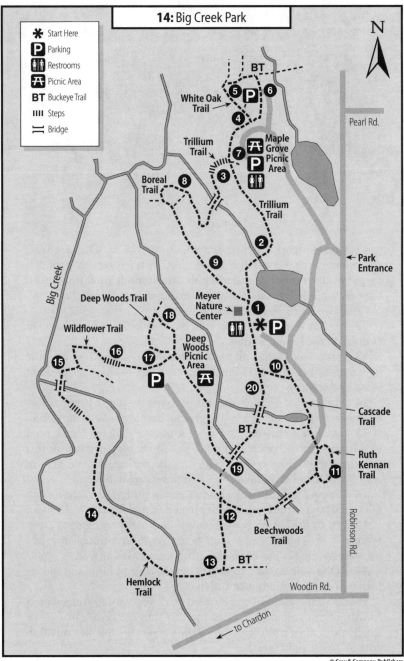

14: Big Creek Park

* Start Here
P Parking
👫 Restrooms
🎪 Picnic Area
BT Buckeye Trail
|||| Steps
⊨ Bridge

N

BT

White Oak Trail

5 P 6

4

Trillium Trail

7 🎪 Maple Grove Picnic Area

3 P 👫

Boreal Trail 8

Trillium Trail

2

9

Deep Woods Trail

Meyer Nature Center

18

Wildflower Trail

16

15

17

Deep Woods Picnic Area

P

🎪

1 * P

10

20

Cascade Trail

BT

Ruth Kennan Trail

19

11

14

12

Beechwoods Trail

13 BT

Hemlock Trail

Woodin Rd.

to Chardon

Pearl Rd.

Park Entrance

Robinson Rd.

Big Creek

© Gray & Company, Publishers

11 Cross the park road to the paved, all-purpose Ruth Kennan Trail, commemorating a naturalist and teacher. Turn left on this path that loops through the woods and meets the Beechwoods Trail. Turn left on the Beechwoods Trail and continue walking in a southwest direction.

Cross two small wooden bridges.

12 Reach a trail intersection with the Hemlock Trail and turn left (south) on the Hemlock Trail.

13 Pass a service road on the left where the Buckeye Trail exits the park. A park bench also on the left invites a rest to enjoy the pleasant woodland scenery.

14 At about the 3-mile point, the trail goes through a hemlock forest, passes a ravine on the left, and reaches another view of Big Creek.

15 Descend a staircase and cross a tributary of Big Creek on a wooden bridge, then ascend another hill. At the top, turn left (north) to enter the Wildflower Trail. This trail is particularly enjoyable in April and May when many spring wildflowers are in bloom.

16 Descend a set of steps, cross a wooden bridge, and continue up the rise of land to the Deep Woods picnic and parking area (3.5 miles).

17 Just to the left of a small playground is the entrance to Deep Woods Trail. This 0.3-mile loop takes the hiker through a lovely wooded area and is also a popular cross-country skiing trail.

18 At the trail junction sign, turn right to continue the loop and return to the Deep Woods picnic shelter.

19 Continue alongside the paved park road south, turning left (north) off the road onto the Beechwoods Trail/Buckeye Trail. Cross a small bridge, then pass a trail intersection where the Beechwoods Trail goes off to the right (east).

20 Continue north on the Buckeye Trail; cross a stream and the paved Cascade Trail just before reaching Meyer Center parking lot. ■

15 Swine Creek Reservation
Middlefield Township

Distance: 3.5 miles

Moderate

Hiking time: 1½ to 2 hours

Description: This park contains several small tributaries that flow southeast to Swine Creek. Many marked trails in the hardwood forest lead up and down ravines that were formed by these streams, providing a varied terrain for hikers and skiers. At times, horseback and wagon riders will use some of the trails, so hikers should use caution, particularly when on the Gray Fox and Wagon trails. Thirty acres of the park are managed as a sugarbush.

Directions: From I-271, take Exit 29 (Chagrin Blvd./SR 87); east on SR 87 into Geauga County and through Newbury, Burton, and Middlefield; continue about 2 miles past Middlefield; right (south) on Hayes Rd. for 1.5 miles; pass Bridge Rd.; right into park entrance; immediate left (south) past parking area on right to parking area at end of road.

Parking & restrooms: Parking is at the end of the park road. On the right is a large pond crossed by a bridge leading to Swine Creek Lodge. Restrooms are behind the lodge. The lodge is open only for park-sponsored programs.

Swine Creek Reservation, located southeast of Middlefield, was once part of a private 1,200-acre hunting preserve belonging to Windsor Ford of Mesopotamia. In 1981 this 331-acre reservation became a unit of the Geauga Park District. The property contains a hunting lodge now used as an education center. Swine Creek Lodge is open for park programs. On Sundays in March, the history of maple sugaring is displayed and demonstrated at the sugarhouse near Woods Edge Picnic Area. Horse-drawn wagon rides are offered to the public on autumn Sundays in Swine Creek Reservation. Call 440-286-9516 for event times.

Fishing (with a license) can be enjoyed in Lodge and Killdeer ponds. The reservation has six miles of trails. Horseback riding is permitted on three trails, and trails appropriate for cross-county skiing are so marked. Swine Creek Reservation is in the heart of Amish country. Use caution driving, as there are many horse-drawn buggies sharing the roads. A visit to some of the Amish shops and restaurants in the villages, particularly Middlefield, will enhance your visit to this part of Geauga County.

1 From the lodge and restroom buildings go north on a path that leads to Squawroot Trail. At the intersection, turn right on the north loop of the Squawroot Trail and pass an active, fenced-in oil well pump on the left.

2 At the next intersection, stay on the Squawroot Trail, to the right. The stream below on the left is a tributary of Swine Creek.

3 Bear left (west) onto the left branch of the Siltstone Trail. Cross the creek on rocks, taking care not to slip on these mossy stones. The trail leads to the right and uphill.

4 Continue along this easy trail until you reach another small tributary of Swine Creek. At the top of the small rise meet the gravel Wagon Trail and bear right (0.5 mile). Pass the north branch of the Siltstone Trail on the right.

5 Cross the paved path (Sugarbush Trail) where a sign indicates that this paved path leads to the Gray Fox Trail. Woods Edge Picnic Area, with drinking fountain and restrooms, is off to the right. Follow the path to the sugarhouse. Continue on the Sugarbush Trail loop.

6 Just off the path enter the Gray Fox/Glen Trail on the right. Enter a hardwood forest, pleasant especially in fall.

7 Cross another tributary of Swine Creek and immediately go to the right uphill on the unmarked Gray Fox Trail. (Another section of the Gray Fox Trail also goes to the left.) At the next intersection, bear right, still on the Gray Fox Trail. Cross the same stream again.

8 At 0.9 mile reach an open meadow with a view to the north across a field to a large white Amish farm on Bridge Rd. Walk along the west edge of the meadow where bluebird boxes have been placed. This is also the Meadowlark Trail used by horsemen and cross-country skiers.

9 Bear left at an intersection of the Meadowlark and Gray Fox trails, staying left on the latter trail going south.

The field may be wet and swampy during some seasons, as a stream rises here and wends its way down to Swine Creek. Meadow wildflowers such as asters and goldenrods attract butterflies here in late summer. The field also provides cover for nesting birds such as meadowlarks and bobolinks. The trail reenters the woods.

10 Bear right at the next intersection, where a sign points toward a continuation of Gray Fox Trail. Cross-country ski signs are posted high up on trees along the trail. The trail passes along the fenced western edge of the reservation.

11 At the next intersection, bear right to stay on the Gray Fox Trail. Below on the right is a deep ravine. The trail winds east, then north through a beautiful beech/maple/oak forest with tangled grape vines scattered throughout.

12 Stay on the marked Gray Fox Trail, avoiding intersecting sap-collecting trails used by the sap sled and wagon for gathering maple syrup. Pass the Glen Trail on your right.

13 Continue north on the Gray Fox Trail (avoiding all side trails) to the same intersection described in Note #7, and turn right to go

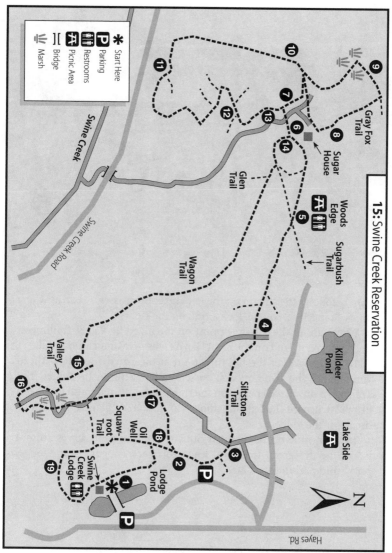

© Gray & Company, Publishers

uphill to the gravel road (Wagon Trail) just south of the sugarhouse (2 miles).

14 Turn right on the gravel Wagon Trail heading southeast. Pass the Glen Trail on the right where it goes down some steps into the ravine.

15 Follow the Wagon Trail south to its intersection with the Valley Trail (2.5 miles). At the bench, turn right and follow the Valley Trail as it gradually descends to the stream valley.

16 Cross a brook close to Swine Creek Rd. The Valley Trail now

closely follows the stream on the left and soon crosses wet areas where it has changed its course. Pass a trail on the right.

17 At about the 3.1-mile point on the hike, the Valley Trail meets the Squawroot Trail on the right. Turn right here and climb uphill.

18 At the top of the hill turn right at the Squawroot sign. Ahead you will see the same oil well passed earlier. Still on the Squawroot Trail, keep the oil well below on the right and continue south to a stand of tall spruce on the left that appear to have been planted as a windbreak for the lodge.

19 Continue on the circular Squawroot Trail as it curves around below the evergreen trees and leads you back (north) to the lodge, pond, and parking area. ∎

My "best" room, however, my withdrawing room, always ready for company, on whose carpet the sun rarely fell, was the pine wood behind my house. Thither in summer days, when distinguished guests came, I took them, and a priceless domestic swept the floor and dusted the furniture and kept things in order.

—Henry David Thoreau, *Walden*

16 Burton

Distance: 2 miles

Easy

Walking time: 2 hours

Description: This easy hike is on sidewalks through the center of town and includes the Burton Village Historic District and part of the Geauga County Fairgrounds.

Directions: From Cleveland, take I-271 to Exit 34 (Mayfield Rd./SR 322); east on Mayfield/SR 322; south on SR 44 for 4.25 miles; left (east) on SR 87 for 2.5 miles to Burton.

From Akron, take I-76 east to SR 44; north on SR 44; right (east) on SR 87 for 2.5 miles to Burton.

Parking & restrooms: Park in the public parking spaces around the central green. Restrooms are located in the Burton Log Cabin on the green.

Approaching Burton from the west, the road rises sharply to reach it. Burton sits on a 1,320-foot-high hill between the East and West Branches of the Cuyahoga River. From a point near the town green there is an impressive view to the east across the East Branch valley to the far hills. When the first white settlers drove their wagons to this hilltop in 1798 they probably did not have the view we find today, for they were in the midst of an endless, dense, mature sugar maple/beech forest, through which they had traveled from the mouth of the Grand River many miles to the north. Could they have known that many of those forest trees would yield the sugary sap for which Burton is known today? And could they have guessed that this hilltop would catch and collect some of the highest snowfalls in the yet-to-be-established state?

It is Burton's blessing that as settlement grew in the state, the town remained removed from major transportation routes and mega-development, and it is to the townspeople's credit that they have cherished their history and their tradition of maple syrup production. The very heart of the town is the Burton Log Cabin and Sugar Camp, located on the town green. Here you can see maple syrup being produced in season and find maple sugar products, including syrup, candy, and gifts, year round. The Log Cabin is also home to the Burton Chamber of Commerce, center of tourist information for visitors. The Log Cabin is open Tuesday through Sunday, February 15 through December 23, 9:30 A.M. to 4:30 P.M.

Burton prides itself on being the town "Where History Lives," and rightfully so. The town green has not changed much over the village's 200-plus years, and surrounding the green is the Burton Village Historic District, which includes 200 acres and 14 buildings dating to two important phases in the village's history: early settlement and the commercial growth of the 1880s. The first family to settle in what was to be Burton arrived in 1798 from Cheshire, Connecticut, making Burton the first settlement in what would become Geauga County. Almost all the early settlers of the town were from Cheshire as well, and you can see the Connecticut influence throughout the town's streets.

At the south end of the green is the Geauga County Historical Society's Century Village Museum, a 63-acre collection of historic structures full of an impressive array of historic furniture, tools, documents, and other fascinating artifacts gathered from the surrounding region. Many of the structures were moved here from other locations to simulate a village around the Hickox Brick Home, built on this location in 1838 and a fine example of Western Reserve architecture. The Century Village Museum provides an excellent introduction to the history of Burton and to life on the Western Reserve frontier. Village tours are offered May 1 through November 15, Tuesday through Sunday, for a small admission fee. Call the museum at 440-834-1492 for tour times.

At the north end of town are the Geauga County Fairgrounds, site of the Great Geauga County Fair, the oldest continuously running fair in Ohio. Every year on Labor Day weekend, it offers everything that you would expect at a fair (and more), including a junior fair and senior fair with 12,000 displays of skills and products, a natural resources area, a band, a horse-pulling contest, midways with games, rides, and food, plus sky divers, a petting zoo, flower shows, and even "Cow Racing." The first county fair was held in 1823 in Chardon, put on by one of the earliest agricultural societies, the Geauga County Agricultural and Manufacturing Society, which is still in existence today (without "manufacturing" in its name). The fair alternated between Chardon and Burton, then in 1853 moved permanently to the Burton site, where it has been held every year through good times and hard times. For more information on the Great Geauga County Fair, call the fair office at 440-834-1846 or visit the fair's website at www.geaugafair.com.

Geauga County has a large Amish population, which contributes to the serenity and beauty of the countryside surrounding Burton. The area is also known for its fruit production and its cheese factories. Both factories near Middlefield, just a few miles east of Burton, feature a wide variety of cheeses, other foods, and gifts. Burton is also close to Punderson State Park and Headwaters Park. The Buckeye Trail passes directly through Burton as well.

Because Burton has retained much of its historic appearance and small-town amenities, it has great appeal for visitors. Burton welcomes visitors and provides numerous ways to enjoy the town, from pancake

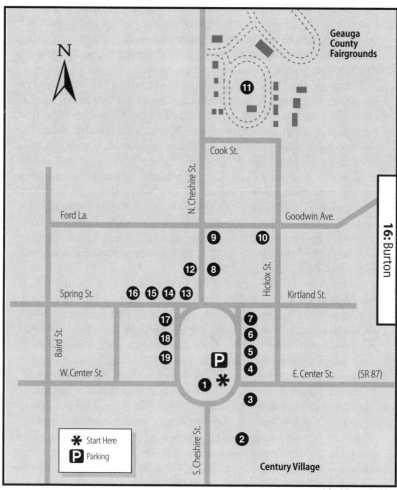

breakfasts to ice-cream socials, from its Apple Butter Festival to its Country Hearth Christmas. In fact, it's a good idea to come to Burton hungry! For more information on events and festivals throughout the year, contact the Burton Chamber of Commerce: 440-834-4204.

1 Begin the hike at the Burton Log Cabin and Sugar Camp Information Center, where you can purchase maple syrup products, souvenirs, and treats for your hike. Here and around town, from mid-February through early April, Burton celebrates Pancake Town U.S.A. Since 1951, Burton has welcomed visitors to town to enjoy seeing how the treasured syrup is produced and to savor it poured over pancakes. As of 2002, over one million pancakes have been prepared for over 338,050 hungry visitors. And over those pancakes have flowed 20,950 gallons of maple syrup. This figure is especially impressive since it takes 30 to 40 gallons of sap to make 1 gallon of syrup, and a good tree might yield up to 10 gallons of sap over four weeks of tapping. During sugar season visitors can warm themselves by the fire and watch the thin sap being boiled down into prized syrup.

2 Leaving the Log Cabin, cross the road to the southeast corner of the green, to Century Village. Here the Geauga County Historical Society has re-created a typical Western Reserve village by collecting homes and other structures from Burton and nearby locations. Twenty-two buildings on 63 acres illustrate what life was like in pioneer times in Northeast Ohio. The various homes, as well as the church, school, store, and other buildings house thousands of interesting artifacts that the historical society has been collecting since 1938. Youngsters of all ages are especially intrigued with the nationally recognized Thoburn Toy Soldier Collection, a collection of over 9,000 miniature lead toy soldiers and other figures. The oldest home on the grounds is the Cook House, built in 1806 and possibly the oldest frame house in Geauga County.

To the right, on the corner of S. Cheshire St. and the town green, is the Hickox Brick House. This home, built in 1838 by Eleazer Hickox, is in its original location; the barn was added in 1840. Hickox was a colorful character, full of the energy and enterprise for which the Connecticut settlers were known. At first he made trading expeditions to the Western Reserve, then settled here in 1804. He continued as a trader, commanded a battalion of militia, had a mill at Punderson Pond, preached, served in the state legislature, and helped build the Ohio & Erie Canal at Roscoe. When he was 80 years old, he and his sons drove a herd of cattle to California, where the sons would establish farms. At 90 he was injured while training a horse and died the next year. He is buried in the cemetery south of town. The Hickox Brick House is furnished as it would have been during the time Hickox and his family occupied it. It also houses the Thoburn Toy Soldier Collection.

Hickox married Stella Umberfield, daughter of Thomas Umberfield. A Connecticut Land Company surveying crew and several settlers, including Umberfield, arrived in the vicinity of what would become Burton in the summer of 1798, less than two years after Moses Cleaveland and his surveying party first arrived at the mouth of the Cuyahoga River. Umberfield, from Cheshire, Connecticut, is credited with bringing the first family to the settlement. A frame addition on the east side of the house is actually part of Thomas Umberfield's log cabin. Umberfield, widowed and ill, refused to leave his cabin and come live with his daughter, so Stella solved the problem by moving father and cabin to this site in 1848. The cabin wing is furnished as a frontier cabin would have been.

From the Hickox House you can see another early home, the Peffers House on the southwest corner of the square. This Greek Revival house was built in 1840 for James Peffer once the postmaster of Burton. The post office was in a room in the home.

If time permits and Century Village is open, take advantage of the guided tour. For a small fee you can visit inside many of the historic buildings. The view to the east from the grounds is spectacular, especially in autumn, when the vast woodland is ablaze with color. The East Branch of the Cuyahoga River, though unseen, winds through its valley a half-mile below the hill, and Middlefield can be glimpsed farther away to the east.

Whether you take the tour of Century Village or not, you can visit the old-fashioned Crossroads Store, located down the lane from the Hickox Brick House. The store is the museum's shop; it offers fun gifts for all ages, including old-time toys, penny candy, and apple butter and maple syrup made on the grounds.

3 From the Crossroads Store, turn back and walk north toward the village green, bearing right on the sidewalk. On the right just before E. Center St. is the E. P. Latham House, a frame house built in 1881. It exhibits features of the Second Empire style of architecture that was popular in the late 1800s and was inspired by the architecture of France at the time. Typical of this style is the mansard roof with cast-iron cresting, the decorative brackets below the eaves, the entry porch, and the three-sided bay window on the side of the house.

Pace Latham was a cannoneer in the Civil War, serving in the 14th Division. During a celebratory firing of cannons after a victory at Cumberland Gap, Latham lost both arms and the sight in one eye when his cannon misfired. He was fitted with metal hooks, the prostheses of the time, and had his home furnished with L-shaped handles on the doors instead of round doorknobs. It is reported that he adapted well to his disability, learning to write with his teeth and becoming well known throughout town for his skill in driving his team of horses.

4 Cross E. Center St. and walk north on E. Park. At 14605 is the A. B. Carlton house, a private residence. It was built in 1863. The south wing of the house was removed to provide space for the restaurant on the corner.

5 At the center of the block is the G. H. Ford House, a magnificent Queen Anne–style home built in 1891. The many gables and spacious veranda are typical of the Queen Anne style. George Ford was the first mayor of Burton and also served as a state senator. He was the son of Seabury Ford, governor of Ohio from 1849 to 1850. Distinguished guests at Ford's house included President William McKinley and Cleveland industrialist Marcus Hanna.

6 The next house to the north is the E. Griswold House, a Western Reserve farmhouse dating to 1835. This structure typifies the style of many dwellings built by settlers in the Western Reserve—a Greek Revival house distinguished by having a two-story section with a one-story wing to one side. Edward Griswold and his partner Silas Gaylord, both from Cheshire, Connecticut, made copper kettles and other goods. This home was later occupied by Dr. Chloe Cleaveland, maker of Compound Extract of Pond Lily, purported by Dr. Cleaveland to aid all sorts of distress including "Dysentery, Diarrhoea, Cholera Morbus . . . Flatulency, Cholic, Paines in the Stomach . . . and that peculiar kind of Diarrhoea attending Children during Teething."

7 To the north of the Griswold House is the Silas Gaylord house. Gaylord, business partner of Edward Griswold, built this house the same year Griswold was building his, in 1835. It was originally built in the Western Reserve style, but was changed to a bungalow by a later owner.

8 Cross Kirtland St. and turn left (west) to reach the corner of N. Cheshire and Kirtland streets. Turn right to walk along the block of stores on the east side. As is the case with many of Ohio's early towns, the original commercial buildings were destroyed by fire. Burton's bucket brigades were no match for the devastating blaze that occurred on the windy, stormy night of December 5, 1871. The wood frame buildings were totally destroyed, and replaced with this brick block, built in 1873. The block now includes a variety of businesses, including a hardware store.

9 Continue north on N. Cheshire St. to Goodwin Ave. At this corner is another handsome home that dates back to Burton's early history. Known as the Goodwin House, it was the home of Dr. Erastus Goodwin and is a brick Greek Revival dating to 1825.

10 Turn right and go east for one block on Goodwin St., to Hickox St. The Buckeye Trail also turns here and soon leaves Burton heading northeast. Note the gallery on Goodwin St., home and studio of local artist Gerald Rouge. Turn left on Hickox St. and go one block to Cook St. Both these residential blocks have a combination of attractive older homes and newer, more modern ones.

11 On Cook St., reach Gate 6 of the Geauga County Fairgrounds. Visitors are welcome on the fairgrounds at any time; admission is charged for special events. If you wish to tour the grounds, enter at Gate 6 and bear left to see some of the exhibition buildings. The fairgrounds include two historic buildings listed in the National Register of Historic Places: the Domestic Arts Hall and the Flower Hall. Walk west toward Cheshire St., and these two halls will be on your right along the westernmost lane of the fairgrounds. The two halls sit side by side; the Flower Hall will be closer to you, while the Domestic Arts Hall is the more northerly one. They date from 1890 and 1889 respectively. Both are simple frame buildings, with walls sheathed with board and batten siding painted white. They are significant for their association with the oldest continuous fair in the state and are excellent examples of this type of building. To the north of the two halls are several more fair buildings, including the administration building, which incorpo-

rates part of a railroad station from the Cleveland & Eastern Traction Company, an interurban line. Leave the fairgrounds by the gate at the corner of Cook St. and N. Cheshire and cross to the west side of N. Cheshire.

12 Go south to reach the commercial block northwest of the square. This block of buildings is more varied than that on the east side of the street. The corner building, nearest the square, was built in 1881 for Parmalee Brothers Hardware and has been occupied by a variety of businesses over the years. The building is an excellent example of the High Victorian Italianate style as used in commercial buildings.

13 At the end of the commercial block, turn right and go west on Spring St. Immediately behind the commercial block is the home of the Burton Fire Department, famous for its pancake breakfasts as well as for its heroic lifesaving and firefighting. This building was originally built as the Burton Town Hall, replacing an earlier town hall that sat on the northeast corner of the green. In addition to the usual municipal functions of a town hall, the building also hosted debates, political conventions, and dramatic productions. The Burton Fire Department was organized in 1926 and altered the hall considerably by removing a central tower and adding lift doors, turning it into the present firehouse.

14 The building just to the west of the Burton Fire Department was originally a high school. Built in 1866, it was one of the earliest high schools in Ohio; it originally sat on W. Park St., where the library is today. This building on Spring St. was moved here to make way for a new high school, the building that now houses the library.

15 Who doesn't dream of finding a hidden cache of cash in their home? The story goes that the A. Beach House, just west of the school building, had such a treasure. When a new fireplace was being added to the home, Amish carpenters discovered a tin box of gold coins hidden in the eaves, most likely secreted there by the original owner, Alfred Beach, owner of a local general store. This house was also moved from its original location; it started out on the corner of Cheshire and Spring streets and was moved to this location in 1881.

16 Continue west on Spring St. The building at 13796 Spring St. began as a Methodist Church. It dates to around 1845 and has been changed several times over the years. It is now home to offices. Continue down Spring St. to Baird St. Cross to the south side and turn left, heading back down Spring St. (east).

17 At the southwest corner of Spring St. and West Park is the Congregational Church, another building that was moved from its original location. It has also gone through many renovations and facelifts. Burton's Congregational Church was organized very early in the town's history, in 1808. The congregation constructed this building on the town square in 1836. At the time it was a nearly square, frame meetinghouse painted white, like those found in many New England towns. The church was moved to this location in 1850 and subsequently renovated several times. In the 1890s the present look was achieved by veneering the ground floor with brick, removing the center steeple, adding a corner tower, and replacing stained glass with clear glass.

18 Turn right (south) on W. Park. Just south of the church is the J. R. Hinkston House, built in 1876. It now houses an antique shop.

19 South of the Hinkston House is one of the most attractive and interesting buildings on the square; it was the second building to house Burton High School and since 1937 has been home to the Burton Public Library. The two-story brick structure was constructed in 1884–85 as the "new" high school, replacing the earlier schoolhouse, which was then moved to Spring St. The façade looks much the same as it does in historic photos of the building, except that a tower on the north side was removed and an addition built on the same side.

The Burton Library was established in 1910 by the Civic Improvement Society, a Burton women's organization. The library had several different homes through its early years, at one time being located in a building that is now the Crossroads Country Store in Century Village. It attained a permanent home when it moved into this high school building in 1937. That same year the library was reorganized as a school district library and became the Burton Public Library. The Helen K. Merritt Reading Room was added in 1981. The Friends of the Burton Public Library hold many book sales, often on festival weekends.

Return to the town green to complete the hike. ■

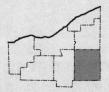

PORTAGE COUNTY

Portage County contains 11 state nature preserves, more than any other county in Ohio. In addition, the Upper Cuyahoga River, a state scenic river, flows through the county. These special natural areas are protected, preserved, monitored, and managed by the Ohio Department of Natural Resources (ODNR).

Only four of Portage County's nature preserves are open to the public, however. These are: Tinker's Creek State Nature Preserve (Ch. 20), Eagle Creek State Nature Preserve (Ch. 21), Frame Lake Fen, and Marsh Wetlands. The rest, including Gott Fen, Triangle Lake Bog, Kent Bog, Tummonds Preserve, Evans Beck Memorial, Flat Iron Lake Bog, and Mantua Bog, are open only by permit because of their extremely fragile nature.

Information about any of these preserves can be obtained from ODNR: 614-265-6453.

The bogs and alkaline bogs (or fens) in Portage County were formed by the melting of large chunks of ice left behind by the last glacier that covered Ohio, about 12,000 years ago. As the glacier retreated, these huge ice blocks settled into the soft ground and made depressions in the soil where boreal plants, shrubs, and trees took hold. These plants, native to more northern temperate zones, still grow in the bogs and fens of Portage County, making ecosystems that are unique for this region. These unspoiled natural areas are living museums that provide habitats for many rare and unusual plants and animals.

Portage County Park District (330-673-9404) offers hiking in Towner's Woods on Ravenna Rd. east of SR 43 in Franklin Township and on Headwaters Trail between Mantua and Garrettsville. Major state parks in Portage County are Nelson Ledges State Park (Ch. 17) and West Branch State Park (Ch. 23). Aurora Sanctuary (Ch. 18) is maintained by the Audubon Society of Greater Cleveland; Mogodore Reservoir (Ch. 22) is maintained by Akron's city water district.

Portage County is also home to some very different attractions, including the following: Six Flags Worlds of Adventure, Aurora Premium Outlets, Kent State University Museum, and the Portage County Historical Society Museum. Additional information about Portage County is available from the Convention and Visitors Bureau: 800-648-6342; www.portagecountycvb.com.

17 Nelson Ledges State Park
Newbury

	Easy

Distance: 1.7 miles

Hiking time: 1¼ hours

Description: This hike requires climbing up and down over rocks and ledges. One opening through a narrow passage may require crawling on hands and knees, and another, squeezing through a tight passage (not recommended for the claustrophobic). These spots can be bypassed by an alternate route. All of the trails are marked with blazes (either a hiker sign or a painted circle in one of four colors: yellow, white, red, or blue). The main features of the park are identified by additional signs. Exercise caution on this hike and stay on the marked trails.
Picnic tables are conveniently located in the forest to the east and north of the parking area.

Directions: From Cleveland: follow US 422 east past the town of Parkman to SR 282, then south 2 miles to Nelson Ledges State Park.

Parking & restrooms: At the park entrance on the east side of SR 282. (The ledges are on the west side of SR 282.)

Nelson Ledges State Park is located in Portage County, close to the watershed divide that separates the Ohio River and Lake Erie. The drive to this park from Cleveland takes you through some beautiful Ohio farmland. Although the park is small, its extensive exposed ledge formations of Sharon Conglomerate sandstone are spectacular. Generations of children have enjoyed scrambling in and around these amazing rock formations.

About 320 million years ago, during the Pennsylvanian Age of the Paleozoic Era—about the time when amphibians developed—the land that is now Ohio was under a shallow inland sea. Quartz, originally from Canada, washed downstream to the edge of the sea and combined with ocean sand to eventually form a conglomerate rock called Sharon Conglomerate. Embedded within it are the abundant small, shiny, quartz pebbles locally called "lucky stones." These pebbles, worn smooth by the ancient action of the water and waves, have in places fallen out of the rock to create what appears to be a pockmarked ledge. As the sandy floor of the ocean was compressed into extremely hard sandstone rocks and the earth shifted, these ledges were exposed. They have been carved by the action of an ancient river and by the advance and retreat of glaciers. Erosion of these ledges proceeds very slowly still.

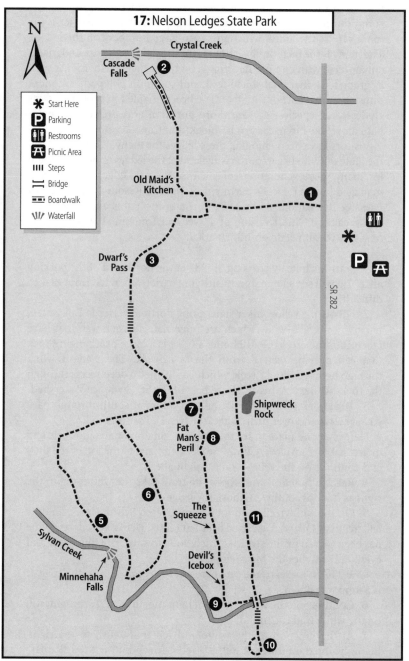

17: Nelson Ledges State Park

N

* Start Here
P Parking
Restrooms
Picnic Area
IIII Steps
Bridge
Boardwalk
Waterfall

Crystal Creek

Cascade Falls ❷

Old Maid's Kitchen

❶

Dwarf's Pass ❸

SR 282

❹

❼

Shipwreck Rock

Fat Man's Peril ❽

❻

The Squeeze

❺

Sylvan Creek

Minnehaha Falls

Devil's Icebox

❶❶

❾

❶⓪

© Gray & Company, Publishers

The shaded and sheltered jumble of rocks comes alive with wildflowers in the spring and hosts ferns nearly year round. Among the common spring wildflowers such as spring beauty and hepatica is the more rare red trillium, which grows in large numbers on the ledges. The many ferns include Christmas fern, which is evergreen, and maidenhair fern, with circular flat fronds on black stalks. Other ferns such as grape fern, marginal shield fern, and common polypody are more unusual in this part of the state. The beech/maple forest overhead includes some species that are more northern and prefer this cooler habitat: yellow birch, eastern hemlock, and Canada yew.

Visitors have been enjoying these ledges for many decades. In 1940 the State of Ohio began purchasing land at the ledges to preserve them for many more generations of visitors. Nelson Ledges State Park is managed by the Ohio Department of Natural Resources, Division of Parks & Recreation. For more information on this and other state parks, call the Ohio Division of Travel and Tourism at 800-282-5393 or visit www.dnr.state.oh/odnr/parks/.

1 Start the hike by crossing SR 282 at the north end of the parking area. You will see a large sign identifying park trails, rated from easy to difficult.

2 Follow the yellow hiker signs going north to Cascade Falls, a tall, narrow waterfall, below which are huge slabs of rock wall that have fallen into the creek. Gold Hunter's Cave is a large overhanging rock that can also be viewed from the boardwalk. The water flowing through here is Crystal Creek, which has formed a deep recess through the rocks. Waters of this creek are part of the St. Lawrence Watershed.

3 Turn back to the yellow trail and follow it south through dark passageways and over boardwalks to Dwarf's Pass (0.2 mile).

Here is a good place to see the Sharon Conglomerate sandstone and quartz pebbles up close. Climb the wooden stairs to the top of the shelf and continue on the yellow trail straight ahead.

4 Reach a junction with the white trail. Take the white trail to the right as it loops southwest above the ledges.

5 On the white trail at about 0.6 mile, reach Sylvan Creek, an outlet stream of Quarry Lake, and bear left (east). Here a very deep ravine has been carved by the stream, which flows toward the Ohio River and eventually reaches the Mississippi.

CAUTION: Use extreme care here not to get too close to the edge. It is a long way down!

6 Continue on the white trail as it loops northward. Turn right, still on the white trail (0.7 mile).

7 At the junction of the white and red trails, turn to the right. Below, painted on the rock wall is a red arrow pointing toward a narrow, rocky entrance. Turn downhill here to follow the red trail south. This is the most challenging of all the park trails.

CAUTION: For those who do not like tight places, it is best to avoid the red trail entirely and take the blue trail instead. It lies to the east of the red trail and parallel to SR 282; it can be reached by following the white trail a little farther east.

The red trail is well marked as it snakes up and down deep inside the ledges and past Sharon Conglomerate walls. At one point you will see long tree roots reaching down the sandstone walls on the left, gaining a foothold wherever they can.

8 The trail reaches a narrow squeeze called Fat Man's Peril under the rocks, then rises. At the top turn left, then right (south), and follow the red marks down over some large boulders.

9 Devil's Icebox (0.9 mile) is a cool, deep natural cavelike fissure through which Sylvan Creek runs. Go inside, stepping on small stones over the water, to enjoy the cool air that remains at this temperature all year round.

10 Follow the stream and cross a wooden bridge going south. A blue hiker sign identifies this path as the blue trail. Follow it up some stairs and continue southward until the path reaches a dead end.

11 Turn around and return on the blue trail. It parallels SR 282 and takes you back to the white trail. Turn right to reach the pedestrian crossing to the parking area. ■

18 Aurora Sanctuary

Aurora

Distance: 2.4 miles

Hiking time: 1½ hours

Description: This loop hike is initially on a wide, mulched trail but soon narrows down to an easily followed path. Some of the trail is marked by 2-foot-square metal tags nailed to trees. Because there are very few trail signs, and some of the red-painted tree blazes are barely visible, it can be difficult to follow the hiking loop without using the trail descriptions below. There are also several side trails in addition to the main trail. Despite considerable growth on either side of the trail, the path is usually evident. All the stream crossings in the sanctuary are on wooden boardwalks or bridges.

Directions: From I-271 take Exit 27 for US 422 east (Solon); east on US 422 to exit for SR 91 (Solon); south on SR 91 past the underpass; left (southeast) on SR 43 to Aurora; continue past SR 82 intersection to SR 306 (Chillicothe Rd.) in Aurora; left (east) on E. Pioneer Trail (opposite the tall, white Church of Aurora) for about 1.5 miles; cross N. Page Rd.; park entrance on right.

From I-76 east take exit for SR 43; north on SR 43 through Kent and Streetsboro; right (east) on E. Pioneer Trail Rd. (just before gazebo in center of town) for about 1.5 miles; park entrance on right.

Parking & restrooms: Park in the small gravel parking lot on the south side of E. Pioneer Trail Rd. The parking lot is on the right side of a private driveway that leads to 896 E. Pioneer Trail Rd. There are no restrooms here.

The Aurora Sanctuary is a 162-acre wildlife sanctuary located east of the town of Aurora on E. Pioneer Trail Rd. The park is owned and maintained by the Audubon Society of Greater Cleveland and its cadre of volunteers. Improvements added by the Audubon Society include wooden footbridges and boardwalks over marshes and formerly impassable areas. The trail here is not to be rushed through. The ambiance of the sanctuary invites visitors to slow down, sit a while, and enjoy its beauty and tranquility.

The Audubon Sanctuary contains two ponds that attract waterfowl (and bird-watchers), especially during bird migration seasons. The Aurora Branch of the Chagrin River flows past the southern boundary of the sanctuary and is fed by many small tributaries, including Kinky Creek. (Fishing is not permitted in the sanctuary.)

NOTE: In the spring this sanctuary tends to be very wet and muddy; boots are recommended.

Sunny Lake Park (see Ch. 19) is very close by and just upstream on

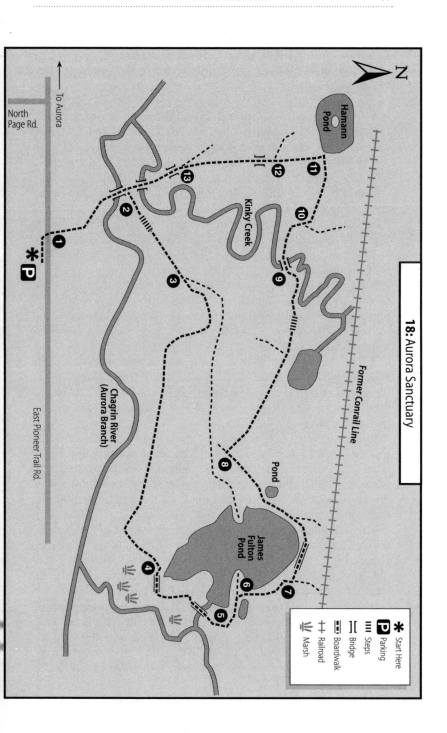

18: Aurora Sanctuary

the Aurora Branch of the Chagrin River. To reach it, take Page Rd. south about one mile to Mennonite Rd., then turn left (east) to Sunny Lake Park on the left. Tinker's Creek State Nature Preserve is also nearby, about 4 miles west of Sunny Lake, but in the Cuyahoga River Watershed (Ch. 20).

1 The entrance to the sanctuary is on the north side of the road. From the parking lot, follow the "Audubon Entrance" sign and walk west about 100 yards, then cross to the opposite side of the road.

CAUTION: Cross E. Pioneer Trail Rd. carefully as fast-moving traffic comes up over the hill suddenly.

Cross a small footbridge to an opening in the hedgerow to reach the entrance to the trail. There is a small sign for the sanctuary here, though it may be hard to see from the road. Follow the wide, mulched trail north, going past a path on the left. The trail gradually descends and narrows to a path that crosses a bridge over the Aurora Branch of the Chagrin River.

2 At about 0.2 mile, watch carefully for a trail on the right. Here there is a sign marked "Cleveland Audubon Society Aurora Sanctuary" posted on a tree and a large bulletin board. Turn right at this trail intersection. This point marks the beginning and end of the loop through the sanctuary.

3 The trail leads uphill on a set of wooden steps through a thick beech/maple forest. At 0.3 mile bypass another trail junction. (This trail goes to the west side of James Fulton Pond, to a bench named in memory of Myrtle Astracan, Audubon Society member and supporter of Aurora Sanctuary.)

Continue ahead (east). Some of the trees are marked with red paint.

4 At about 0.7 mile reach the south corner of James Fulton Pond, named for a longtime member of the Audubon Society and Chairman of the Aurora Sanctuary Committee. Go left a few steps for a view of this large, plant-filled pond. Often there is a variety of waterbirds on the pond.

The trail follows the south shore of the pond and crosses several wooden boardwalks over wet and marshy land and the pond's outlet stream.

5 Next, ascend a hill on a pallet stairway with a rope handrail, bear left, then right, cutting across a small point of land.

6 The bench here (named for Gordon Walker, another supporter of Aurora Sanctuary) is a good place to observe the lake. It is a joy to come here during migration to see the many birds that feed and rest on the pond and in the surrounding habitat. In the past, beavers have been active in this part of the lake—the remains of two beaver lodges can be seen along the bank.

Continue around the pond, through dense overgrowth.

7 At about 1.0 mile pass a trail spur on the right and continue on the main trail going northwest across another boardwalk from which there is another good view of the pond. At the end of the boardwalk, the path goes uphill and bends around to the south. Avoid taking the trail at the top of the hill, as it goes out to the abandoned rail line.

8 At 1.2 miles reach a junction to the right (west).

NOTE: Be sure to take this right turn (west), because the path ahead just goes around in a circle.

Continue on the trail, overgrown and grassy, another 0.1 mile. Next the trail bears right (northwest) at an open area and passes a trail on the left. Enter a beech/maple forest (1.3 miles).

9 Soon the path descends on a wider trail to reach Kinky Creek. Cross the stream on a bridge.

10 At 1.5 miles is another trail junction. Follow the trail to the left (west). The trail on the right (north) goes out to the railroad tracks.

11 At about 1.6 miles reach an open field. Straight ahead is small Hamann Pond. Turn left (south) and follow a path through a field. Bluebird boxes are scattered throughout the field.

12 After another 0.2 mile, reenter the woods where the trail jogs right then left to a double stairway and bridge over a ditch. This southeast–northwest ditch, running diagonally through the sanctuary, is an old railroad right-of-way for the Clinton Airline, named for New York Governor DeWitt Clinton in 1852. This railroad was to run from New York to Missouri but was never completed because of high costs and the Depression of 1856. Only the partially dug ditch remains here.

The trail now goes south on a hogback ridge above a ravine with Kinky Creek below on the left.

13 The path descends and crosses a small bridge over a tributary, then a larger bridge over Kinky Creek. There are some stone remnants of an old bridge abutment.

At 2.0 miles reach the same junction as in Note #2 above to complete the loop. Continue ahead (south), crossing over Aurora Branch. The path gently ascends and exits to E. Pioneer Trail Rd. ■

19 Sunny Lake Park
Aurora

Distance: 1.75 miles

Hiking time: 1 hour

Description: The flat trail around Sunny Lake is partly asphalt-paved. This is a good exercise trail with constant views of the lake.

Directions: From I-271 take Exit 27; east on US 422 to exit for SR 91 (Solon); south on SR 91 to center of Solon; pass underpass; left (east) on SR 43 past SR 82 to center of Aurora; right (south) on SR 306 (Chillicothe Rd. and still SR 43) for about 1.5 miles; left (east) on Mennonite Rd.; continue past Page Rd.; park entrance on left.

From Akron take I-76 east to exit for SR 43; north on SR 43 through Kent and Streetsboro; right (east) on Mennonite Rd. (about 2 miles north of I-80 underpass) for about 1 mile; park entrance on left.

Parking & restrooms: Park just inside the entrance; restrooms are in the brick concession building.

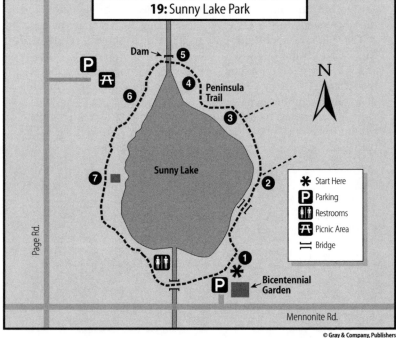

19: Sunny Lake Park

Dam

Peninsula Trail

N

Sunny Lake

Page Rd.

Bicentennial Garden

Mennonite Rd.

* Start Here
P Parking
Restrooms
Picnic Area
Bridge

Sunny Lake Park is a unit of Aurora's Department of Parks and Recreation. It is a popular lake for fishing and boating, but swimming is not permitted. Picnic shelters, a children's playing area, a sand volleyball court, a bocce court, and a boat rental concession are located near the entrance to the park off Mennonite Rd. The Bicentennial Garden next to the parking area was dedicated in 1999. There is one hiking trail that encircles the lake. The path passes through the Memorial Tree Garden.

1 Start east of the parking lot on the asphalt-paved trail to circle Sunny Lake in a counterclockwise direction. At 0.5 mile cross a wooden bridge over a stream.

2 Stay left at a fork in the trail (0.6 mile).

3 Stay left again when another trail comes in from the right. The main trail is marked with white rectangular blazes on the trees.

4 To the right of the trail is an open picnic spot at the lake's edge. The path ascends a slope and at 1.0 mile a sign indicates that this is the Peninsula Trail.

5 Cross a mowed field (under a power line) to the dam at the north end of the lake.

6 The trail continues now on a gravel road past the Page Rd. parking and picnic area on the right (1.3 miles).

7 Continue on the gravel road (closed to traffic) past benches and picnic tables on the left, overlooking the tranquil lake. Just after the boat rental building the trail crosses the lake's inlet stream on a footbridge and ends at the parking lot. ■

20 Tinker's Creek State Nature Preserve Aurora

Distance: 2 miles

Easy

Hiking time: 1¼ hours

Description: Three flat trails are well delineated and use high ground and boardwalks to take hikers to each of the seven ponds in the preserve and to an observation platform for a beautiful view of the creek and marsh.

Directions: Take I-480 to exit for SR 91 (Twinsburg); south on SR 91 for 1.4 miles; left (east) on Old Mill Rd.; cross over I-480; Old Mill becomes Davis Rd. in Portage County; continue east; at 0.7 mile past Ravenna Rd., cross railroad tracks; parking area for preserve on left.

From Akron take I-76 east to SR 43; north on SR 43 past Streetsboro; left on Frost Rd.; right on Aurora-Hudson Rd.; left on Davis Rd.; preserve parking lot on right just before Ravenna Rd.

Parking & restrooms: Park in small lot on the north side of Davis Rd.

Tinker's Creek State Nature Preserve, a 786-acre marsh and swamp forest named for the creek flowing through the marsh, is located close to the Portage–Summit county line near Twinsburg. Tinker's Creek is a long, irregular stream that rises in northern Portage County and flows across a plateau of swamps and marshes. It then courses northwest through Summit County to Bedford Reservation in Cuyahoga County and finally empties into the Cuyahoga River in Cuyahoga Valley National Park.

The area around these wetlands was a source of great fear to pioneers and early settlers because there were rumors of sinkholes and quicksand. In the late 1800s the New York, Chicago, & St. Louis Railroad built a line through the western edge of what is now the preserve and constructed an embankment that created even more swampland and marsh than was there originally.

Dedicated as a scenic nature preserve in 1974 by the Ohio Department of Natural Resources, about three-quarters of the area is marshland with cattail, willow, buttonbush, alder, and other moisture-loving plants and trees. In the small forest are dogwood, maple, oak, pine, aspen, and wild cherry trees. Seven spring-fed ponds dot the forested land and provide habitat for beaver, ducks, Canada geese, great blue herons, fox, deer, reptiles, and amphibians.

The park is open only during daylight hours, and visitors are asked to remain on the trails in this watery nature preserve. It is wise to bring insect repellent if you visit the park in the summer. Watch carefully for

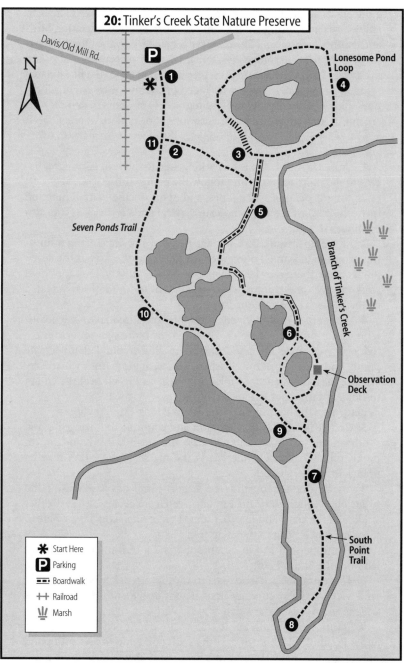

20: Tinker's Creek State Nature Preserve

Davis/Old Mill Rd.

N

Lonesome Pond Loop

Seven Ponds Trail

Branch of Tinker's Creek

Observation Deck

South Point Trail

* Start Here
P Parking
Boardwalk
Railroad
Marsh

© Gray & Company, Publishers

poison ivy, which is abundant. Binoculars and bird, tree, and wildflower guidebooks are quite useful here. In the spring, visit Tinker's Creek to enjoy birds and spring wildflowers; in the fall, to see migrating birds and colorful tree foliage. The preserve is managed by the Ohio Department of Natural Resources (ODNR), Division of Natural Areas and Preserves. Ohio's 123 nature preserves protect some of the finest natural areas in the state. They are intended primarily for research, education, hiking, nature study, and photography. Pets, horses, and bicycles are not permitted on the trails. For more information, phone ODNR at 614-265-6453; TDD 614-265-6994; or visit www.dnr.state.oh.us/.

1 Cross Davis Rd. from the parking area to the trail entrance adjacent to the railroad tracks and follow the path south.

2 Enter a stand of white pines, and upon reaching a trail junction turn left (east) where a sign indicates Seven Ponds Trail. (This trail also continues straight ahead.)

3 At the boardwalk turn left again (north) to walk along a hummock on the 0.5-mile Lonesome Pond Loop to the first of the seven ponds. Here there may be evidence of beaver activity; look for chisel work on trees and stumps. These prominent tooth marks are created by the beaver's ever-growing front teeth.

4 Lonesome Pond Loop encircles this spring-fed lake, which contains exceptionally clear water. There may be more signs of beaver activity as you circle the pond clockwise. Beaver build dams, create ponds, and erect lodges out of aspen, willow, or birch trees, which they also use for food. A partially filled-in marsh on the left near the end of the loop is a fine spot to look for birds and waterfowl.

Return on the boardwalk to the Seven Ponds Trail junction.

5 Go left (south) at this junction and continue following the trail south on and off boardwalks to pass the second, third, and fourth ponds on the right. On the left is the marsh and a south-flowing branch of Tinker's Creek.

6 Just beyond the fourth pond, a short path leads past a fifth pond to an observation deck on the left. Watch for waterfowl and other wildlife in the creek and marsh. Canada geese often congregate here to feed and rest. Return to the main trail.

7 Continue south to the sixth pond and a trail intersection. Bear left onto the South Point Trail.

8 This hummock of land extends through an oak forest to another wide view of the swamp and marshlands at the end. Here the creek widens and bends to the north.

9 Return along South Point Trail to the trail junction. Bear left on Seven Ponds Trail. You will pass the sixth pond and the seventh pond on the left. Continue straight (north) toward Davis Rd. and the parking lot. Halfway back, on the right, is the opposite side of the third

pond passed earlier. Farther along on the right is the second pond, also passed earlier.

10 Between the third and second ponds watch for possible beaver activity, especially at dawn and dusk. Here look for a very large beaver lodge at the north end of the second pond. There might also be beaver swimming and busily working in this pond, engaged in dam building or wood harvesting.

11 Continue north to the end of the trail on Davis Rd. ∎

21 Eagle Creek State Nature Preserve Nelson Township

Distance: 4.7 miles

Moderate

Hiking time: 3 hours, for leisurely enjoyment.

Description: The terrain is easy to walk but wet and muddy in some places, making waterproof boots useful. There are two loop trails: the 1.5-mile Clubmoss Trail loop and the 2.5-mile Beaver Run Trail, including the short Beech Ridge Trail loop. Because of the unusual flora and fauna here, it is instructive to have binoculars and bird, fern, wildflower, and tree identification books along on the hike.

Directions: From US 422 take exit for SR306 (Bainbridge); south on SR 306 to Aurora; left (east) on SR 82 to Garrettsville; northeast on Center Rd. (CH 293) for 2 miles; south on Hopkins Rd. for about 1 mile; on right.

From SR 8 north take exit for SR 303; east on 303; northeast on SR 88 (at Freedom/Drakesburg) to Garrettsville; right (east) on SR 82 for two blocks; left on Center St. for about two miles; south on Hopkins Rd. for about one mile; park entrance on right.

Parking & restrooms: There is a small parking area at the park entrance; there are no restrooms here.

Eagle Creek State Nature Preserve is in Nelson Township near Garrettsville. This 470-acre preserve opened in 1974 and is owned and managed by the Ohio Department of Natural Resources, Division of Natural Areas and Preserves. Trees here include cucumber magnolia, yellow birch, and swamp-loving buttonbush. A bird observation blind enables visitors to view waterfowl and many kinds of songbirds, especially during the migration season. Eagle Creek itself meanders through a floodplain from north to south and eventually enters the Mahoning River east of here. Within the preserve are cranberry bogs, swamps, marshes, and beaver ponds. Boardwalks and trails allow close-up study of many wildflowers, moisture-loving ferns (such as the royal, cinnamon, and ostrich), and the insectivorous sundew and pitcher plant.

Because its many marshes are a great breeding ground for mosquitoes, this preserve is best enjoyed in the spring or fall. Insect repellent is essential for summer hikes. The park is open only during daylight hours; dogs, picnicking, alcoholic beverages, and camping are not permitted.

1 Start the walk from the parking area, heading west across a grassy field. Pass a turnoff to the amphitheater and continue straight ahead.

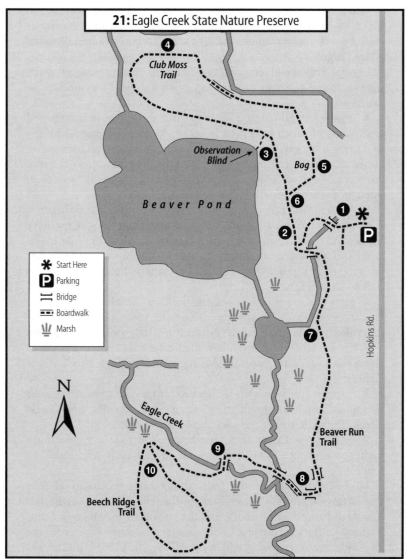

21: Eagle Creek State Nature Preserve

Club Moss Trail

Observation Blind

Bog

Beaver Pond

Start Here
Parking
Bridge
Boardwalk
Marsh

N

Hopkins Rd.

Eagle Creek

Beaver Run Trail

Beech Ridge Trail

© Gray & Company, Publishers

After entering the woods, cross a small boardwalk. Note the buttonbush swamp on the left. The buttonbush shrub can be identified in the summer by its spherical cluster of small, fragrant white flowers.

2 At 0.2 mile reach a trail intersection, and turn right (north) onto the Clubmoss Trail. The pathway bends north, passes a bog and small pond, and meets the end of the trail loop on the right (0.5 mile).

3 Continue straight ahead on the Clubmoss Trail going toward Beaver Pond. On the right is a small stand of clubmoss, which looks like tiny, erect, dark-green evergreen trees.

Reach the path on the left leading down to the bird observation blind. Pause here to enjoy the variety of wildlife on this picturesque beaver pond. You may notice the shy swamp sparrow feeding along the water's edge.

Leave the blind and return to the Clubmoss Trail, turning left at the intersection to continue on the loop as it winds gently around to the northeast.

4 Follow the trail around the loop through a forest of cottonwood trees, some of which have been felled by storms and aging. The ruins of farm foundations and the remnants of a farmhouse and barn are on either side of the trail along this stretch of the pathway. As the trail curves eastward, you will pass small ponds and cross a boardwalk to an open field where the path begins to turn south.

5 At about 0.9 mile a sign on the right identifies the Sphagnum Bog; a short boardwalk leads into this interesting bog. Cranberry bushes and the carnivorous pitcher plant and sundew thrive here. The latter two ensnare small insects for their nourishment—the sundew with its sticky leaf hairs and the pitcher plant by holding water in its hollow-shaped leaves.

6 Return to the trail and complete the loop. Turn left (south) at the trail intersection and follow the path until it meets the trail junction described in Note #2. Begin the Beaver Run Trail by continuing south.

7 Cross a footbridge and follow the Beaver Run Trail up and down above the edge of a stream and the marshlands of Eagle Creek on the right (west).

8 After the trail bends west, cross two bridges and a boardwalk over floodplain before reaching a bridge over a side stream that enters Eagle Creek. The path may be wet and marshy along here.

9 Cross Eagle Creek on a long bridge and follow the route on higher ground now. The path goes uphill to start the Beech Ridge Trail loop.

10 Follow the Beech Ridge Trail looping counterclockwise. Here in this forest of many beech trees, look for the yellow birch tree, with yellowish-to-bronze peeling bark, and the cucumber magnolia (cucumbertree) with its springtime yellowish-green blossoms. The cones are cucumberlike when young, and in the fall they drop to the ground and release dark-red seeds.

Some of the spring wildflowers you might see along this trail are blood root, trillium, cut-leaved toothwort, spring beauty, trout lily, purple, white, and yellow violets, squirrel corn, and Dutchman's breeches.

Complete the loop and retrace your steps along the trail. Cross the bridge over Eagle Creek and the other bridges to the same trail junction described in Note #2. Turn east (right) to return to the parking area. ■

22 Mogodore Reservoir
Mogodore

Distance: 6 miles **Strenuous**

Hiking time: 3 hours

Description: The Buckeye Trail is clearly marked with 2-by-6-inch blue blazes painted on trees and posts and occasionally with a blue arrow on a post. The terrain is generally flat with several bridged stream crossings. There are many pleasant views of the water on this hike; they are especially rewarding in early spring or late fall when the trees are bare.

Directions: From I-480 east (becomes SR 14 at I-80 interchange); continue on SR 14 to Streetsboro; south on SR 43 through Twin Lakes, Kent, and Brimfield; park entrance on left 3.3 miles south of I-76 (small sign).

From I-76 take exit for SR 43; south on SR 43 for 3.3 miles; park entrance on left.

Parking & restrooms: Park adjacent to the small administration building. Primitive restrooms near park entrance.

Mogodore Reservoir, just east of Akron, was created in 1936 by impounding water of the Little Cuyahoga River to form a water-supply lake. The city of Akron Water Division owns the reservoir; the Akron Area YMCA manages the recreational program here. A campground, Mogadore Park, is located west of SR 43, along the south shore of the lake. It is open Memorial Day to Labor Day and offers camping, swimming, ball courts, a playground, picnic area, and hiking trails. The Mogadore Boathouse on SR 43 rents boats and canoes. A permit is required for boating.

Mogodore Reservoir contains 19 miles of shoreline and about 900 acres of water surface. It is carefully managed for high water quality (gasoline motors are prohibited), and the many coves and forested shoreline contribute to the serenity of this lake. On this hike you will follow the blue-blazed Buckeye Trail on the north side of the reservoir, east of SR 43. (The Buckeye Trail also follows the north edge of the reservoir west of SR 43.)

Mogodore Reservoir is a prime location for fishing, boating, and canoeing during most of the year, and for waterfowl hunting in fall. No hiking or fishing is permitted during the November hunting season. Check with the park office for information: 330-628-2672.

1 Start the hike at the gate in the northeast corner of the parking lot. The Buckeye Trail (BT) leads past an old trailer camp on an as-

phalt-paved trail. Leave the paved trail to go east (right) on a footpath. The BT quickly makes a sharp left turn (at a blue arrow) and goes up a small slope.

2 The path bends left and crosses a bridge over a small stream. (Note that a double blue blaze on a tree indicates a turn in the trail; the upper blaze indicates the direction of the turn, right or left.)

3 Continue heading generally east through a forest of red and white oaks, beeches, and maples. Mogodore Reservoir is on the right (south). Canada geese are a common sight in the reservoir. Occasionally a great blue heron might be seen wading in the shallow water searching for fish, frogs, or other aquatic animals.

The trail veers slightly away from the reservoir, then goes uphill onto an embankment overlooking the water, providing long, scenic views of the lake. Next it descends to the water's edge. After passing a fallen tree, the path heads in a generally northeast direction. On the left is a wire fence marking private property, beyond which are houses on Saxe Rd.

4 Cross another stream on small logs and continue on the BT along the reservoir. The path now veers away from the water. Cross another small stream on logs and reach Congress Lake Rd. at 1.2 miles.

5 Cross the road and reenter the BT directly opposite. The trail turns toward the reservoir initially and then bends away. Watch carefully for BT blazes in this sometimes overgrown area.

6 Reach Pipe Line Rd. at 1.5 miles. This is an open two-lane, grass-and-cinder road now closed to vehicles. Follow it as it bends away from the reservoir. Avoid taking any of the grassy trails leading off both sides of the road.

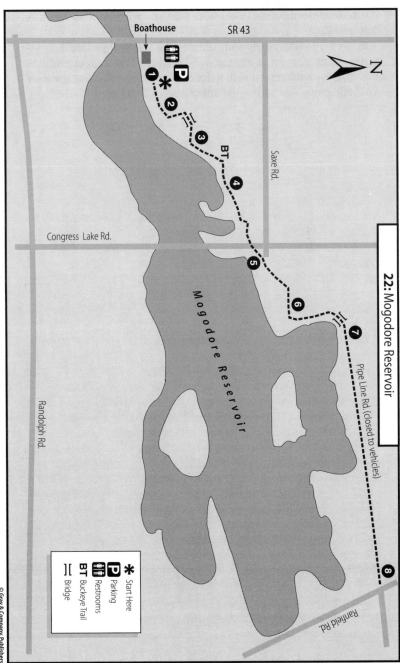

7 Cross a small bridge and continue to follow the road as it turns east and is bordered by tall pines.

Continue to the gate at Ranfield Rd. (The BT continues north on Ranfield Rd.)

8 At 3.0 miles, reverse your direction to follow Pipe Line Rd. west to the point where it enters the woods (Note #6). Watch carefully for blue blazes on the return path to follow the trail overlooking the reservoir, and enjoy views from the opposite direction. ∎

23 West Branch State Park
Ravenna

Distance: 9 miles

Strenuous

Hiking time: 4½ hours

Description: Somewhat strenuous due to its length and its traverse of rolling hills. About 20 percent of this hike is on roads.

Directions: From I-271 take exit for I-480 east/SR 14; east on SR 14 toward Ravenna; pass SR 44 and SR 88; east on SR 5; right (south) on Rock Spring Rd. for about 1 mile; park entrance on right.

Parking & restrooms: At the boat launch area off Rock Spring Rd.

Managed by the Ohio Department of Natural Resources, West Branch State Park surrounds Michael J. Kirwan Reservoir near Campbellsport. This loop hike around the western third of the reservoir on the Buckeye Trail traverses gently rolling terrain on the glaciated plateau of northeastern Ohio. In 1965, the U.S. Army Corps of Engineers created the reservoir by damming up the west branch of the Mahoning River for flood control as well as recreation, water supply, and wildlife management. The state park consists of more than 5,300 acres of land and 2,650 acres of water. From along Knapp Rd., remnants of the canal and railroad that once ran alongside the Mahoning River can be seen sticking up above the water out in the middle of the reservoir.

This hike offers scenic views of the reservoir and passes through some interesting habitats. Beaver live around the reservoir and in some places have "managed" wetlands adjacent to the reservoir. Boggy wetlands, a legacy of the glaciers, support an interesting mix of plants including skunk cabbage, alder, buttonbush, and swamp white oak. Part of the trail goes through a beech/maple forest, a remnant of the once-extensive beech/maple band that stretched across the plateau from Mansfield to Pennsylvania. The woodlands are rich with wildflowers, songbirds, and mammals.

In addition to hiking trails, the park offers bridle trails, camping, fishing, hunting, picnicking, swimming, boating, and winter sports. Note that the Buckeye Trail passes through areas that are open to public hunting in season. For information, call the park office in Ravenna at 330-296-3239 or see the ODNR website at www.dnr.state.oh.us.

1 Start the hike from the boat launch parking area and Buckeye Trail signs by going north on the well-worn path of the blue-blazed Buckeye Trail. At 0.2 mile enter a pine forest, and at about 0.4 mile cross a small bridge. Passing a small pond on the right, the Buckeye Trail bears to the right and climbs.

2 Views of the reservoir appear, and soon the trail crosses an inlet and small bridge (1.4 miles), then a power line right-of-way (1.5 miles). Follow the blue blazes and avoid taking any side trails that cross the main trail.

3 At about 1.7 miles the trail follows a steep, downhill washed-out gully, then passes through a wet area that may be flooded at times. The blue blazes may be difficult to follow in this section. The trail goes to the right, uphill.

4 Ascend the slope of black cinders to the top of a culvert, crossing it carefully over the stream below.

CAUTION: Do not go onto the railroad tracks as this is an active railway and trains pass here often.

5 At about 2.1 miles the trail bears left, goes under the power line, and then widens (2.2 miles). Stay left toward the reservoir and views of the water.

6 Pass two shelters built by the Kent State University Outing Club. From the second one the trail goes downhill, east of the shelter. You might see signs of beaver activity in this area.

7 At about 2.6 miles the trail veers away from the reservoir and travels through an overgrown field.

8 At 3.3 miles the trail emerges onto Knapp Rd.

9 Leave the Buckeye Trail behind for about 1.5 miles and follow the white blazes placed on utility poles along Knapp Rd.

10 Go south past the boat launch area, cross the bridge over the reservoir, and bear left onto the berm of SR 14.

CAUTION: Because of fast traffic on this highway, walk in single file facing the cars.

11 On SR 14, just past Cable Line Rd., look for the blue Buckeye Trail blazes on the left marking the trail entrance. There is a large pile of gravel and a Buckeye Trail sign at the entrance to the woods (4 miles). Take an immediate left (southeast) and continue following the blue blazes.

12 The trail in this area passes through private property. Here and elsewhere throughout the state, private property owners have kindly given permission for the Buckeye Trail to cross their land to allow for continuity of the trail.

The trail reaches a shrubby area and passes a pond. There might be beaver activity at this small pond. At about 5 miles the trail enters some pines.

13 Cross a small brook, climb up to a lane, and turn right onto the lane. After a short walk, leave the lane and turn left at the Buckeye Trail

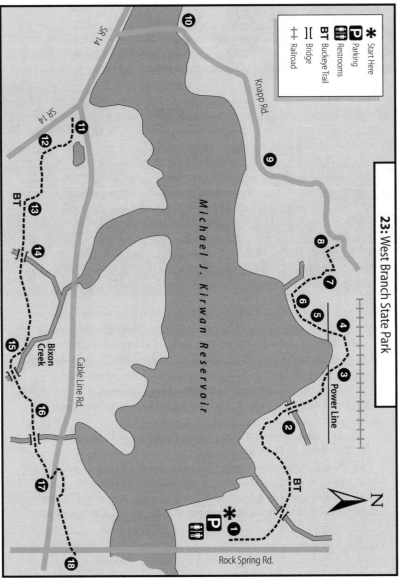

© Gray & Company, Publishers

post, just before a gasline right-of-way. Then descend to cross another brook. This section of trail goes through part of the older forest of mature beeches, maples, oaks, and shagbarks, some impressively large. Several species of woodpeckers are active year round in this woodland and are easier to see and identify than some of the smaller birds. The pileated woodpecker is the largest, with a length of 16.5 inches and a wingspan of 29 inches. Pileated woodpeckers excavate large rectangu-

lar holes in trees, looking for insects to eat. You may hear their loud drumming or catch sight of one maneuvering through the forest.

14 The trail continues on generally level ground interspersed with dips and climbs when crossing side drainages that flow toward the reservoir. A fairly large beaver pond is to the left of the trail.

15 At about 7 miles the trail crosses a small ravine and stream, then a wider stream, Bixon Creek. Recross Bixon Creek on a log bridge (7.4 miles).

16 The trail passes an open cornfield on the left and crosses another small brook (8 miles).

17 Reach a dirt road (Cable Line Rd.) and cross it diagonally left where the Buckeye Trail reenters at the edge of the woods.

18 At Rock Spring Rd. turn left (north). Follow the road across the causeway to return to the starting point at the boat launch area. ■

24 Kent
and Riveredge Park

Distance: 3 miles

Easy

Walking time: 2 hours

Description: This hike combines a city sidewalk tour of Kent's historic West River neighborhood with a walk along the Cuyahoga River. On the river walk, pathways, steps, and decks connect four small city parks situated along a mile-long stretch of the river.

Directions: From Cleveland, take I-480 east to exit for SR 14; SR 14 joins I-480 in Bedford; stay on I-480/SR 14 until I-480 ends; exit on SR 14 (Streetsboro); follow SR 14 to SR 43; right (south) on SR 43 to Kent; left on W. Main St.; cross Cuyahoga River; immediate right on Franklin Ave. for about a quarter mile; right on Stow St.; continue back across river; immediate left into John Brown Tannery Park parking lot.

From Akron, take I-77 or SR 8 to I-76 east; east on I-76 to Exit 33 for SR 43, (Kent/Hartville); left (north) on SR 43 for 3 miles; left on Summit St. (becomes Stow St.) for about two blocks, cross Cuyahoga River; left into Tannery Park parking lot.

Parking & restrooms: Park at the John Brown Tannery Park trailhead located on the south side of Stow St. There are no restrooms at the parking lot. Seasonal restrooms are located in Fred Fuller Park near by.

As was the case with other early Ohio towns, the location of water power determined the location of Kent. The first permanent settlers, John and Sally Haymaker, arrived at the Cuyahoga River in 1805 and soon harnessed the power of the river to grind grain. Other settlers and mills followed, and a young settlement grew up along the banks of the river. The early town where this hike begins was called Franklin Mills. Another settlement, called Carthage, was formed upstream, and eventually the two merged into one town known as Franklin Mills. The Kent name was to come later.

Most of the earliest development in town took place on the west bank of the river, but in the 1830s word spread that the Pennsylvania & Ohio (P & O) Canal would pass through town, and attention shifted to the east side of the river, where the canal would be built. Development there formed the beginnings of the town's central business district. The P & O Canal, which tied the Pennsylvania Canal System to the Ohio & Erie Canal in Akron, was a highly successful link in Ohio's canal system. The P & O operated for a good decade before it gave way to the faster railroads.

The name Franklin Mills stayed with the town through the canal era. It was changed in 1867 to honor Marvin Kent, a prominent citizen who was influential in making sure that the Atlantic & Great Western Railroad came to town. With the coming of the railroad, Kent's commercial district flourished. Many businesses were established near the railroad station, and the railroad itself offered opportunities for employment in the rail yards.

The contributions of another Kent citizen earned the town the nickname of "Tree City." In 1880 John Davey, an Englishman who immigrated to Ohio, formed a company for the proper care and conservation of trees. In 1901 he wrote a book called *The Tree Doctor,* in which he explained how his methods of caring for shade trees were based on science and observation. By 1908 he was receiving many requests for his services and incorporated the Davey Tree Expert Company a year later, with headquarters in Kent. One of John Davey's three sons, Martin L. Davey, served as the company's first general manager and in 1913, at the age of 29, was elected mayor of the city. He was reelected twice and then won a seat in the U.S. House of Representatives, followed by two terms as governor of Ohio.

Today Kent is perhaps best known as the home of Kent State University. Although the university campus is not included in this hike, it is a worthwhile destination as a side trip. The university is located just east of the downtown business district and can be reached by traveling east on Main St. In the early 1900s the state was experiencing a severe shortage of teachers. In 1910 two teachers' colleges were established in the northern half of the state, one here in Kent, to be called Kent State Normal School, and one in Bowling Green, now Bowling Green University. The cornerstone of Merrill Hall, the first building on the Kent campus, was laid in 1912. In 1935 the college added graduate programs and became Kent State University. Today the university has an enrollment of over 20,000 (in a city of 30,000).

There are several things of special interest for those visiting the 824-acre university campus. The May 4 Memorial commemorates the events of May 4, 1970, when four students were killed and nine wounded during a demonstration protesting the U.S. invasion of Cambodia. A year following the tragic events, the university established the Center for Peaceful Change, now the Center for Applied Conflict Management, as a living memorial. More recently, Kent State has been holding annual symposia on democracy, drawing on the work of leaders throughout the world.

The Kent State University Museum offers one of the finest and most complete costume collections in the world, as well as thousands of pieces of decorative art. In keeping with the town's reputation as an early center of glass-making, the museum also displays an extensive collection of American glass. The museum is located in Rockwell Hall, a 1927 Beaux Arts building that originally housed the university's li-

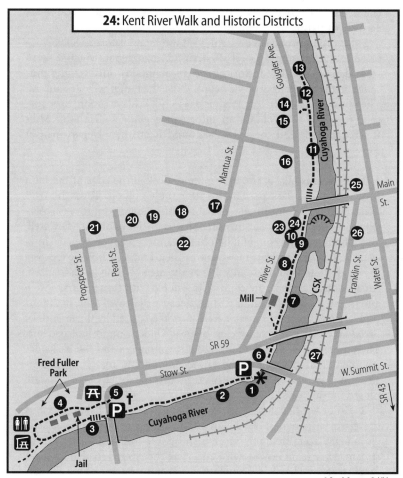

24: Kent River Walk and Historic Districts

© Gray & Company, Publishers

brary. It is open Wednesdays through Sundays; for more information phone 330-672-3450. The Kent State University Library is located in a 12-story building on the south end of the campus. Notable on campus are the many black squirrels. In 1961 a grounds superintendent brought 12 of them back from London, Ontario. They have since expanded their range throughout the town and well beyond. An annual event on campus, the Black Squirrel Festival, celebrates these local celebrities.

The Kent Parks and Recreation Department has honored the early history of the town and its natural setting by establishing Franklin Mills Riveredge Park along the Cuyahoga River in the heart of Kent. Paths, stairs, and observation decks allow visitors to get close to the river and visit the sites of some of the town's earliest enterprises. In the places where the early mills and factories are gone, nature has reclaimed the riverbanks. This part of the hike is well shaded and offers an oasis of nature in this historic town.

For more information on Kent, visit the Kent Historical Society located in the Atlantic & Great Western Railroad depot, which it saved from demolition. The historical society maintains offices and a museum on the upper level of the depot, above the Pufferbelly Restaurant. The museum is open on Wednesdays and Fridays, noon to 4 P.M. (330-678-2712). To obtain an informative guide to Franklin Mills Riveredge Park, call the Kent Parks and Recreation Department at 330--673-8897.

1 Begin this hike at the information kiosk at the edge of the John Brown Tannery Park parking lot near the Cuyahoga River. In 1835 Zenas Kent and John Brown, the abolitionist, entered into a partnership to build a tannery at this site. The partnership did not fare well, and John Brown was out of it before the tannery was completed. However, he invested in land in what was then Franklin Mills, expecting that real estate would rise in value as the area became industrialized. An economic crisis in the country interfered with those plans as well, and he eventually left Franklin Mills. Because of Brown's role in the antislavery movement, Tannery Park is now recognized by the Friends of Freedom Society as a significant historic Underground Railroad site. The tannery itself was demolished, but volunteers and the parks department reused some of the tannery's building materials in constructing a gazebo on the tannery site. Across the street, old bricks were reused in walkways.

2 Go down the steps, past the small gazebo, to a fishing deck. A gravel-surfaced nature trail begins at the fishing deck and parallels the Cuyahoga River. Facing the river, turn right to follow this path downstream, away from downtown Kent. Here the river is shaded by silver maple trees and black willows. Fishermen enjoy catching blue gill, catfish, rock bass, and other freshwater fish. A stone marker to the right of the trail honors Ruth Meade, a respected environmentalist who was a key leader of the Kent Environmental Council (KEC) and pioneered the city's recycling efforts. KEC volunteers helped establish this park by beginning the reclamation of the site in the 1970s.

This path can be very muddy, and might be under water if the river is high. If impassable, skip this part of the hike and pick it up at #6, just across the street from the Tannery Park parking lot.

3 Reach the Harvey Redmond Bridge and the eastern edge of Fred Fuller Park. Cross the road and walk up a few steps to the continuation of the river-edge path. Continue on this path, now at a slightly higher level above the river, still paralleling it. After a short distance, the trail splits. Take the right fork, uphill, into the main picnic area of Fred Fuller Park. The Lamson & Sessions Company donated about 56 acres for the park in 1934, and it has since been developed into Kent's largest

park, with recreational facilities on both sides of the Cuyahoga River. This part of the park has several small picnic shelters and play areas situated on an oak-shaded hill.

4 Once you reach the top of the hill in the picnic area, turn right to reach the Roy H. Smith Shelterhouse, a popular site for meetings and other gatherings. Go past the shelterhouse, then past the Kent Parks and Recreation Department headquarters, to reach the Old Kent Jail. This historic jail was originally on Day St., near the center of town, but it was in the path of a new downtown retail business and so was moved to this location in 1999. The building was constructed in 1869 and served as a jail until the 1930s, and then for a while as office space for the city service director and engineer. The jail was typical of small-town jails of its day, often busiest on Saturday nights with an influx of "drunks, horse and buggy speeders, rowdies, and unethical traveling salesmen." The architectural details of the little building, such as the small porch with undulating wooden brackets, seem to belie its mundane function, though the accommodations were probably just what you would expect. The Kent Parks and Recreation Department added certain conveniences to the building, which is listed in the National Register of Historic Places, and now makes it available for meetings and event rentals.

Leaving the jailhouse, go down the slope, past another shelter and playground, to reach the park road. Turn left and climb the hill to Stow St.

5 Turn right on Stow St., heading east and back toward the John Brown Tannery Park. On the right is Pioneer Cemetery, dating to 1810.

The Kent Historical Society has dedicated this cemetery to the Haymakers and other pioneer families that settled here along the Cuyahoga River. You might wish to spend some time here looking at the very old gravestones in this quiet spot above the river.

6 Continue east on Stow St., going down the hill to Tannery Park. Cross to the north side of Stow St. where there is a small parking lot and the entrance to Franklin Mills Riveredge Park. This long, narrow park parallels the Cuyahoga River for about half a mile, from this point to Brady's Leap Park. The trail here is made up of paths, decks, and steps. In a couple places steps lead down to the river's edge. This short stretch of trail enters into the heart of the oldest part of what is now Kent, and remnants of the area's history stand as casual monuments to the town's beginnings. On the right at the river's edge is one of these, the partial wall of the Kent Mill, a flour mill built by Zenas Kent in 1838. Terraced steps lead down to the mill ruins. The mill was in operation for many years and stood until 1931, when it was torn down. Other enterprises located here along the river were a sawmill, a forge, and a hemp business. But these water-powered businesses were all prone to destruction by floods, and as other forms of power became available, all industry left the river's edge for higher ground. Nature has reclaimed the riverbank, and it is now a surprisingly wild spot in the middle of the city.

7 Go under the SR 59 bridge. Immediately beyond the bridge the trail splits. Take the right fork down a few steps, and after a few more steps you can get a good view of a white, five-story factory building above and to your left. In the 1830s a number of investors in Franklin Mills planned to create a silk industry in the young town, with hopes of turning Franklin Mills into a major industrial city. Though mulberry trees, the silkworms' food source, were plentiful along the banks of the river, the climate of Northeast Ohio was too harsh for the cultivation of the Asian silk-producing moths. The building went through other incarnations, eventually housing another seemingly incongruous enterprise, an alpaca mill, the town's second-largest industry during its heyday. Local farmers supplied the wool for the mill. Today the building houses the Portage Packaging Company.

8 Climb a few more steps; at the top an asphalt trail joins in from the alpaca mill building. Continue north on the trail, through this narrow green space hugging the river. This band of trees and shrubs near the water provides a favorable habitat for a number of different bird species. Birds to watch for include cardinals, here throughout the year, and swifts and swallows in warmer months, hunting insects over the river. Great blue herons can be seen wading in search of food below the dam and in the shallows downstream. During spring and fall migrations, various warblers alight here to feed and rest.

Buttonbush, an aquatic shrub, grows along the river. The plant's fragrant white flowers are clustered into round ball-like heads. Both wild and cultivated species of plants grow alongside the trail.

9 From the observation decks just south of the Main Street Bridge, you can see a number of historic features that make up the Kent Industrial District, listed in the National Register of Historic Places. The gracefully arched dam across the river was built in 1836; it is one of the oldest stone-arch dams in the country, and the only one with a canal lock attached. Irish immigrants, recruited as canal laborers, constructed the dam from locally quarried sandstone. It served to impound water for the Pennsylvania & Ohio Canal. At this location, the canal ran along the east bank of the Cuyahoga River. Only a remnant of a canal lock remains. Though the dam was useful in its day, it no longer serves its original purpose, and it impedes the free flow of the Cuyahoga River. In 2002 Kent officials decided to lower the impoundment and allow more river water to flow, in an effort to improve water quality in the Cuyahoga River. A special design will preserve the historic structures while allowing for the improvements.

After the demise of the canal, trains replaced canal boats on tracks laid in the filled-in canal bed. Those tracks, originally built for the Baltimore & Ohio Railroad and now used by CSX, are below another set of tracks. The upper-level tracks were for the Atlantic & Great Western Railroad, whose station now houses the Kent Historical Society and the Pufferbelly Restaurant.

The stone Main Street Bridge is also notable. In 1837 a covered bridge was erected upstream of the dam. It remained until replaced by this masonry-arch bridge, built in 1876. It is one of the few remaining stone-arch bridges in the state.

10 Continue north on the walkway, down the steps and toward the Main Street Bridge. At the trail bridge, just before the street bridge, is an interesting niche where a five-foot-high natural waterfall flows over a rock ledge to the left. In this small space you can see evidence of construction from previous eras—bricks and sandstone and concrete layered on top of natural bedrock. A large red mulberry tree overhangs the bridge. Red mulberry trees, native to Ohio, produce fruits favored by squirrels and birds. White mulberry trees are an Asian species introduced in the eastern United States in colonial times in an effort to cultivate a silk industry.

Go under Main St. At the north side of the bridge, a brick trail on the left leads to a stairway to Main St.

11 From this spot you can see grain silos and mill buildings on the opposite bank of the river. These buildings were originally the Peerless Roller Mills, named for the "roller process" of milling grain, which succeeded the use of water-powered millstones. From 1879 on, the mills were operated by the Williams Brothers Company, and they continue to be family owned and operated today. The company mills cake and pastry flours from Ohio-grown wheat. Many popular brands of cookies and cakes use flour produced at these mills.

Behind the viewing platform is an alcove built from sandstone blocks. The bedrock along the river is Sharon Conglomerate, a sandstone imbedded with quartz pebbles. During Kent's early days there were many quarries along the river supplying building stone for the developing town.

12 Pass a brick walk on the left; you will return here shortly. Continue north, passing behind a brick building. This is the L. N. Gross Building, which originally housed a shirtwaist factory. It is now home to a vintage automobile-restoration business.

13 Continue ahead to where the trail ends at Brady's Leap Park. A rock marks this legendary spot where a man named Samuel Brady was reported to have leapt across the Cuyahoga River. Captain Brady was an army scout sent to the Ohio territory following the Revolutionary War to gather information about Indian activities in the region. As the story goes, Brady was being pursued by a band of Indians and, at this spot, jumped across the river to escape capture. The Indians crossed the river farther upstream and continued in pursuit to the lake east of here that now bears Brady's name. Brady reportedly eluded capture by hiding in the trunk of a tree and later walked back to Pittsburgh. Although he is best remembered for this story, his life undoubtedly had other interesting episodes—he was known to be an adventurous figure during the tumultuous time of the Revolutionary War and subsequent westward expansion by settlers into Indian territories.

14 Turn back south and then turn right to climb the gently sloping brick walk to Gougler Ave. (the L. N. Gross Building is on the right). As there is no crosswalk here we suggest you stay on the east side of the street, from which you can see several historic buildings. Straight across the street is the Unitarian-Universalist Church, dedicated in 1868. The building was built on land donated by Marvin Kent and has housed the same church continuously throughout its history.

15 To the left of the church is the Franklin Township Hall. This hall was built in 1837 and continues to function as the township government seat. It was modeled after a building in Connecticut and built from local materials: sandstone from the riverbank, wood from nearby forests, and bricks made at a location near the start of this hike. Besides being a center for local government, the building served as the township's first high school and has the distinction of being the place where James A. Garfield began his political career—here, in 1859, he was nominated for the Ohio senate. He would later become the 20th president of the United States, though he served for only six months before he was assassinated.

16 Walk south on Gougler Ave. At the corner of Gougler Ave. and Park Ave. is the Congregational Church, built in 1858. An 1868 photo shows the church's tall steeple, which in 1905 was blown off in a winter storm. The church's congregation moved to a new location in 1955, and this building has since been adapted for commercial use.

17 At W. Main St., turn right (west) and cross Gougler Ave. On the right is the Kemp building, renovated by a group of physicians. Next to it, a popular coffee shop has recycled a former restaurant building. Continue to N. Mantua St. and cross to the northwest corner. From this corner, looking back east, you can see the tops of Kent State University buildings on the hill in the distance.

Now turning back toward the west, note the large brick house sitting back from the street behind a brick wall. Marvin Kent, after whom the town was named, built this Italianate mansion between 1880 and 1884. It is listed in the National Register of Historic Places and today serves as a Masonic temple. Marvin Kent sought out and employed the best craftsmen he could find, including Isaac D. Tuttle of Ravenna for the stonework and wood carvers from New York and Cleveland. The intricately carved woodwork in the home is extraordinary and contains many details specific to the Kent family. An arched pane of etched glass over the double front doors and two etched panes in the interior doors depict medieval country scenes.

The three stories include a ballroom on the third level, a library and billiard room on the second level, and high-ceilinged parlors on the first level. In its time, these features all earned the building a reputation as one of northern Ohio's most "elegant and palatial" residences. Many notables were guests in the home, including four U.S. presidents. The house was last occupied by Marvin Kent's son, William, until he died in 1923, when heirs sold it to the Rockton Lodge #316, Free and Accepted Masons. Marvin and two descendants were members of the Masonic Fraternity, and the current Masons have continued to preserve this historic home. It is open for tours during the Kent Fest around July 4th, and by appointment.

18 The West Main Street Historic District stretches from the Marvin Kent home west to 625 W. Main St. and includes 24 buildings. At 443 W. Main St. is a dark-red brick home built in a later era than the Kent mansion and in a quite different style. Known as the John Getz House, it dates to 1916, and its design shows the influence of Frank Lloyd Wright's Prairie Style, with low horizontal lines, projecting eaves, and tile roof.

19 West of the Getz house is the Charles Williams House, built around 1890 in the Queen Anne style. Marvin L. Davey of the Davey Tree Expert Company, a former governor of Ohio, lived in this home.

20 At the end of this block, just before Pearl St., are two homes built in the Eastlake style. The William Getz House at 471 W. Main St. was built in 1890, and the Hardy/Chellen house at 477 was built about 10 years earlier. They both show some nice elements of the Eastlake style, such as the "gingerbread" details and porches.

21 Cross Pearl St. and continue west one more block, past more century homes, to the Patton House on the corner of W. Main and N. Prospect streets. At this corner, cross W. Main St. to the south side and turn to go back east. Cross S. Pearl St.

22 Midway down the next block, at 450 W. Main St., is one of the oldest homes in this historic district, the Simon Perkins Wolcott House, built in 1868. Wolcott, born in Northfield, was a well-educated man who became the second mayor of Kent in 1866.

23 Continue east, crossing S. Mantua St. In the next block, at 312 W. Main St., is the Kent Free Library, one of over 2,800 libraries that were made possible through the generosity of industrialist Andrew Carnegie. This library was completed in 1903.

24 Cross River St. On the corner, at 272 W. Main St., is the Gifford Building. The first building on this site was a livery stable, succeeded by the present structure, which was constructed in 1916. It was a car dealership until the 1970s and now houses law offices.

25 Continue east to cross the Cuyahoga River on the historic Main Street Bridge. From the east end of the bridge you can look down on the river, the dam, and the railroad tracks where the P & O Canal used to be. At the corner of W. Main St. and Franklin Ave. is the town's gazebo. Across W. Main St. is a small park, the Home Savings Plaza, donated to the people of Kent by Home Savings Bank. The Kent Exchange Building was here until it burned down in 1972. Now summer concerts and other events take place on this prominent downtown corner.

26 Turn right (south) on Franklin Ave. to reach the Atlantic & Great Western Railroad station, home of the Pufferbelly, Ltd., restaurant and the Kent Historical Society. This station was due to be demolished in 1975 when the Historical Society stepped in and saved it from the wrecking ball. The society leases the lower floor to the restaurant and maintains its offices and museum upstairs. The brick depot was built in 1875 in a style known as Tuscan Revival and is listed in the National Register of Historic Places. Kent was strategically located at the midway point of the railway's route from New York City to St. Louis, and the subsequent rail-related industry and commerce gave Kent a great economic boost in the late 1800s.

27 Continue south past the depot and under SR 59. In the summer months the Haymaker Market, an open-air farmers' market, is open for business in this lot.

Turn right (west) at Stow St. (called Summit St. to the east); cross both sets of railroad tracks and the Cuyahoga River to return to the starting point of the hike. ■

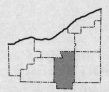

SUMMIT COUNTY

Summit County is dominated by the city of Akron, which grew with the establishment of the Ohio & Erie Canal across the summit of land between the Tuscarawas and Cuyahoga rivers. Scores of enterprises sprang up along the canal as boats traveled in both directions through the locks. Later milling and manufacturing helped the city grow—eventually it became a major rubber-producing center.

Prior to pioneer settlement, Indians inhabited this region and established a route for portaging their canoes to connect the south-flowing Tuscarawas River and the north-flowing Cuyahoga River. In 1785, the Treaty of Fort McIntosh established the Portage Path as one of the boundaries demarcating native American territories from land claimed by the United States.

Within Summit County lies the major portion of the 33,000-acre Cuyahoga Valley National Park (CVNP), which preserves 22 miles of green space between Cleveland and Akron. Hale Farm and Village, located within CVNP, preserves the farmstead of settler Jonathan Hale and includes a re-creation of a typical 19th-century Western Reserve village using buildings and furnishings from all over Northeast Ohio (800-589-9703). Four of the Metro Parks, Serving Summit County are also within this pastoral corridor.

This park system consists of more than 6,600 acres of land including 11 developed parks, the F. A. Seiberling Naturealm, the 23-mile Bike & Hike Trail, the Towpath Trail, and several large conservation areas. Selected hikes in these parks are described in Chs. 32–41. Metro Parks, Serving Summit County publishes a quarterly newsletter, *Green Islands*, and a quarterly programs and events guide.

In 2001, Metro Parks and eight other community partners released the Summit County Trail and Greenway Plan. The plan builds on the county park system and shows the potential for future park lands and links to the Ohio & Erie Canal Towpath Trail and other existing trails.

For information about Metro Parks, Serving Summit County, call 330-867-5511. For program information, phone 330-865-8064.

Additional information about Summit County is available from Akron/Summit Convention & Visitors Bureau: 800-245-4254.

25 Hudson Village
and Western Reserve Academy

Distance: 2 miles

Easy

Walking time: 1½ hours

Description: Hikes A and B are easy, pleasant walks through historic Hudson Village and the campus of Western Reserve Academy. They are almost entirely on sidewalks and will introduce the visitor to beautifully restored 19th-century homes and public buildings and provide an introduction to the town's historical past.

Directions: From Cleveland take I-480 to Exit 37 (Hudson/Twinsburg); south on SR 91 for 4 miles to Hudson (pass Western Reserve Academy on left just before entering town); SR 91 becomes N. Main St.
From Akron, take SR 8 north to Streetsboro Rd. (SR 303); right (east) on Streetsboro Rd. into Hudson; left (north) on SR 91.

Parking & restrooms: Just before the clock tower, turn west into the Municipal Parking Lot behind the row of business buildings on N. Main St.; restrooms are available at the library.

Hudson Village has been mentioned as one of the top 100 historic places in the U. S. because so many of its residences and other structures are listed in the National Register of Historic Places. Many buildings on the campus of nearby Western Reserve Academy (originally Western Reserve College) also boast this prestigious listing. Hudson Village is reminiscent of a small Connecticut town because of its architecture and neat village green containing a bandstand and clock tower. This "New England look" is not surprising. The first settler here was David Hudson (1761–1836) of Goshen, Connecticut, who arrived in 1799 to view land in the Connecticut Western Reserve that he and two others had purchased, sight unseen.

Hudson had traveled with a small party through New York State to Lakes Ontario and Erie, then to Lorenzo Carter's cabin at the mouth of the Cuyahoga River. Heading south on the Cuyahoga to Brandywine Creek, he found he could go no farther and so continued on foot, using surveyor's tools to find his 5-mile-square parcel of land, identified only as Township 4, Range 10.

After returning home to retrieve his family and bring other settlers, he and his men began to cut a crude road in from the Cuyahoga River to Hudson (as the settlement became known in 1802), over which the settlers came. This path became the David Hudson Trail, and evidence of its beginnings can still be seen in a wide track crossing the Stanford

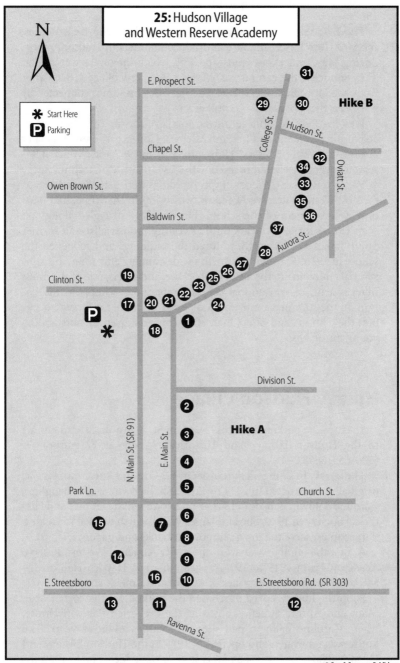

© Gray & Company, Publishers

Trail in Cuyahoga Valley National Park (Ch. 29). David Hudson's descendants lived in the Hudson family home at 318 N. Main St. until 1967.

The first settlers were sturdy New Englanders who built homes, shops, a church, schoolhouse and other buildings in Hudson, reproducing the Connecticut landscape with which they were so familiar. They modeled the campus of Western Reserve College (1826) after Connecticut's Yale College, constructing brick buildings connected by walkways that crisscross a central green.

Western Reserve College moved to Cleveland in 1882 because of economic problems and became Adelbert College; its name was later changed to Western Reserve University, and, in 1967, Case Western Reserve University, when it merged with Case Institute of Technology.

Western Reserve College's empty buildings were subsequently occupied by Western Reserve Academy, which, up to that time, had been only a department of the school. The academy struggled along and even closed for a few years until a wealthy industrialist and former pupil, James W. Ellsworth, restored the buildings and reopened the school in 1916. Through Ellsworth's wide-ranging efforts and his substantial endowment, the academy became, and still is, one of the finest independent, co-educational college preparatory schools in the nation. In the summer, a music school, Encore School for Strings, occupies the campus and offers many free concerts given by outstanding young musicians.

Hike A. Hudson Village

1 From the parking lot, cross N. Main St. at Aurora St. and go east to the Hudson Library and Historical Society at 22 Aurora St. (330-653-6658).

The library building on the corner of E. Main and Aurora streets was originally constructed in 1834 by Frederick Baldwin, whose daughter, Caroline Baldwin Babcock (1841–1921), founded the Library and Historical Society in 1910. She and James W. Ellsworth wanted to create a library to preserve the town's important books and papers.

At first the library was part of the newly reopened Western Reserve Academy. From 1919 to 1924 it was housed in Hayden Hall on the academy campus at the corner of Aurora and College streets.

Soon the library board purchased the building at the corner of E. Main and Aurora streets, known as the Frederick Baldwin House, where Caroline Baldwin had spent her early childhood years. The house was renovated and opened in 1925 as the Hudson Library and Historical Society. In 1954 a new east wing was added, and in 1963 another major expansion took place. The most recent interior renovation occurred in 1995.

The library has a reputation for its excellent collection of books and manuscripts. It is a major research center for scholars studying the life and times of one of Hudson's best-known citizens, abolitionist John Brown (1800–1859).

2 Turn south on E. Main St. crossing Division St. At 41 E. Main is the former Edgar B. Ellsworth Store, built in 1841 and now a dental office. Ellsworth's son, James, worked in this store as a child.

James W. Ellsworth (1849–1925) acquired great wealth in Chicago as a major coal dealer and distributor. His contributions to Hudson are numerous. He provided the resources for street paving, the planting of elms, new power and water plants, a sewer system, a telephone system, renovation of homes and land, and shored-up banking and school systems. The clock tower was one of Ellsworth's final philanthropic gifts to the community. Upon his death in 1925 he left most of his wealth to Western Reserve Academy, which he had restored and reopened in 1916.

3 At 35 E. Main St. is the 1889 A. W. Lockhart House. Lockhart was a local saloon keeper whose tavern across the green on Main St. caught fire in April 1892 and caused the entire business block to burn, leaving no early buildings remaining on the west side of Main St.

4 Next is the Town-Shields House at 33 E. Main. Inside the Queen Anne–style façade of this structure is a Greek Revival house built in 1824 by Dr. Israel Town. The Queen Anne façade, built in 1890 by the Shields family, wraps around the original home. (The attic roof of the earlier building remains.)

5 Just before Church St., at 27 E. Main St., is the 1879 Hudson Town Hall. It became the home of the fire department in 1896. The First Congregational Church, founded by David Hudson in 1802, was originally located on this site. The building now serves as office space for the city of Hudson.

6 The building identified as a funeral home at 19 E. Main St. is the Town-Neibel House, Dr. Israel Town's 1836 home. It was remodeled in 1877 by the Neibel family.

7 On the green to the right (west) is the site of Hudson's original 1802 schoolhouse. On the south side of Church St. is a sign about Landsberg am Lech, Hudson's sister city in Switzerland.

8 Sebastian Miller, an important Main St. merchant, built his 1878 home at 13 E. Main St. in the popular Italian Revival style.

9 Capt. Heman Oviatt was an early pioneer who built this house at 7 E. Main St. in 1825. It later became the parsonage for the First Congregational Church and, still later, the rectory for old St. Mary's Church next door.

10 St. Mary's Church (1860) originally stood at Oviatt and Maple streets three blocks east of here. In 1888 the building was moved to this location and greatly expanded. St. Mary's parish left in 1970 to build a new church, and now this beautiful old landmark is occupied by Temple Beth Shalom and the Spiritual Life Society, who both share worship space.

11 At 5 E. Main St., on the southeast corner of Main St. (SR 91) and E. Streetsboro St. (SR 303), is an imposing white three-story structure. It was originally the Free Congregational Church, built in 1841 by abolitionist Owen Brown, father of famed abolitionist John Brown. The old church has been raised up over new first-floor construction and expanded to house offices.

Owen Brown (1771–1856), a member of a prominent New England family, settled in Hudson in 1805. Of Owen's 17 children, John is by far the best known. The entire Brown family was strongly antislavery and all were active in the Underground Railroad movement to help runaway slaves gain freedom in Canada. The family lived in a wooden home at 9 Aurora St. (where the Brewster Mansion now stands).

There is a memorial plaque for John Brown in the park between E. Streetsboro and Ravenna streets, near the spot where he made one of his last Hudson speeches before going to Harpers Ferry, Virginia. His fiery antislavery rhetoric culminated in a raid on the federal arsenal there in 1859. Brown was hanged in December of that year, an event that helped instigate the Civil War.

12 To the east of this park is the Inn at Turner's Mill (36 E. Streetsboro), a restaurant and historic landmark. It was built in 1852 as a steam mill by Edgar B. Ellsworth (see Note #2) and Henry N. Day. Originally, it was known as the Hudson Planing and Lumber Co., but by 1873 it became the Hudson Mill Co., and later Turner's Mill. This landmark structure has been beautifully restored from top to bottom—from the third floor where shakers originally removed husks from the grain to the first floor where grinding took place.

13 Turn back (west) across the green to SR 91 and SR 303 (N. Main and E. Streetsboro streets). Cross SR 91 to see the small Boy Scouts of America Cabin built by Troop 321 in 1931 (not open to the public) and Hudson's World War I Monument (1917–18).

14 Cross SR 303 (E. Streetsboro St.) and walk north to another open green. In the center of this green space is a small plaque placed by the Hudson Library and Historical Society and the First Congregational Church to mark the site of the first Thanksgiving service in Hudson.

15 Toward the rear (west) of the green at 36 N. Main St. is the Greek Revival–style Augustus Baldwin House built in 1825.

16 At the south end of the green is the 1976 Hudson Bandstand, built to celebrate our country's bicentennial. Continue walking north on N. Main St. past interesting shops and businesses.

17 Continue north to 160–164 N. Main St. and Saywell's Drug Store, built in 1913. Its old-fashioned soda fountain is a Hudson tradition.

18 Hudson's landmark clock tower was built on the town green in 1912 by James W. Ellsworth as his gift to the community of his birth. The still-functioning, gravity-run clock is the original one made by the E. Howard Clock Company. The tower also served as a public water fountain. Note the watering trough for horses on the north side and fountains for people and small animals on the west side. A marker on the south side of the clock tower notes that it was a gift from James W. Ellsworth, and that Percy Dresser, town marshal, faithfully wound the weights and chimes from 1935 to 1950.

19 On the northwest corner of Clinton and N. Main streets (178 N. Main) is the 1833 Walter Wright Store, now Hudson General Store. This building and all those in this block north to Owen Brown St. escaped the 1892 fire and date from the 1830s to the 1850s. This store is typical of the old wooden buildings that formerly lined all of the west side of N. Main St.

20 Cross N. Main St. and go east on Aurora St. On the corner at 5 Aurora St. is the old Brewster Store, now Republic Bank. Next to it is the Brewster Mansion at 9 Aurora St., presently housing shops and offices. Anson Brewster (1807–1864), a native of Connecticut and direct descendant of the Mayflower's William Brewster, came here in 1825 and opened his brick, Federal-style store in Hudson in 1839.

In 1853 he built the mansion next door on the site of Owen Brown's old wooden home (Note #11), which had burned to the ground in 1842. The mansion is the only stone Gothic Revival building left standing in the Western Reserve.

21 Next, to the east, is Christ Church Episcopal Chapel (1930), which was constructed when the original 1846 Gothic-style sanctuary was torn down. It occupies the same foundation as the original church.

22 The 1834 Isham-Beebe House at 21 Aurora St. is Christ Church Episcopal's Guild Hall. Warren Isham was an early Hudson newspaper publisher. The Beebes became owners of the house when Anson Brewster's daughter, Ellen, married D. Duncan Beebe, who entered his father-in-law's store and later became sole proprietor of the business. "Brewster Row," as it was then called, extended along Aurora St. from the family store to the Beebe House.

23 The new, enlarged Christ Church Episcopal, completed and opened on Christmas Eve 1994, connects with the rest of the church's buildings.

24 East of the library, at 30 Aurora St., is the 1826 Whedon-Farwell House. This structure was originally built in Greek Revival style, but an 1870 renovation made it look more like a Victorian home.

25 At 37 Aurora St. is the 1847 Brick Academy. At one time it housed women students who were taught by Western Reserve Academy professors—in their free time, because women were not then permitted on the all-male campus.

26 Next along Aurora St. is First Congregational Church of Hudson. A plaque affixed to the side of the original building describes its long history.

Hike B. Western Reserve Academy

27 Continue walking northeast on Aurora St. to College St. and turn left (north). On this corner is Hayden Hall (1870), the original home of the Hudson Library. Six grand pillars front this imposing building surrounded by beautiful gardens. Once a cheese warehouse, then a community center, this building later became the school's fine arts center. Presently it houses the music department, containing studios, a recital hall, and practice rooms.

28 On the northwest corner of Aurora and College streets is Loomis Observatory, established and built by Professor Elias Loomis in 1838. It is the oldest observatory on its original foundations in the United States. Loomis, a professor of mathematics and philosophy, was one of America's preeminent 19th-century astronomers. The observatory has been restored several times but still has its original telescope, transit, astronomical clock, and chair.

Continue north on College St. On the right are the John D. Ong Library, Seymour Hall, the Chapel, and four-story North Hall. Between Baldwin and Chapel streets are faculty homes.

29 Pass the playing fields and Hudson St. as you head to Ellsworth Hall on the southwest corner of College and E. Prospect streets. Built in 1922, this structure was named for the school's major benefactor, James W. Ellsworth. It contains a dormitory, dining room, student center, publications office, radio station, laundry, and meeting rooms.

30 On the east side of College St., opposite Prospect St., is the four-story Athenaeum (1843), a girls' dormitory and the largest of the college's original buildings. At first it was the natural science building, becoming a dormitory in 1917. Its name came from a literary society once housed there. Ohio's first Phi Beta Kappa chapter received its charter in this building in 1847.

31 Beyond the Athenaeum is Bicknell Athletic Complex, originally built in 1920 with subsequent additions. In 1930, a swimming pool was added, and then a gymnasium in 1951. In 1983, renovations added a new swimming pool and diving well, squash courts, indoor tennis courts, and a wrestling room.

32 On College St., backtrack to Hudson St. and go east past faculty homes. At Oviatt St. turn right (south). More faculty homes are on the left (east) side of the street. On the right (west) side of Oviatt is Harlan Wood House (1953), a boys' dormitory named for a former teacher, dean, and headmaster.

To the south of Wood House is Knight Fine Arts Center (1986), a major teaching and performance facility. It houses a 400-seat auditorium with a full stage and classrooms for drama, dance, art, stagecraft, publications, and photography, as well as the Moos Gallery.

33 Just past Knight Fine Arts Center and before Aurora St., enter the campus on the drive off Oviatt St. and walk toward the Chapel, the focal point of Brick Row.

The Chapel, built in 1836, is now the site of school meetings, concerts, and lectures. In the summer, Encore School for Strings holds its recitals here. The building has undergone many renovations and improvements over the years. A new Holtkamp organ was installed in 1966 and the third tier of the steeple was replaced in 1989.

34 North of the Chapel is North Hall (1837), a girls' dormitory and one of the original college buildings. Despite a major restoration in 1986, it has undergone the fewest changes of any of the old buildings.

35 South of the Chapel is Seymour Hall, housing administrative offices and classrooms. It was built in 1913 on the sites of Middle College (1826) and South College (1830).

36 At the end of the green is Wilson Hall (1963), containing classrooms, laboratories, and a 100-seat lecture hall. South of Wilson Hall is the John D. Ong Library, opened and dedicated in 2000. This library is the first new structure on Brick Row since 1914. The architects, Albert Filoni and Terry Shannon of MacLachlan, Cornelius & Filoni in Pittsburgh, designed the building to fit in with the 19th-century look of the row. However, the interior is state of the art with regard to technology, with a bibliographic classroom, large computer lab, computer workstations throughout, and power and data hookups in nearly every study carrel, table, and study room. The collection of 50,000 volumes serves the 400 students, 60 faculty, staff, and their families.

Continue southwest on the sidewalk past the Loomis Observatory and again reach Aurora St. Continue southwest on Aurora St. to N. Main St. and the parking area. ■

26 Hudson Springs Park and Bicentennial Woods Hudson

Easy

Distance: 3 miles

Hiking time: 1½ hours

Description: The 1.8-mile Lake Trail in Hudson Springs Park follows the north shoreline of Hudson Spring Lake and continues through the woods along its southern edge to return to the starting point. The wide path is surfaced with fine gravel, and the terrain is mostly flat or gently rolling.
The 0.5-mile Bicentennial Woods trail is also surfaced and winds up an easy slope to Victoria Pkwy., returning on the same path.

Directions: From I-271 take Exit 21 for I-480; east on I-480 to Exit 37 for SR 91; south on SR 91 for 4 miles to Hudson Village; left (east) on SR 303 just past town green; continue 2 miles; left (north) on Stow Rd. for 1 mile; park entrance on right.

From Akron, take SR 8 north to SR 303; right (east) on SR 303 to Hudson; north on Stow Rd.; park entrance on right.

Parking & restrooms: At the parking area inside the entrance.

Hudson Springs Park lies three miles northeast of Hudson Village adjacent to the Ohio Turnpike. This 260-acre park, owned and operated by Hudson's Park Commission, offers boating and fishing for bass and bluegill in its 50-acre keyhole-shaped lake. Other facilities in the park include picnic tables with grills, two picnic pavilions, a children's playground area, a playfield, and a hiking trail that surrounds the lake. Among the wildlife inhabiting the lake, woods, and fields of Hudson Springs Park are ducks, geese, fox, beaver, muskrat, and deer.

Bicentennial Woods is a small 33-acre parcel of land directly opposite (west of) Hudson Springs Park. It was acquired in 1970 by some of Hudson's citizens and organizations for the enjoyment of all the town's residents. Children from local schools frequently use Bicentennial Woods for nature and environmental studies.

1 At the Lake Trail sign, enter the trail to hike clockwise around the water on a wide gravel walkway that starts toward the east. Pass a playground on the left; views of the lake open ahead on the right. Picnic pavilions and a boat launch area are near the shoreline. Early spring and late fall, when the leaves are down, are fine times to enjoy lake views from here.

Please be aware that the trail is shared with bicyclists.

2 At 0.7 mile pass a bird observation deck on the left. At a trail junc-

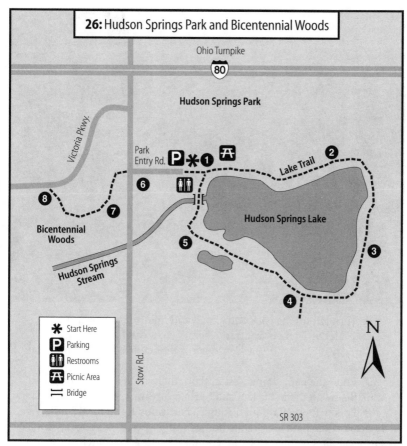

26: Hudson Springs Park and Bicentennial Woods

Ohio Turnpike

80

Hudson Springs Park

Victoria Pkwy.

Park Entry Rd. P ✱ ❶ 🛖   ❷ Lake Trail

❻ 🚻

Hudson Springs Lake

Bicentennial Woods

❽   ❼   ❺   ❸

Hudson Springs Stream

❹

✱ Start Here
P Parking
🚻 Restrooms
🛖 Picnic Area
⊐⊏ Bridge

Stow Rd.

N

SR 303

© Gray & Company, Publishers

tion bear right, paralleling the lake for a very short distance. The path now rises and winds away from the lake at its far east (dammed) end. The trail passes through a young beech/maple forest.

3 A bench on the left at 1 mile invites a restful pause for pleasant enjoyment of the woods. The path now winds south through woods as it veers away from the lake and gently rises uphill.

4 A dirt trail joins from the left (1.2 miles), but continue northwest on the gravel trail. Deer may be spotted in this park in the morning or late afternoon. Here many springs rise and flow down to the lake, giving it and the park their name.

The path now winds west and goes down to lake level.

5 Continue past a small pond on the left (1.7 miles), cross a wooden bridge over Hudson Springs Stream, and follow the gravel path uphill past several more park benches. When you come to a Y in the trail, stay to the right. Continue on the trail past the boat launch and picnic pavilion to return to the parking area.

6 Turn left on the park entry road and follow it to Stow Rd. CAUTION: There is fast traffic here—cross carefully!

Directly opposite the park entrance is the trailhead for Bicentennial Woods.

7 Enter the path, going west initially, then south on the wide gravel trail. Below on the left is Hudson Springs Stream.

8 Follow the trail uphill through a hardwood forest for 0.5 mile. At the end of the path are private homes and property on Victoria Pkwy. On a public green is a plaque commemorating the purchase of the woods in 1970 by Hudson citizens and businesses in time for our nation's bicentennial celebration.

Retrace your steps along the path to return to the parking area in Hudson Springs Park. ■

27 Portage Lakes State Park
Akron

Distance: 3.2 miles
Easy

Hiking time: 2 hours

Description: This easy hike is on a flat trail that skirts the shorelines of Turkey-foot Lake and Latham Bay and crosses several picnic areas. There are many views of the lake from several vantage points along the trail. Since the picnic areas and beach are heavily used in the summer, the park is much quieter in the spring, fall, and winter.

Directions: Take I-77 south to exit 129 for I-277; east on I-277 to Exit 2 for Manchester Rd./Waterloo Rd.; left on Waterloo; right (south) onto Manchester (SR 93) for 4.5 miles; park entrance on the left, just past Vanderhoof Rd.

Parking & restrooms: After entering the park, pass the road to the park office and continue to the first parking lot on the right at the turnoff to Big Oaks Picnic Area. Restrooms are near the parking area.

Portage Lakes State Park, located south of Akron, is on one of the highest points in the state, from which water flows either north to Lake Erie or south to the Ohio River. Boating, swimming, camping, and fishing are the main attractions of this state park, but there are several miles of scenic hiking trails in its developed portion. Because this recreation area contains 2,520 acres of water to 1,000 acres of land, it attracts many kinds of waterfowl, shorebirds, and mammals. At various times you may spot mallards and wood ducks, Canada geese, herons, deer, skunks, raccoons, hawks, owls, and many species of songbirds.

The Portage Lakes are a chain of natural, glacier-formed lakes, of which there are very few in Ohio. Large chunks of ice broke off the glacier, settled into depressions, melted, and formed kettle lakes—the bogs and marshes located here are aged kettle lakes.

Lying on a major watershed divide, the lakes played a key role in the lives of the Indians. From the lakes, which sit near the headwaters of the south-flowing Tuscarawas River, it was only an eight-mile portage to reach the north-flowing Cuyahoga River. This made navigation possible from Lake Erie to the Ohio River with only one relatively short overland portage. Later this area became an important settlers' trading post and was a rendezvous point for troops during the War of 1812. During the canal era, some of the lakes were modified to serve as reservoirs, supplying water to the canals. Since 1949, the Ohio Department of Natural Resources, Division of Parks and Recreation, has managed the Portage Lakes area, including maintenance of the boat channels between the lakes. For more information contact the park office: 330-644-2220.

1 Begin the hike by heading southeast through the parking lot to the sign for the Shoreline Trail. Enter the trail to the left of the restroom building.

2 After 0.2 mile reach another parking lot and turn left (east). Continue through the parking lot to the trail entrance at the signpost with a yellow arrow. The path follows the south border of the park through a band of white pines and past backyards of private homes.

3 Continue eastward and at 0.6 mile cross a gas line right-of-way, then a park service road. Although the trail twists and turns, the pathway is distinct.

4 At 1.3 miles bear right and pass through an opening in a fence, then bear left, following the trail marker. Cross an asphalt drive. It leads to Tudor House (Franklin Park Civic Center), a facility used for business meetings and private parties (330-644-1728).

5 Continue straight on the trail, again posted with a yellow arrow. On the left is a huge parking lot used in the summer for visitors to Turkeyfoot Beach.

6 At a T intersection, with the lake directly ahead, turn left (north). (The trail to the right dead-ends at the lake.) Reach Turkeyfoot Beach. Now the trail follows the edge of Turkeyfoot Lake, parallel to a dirt road on the left, and goes out around a point of land.

7 Reach Mosquito Point, the end of the peninsula (2 miles); in the summer, it's a good place to watch boats on the lake. To the east is Samoa Bay; directly north is a golf course. This peninsula, once an island, was filled in about 40 years ago to provide easy access to the point.

Turn left (west) and follow the opposite side of the peninsula back to the beach.

8 Follow the shoreline to the end of Turkeyfoot Beach and enter the woods at the far northwest end of the beach. Oak trees dominate the woods here and much of the shoreline, points, and knolls around the lakes. Pass a trail on the left that goes to a parking lot; continue straight ahead (north).

As you approach Latham Bay, watch for a sharp left turn where the arrow sign points uphill. (The path ahead goes to the bay and circles uphill.) Turn left at the top of the hill to the parking lot for High Point Picnic Area.

9 Follow the arrow posts to the south end of the parking lot. Continue on the paved road to the trail entrance off the road on the right (2.8 miles). A sign at the trail entrance reads "Emergency and Authorized Vehicles Only."

At the concrete restroom, stay to the left to follow the trail heading

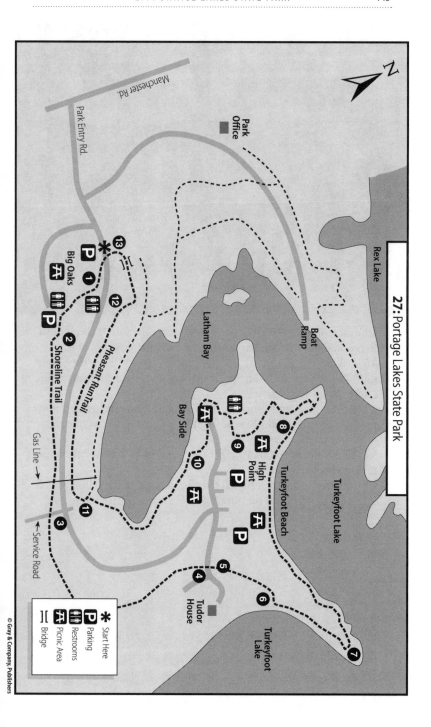

27: Portage Lakes State Park

Manchester Rd.

Park Entry Rd.

Park Office

Rex Lake

Big Oaks

Shoreline Trail

Pheasant Run Trail

Latham Bay

Boat Ramp

Bay Side

Gas Line →

High Point

Turkeyfoot Beach

Turkeyfoot Lake

Service Road →

Tudor House

Turkeyfoot Lake

* Start Here
P Parking
Restrooms
Picnic Area
)(Bridge

© Gray & Company, Publishers

southwest alongside the attractive coves of Latham Bay. At about the 3-mile point, the trail turns left (east) to the road and parking lot.

10 Follow the road past the parking lot on the left. Turn right (south) at the sign for Shoreline Trail. Now the trail is in more open, brushy parts of the shoreline.

11 At the next trail junction the shoreline trail reaches and joins the red-marked Pheasant Run Trail. Turn left, cross the gas line right-of-way, and continue west.

12 The trail takes a sharp right turn, enters a new-growth forest, then crosses a small bridge.

13 At a trail juncture, turn left (south), staying on the yellow Shoreline Trail, which leads to the parking area where the hike began. ■

28 Peninsula
and Deep Lock Quarry Metro Park

Distance: 2.8 miles

Easy

Hiking time: 1½ hours

Description: The Towpath Trail is generally flat and is exceptionally scenic as it follows alongside the Cuyahoga River. Within the Metro Park is a moderately steep hill to climb to see the quarry itself and a steep set of steps to climb down into the quarry for a clearer view.

Directions: From I-271, take Exit 12 for SR 303; east on SR 303 to Peninsula; follow signs to Lock 29 Trailhead; north on Locust St. (at the Peninsula United Methodist Church) for 1 block; continue one block west past Peninsula Depot; cross railroad tracks to enter the Lock 29 Trailhead.

Parking & restrooms: Located at Lock 29 Trailhead.

Peninsula and Deep Lock Quarry Metro Park provide visitors with interesting history pertaining to the Ohio & Erie Canal. Metro Parks, Serving Summit County manages Deep Lock Quarry Metro Park. It is within the boundaries of Cuyahoga Valley National Park (CVNP).

Constructed between 1825 and 1832, the 309-mile Ohio & Erie Canal extended from Cleveland and Lake Erie to Portsmouth and the Ohio River. A disastrous flood in 1913 destroyed much of the canal and hastened the end of a colorful era of transportation. Cascade Valley Metro Park also preserves significant canal history (Ch. 33).

The hike begins in Peninsula, at Lock 29 Trailhead. Here you will find an expansive view of a small waterfall on the Cuyahoga River. This waterfall flows over the remains of a dam that was built to power an 1823 gristmill on the west side of the river near Lock 29. A parking area provides easy access to the lock and the Towpath Trail.

At Lock 29 CVNP has erected an information kiosk, interpretive signs, and a view point from which to study the old lock. It is here that the Ohio & Erie Canal made its crossing on an aqueduct, from the west to the east side of the Cuyahoga River (now replaced by an arched footbridge).

Before starting the walk, you may wish to explore Peninsula and its interesting shops housed in canal-era buildings. The small town of Peninsula was a very busy canal port from the 1820s onward, with hotels, bars, boatyards, mills, stately homes, and a full complement of shops and stores. When the railroad came through this valley in 1880, Peninsula's importance as a canal town quickly diminished. It has long been a mecca for artists, and today is a popular stop for visitors to CVNP.

The interesting Fox House (c.1880), just above the river at 1664 W. Main St. (SR 303), was restored by CVNP in 1985. The house stands at the site of what was one of Peninsula's busiest boatyards. It is easy to imagine what an active canal port this village must have been in its heyday!

The historic district of Peninsula is listed in the National Register of Historic Places. For more information about its history, visit the Peninsula Library and Historical Society at 6105 Riverview Rd., just south of SR 303, and the Cuyahoga Valley Historical Museum, located in the Boston Township Hall at the northeast corner of SR 303 and Riverview Rd.

A seasonal visitor contact station is located near Lock 29 Trailhead, in the railroad depot. The Cuyahoga Valley Scenic Railroad (CVSR) operates many train trips throughout the year through CVNP, from Independence near Cleveland, to Peninsula and Akron (800-468-4070).

Deep Lock Quarry Metro Park is just south of Peninsula on the Towpath Trail and adjacent to both the Cuyahoga River and the CVSR. Both the canal and railroad carried Berea Sandstone excavated from the quarry. Huge blocks of stone were used to make locks and bridges and for other canal construction, as well as for homes and public buildings.

The deepest lock along the entire length of the canal is found within this park. Normally locks were dug to a 10-foot depth, but here Lock 28 reaches 17 feet—it's the "deep lock" for which this park was named. The Towpath Trail follows the original towpath of the Ohio & Erie Canal. This path is also part of the statewide 1,200-mile-long Buckeye Trail.

1 Start the hike at Lock 29 Trailhead. Climb the steps to the top of the lock and turn left (south) to begin the Towpath Trail. An interpretive sign describes the former eastward bend of the Cuyahoga River that once isolated the town on a "peninsula" of land. At a later time the river was dammed and a new channel cut through to give the river its present course, eliminating the peninsula.

The trail crosses under Main St. (SR 303) and continues south along an attractive stretch of the river. Bicyclists also use this trail and may whiz by at great speed. Hikers should stay to the right of the trail.

Here you may see wildlife such as great blue herons, mallards, painted turtles, downy woodpeckers, and other birds. Wildflowers and neotropical warblers are abundant in the spring. There are many specimens of the state tree, the Ohio Buckeye, whose five leaflets differentiate it from the horse chestnut, which have seven leaflets. The Ohio Buckeye has a tall, white, upright cluster of blossoms and a shiny brown seed that resembles a buck's eye.

The canal is to the right (west) of the trail and in some places is overgrown with brush and trees. The towpath—once used by mules

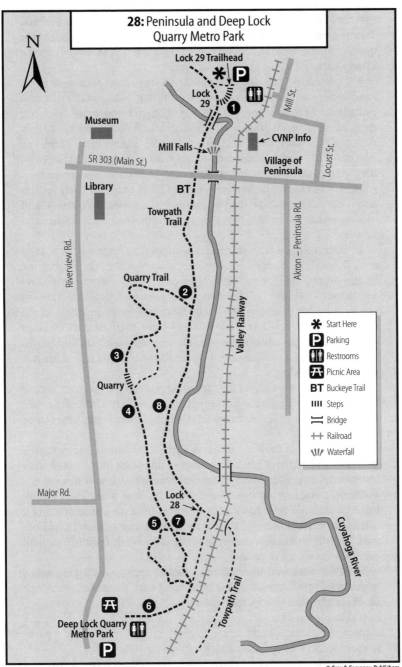

28: Peninsula and Deep Lock Quarry Metro Park

N

Lock 29 Trailhead

* Start Here

Lock 29

Museum

Mill Falls

CVNP Info

SR 303 (Main St.)

Village of Peninsula

Library

BT

Towpath Trail

Quarry Trail

Riverview Rd.

Akron – Peninsula Rd.

Locust St.

Mill St.

Valley Railway

Quarry

Major Rd.

Lock 28

Cuyahoga River

Deep Lock Quarry Metro Park

Towpath Trail

* Start Here
P Parking
Restrooms
Picnic Area
BT Buckeye Trail
IIII Steps
Bridge
++ Railroad
Waterfall

© Gray & Company, Publishers

pulling canal boats—was usually located between the canal and the river so it would act as a barrier, separating the two streams of water.

2 At about 0.5 mile the trail reaches Deep Lock Quarry Metro Park. Take the trail to the right to make a zigzag ascent of a steep hill to the quarry. At the next sign continue straight ahead (westward) to the quarry rim.

3 Opened in 1829, the quarry was an important source of Berea Sandstone, used for many types of construction: canal locks and bridges; home foundations; millstones; railroad bridges and roadbeds; shelters, steps, and bridges in Cleveland and Akron parks; harbor structures in Cleveland; and other uses in many local buildings. Akron's Ferdinand Schumacher, a part owner of the quarry in 1879, used millstones from it for milling oats at his well-known factory, which later became the famous Quaker Oats Company. Early settlers also used this sandstone for fashioning grindstones, pulpstones, and hulling stones to process their crops and to sharpen their scythes and knives.

To extract the slabs, workmen at the quarry cut large blocks of solid rock by drilling, wedging, channeling, and blasting. Looking at the quarry now, more than 125 years later, one can imagine the vast activity that took place here. This dangerous work was slow when blocks were cut by hand, and by the 1880s machines were employed in the quarrying process. Channeling devices were used to cut openings about three inches wide in the solid stone, from which smaller blocks were then wedged or blasted out. Some of the channel marks are still visible in the rocks.

The Quarry Trail follows the top of the pit for a short distance, then leaves the quarry going south down steep, slippery stone steps. Use CAUTION during wet or snowy weather or if fallen leaves cover these steps (1 mile).

4 At the foot of the steps continue to the right (south) following the main trail. The quarry can be explored at this point but is now a shallow swamp. Two plants rarely found in area parks do enjoy this wet environment: the narrow-leaved cattail and the rose pink. The narrow-leaved cattail not only has narrower leaves than the common cattail, but its upper and lower spike parts are separated by a distinct gap. Rose pink or bitterbloom blooms in the summer and early fall and has small pink flowers with five petals.

5 At the next trail intersection, take the spur to the right (west), which goes uphill on a wooded path lined with discarded sandstone blocks left by the quarrying operation.

6 The loop path ends on the main trail. Turn right and head up the slope to the picnic area. Here are restrooms, picnic tables, and a parking lot for Deep Lock Quarry Metro Park (1.5 miles).

7 From the picnic area return on the same Quarry Trail to the second trail intersection. Turn right (east) at this junction going down to-

ward Lock 28. Along the trail are several large millstones abandoned by mill workers; perhaps these were not suitable for grinding because of cracks or other defects. It is thought that the small mounds of earth along the trail may have been left by workmen scraping dirt from underneath stones removed from the quarry. An interpretive sign indicates that some of the large sandstones scattered throughout the woods are not only millstones, but spalls (fragments) and foundations of old buildings. Another sign points out that a railroad once ran along this path carrying flatcars loaded with millstones from the hill above.

Just ahead lies Lock 28 alongside the Towpath Trail. At 17 feet, it is the deepest of the 42 locks built between Cleveland and Akron and is in remarkably good condition after more than 175 years. A bronze historic marker is located on its inner side.

Constructing the canal was painful, backbreaking, and dangerous work. Many men (and boys) of the Western Reserve, augmented by German and Irish immigrants, lost their lives in the process. They died either from the treacherous digging job itself—in all seasons and in all kinds of weather—or from rapidly spreading "canal fever" (malaria). Canal workers suffered the additional hardships of poor working conditions and poor pay.

During the early and mid-19th century, the lock system on the 309-mile-long Ohio & Erie Canal was vitally important to navigation between Lake Erie and the Ohio River, as well as ports in the southern and eastern U. S. Because the high point of land in Akron was 395 feet above that of Lake Erie, 44 locks (later reduced to 42) were necessary to raise and lower boats traveling between these two cities.

Visible on Lock 28 are the remains of some of the iron work used to open and close the gates at each end of the lock. Holes at the tops of the walls held mooring posts to tie up boats as they were being raised or lowered inside the lock. The square openings farther down in the walls were internal culverts used to drain water out of the lock when the gates were closed.

8 Follow the Towpath Trail north along the river to return to Peninsula and Lock 29 where the hike began. ■

To see a world in a grain of sand
And Heaven in a wildflower
To hold infinity in the palm of your hand
And eternity in an hour.

—William Blake

29 Brandywine Gorge and Stanford Trail Boston Heights

Distance: 1.5 miles for Brandywine Gorge; 2 miles to
    Averill Pond (Option 1); 4.5 miles to the Stanford House Hostel (Option 2)

Moderate

Hiking time: 1–3 hours (depending on optional trails)

Description: Two options (see Notes 5 and 6) on this hike offer alternatives for
    extending the walk. After a view of Brandywine Falls, the hike begins on the
    Brandywine Gorge Trail near the Inn at Brandywine Falls. The path goes
    downhill above Brandywine Creek (on the north side of the gorge) to a
    creek crossing on large sandstone blocks. (After a heavy rainfall, the stream
    can become too high to cross on these blocks; when that's the case, there is
    no alternative but to return uphill on the same trail.) The hike continues on
    the south side of Brandywine Gorge with moderately steep up and down
    climbs on the well-marked trail. Option 1 continues south to Averill Pond
    and Option 2 continues even farther south to the 30-bed Stanford House
    Hostel. There are several moderately sized hills to climb on all three hikes.

Directions: From Cleveland take I-77 south to Exit 149 for SR 82; east on SR 82;
    south on Riverview Rd. to Jaite (CVNP Headquarters); left (east) on
    Vaughn/Highland Rd. to blinking light; right (south) on Brandywine Rd.;
    pass Inn at Brandywine Falls (on right); cross bridge; right on Stanford Rd.;
    entrance to Brandywine Falls parking area just past exit road, on left.

From Akron take I-77 north to exit for SR 21; north on SR 21; cross over Ohio
    Turnpike (I-80); right (east) on Snowville Rd.; left (north) on Riverview Rd.
    for one block to Jaite; right (east) on Vaughn/Highland Rd. to blinking light;
    right (south) on Brandywine Rd.; pass Inn at Brandywine Falls (on the right);
    cross bridge; right on Stanford Rd.; entrance to Brandywine Falls parking
    area just past the exit road, on the left.

NOTE: Stanford Rd. is permanently closed to vehicles between the Brandywine
    Falls parking area and Stanford House Hostel.

Parking & restrooms: At the Brandywine Falls parking area.

Brandywine Falls is one of the most popular spots in Cuyahoga Valley National Park (CVNP). A series of wooden walkways, stairs, and two viewing platforms enable visitors to enjoy the scenery of the beautiful 65-foot-high waterfall of Brandywine Creek. The foundation of an old gristmill is at the east end of the walkway. Brandywine was once a town of a dozen households, with the mill employing 20 workers. Today very little remains of the old village, which reached its zenith in 1852.

History records that George Wallace, a New England entrepreneur, saw the potential for creating an industrial village at this spot by harnessing the water power of the falls. He first built a sawmill on the north side of the creek in 1814, followed a year later by a gristmill on the south side that produced flour and cornmeal. A profitable whiskey distillery was built a half-mile north of the sawmill, and a few years later Wallace opened a woolen mill, school, post office, and village store. The construction of the Ohio & Erie Canal, and the subsequent growth of railroads, contributed to the demise of this once-thriving village. Business went to larger commercial centers with better transportation.

In 1848 George's son, James Wallace, built a farmhouse on the north side of the falls, now restored as the Inn at Brandywine Falls. Open year round, it is operated by Mr. and Mrs. George Hoy as a bed and breakfast. The six-bedroom main building and barn are listed in the National Register of Historic Places. For more information call 330-650-4965.

1 Begin the walk by crossing Stanford Rd. from the Brandywine Falls parking area to the walkway entrance. Walk down the steps to the lower viewing area, enjoying vistas of the hemlock-lined gorge and creek along the way. The platform at the foot of the stairway is a popular place for wedding ceremonies and is closed to the public when services are being held here.

NOTE: The stairs to the waterfall are closed when there are icy conditions.

The waterfall cascades over eroded shale of varying degrees of hardness. The shale is composed of mud and silt laid down in successive layers by an ancient sea that once covered what is now Ohio. At the top of the falls is 360-million-year-old, erosion-resistant Berea Sandstone capping the older gray Bedford Formation (shale) beneath it. Farther downstream are large blocks of Berea Sandstone that have fallen from above, having broken off at fracture lines.

Walk back up the steps, turning left at the top to follow the walkway to its far eastern end. Signs along the way point out interesting historical features. At the ruins of the gristmill you reach the lip of the waterfall.

Here in the creekbed you can see potholes in the sandstone caused by swirling sand and water, and grooves worn in the rock from the water's swift flow. The groove that extends all the way across the top once diverted water to the gristmill and its water wheel.

2 Walk eastward up the steps to another, smaller parking area and cross the bridge over Brandywine Creek to its north side where picnic tables and park benches invite a pause to admire the picturesque scene.

Follow the path along the fence to the trail entrance marked with a sign at the far west end of the lawn. The Brandywine Gorge Trail descends 0.75 mile to the creek crossing below. This trail was built mainly by volunteers from the Cuyahoga Valley Trails Council with support from CVNP. The path follows an old road that originally went down to the Cuyahoga River from Brandywine Rd.

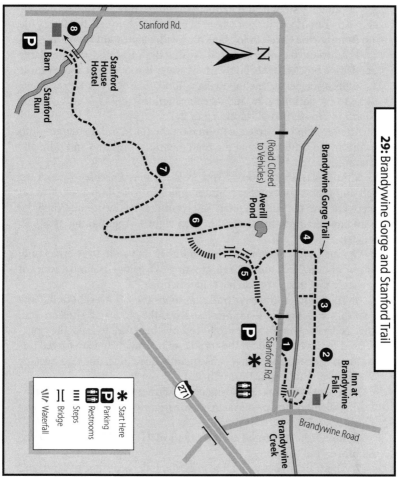

© Gray & Company, Publishers

Brandywine Creek is visible below on the left. In the spring and summer a variety of wildflowers thrive in this cool, moist gorge.

CAUTION: Stay back from the cliff, because constant erosion loosens soil along the edge.

3 As you continue down, note the ancient sedimentary rock layers on the boulders along the north side of the trail. Water ripple marks, alternating ridges and troughs, are prominent in the Berea Sandstone evident on some of the rocks that have slumped from above. Some of the sandstone blocks also reveal cross-bedding, characterized by sedimentary layers that run at an angle to normal horizontal bedding. They indicate the direction of water currents at the time the sandy layers were deposited.

Mature maple, oak, beech, and hemlock trees are dominant in the woods along the trail.

Just after log steps near the foot of the gorge, turn left on a short spur to reach a photogenic spot where hemlocks arch over a small cascade on Brandywine Creek. A log bench provides a pleasant rest stop.

4 At about 0.6 mile the trail crosses Brandywine Creek on large sandstone blocks. (CAUTION: If the water is too high or if the blocks have been washed askew following a flood, do not cross. Retrace your steps to the parking area, and take the Stanford Trail to Averill Pond or Stanford House Hostel [Option 1 or 2]).

After crossing the creek, continue on the trail until it emerges onto Stanford Rd. After crossing the road, the trail continues and joins the Stanford Trail.

5 At this trail junction (if you are not taking Option 1 or 2), turn left and follow the Stanford Trail uphill. You will climb a set of wood steps cut into the embankment and continue steeply uphill. When the trail emerges onto Stanford Rd., turn right to the parking area (1.5 miles).

Option 1: To continue the hike another half-mile to Averill Pond, turn right on the Stanford Trail, crossing two bridges. Climb a series of steps up the hillside to reach a trail junction.

6 Turn right at the next trail sign to visit small Averill Pond. Note that this trail is wider than the others. It is the old David Hudson Trail that New England pioneers followed on their way to land they purchased in the Connecticut Western Reserve. David Hudson forged this route to the settlement that subsequently bore his name and became the town of Hudson in 1802 (Ch. 25).

To return to the hike's starting point, retrace your steps on the Stanford Trail, following posted signs to the Brandywine Falls parking area (2 miles).

Option 2: To continue to the Stanford House Hostel, follow the Stanford Trail south.

7 The trail crosses a small boardwalk, follows a ridge of land, and descends to Stanford Run.

After crossing the bridge, turn right on an open grassy trail. A large barn on the Stanford property appears ahead. Take the path toward the barn (southeast).

8 The historic Stanford House (1843) was restored and opened in 1986 by the National Park Service and the Northeast Ohio Council of Hosteling International. This 30-bed hostel is closed during the day but open 7–9 A.M. and 5–10 P.M. to accommodate hikers, bicyclists, skiers, and the general public. There is a kitchen to allow guests to prepare their own meals. There is a small parking lot at the hostel. For information call 330-467-8711.

To return to the car, retrace your steps along the well-marked Stanford Trail and follow signs to the Brandywine Falls parking area. ■

30 Kendall Lake and Cross Country Trail Boston Heights

Distance: 3.5 miles

Hiking time: 2 hours

Description: This hike begins at the Kendall Lake Shelter, where there are picnic facilities and a fishing dock. The hike starts by encircling the lake on the
1-mile Lake Trail, then loops southeast and northwest on the 2.5-mile Cross
Country Trail. The latter trail is a front-country hiking/skiing trail through
woods of tall pines, oaks, and hemlocks. It traverses a broad meadow,
crosses Salt Run, and, at the end, descends a long, open hill—all of which
provide hikers with a great variety of habitats. You might catch a glimpse of
wild turkey, deer, or coyote roaming through the upland forest.

Directions: From Cleveland, take I-271 to Exit 12 for SR 303; east on SR 303 to
Peninsula; cross Cuyahoga River bridge; right (south) on Akron-Peninsula
Rd. for about 1 mile; left (east) on Truxell Rd./Kendall Park Rd. for about 1
mile to Kendall Lake parking area on right.

From Akron take Akron-Peninsula Rd. north; right on Truxell Rd. to Kendall Lake.
(Or follow directions from I-271 above.)

Parking & restrooms: At Kendall Lake parking area and on Quick Rd.

The Virginia Kendall area is noted for its spectacular Ritchie
Ledges—composed of Sharon Conglomerate sandstone—and its
beautiful hardwood forest with abundant wildlife. This park was established with 420 acres of farm and forest land that had served as a
country retreat for Clevelander Hayward Kendall. He willed this magnificent spot to the state of Ohio in 1929 in memory of his mother, Virginia Kendall. Originally administered by the Akron Metropolitan
Park District, it is now part of Cuyahoga Valley National Park (CVNP).
It was the first area incorporated into CVNP after its creation in 1974.
Several of its shelters and other buildings were constructed in the
1930s by the Civilian Conservation Corps.

Salt Run and its several tributaries course through the area of this
hike. The Cross Country Trail is not only a pleasant hiking trail but
also a popular ski trail. Kendall Lake Winter Sports Center is open
weekends in January and February with information available about
skiing, snowshoeing, sledding, and tubing (800-445-9667).

NOTE: A 4-mile hike to Ritchie Ledges is described in *Cleveland On
Foot, 3rd Edition* (1992–2001), Ch. 43 (see Bibliography).

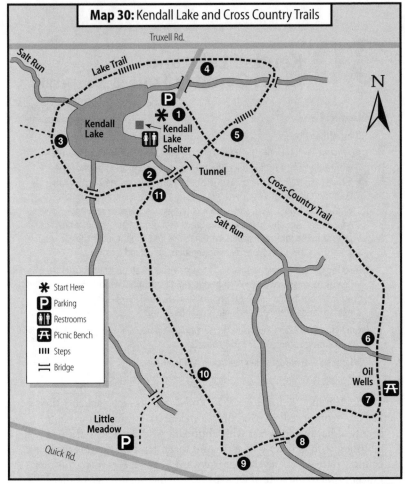

Map 30: Kendall Lake and Cross Country Trails

Truxell Rd.

Salt Run

Lake Trail

Kendall Lake

Kendall Lake Shelter

Tunnel

Cross-Country Trail

Salt Run

N

Start Here
Parking
Restrooms
Picnic Bench
Steps
Bridge

Oil Wells

Little Meadow

Quick Rd.

© Gray & Company, Publishers

1 Enter the trail from the parking lot at the southeast corner near the trailhead kiosk. Follow the Lake and Cross Country trails partway uphill. Turn right on this open slope (about midway uphill) to pass through the tunnel (on the right), following Lake Trail signs.

2 Cross Salt Run on a bridge and continue straight ahead. At the next intersection, where the Cross Country Trail goes to the south (left), continue ahead on the Lake Trail at the edge of Kendall Lake, where you might see ducks, Canada geese, or herons. The trail soon reaches the earthen dam built in 1937 by the CCC to create Kendall Lake.

3 As you approach the dam, you will see on the left the intersection for Salt Run Trail. Continue on the Lake Trail encircling the lake.

4 Cross the park entrance road and continue eastward along a crushed-stone path. Cross a tributary of Salt Run on a bridge, then climb some steps up to a red pine forest. Soon you will reach the same open slope near where the hike started (Note #1).

5 Turn left (east) to enter the wide Cross Country Trail. A little farther along note the many sweetgum and tulip trees and huge old white oaks. You might also see some of the foundations of farm buildings, a reminder of the area's agricultural history.

6 The gently rolling trail eventually reaches a large field. A single picnic table is on the left.

7 At a trail intersection, stay to the right (west). (The path straight ahead leads out to Akron Cleveland Rd). Two oil well pumps are in the field.

8 Continue westward now on the path cut through the field of goldenrod. At the far end of the field, reenter the woods, following the wire fence on the left, and descend steeply to a bridge over Salt Run.

9 Ascend a hill and follow the trail as it bends sharply right (north). Avoid taking the service road that goes out to Quick Rd.

10 At the next trail intersection, go straight to stay on the Cross Country Trail. The trail to the left goes to the Little Meadow parking area on Quick Rd. Continue down an open meadow of the Kendall Hills until this trail reaches the Lake Trail again.

11 Turn right onto the Lake Trail and follow it back to Kendall Lake Shelter by going through the tunnel and turning left down the slope to the parking lot (3.5 miles). ■

31 Buckeye Trail from Boston Mills to Peninsula

Distance: 7.5 miles

Strenuous

Walking time: 3$\frac{1}{2}$ hours

Description: Although noisy at the beginning and end from nearby interstate traffic, this long walk is well worth the effort. You will climb up and down hills, hike through a cool pine forest, and cross the valley of Boston Run on the first part of the hike. At midpoint you will have an opportunity to visit the historic town of Peninsula and the Lock 29 Trailhead (Ch. 28). The return section of the hike goes along the flat canal Towpath Trail with views of the Cuyahoga River and wildlife along the way.

Directions: From Cleveland take I-77 south to exit for Miller Rd.; east on Miller; south on SR 21; east on Snowville Rd.; south on Riverview Rd. to Boston Mills Ski Resort; east on Boston Mills Rd.; cross Cuyahoga Valley Scenic Railroad tracks and Cuyahoga River bridge; Boston Store Trailhead parking area on right immediately past the bridge.

From Akron take I-77 north to I-271; north on I-271 to exit for SR 303; east on SR 303; north on Riverview Rd. in Peninsula; east on Boston Mills Rd.; cross Cuyahoga Valley Scenic Railroad tracks and Cuyahoga River bridge; Boston Store Trailhead parking area on right immediately past the bridge.

Parking & restrooms: At Boston Store Trailhead and Lock 29 Trailhead.

Cuyahoga Valley National Park (CVNP) preserves a 33,000-acre green space between Cleveland and Akron, and its visitor centers contain a repository of the early history of the Western Reserve of Connecticut. The village of Boston Mills was once a thriving community of boatyards, shops, a tavern, and a hotel that almost disappeared in a great flood in 1913.

The 1836 Boston Store alongside the canal on Boston Mills Rd., just east of the Boston Store Trailhead, functioned as a general store throughout most of the 19th century. Artifacts have been recovered from this site that served canal boats plying the Ohio & Erie Canal. A museum depicting 19th-century canal life and boat building is housed in the Boston Store.

On this hike you will visit the villages of Boston Mills and Peninsula, enjoy walking in deep woods on the Buckeye Trail, see remnants of canal locks, and hike along the scenic Cuyahoga River on the Towpath Trail.

1 Begin on the blue-blazed Buckeye Trail (BT) at the Boston Store Trailhead going south. (Use CAUTION on this wide paved path; it is

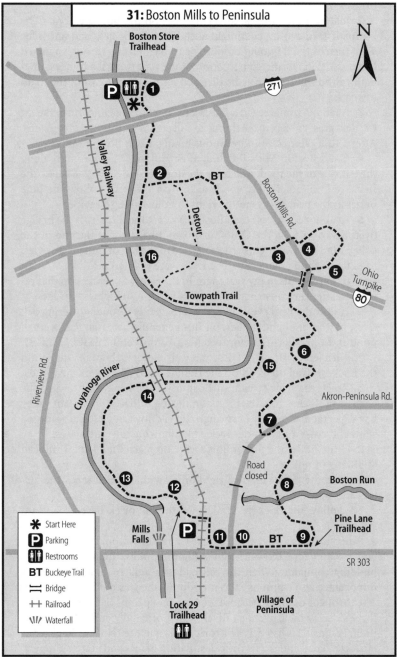

31: Boston Mills to Peninsula

N

Boston Store
Trailhead

P 👫 ✱ ❶

271

Valley Railway

❷

BT

Detour

Boston Mills Rd.

❸   ❹

❺

Ohio
Turnpike

80

❶❻

Towpath Trail

❻

Riverview Rd.

Cuyahoga River

❶❺

❶❹

Akron-Peninsula Rd.

❼

Road
closed

❽   Boston Run

❶❸   ❶❷

Mills
Falls 〰

P

❶❶ ❶❶⓿ BT   ❾

Pine Lane
Trailhead

SR 303

Legend:

✱ Start Here
P Parking
👫 Restrooms
BT Buckeye Trail
⊐⊏ Bridge
+⊢ Railroad
〰 Waterfall

Lock 29
Trailhead
👫

Village of
Peninsula

© Gray & Company, Publishers

also used by fast-traveling bicyclists.) Pass under the twin highway bridges of I-271.

2 Just past the bridges, turn left (east) on the Buckeye Trail. (The Towpath Trail continues straight ahead.) Cross the field and watch for a left turn of the BT going uphill. The trail climbs up through a mixed forest. NOTE: During construction of the new turnpike bridges, towpath traffic will frequently be diverted onto a detour east of the main towpath.

3 At about 1 mile reach a grassy area next to the Ohio Turnpike. At the next grassy area, cross a drainage culvert and climb a set of log steps. After a short stretch of more woods hiking, reach Boston Mills Rd.

4 Cross Boston Mills Rd. and, after walking 0.1 mile south along the left side of the road, watch for the double blue tree blaze where the Buckeye Trail enters the woods again (on the left). Follow the blue blazes as the trail swings to the right to follow along a ravine.

5 At about 1.5 miles reach Boston Mills Rd. again. Cross the bridge overpass (over I-80, the Ohio Turnpike), turn right at the end of the bridge, and follow the construction road to the top of the rise. Turn left to enter a white pine forest. The trees were planted neatly in straight rows by Girl Scouts many years ago. To the right is a depression that remained after the construction of the original I-80 highway bridges.

6 Follow the Buckeye Trail as it curves gently through towering oak trees, past ravines and gullies, on this generally flat trail. Pass a small pond and a clearing just before reaching Akron-Peninsula Rd. (3 miles).

7 Turn left (east) on A-P Rd. and walk along it about 0.3 mile until the Buckeye Trail turns off on the right (south) and enters the woods.

8 Reach the wide stream of Boston Run flowing west toward the Cuyahoga River. Cross the brook on the log bridge. This stream valley has a spectacular display of springtime wildflowers. Descend some log steps and cross a small side creek, still following the blue blazes.

9 Cross under the power line, and soon reach Pine Lane Trailhead at SR 303 (4 miles).

Leaving the trailhead, turn right onto an abandoned road (the former Rte. 303).

10 Follow the Buckeye Trail down the old brick-paved road into Peninsula.

Peninsula was a busy Ohio & Erie Canal town from the 1820s on—larger than Cleveland—with many homes, mills, hotels, and a boat-building company. When the railroad was built in 1880, Peninsula's importance as a commercial center diminished, as did its population. The town got its name because it once was a peninsula surrounded on three sides by the Cuyahoga River, which originally curled back upon itself. Peninsula is listed as a historic district in the National Register of Historic Places and is a favorite destination of arts and crafts shoppers.

11 No longer following the Buckeye Trail, turn right (north) just past the railroad tracks, following the signs to the Towpath Trail. A

CVNP Visitor Center is located in the depot alongside the tracks. (The Cuyahoga Valley Scenic Railroad offers excursion rides through Cuyahoga Valley National Park. For ticket information and schedules call 800-468-4070.)

Turn left into Lock 29 Trailhead. The Towpath Trail leaves the trailhead from the west end of the parking area. Here the Ohio & Erie Canal crossed the river via an aqueduct. Exhibits describe the aqueduct, the lock, and a mill. Lock 29 can be viewed both from above and from inside the lock itself.

12 Take the paved Towpath Trail to the right (north). There are bicyclists on this multi-use trail most of the time; hikers should keep to the right.

13 Pass another lock on the right (Lock 30).

14 Continue through a tunnel under the Valley Railway (6.3 miles).

15 Pass another lock and reach a long boardwalk that passes through swamp and marshland alongside the Cuyahoga River. This wide area, known as Stumpy Basin, allowed enough space for canal boats to pass each other and turn around. I-80 is to the right (northeast). NOTE: During construction of new turnpike bridges, Towpath Trail traffic will frequently be diverted onto a detour trail east of the main towpath.

16 Pass under the I-80 bridges and rejoin the Buckeye Trail. Continue under the twin bridges of I-271 and return to the Boston Store Trailhead and parking area. ■

32 Cascade Valley Metro Park
Oxbow and Chuckery areas / Akron

Directions: From Cleveland take I-271 to Exit 12 (SR 303); east on SR 303; pass Cuyahoga River bridge in Peninsula; right (south) on Akron-Peninsula Rd. through Cuyahoga Valley National Park; left (east) on Portage Trail Ext. W; right (south) on Northampton Rd. (changes to Cuyahoga St.); entrance to Cascade Valley Metro Park's Oxbow Area (Hike A) is off Cuyahoga St. on the left, opposite Valley View Golf Course. (For Hike B, continue south on Cuyahoga St. another 0.75 mile to the park entrance on left marked for Chuckery Area).

From the I-77/76 merge in Akron, take SR 59 (Innerbelt); north on N. Howard St.; north on Cuyahoga St.; park entrances for Chuckery Area and Oxbow Area on right.

In the 1970s local citizens and planners from the city of Akron and Metro Parks, Serving Summit County, conceived the idea of an urban park extending from downtown Akron north along the Cuyahoga and Little Cuyahoga rivers, toward Cuyahoga Valley National Park. The park plan calls for developing a number of park units, totaling 1,500 acres. To date, four units have been completed, two of which are explored in this chapter. Additional units will be completed as funds become available.

The name Cascade Valley historically referred to the valley of the Little Cuyahoga River, which joins the main Cuyahoga just west of the area covered in this chapter. In the 1800s the Cascade Race, running parallel to the Little Cuyahoga River, powered numerous mills, contributing to the growth of the young town of Akron.

In 1982 the 89-acre Oxbow Area to the west of the river was opened, and in 1986 the 310-acre Chuckery Area opened, featuring remains of a manmade water channel called Chuckery Race, now listed in the National Register of Historic Places. In 1844, Dr. Eliakim Crosby devised an ambitious plan to divert the Cuyahoga River through a small channel, or race, to provide power for a planned industrial town to be called Summit City. Economics forced him to abandon this project before it could be completed. Although it is now filled in, remnants of the old race can be seen on the Chuckery Trail.

At Gorge Metro Park east of here, the Cuyahoga River makes a sharp turn westward from its long southerly course through Geauga and Portage counties as it encounters the higher land of Summit County. Here in Cascade Valley Metro Park, the river flows south again, briefly, before turning north to flow through Sand Run Metro Park, Cuyahoga Valley National Park, and on to Lake Erie.

The Indian Signal Tree, a feature of Cascade Valley Metro Park, is an unusually shaped Bur Oak tree with horizontal limbs on either side of a massive trunk. Legend says that Indians dwelling here may have shaped the tree as a directional signal or perhaps used it for ceremonial purposes. Common belief is that the tree was a marker for the beginning of a canoe portage overland from the Cuyahoga River to the Tuscarawas River; others dispute this. It is, nonetheless, a magnificent tree.

The floodplain of the Cuyahoga River valley supports numerous wildflowers in this park, especially the white trillium. Excellent views of this river, with its cascades and rapids, are available from several vantage points in both the Oxbow and Chuckery Areas. The park offers baseball, softball, soccer, tobogganing, and sledding.

The trailheads for the two marked trails—the 1.2-mile Oxbow Trail (Hike A) and the 2.4-mile Chuckery Trail (Hike B)—are separated by the Cuyahoga River and require a short car trip if you wish to hike both loops.

Hike A: Oxbow Area

Distance: 1.2 miles

Easy

Hiking time: Less than 1 hour

Description: The first half-mile of the Hike A loop is on a flat path through a beautiful stretch of floodplain alongside the Cuyahoga River. If the river water is high, alternate paths are available. There are views of the small cascades that give the park its name. The second half-mile ascends a steep hill for a long view of the valley before descending to the parking area.

Parking & restrooms: After entering the park, drive past the first parking area on the left (sledding hill) and past the next one (ball fields), to the parking area at the end of the road. Restrooms are at the sledding hill and the ball fields.

1 Enter the Oxbow Trail, marked by a sign with a pair of parallel ripple marks, at the northeast end of the parking area. Immediately turn right (south). The path leads across the flat floodplain of the Cuyahoga River, rich with small vernal wetlands and wildflowers. Many oaks, maples, and cottonwoods flourish in this environment. Because the plain is frequently flooded, the soil is thick, moist, and silty. Sycamore, silver maple, and, especially, cottonwood trees are the dominant species here, because they are shallow-rooted and fast-growing.

2 At 0.25 mile reach the south-flowing Cuyahoga River. A short side trail leads to the river for a nice view up and downstream.

The path now goes north and reaches a trail junction. If the high-water bypass is needed, turn left. Otherwise, go right for the riverside path. The bypass trail will join the main trail along this very pleasant river walk.

3 After another high-water bypass, continue north past a picnic area. The trail bends west, crosses a small footbridge, and ascends a steep hill on 104 timber steps.

4 At the top, the path bends west to a bench from which you can enjoy a long view of the Cuyahoga River Valley below. Continue through a forest of trees that thrive in high, well-drained soils: oaks, maples, and white pines.

5 At 0.7 mile begin to descend to the valley on 47 timber steps, then 19 more, and yet another 20 steps before reaching an open field and the sledding hill on the right. Cross the field to the parking area.

Hike B: Chuckery Area

Distance: 2.4 miles

Easy

Hiking time: 1½ hours

Description: The Chuckery Trail is well marked and wide in most places, and follows a short section of the Cuyahoga River. The first part of the hike is on a flat pathway. Then it ascends a steep hill on the former Chuckery Race and finally descends to the river level on sets of stairs.

Parking & restrooms: From Oxbow Area, drive south on Cuyahoga St. to the Chuckery Area entrance on the left. Follow the park road to the first parking area on the left. Restrooms are located here.

6 Enter the path to the left of the restroom building. It leads to the impressive Indian Signal Tree. A plaque describes the tree's history.

7 Go west across the field to the Chuckery Trail entrance, marked with an arrowhead symbol on the left. The swift Cuyahoga River soon appears on the right. Note the many large eastern cottonwood trees, which are often found beside streams. Their leaves are roughly triangular with toothed margins. American sycamore trees also grow along these streams and are characterized by peeling bark that leaves irregular patches of whitish-brown color on their trunks. Their leaf resembles a very large maple leaf.

On the opposite side of the river a stone retaining wall has been built at a strategic spot to retard erosion where the river makes a sharp oxbow turn.

8 The trail bends south away from the river and passes through an open meadow, a reclaimed landfill from the 1950s and 1960s.

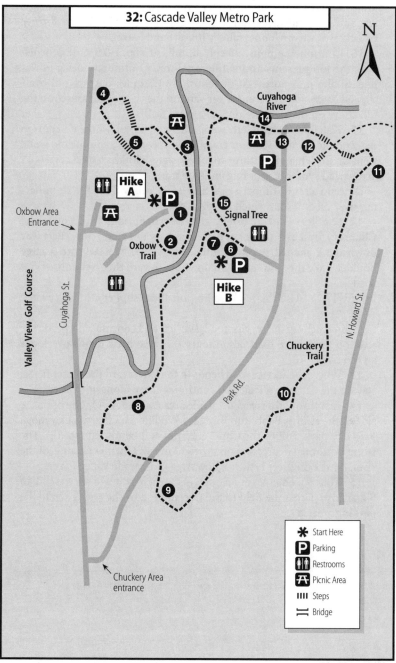

32: Cascade Valley Metro Park

N

Cuyahoga River

Oxbow Area Entrance

Hike A

Oxbow Trail

Signal Tree

Hike B

Valley View Golf Course

Cuyahoga St.

N. Howard St.

Chuckery Trail

Park Rd.

Chuckery Area entrance

✳ Start Here
🅿 Parking
🚻 Restrooms
🛖 Picnic Area
IIII Steps
⚌ Bridge

© Gray & Company, Publishers

9 At 0.7 mile cross the park road and continue on the Chuckery Trail. Ascend a steep hill through an oak/maple forest. The trail bends left and goes northeast on a wide gravel trail. This is the former Chuckery Race ditch now filled with dirt and gravel.

10 Continue climbing steeply uphill. At about 0.9 mile a bench near the top presents an inviting rest stop. Continue under a power line, hiking in a northeast direction. At 1.2 miles pass an old oval-shaped brick-and-concrete sewer vent on the right. The houses on the hill above on the right are on N. Howard St.

11 Watch for a sharp left (west) turn in the trail, where it begins to descend the hill and winds through lovely woods. Pass some old stone steps on the left and continue to follow signs with the Chuckery Trail's arrowhead symbols, avoiding any side trails.

Descend a set of timber steps, and again you will see the shimmering river cascades for which the park has been named.

12 (2 miles) The trail briefly joins the Highbridge Trail. Follow the Chuckery Trail as it turns left to descend a set of stone steps. Part way down the Y-shaped steps, note the "WPA-1937" carved into a large boulder. Take the stone steps on downhill toward the river and service road.

CAUTION: Use the hand railing on these slippery, moss-covered steps.

Upon reaching the service road, stay left and continue alongside the river on the service road (also the trail). A riverbank bench overlooks an old river ford.

13 Where the service road bends to the left toward the soccer fields, stay on the Chuckery Trail as it continues ahead alongside the river.

14 Pass through a riverside picnic area (2.1 miles). On the opposite side of the river is Babb Run Bird and Wildlife Sanctuary, a Cuyahoga Falls city park. Follow the Chuckery Trail as it bends left (south). The stone-bottomed depression on the right marks a former channel of the river. Across the river is the Oxbow Area of Cascade Valley Park.

15 The trail emerges at an open field where you will see the Indian Signal Tree. Cross the field to the tree and follow the path back to the parking area. ■

33 Cascade Valley Metro Park
Cascade Locks/Mustill Store Area / Akron

Directions: From I-77 take Exit 21C for SR 59 (Innerbelt); east on SR 59; left (north) on N. Howard St.; left (west) on North St. at first traffic light; cross bridge over canal; Mustill Store trailhead on right.

From Akron take N. Howard St. north; left (west) on W. North St.; cross bridge over canal; right into the Mustill Store trailhead.

Parking & restrooms: At the Mustill Store trailhead.

Cascade Valley Metro Park is composed of four units: the Schumacher Valley Area, the Chuckery and Oxbow Areas (Ch. 32), and the Cascade Locks Area, which includes the historic Mustill Store. Cascade Valley Metro Park, a joint project of the city of Akron and Metro Parks, Serving Summit County, will eventually consist of eight units totaling 1,500 acres, all connected by the Ohio & Erie Canal Towpath Trail.

The 309-mile Ohio & Erie Canal once extended from Lake Erie at Cleveland to Portsmouth on the Ohio River and for 80 years was the most important means of transportation in this part of the state; the height of activity was 1827–1850. The entire length of the canal from Cleveland to Portsmouth was opened in 1832 with great fanfare because it transformed this part of Ohio from a rather primitive wilderness into one of the nation's most prosperous areas. Products from this region could now be shipped north to Cleveland and from there to E. Coast markets by way of Lake Erie, or south to the Ohio River and then as far south as New Orleans.

The 38-mile Akron-to-Cleveland section of the canal was built in record time between 1825 and 1827. It required 44 locks (later reduced to 42) to lift or lower canal boats over the 395-foot difference in elevation between the two cities. Because Akron's Locks 1 through 21 were close together (within a two-mile span) and were the steepest on the canal, they have been called the "giant staircase." Cascade Locks includes Locks 10 through 16 of this historic waterway. Canal water (and excess storm-sewer water) cascades over the sills of Locks 10 through 15, where it is diverted into the Little Cuyahoga River near Mustill Store.

Many of the Ohio & Erie Canal locks were severely damaged in the great flood of 1913. They were subsequently abandoned and some became filled with debris and trash. The canal's demise had already been sealed when railroads became the dominant mode of transportation for both goods and people soon after the Civil War.

In order to preserve an important part of Ohio's history and create new opportunities for recreation, a short segment of the lock staircase was opened to the public in 1994 by the city of Akron. Cascade Locks Park Association (CLPA) spearheaded this effort, and the park is now under the management of Metro Parks, Serving Summit County.

Hike A extends from Mustill Store south to Akron's Innerbelt. Hike B, along the restored Towpath Trail, starts at the Mustill Store and runs north to the confluence of the Little and main Cuyahoga rivers. Both hikes return on the same trail to the parking lot.

For more information about Cascade Locks Park Association call 330-374-5625. To reach Metro Parks, Serving Summit County, call 330-867-5511 or visit their website at www.summitmetroparks.org.

Hike A: **Cascade Locks**

Distance: 1 mile

Easy

Hiking time: 1 hour

Description: This walk is mostly on a marked mulched trail and entails climbing up and down several sets of stairs from which to view the canal and each of the locks. It begins at North St. and climbs 0.4 mile from there to Lock 10 and back.

1 Follow the Ohio & Erie Canal Towpath Trail north 150 feet to the Mustill Store and, east of the store, Lock 15. With 10 feet of lift, Lock 15 is the northernmost watered lock of the Cascade. The Mustill Store and house have been restored to their canal-era appearance through a unique cooperative effort among the city of Akron, Cascade Locks Park Association, Metro Parks, Serving Summit County, and the National Park Service. The Mustill Store houses one of the visitor centers along the Ohio & Erie Canal National Heritage Corridor (see Hike B).

The locks here were built of locally quarried sandstone. The 90-foot-long lock chambers were 15 feet wide to accommodate the 70-to-80-foot-long, 14-foot-wide canal boats. Boats traveled only four miles per hour and, even riding low in the water with 50–80 tons of cargo, drew only three feet of the water.

The locks were closed at either end with oak gates that formed a V pointing upstream to resist the pressure of water.

Lock hydraulics worked by gravity. A "wicket" operated by means of an iron crank handle at the top of the gate permitted water to flow into or out of the lock. As the water entered or left the lock, the boat was then carried either up or down to the next water level.

There were several kinds of canal boats: freight boats (the most valuable), passenger packets, and state boats for the maintenance of the canal.

The boat was pulled by mules on the towpath. In this area the towpath switched from one side to the other. Here at Lock 15 the towpath is on the west, the same side as the store. South, at Lock 11, the towpath crossed to the east side of the canal.

2 Turn south on the Towpath Trail and cross North St. and the bridge over the canal, to the trailhead for the south section. Enter the trail at the kiosk sign for Cascade Locks Park. The sandstone wasteway near the bridge was used for runoff of excess water that flowed around Lock 14.

In 1907, the original sandstone-block walls inside Lock 14 were chiseled and faced with concrete to waterproof them yet still maintain the 15-foot width. Near the bottom of the lock the original 1827 stone blocks (not faced with concrete) are still exposed.

Lock 14 is located in what was once a very busy valley. East of the trail is an open field, a former water basin. A mill race separate from the canal powered mills here and at other sites near the canal. Cascade Mills was owned and operated by Ferdinand Schumacher, the innovator and industrialist who ultimately became president of Quaker Oats Co. Schumacher's 1876 mill was powered by an immense, 37-ton, iron overshot wheel with a 10-foot face. It was 36 feet in diameter, with 96 steel buckets receiving canal water through an underground pipe system called Cascade Race. The ruins of the race may be seen near Lock 12. Wastewater and water discharged from the wheel flowed out through underground conduits to the Little Cuyahoga River. This huge wheel powered purifiers, iron rolls, cockle machines, ending stones, brush machines, and other appliances used in the manufacture of flour. The mill retained the large water wheel and also added tall chimneys for coal-burning steam engines when steam power eventually replaced water power.

Local historians have uncovered the interesting history of the 37-ton water wheel. Apparently the wheel was turned on its side and buried in the basin in the 1920s when it was no longer useful. In the 1950s, when Ohio Edison constructed a steel transmission tower on the site, it was lifted by crane to a location a short distance east of the pit. In all likelihood it lies buried there still.

3 The concrete conduit near the path carries voltage lines for First Energy.

The railroad trestle farther ahead supports the historic Valley Railway. The Cuyahoga Valley Scenic Railroad operates an excursion service to carry visitors from Independence to Akron, going through the heart of Cuyahoga Valley National Park. (For train information, call 800-468-4070.)

The three stone arches on the east once supported a wooden bridge over Lock 13, originally constructed by the Valley Railway in 1879–80.

When the Valley Railway went bankrupt in 1895, it was reorganized as Cleveland Terminal & Valley Co. In 1909 the railroad was taken over by Baltimore & Ohio, which, in a 1910–1916 capital improvement program, replaced the original wooden trestle with a steel railroad trestle to carry freight. In 1963, B&O merged with Chesapeake & Ohio and became CSX. This bridge is about 300 feet long and crosses 40 feet above Lock 13.

Lock 13 also contains exposed original sandstone blocks at its bottom. The concrete walls connecting some of the locks were built in 1937 to prevent erosion of the canal banks.

4 Down a few steps and up another set of steps is Lock 12 on the right and Ace Rubber Co. on the left.

At the top of the steps at Lock 12, look left (east) to see the old Cascade Race. The water for the race originated from a dam on the Little Cuyahoga River in Middlebury (near Goodyear headquarters). Dr. Eliakim Crosby built the race (sometimes called "Crosby's Ditch"), taking advantage of the downhill terrain to power his Old Stone Mill at Lock 5 (now covered by Cascade Plaza). Along the race were mills, factories, an iron furnace, a distillery, and other businesses that enabled Akron to thrive.

CAUTION: Watch for vehicles in the open area behind the factory.

Ace Rubber Co., built as American Rubber Co. in 1919, is still in operation and produces rubber floor mats for industry. It is located on the site of the old Aetna Mill (1843), which was built near the even earlier Aetna Iron Furnace.

South of the multistory Ace building is a sump, surrounded by a screened-in shed. The water inside is used for cooling during the manufacturing process and is constantly recirculated.

Originally the millrace water powered two more mills and eventually flowed down to the Little Cuyahoga River.

At the north end of Lock 12 are the remains of a canal basin where boats tied up to take on cargoes. West of Lock 12 is a water wasteway that took excess water around the lock.

5 Continue up the next set of steps and under the next railroad trestle to Lock 11.

The concrete structure that crosses the canal at this point is another conduit for First Energy power lines.

The railroad trestle above Lock 11 is an active freight line of the Wheeling & Lake Erie Railroad. The bridge is about 875 feet long and crosses 70 feet above Lock 11.

The old stone towers on the left and right are pilings that remain from a trestle built by Pittsburgh, Akron & Western RR in 1890–91.

The present bridge, with its steel supports, may have been built after the 1913 flood when stone piers had been undermined.

Continue on the trail. At the far end of Lock 11 the date "1907" is cast into the wall, indicating when the concrete lining was added to the locks. The opening to an internal sluiceway can be seen on the west

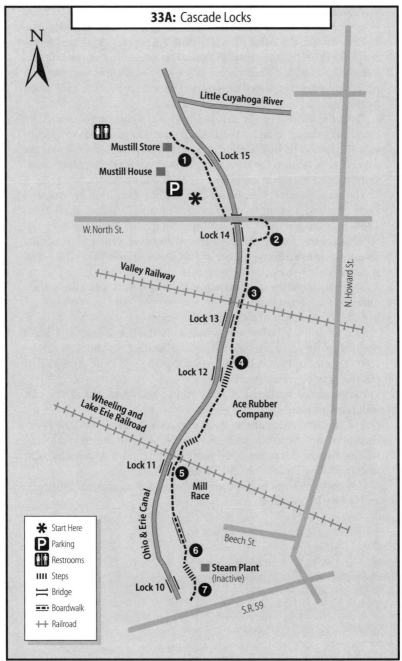

33A: Cascade Locks

N

Little Cuyahoga River

Mustill Store

Lock 15

1

Mustill House

P

*

W. North St.

Lock 14

2

Valley Railway

3

Lock 13

Lock 12

4

Wheeling and
Lake Erie Railroad

Ace Rubber
Company

N. Howard St.

Lock 11

5

Mill
Race

Ohio & Erie Canal

Beech St.

6

Steam Plant
(Inactive)

Lock 10

7

S.R. 59

* Start Here
P Parking
Restrooms
IIII Steps
⊨ Bridge
▭▭ Boardwalk
++ Railroad

© Gray & Company, Publishers

wall of Lock 11; the sluiceway acted as an alternative water control device. Note another open boat basin at the end of Lock 11.

6 The ditch for the millrace is now obvious on the left (east). Also to the east are the ruins of what some authorities think was Schumacher's Dam, built to create the necessary "head" (or altitude) for his overshot mill wheel. Constructed in the early 1870s, this concrete dam may have provided water through a 48-inch pipe to the mill wheel below.

From the left side of the boardwalk, view the concrete dam and box containing the opening for the 48-inch pipe. The bolts that you see inside the hydraulic box supported a screen to keep debris out of the pipe. A pool behind the dam accumulated water for the pipe; excess water flowed over twin spillways on either side of the box.

The walls alongside the boardwalk and the dam itself are made of early portland cement, a product first manufactured in the U.S. in 1868. Schumacher must have realized that this new construction material was ideal for the dam he wanted to build. One has to admire Schumacher as an entrepreneur and an innovator on the cutting edge of industrial progress.

7 After ascending the next set of steps, you will reach the former Ohio Edison Steam Plant.

CAUTION: Stay well away from the fence.

This large brick building was originally the Beech St. Steam Plant and for many years produced steam for heating buildings in downtown Akron. An even earlier plant on this site produced Akron's first electricity to operate a street railway.

Although the west wall of Lock 10 has been demolished, the east wall remains totally intact.

The trail ends here at the fence. The Ohio & Erie Canal, however, continues under the Innerbelt and Market St. Soon the Towpath Trail will climb past this point on its way into downtown Akron and, ultimately, to New Philadelphia in Tuscarawas County.

Retrace your steps back down the "staircase" of locks to North St. and the parking area. ■

Hike B: Mustill Store and Towpath Trail

Distance: 4 miles

`Easy`

Hiking time: 2 hours

Description: The hike from Mustill Store north on the Towpath Trail provides a mix of history and nature, two key elements that make the trail so universally well liked. This walk is entirely on smooth, flat surfaces of asphalt and crushed limestone. It follows the route of the canal and passes two remaining locks, ending at a platform overlooking the confluence of the Little Cuyahoga River and the main stem of the Cuyahoga River before returning on the Towpath to the Mustill Store and the parking area. Although many travelers of the Towpath Trail are on bicycle, the best way to explore this popular trail is on foot. (Remember the Towpath Trail is a shared trail; stay to the right, and hike in single file when with a large group.)

1 The Mustill Store is your first stop after leaving the parking area. The canal-era store and nearby house are believed to have been built in the 1850s. Three generations of Mustills served those that worked and lived on the canal until the late 1880s. The store was in an excellent location since passengers and boatmen waiting their turn to lock up or down the staircase locks (see hike A above) had extra time on their hands. The Mustill Store is open to visitors; hours vary depending on the season. If it's open, don't miss an opportunity to visit the store and see the exhibits inside that tell about the Mustill family, their store, and life on the canal as well as about the canal's importance in the development of the city of Akron.

Head north from the Mustill Store down a gentle paved grade just past Lock 15 to see where the canal waters meet and mix with those of the Little Cuyahoga River coming in from the east. This was not always the case. The flood of 1913 wiped out the canal north of Lock 15, leaving it little more than a small depression adjacent to the towpath. A number of remnant concrete structures—originally used for water control—can be found along the trail here.

2 Lock 16 is on the left of the trail at mile marker 36. Mile markers give approximate distances from the original terminus of the canal in downtown Cleveland. The canal is in a dry or unwatered state from this point north until the Brecksville feeder dam at Lock 36.

3 At 0.5 miles from the trailhead, pass Lock 17. Although the Towpath Trail along this stretch is not always on the exact alignment of the original towpath, here it is, immediately adjacent to the lock and between the lock and the river. Above the trail to the west lies the embankment of the Valley Railway. Built in the 1870s, the railroad dealt a near death blow to the canal. Operating year-round and traveling faster than the canal boats, the railroad could compete for both freight

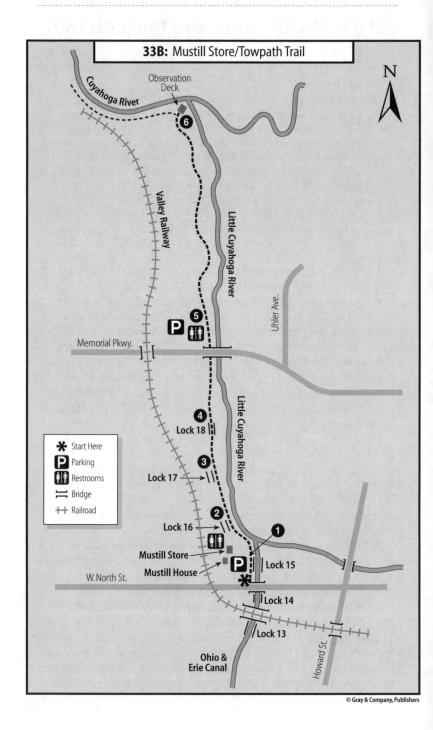

33B: Mustill Store/Towpath Trail

N

Cuyahoga River

Observation Deck

6

Valley Railway

Little Cuyahoga River

Uhler Ave.

P 5 (restrooms)

Memorial Pkwy.

4
Lock 18

3
Lock 17

Start Here
P Parking
(restrooms) Restrooms
)(Bridge
++ Railroad

2
Lock 16

Little Cuyahoga River

1

(restrooms)
Mustill Store
P
Mustill House

W. North St.

Lock 15

Lock 14

Lock 13

Howard St.

Ohio &
Erie Canal

© Gray & Company, Publishers

and passenger traffic. The canal hung on, supplying the needs of a few small industries and a curious recreational trade, until put out of business forever on March 26, 1913, when hit by a disastrous flood.

4 Here the trail passes through Lock 18, giving you an opportunity to get a close look at the lock walls (much as a passenger on a canal packet boat might have seen). The trail has been graded to avoid the 8-to-12-foot drop experienced by canal passengers. A close look at the lock walls will tell much about its history and function. Originally built of sandstone, the locks had deteriorated by the end of the 1800s to the point that the state of Ohio, the canal's owner, had to make major repairs. The new "miracle" product at the time was Portland cement concrete. As you look at the walls, you see where a large portion of the concrete face has fallen off. It reveals the use of "bank run" gravel smoothed and rounded by the streams from which it was taken, in the original concrete mix. Present day engineers avoid using this type of material in favor of more angular crushed rock and stone. The ends of the walls were formed as curves to minimize damage to the boats as they entered and exited the lock.

5 (1.2 miles) The trail passes under Memorial Parkway and past a trailhead parking lot, where you'll find water and restrooms. The trail continues to parallel the Little Cuyahoga River north through young woodlands interspersed with small fields. Although near an urban area and built upon an old landfill, this stretch of trail is remarkably wild. In the spring and summer the areas alongside the trail are lively with birds: Baltimore orioles, rose-breasted grosbeaks, several species of woodpeckers, song sparrows, red-tailed hawks, kingfishers, and great blue herons are just a few of the many birds feeding and nesting here in the river valley.

6 (2 miles) Here a platform overlooks the confluence of the Little Cuyahoga River and the main stem of the Cuyahoga River. Take a moment to watch the waters mix and mingle. The reddish-hued shrub that covers the banks here is Japanese knotweed. This shrub is not native to this valley and spreads so vigorously that it impedes the growth of native species. It typically takes hold in places like this, where the native vegetation has been disturbed. Although here the non-native shrub is dominant, both native and non-native species are revegetating other areas of the old landfill bordering the trail.

Return to Mustill store by retracing your steps. ■

34 Firestone Metro Park
Akron

Distance: 2.8 miles

Easy

Hiking time: 1¼ hours

Description: The flat 1.6-mile Willow Trail begins near the shelter, follows the shoreline of Little Turtle Pond, and goes alongside the small Tuscarawas River and Tuscarawas Race. The 1.2-mile Red Wing Trail ascends and descends a small hill to cross the marsh on a boardwalk and follows the river briefly in the opposite direction. Although both trails are short, they offer a surprising amount of variety, both in terrain and natural beauty.

Directions: From I-271 take Exit 18 for SR 8; south on SR 8 past I-77/76 to exit for Waterloo Rd.; west on Waterloo; left (south) on Glenmount Rd. past I-277 to end; left (east) on Swartz Rd.; right (south) on Harrington Rd.; pass first park entrance on right (Little Turtle Pond) to second entrance (on right).

From Akron, take I-277/US 224; south on S. Main St.; east on Swartz Rd.; right (south) on Harrington Rd.; pass first park entrance on right (Little Turtle Pond) to the second park entrance (also on right).

Parking & restrooms: Near the Tuscarawas Picnic Shelter.

Firestone Metro Park, a unit of Metro Parks, Serving Summit County (MPSSC), was organized in 1949 when Firestone Tire and Rubber Co. donated 189 acres of land across from Firestone Country Club. Now consisting of 255 acres of rolling terrain, the park includes a fishing and ice-skating pond; picnic areas; a large sledding and kite-flying hill; three short trails; a reservable picnic shelter; and Coventry Oaks, a reservable, fully outfitted, enclosed pavilion (to reserve either facility, call 330-867-5511). The narrow Tuscarawas River runs north through the park before eventually turning south to empty into the Muskingum River in Coshocton. Alongside the Willow Trail is Tuscarawas Race, a canal dug originally to feed water to the Ohio & Erie Canal but now providing water for industrial use and fire protection. A large wetland, the centerpiece of Firestone Metro Park, attracts a variety of migratory songbirds, making this park a popular destination for bird-watchers. One hundred seventy-five species of birds have been identified at Firestone Metro Park. This wetland was formed by a rise in the water table resulting from a dam constructed in 1956 on Harrington Rd. to form Firestone Reservoir.

1 The Willow Trail, marked with a leaf symbol, begins north of the Tuscarawas Shelter on a wide dirt road going north, a track used also

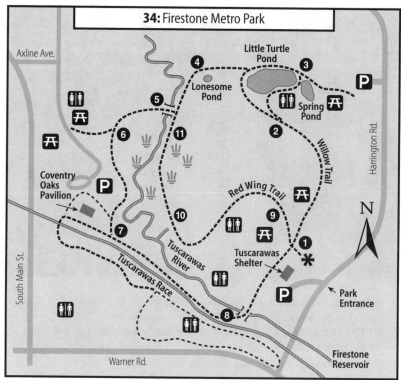

34: Firestone Metro Park

© Gray & Company, Publishers

by park vehicles. Some of the trees carry identification labels.

2 Reach Little Turtle Pond at 0.3 mile and bear right to follow the edge of the pond. Special summer fishing programs for children under 15 years are held in this stocked pond. Lighted ice-skating is available in the winter (330-865-8060).

3 The trail continues between Little Turtle Pond and Spring Pond, where many waterfowl usually congregate. Continue along the north side of Little Turtle Pond until the trail bears west into the forested area.

4 Pass Lonesome Pond (filled with cattails) on the left. The narrow Tuscarawas River is now on the right, flowing north through the park. (This river flows west after it leaves the park, then south to Barberton.)

5 (0.7 mile) At a trail junction turn right to cross the river on a wooden footbridge and follow the trail as it bends west.

6 At a trail intersection, turn left (south). (The side trail ahead goes out to Axline Ave. and a picnic area.) Continue south on the Willow Trail alongside the river, which is now on the left. Pass a side trail on the right (leading out to Coventry Oaks Pavilion).

7 Reach Tuscarawas Race at 1 mile and bear left (southeast). The race, built to channel water to the Ohio & Erie Canal northeast of Bar-

berton, now channels it from Firestone Reservoir to lakes west of here and then on to another part of the Tuscarawas River.

The Tuscarawas River is now on the left below. On this wide embankment a railroad once carried coal from a mine southeast of here. Continue along the race to a trail junction.

8 Turn left (north) at this junction to cross the river on an arched wooden bridge and return on the trail to the Tuscarawas Shelter (1.6 miles).

From the shelter building, cross the field in a northwest direction to the edge of the woods and a sign indicating the Red Wing Trail, marked with a bird symbol.

9 Follow the Red Wing Trail westward uphill through an upland forest of oak, maple, and beech.

10 The trail goes downhill to an open area with restrooms on the left. Continue to the west then north to enter the wet meadow on a plastic boardwalk. According to MPSSC, this is one of the finest protected wetland areas in Summit County. Here it is possible to see frogs, turtles, raccoons, or muskrats. Cross the wet meadow to reach the Tuscarawas River again (2.1 miles).

11 Bear right onto the path to follow the river north. Reach the junction with the Willow Trail and the bridge crossed earlier (Note #5). Stay to the right (north) on the Willow/Red Wing Trail and follow it back northeast alongside the river, past the sign for Lonesome Pond, to Little Turtle Pond.

12 Turn right (south) at Little Turtle Pond. Stay to the right at the next trail intersection and follow the trail back to the parking area. ∎

35 Munroe Falls Metro Park
Munroe Falls

Distance: 3 miles

Easy

Hiking time: 1½ hours

Description: The 2.2-mile Indian Spring Trail undulates over moderately hilly terrain through deciduous forest and past two ponds southeast of the swimming lake. The walk is on a wide, well-marked trail and on grass bordering the beach around the swimming lake.

Directions: From Cleveland, take I-271 to Exit 18 (SR 8); south on SR 8 to exit for Graham Rd./Silver Lake/Stow; east on Graham Rd.; right (south) on SR 91 to Munroe Falls; continue across river and railroad tracks; left (east) on S. River Rd. for 1 mile; park entrance on right.

From Akron, take SR 8 north; right (east) on Portage Trail; immediate left (east) on Munroe Falls Ave.; right (south) on SR 91 for about 0.25 mile; left on S. River Rd. for about one mile; park entrance on right.

Parking & restrooms: After entering the park, continue to the right and circle around the swimming lake to the parking lot marked for trails, just before the Shady Beach Shelter. Restrooms are at Shady Beach picnic area.

Munroe Falls Metro Park, a unit of Metro Parks, Serving Summit County, is located near the Cuyahoga River in the town of Munroe Falls. The central feature of this park is a 13-acre swimming lake, a former private swim club owned by the John Renner family. Metro Parks purchased the property in 1978 and made extensive improvements that included picnic shelters, tennis, volleyball, and basketball courts, and playgrounds. A new bathhouse complex was built in 1995. A park admission fee is charged during the swimming season from Memorial Day to Labor Day. The Indian Spring loop trail through the woods is enjoyed by hikers and, in winter, by cross-country skiers.

1 Enter the Indian Spring Trail at the south end of the parking lot at the trail marked with a tomahawk symbol.

2 At 0.2 mile bear left over the dam at the north end of Beaver Pond. The trail goes to the right (south) and uphill to overlook this small pond, often spotted with ducks and geese.

3 The broad trail bends east through a forest of oak, maple, beech, and cucumber trees.

4 At 1 mile the trail bends slightly toward the north, then east, crosses a small footbridge, and ascends a small rise. Here are bigtooth aspens whose unusual leaves are ovate with rounded marginal teeth.

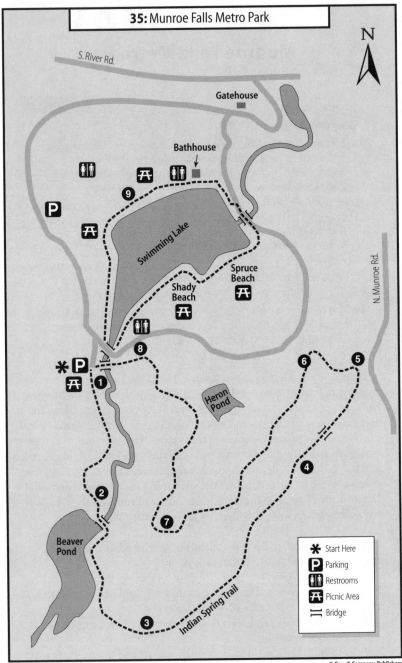

35: Munroe Falls Metro Park

© Gray & Company, Publishers

5 Just before the trail turns west, pass a park bench. The road to the right (east) is N. Munroe Rd. At about 1.2 miles the path gently descends through an oak forest.

6 Turn left. The trail now bends to the southwest as it snakes through the woods.

7 Soon the path turns toward the northeast past an open field. At about 2 miles reenter the woods going eastward through a former farm field now in succession. Pass Heron Pond on the right, where there is a bench overlooking the pond, and continue on the trail.

8 After rising gently then descending down stone steps, the Indian Spring Trail crosses a footbridge to the parking area. This hike can be ended here or may be extended by walking 0.75 mile more around the swimming lake.

9 Continue in a clockwise direction on the grassy area around the swimming lake and past a bathhouse. Cross the bridge at the east end of the lake and continue under a stand of spruce trees shading the Spruce Beach Picnic Area. Reach the parking area just beyond the Shady Beach Shelter. ■

36 F. A. Seiberling Naturealm
Akron

Easy

Distance: 2.75 miles

Hiking time: 2 ½ hours

Description: The trails in the Naturealm are generally short and include flat paved paths and unpaved trails over hillier terrain. Paved walks through the arboretum go past flowering, weeping, and pyramidal trees and shrubs, and a collection of fruit and nut trees. On Cherry Lane Trail an observation deck overlooks Echo Pond, and a suspension bridge over a ravine joins that trail with Fernwood Trail. The longest trail in the Naturealm is the 1.3-mile-long Seneca Trail loop, which begins near Seneca Pond and continues through former farmland, now a deciduous forest, and ends in the rock and herb garden near the visitors' center.

Directions: From Cleveland, take I-77 to Exit 138 (Ghent Rd.); south on Ghent; left (east) on Smith Rd.; continue past Revere Rd. and Sand Run Rd.; entrance on right.

From south of Akron, take I-77 to exit for SR 18; east on SR 18 for about 0.5 mile; east on Smith Rd. to Naturealm.

Parking & restrooms: At the visitors' center.

F. A. Seiberling, co-founder of Goodyear Tire and Rubber Company, donated 400 acres of his land to establish Sand Run Metro Park, of which the F. A. Seiberling Naturealm is a part. Opened in 1964 by Metro Parks, Serving Summit County, this 100-acre nature preserve was set aside specifically to help visitors understand and appreciate the natural environment. It offers an arboretum of 16 acres with more than 300 kinds of trees and shrubs, and a rock and herb garden containing a collection of 85 glacial rocks and more than 100 species of herbs. There are many flowering trees in the arboretum that are especially beautiful in the spring, and three well-designed hiking trails in the forests behind the arboretum.

An underground visitors' center, built into a hill, contains a series of striking nature exhibits portraying plants and animals of woodlands and marshlands. An unusual walk-in display that simulates an underwater habitat is a child's delight, with oversized snails, crayfish, water bugs, and other pond life depicted at 12 times normal size. There is also a bird-watching room (with binoculars provided) and a weather station. Park naturalists offer a variety of programs, classes, and nature walks year round. The center, open Mon.–Sat. 10–5, and Sun. noon–5, is located on Smith Rd. east of Sand Run Rd. (330-865-8065).

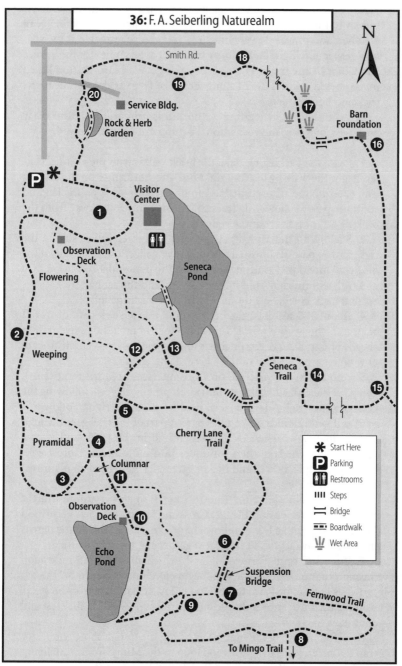

© Gray & Company, Publishers

The Naturealm recommends the following schedule for the best viewing of plants and trees: crabapples in early May; rhododendrons in May to June; azaleas in May to June; herbs in late June; fall foliage in October; and prairie flowers July to October. Also available at the visitors' center and in trailhead boxes are leaflet-type guides for the Seneca and Cherry Lane trails. These guides give detailed information keyed to numbered features found along the trails. There is also a guide to the rock and herb garden.

Because the F. A. Seiberling Naturealm is primarily a nature study area, pets, bicycles, and recreational equipment are not allowed.

1 From the parking lot, take the brick walkway to the visitors' center. Begin the walk by bearing right just after the center on the asphalt trail entering the arboretum. Pass an observation deck on the left and continue past the flowering trees collection. A brick walkway from the parking lot joins in from the right.

2 Staying on the asphalt, at the next trail intersection stay to the right and go past the unusual weeping trees collection. Bear right at the next trail junction. Continue south past the pyramidal collection.

3 A bark-mulched trail intersects here, and the asphalt trail curves around back north. Stay on the asphalt trail, bearing left.

4 About 100 feet past the intersection, one asphalt path bears left back into the arboretum. Do not take that branch, but stay straight ahead. The trail curves again, back toward the visitors' center. You are now on a paved portion of the Cherry Lane Trail.

5 About 300 feet past the previous intersection, turn right (east), going off the asphalt walkway onto a soft pine-bark path, following the Cherry Lane Trail. A large glacial boulder is on the right. Follow this path as it gently winds downhill. The first part of the trail goes through an area that was pasture or plowed ground in the 1960s and is now young forest. The trail then continues into more mature forest with large oak, maple, beech, and hickory trees. Pass a fenced-in plant rescue area on the left.

6 At this point, leave the Cherry Lane Trail and continue straight ahead to the suspension bridge. Cross the bridge to reach Fernwood Trail, marked with a fern symbol. The wild nature of the ravine here is in distinct contrast to the cultivated gardens of the arboretum.

7 Turn left onto Fernwood Trail, which makes a 0.5-mile loop through mature forest. The trail begins to climb; a bench on the left provides a pleasant place to rest and enjoy the ambiance of the steep, wooded ravine below. Continue on the trail as it swings to the west and continues to climb.

8 Before reaching the high point along the trail, a short connector trail to the left joins the Fernwood loop to the Mingo Trail, a challenging 3.3-mile loop through Sand Run Metro Park (Ch. 37).

9 At this intersection the Fernwood Trail loop ends (the suspension bridge is a short distance to the right). Turn left (west). In about 200 feet you reach Echo Pond.

10 At the north end of Echo Pond is a sheltered observation deck with benches, an inviting niche from which to observe this small haven for wildlife. Amphibians and waterfowl frequent this pond.

11 From the pond, follow the pine-bark trail north, rejoining the Cherry Lane Trail, and go on to the asphalt walk you were on a short while ago. Turn right on the asphalt walk, following the sign for Cherry Lane Trail, until you reach the same intersection described in #5. This time, continue straight ahead at this junction, staying on the asphalt walkway.

12 Continue straight ahead on the asphalt, staying to the right of the fruit and nut collection.

13 At this intersection, continue straight ahead to a bench tucked snugly into an alcove overlooking Seneca Pond. After visiting this observation nook, go back a few steps to the start of Seneca Trail, marked with an arrowhead symbol. Turn onto the unpaved path, now going generally east, away from the visitors' center area. This 1.3-mile forest path circles through the woodlands east of the arboretum.

A leaflet available in the visitors' center describes numbered features found along the trail. We have noted some of these below.

Soon after starting on the Seneca Trail, you reach steps leading down to a bridge across Seneca Run, the creek that forms Seneca Pond. Seneca Run flows into Sand Run, one of the larger tributaries of the Cuyahoga River. The forest here is a mature hardwood forest similar to that which the early settlers would have encountered. Dominant trees are sugar maple, American beech, tuliptree, wild cherry, oak, hickory, and aspen. A particularly large tuliptree can be found near the trail. It is about 100 feet tall, and is one of the oldest and tallest trees in Naturealm.

14 Young people and adults alike enjoy using the Tree Finder. Try your skill at identifying the various tree species within sight of the finder.

15 A short side trail leads to the Sand Run valley overlook. Sand Run Metro Park surrounds most of the Sand Run valley. The stream enters the Cuyahoga River about a half-mile from here. This is a good spot from which to watch for woodland birds, such as tufted titmice, chickadees, white-breasted nuthatches, and several varieties of woodpeckers, including the largest, the pileated woodpecker, with a wingspan of 29 inches.

16 Here the trail passes directly through the remains of a barn foundation, 30 feet by 60 feet. Young black walnut trees are now growing within the footprint of the barn, providing a source of food for the many squirrels that inhabit this woodland. Squirrels, with their practice of burying nuts, account for much of the distribution of black walnut trees. These trees were probably "planted" by squirrels.

17 About halfway around the Seneca Trail loop, the trail goes through a wet area where you can find plants typical of swampy areas—skunk cabbage, marsh marigolds, ferns, jewelweed, and golden ragwort. Skunk cabbage is one of the earliest plants to emerge in springtime, at the first hint of warmth, and it grows in abundance here.

A little farther ahead alongside the trail is a spring flowing from the hillside. When this area was farmed, the farmer placed clay tiles to route the water to the barn not far away.

18 The trail now swings west and uphill, back toward the visitors' center. A creek ravine is to the right, and not far beyond is Smith Rd. This road has long been in use—it was originally a military road built by soldiers during the War of 1812.

19 Near the end of Seneca Trail, the path passes through an area being managed as prairie. The Metro Parks managers use controlled burns to help control woody plants and non-native weeds. Associated with the prairie and field plants are many species of butterflies, several of which are pictured and identified on signs along the trail. Grassland and field birds might also be seen here, such as field sparrows and Eastern bluebirds.

Cross a service road and continue on Seneca Trail to the rock and herb garden.

20 Seneca Trail ends in the delightful rock and herb garden. In 2002 Metro Parks, Serving Summit County, completed a major renovation of the garden, redesigning it and building a new paved walkway, footbridge, and ornamental pond with a waterfall. Metro Parks staff, the Naturealm Herb Society, and the master gardeners of Ohio State University Extension all contributed to the renovation. The rock and herb garden helps visitors to see and experience the many herbs that can be grown in gardens in Northeast Ohio.

Leave the rock and herb garden to reach the parking lot where you began. ■

37 Sand Run Metro Park
Akron

Moderate

Distance: 4 miles

Hiking time: 2 hours

Description: This hike in Sand Run Metro Park is a very hilly loop hike on the Dogwood and Mingo trails through the west end of the park. The pathway follows the hills up and down and crosses streams on stone blocks or bridges.

Directions: From Cleveland take I-77 to exit for Ghent Rd.; south on Ghent; left (east) on Sand Run Pkwy. opposite Summit Mall; continue past Revere Rd. and Sand Run Rd. to park; inside park, drive through vehicle ford of Sand Run stream to Wadsworth Picnic Area, on right just beyond Shadowfield Picnic Area. (In heavy rain, cars cannot ford stream and must approach park from the east rather than the west, taking Smith Rd. and Merriman Rd. to Sand Run Pkwy.)

From Akron take Portage Path north past Stan Hywet Hall; left (west) on Sand Run Pkwy. to Wadsworth Area.

Parking & restrooms: At Wadsworth Picnic Area.

In 1930 Sand Run Metro Park became the first park to be acquired by Metro Parks, Serving Summit County, through gifts of land from F. A. Seiberling, the founder of Akron's Goodyear and Seiberling Rubber companies. Seiberling Naturealm, located within this park on Smith Rd., was named in his honor (Ch. 36).

Sand Run is a hilly, 1,106-acre park that stretches on an east–west axis along Sand Run within Akron city limits. The park's steep ravines enclose several streams that empty into Sand Run, which flows northeast into the nearby Cuyahoga River. Sand Run is so named because of the large amount of sand that was once carried downstream here. The highly erodable sandy soil and hillside slumps are noticeable along the trails. Wildflowers and ferns thrive in the valleys of this park, as do many birds in its tall trees. Squirrels, woodchucks, raccoons, and other wildlife populate the wooded areas. Since the forest here has been protected since the time of the Seiberlings, many of the trees have reached impressive size. Thousands of visitors over the years have found the park to be a welcome oasis in the midst of congested urban development.

This park contains several picnic areas, reservable shelters, playing fields, foot and jogging trails, a sledding hill, a skating area, and an exercise parcours and is connected by trail to the Ohio and Erie Canal Towpath Trail. Many of the shelters and other early park buildings, as well as an extension of Sand Run Pkwy., were built by the Civilian Conservation Corps in the 1930s. In 1932 Akron work relief crews built five miles of foot trails to complement existing bridle trails. The bridle trails have since been converted to hiking trails.

The Buckeye Trail (BT) goes through Sand Run Metro Park, though here it is not marked with the trail's usual 2-by-6-inch blue blazes. It is identified on signposts by the letters BT inside a yellow-bordered arrow.

The BT follows the old Portage Path between the Cuyahoga and Tuscarawas rivers. This important pathway was the original route used by natives of the area as they carried their canoes over the land between the rivers. A commemorative sign has been placed at the top of the hill at the junction of Portage Path and Treaty Line Rd. to recognize this historical route. A life-size bronze statue of an Indian portaging a canoe at the intersection of Portage Path and Merriman Rd. marks the northern terminus of the Portage Path. Bronze arrowheads mark the entire 8-mile route. Treaty Line Rd. was named for the 1785 Treaty of Fort McIntosh, which delineated Delaware and Wyandot territory and declared lands outside the boundary "free of Indian claims."

The administrative office for the Metro Parks, at 975 Treaty Line Rd., is open on weekdays to provide information, maps, brochures, and shelter reservations (330-867-5511). The district publishes a quarterly newsletter called *Green Islands* and a quarterly programs and events guide. For seasonal information (sledding and ice-skating) call 330-865-8060; for program information call 330-865-8064.

1 Start the hike from the Wadsworth Area. Cross the field to reach the Dogwood Trail (marked with a tree leaf). Ascend the steep hill (southwest) on the Dogwood Trail. At the top of the hill stay on the Dogwood Trail, passing any of the turns off this trail.

General Wadsworth, who commanded troops in the War of 1812, used this summit as a lookout point when his forces camped near what is now the Old Portage Picnic Area at the intersection of Portage Path and Sand Run Pkwy.

2 Follow the Dogwood Trail westward through the woods until reaching an open area, the North Hawkins Playfield (0.5 mile). Continue following Dogwood Trail signs past the sledding hill on the left and the soccer field, also on the left, as the pathway curves along the edge of the woods. The trail reenters the woods on the right.

3 The trail next goes steeply downhill to Shady Hollow Pavilion (1.1 miles), a log cabin–style, reservable pavilion. Pass the pavilion and continue straight, following the entrance drive toward Sand Run Pkwy. Just before the parkway, turn left onto the Mingo Trail, marked with a triangular tree symbol. (Note that these trail signs have an arrow pointing in the direction opposite from the one you are going in.)

4 As you follow the ups and downs of this trail going west, Sand

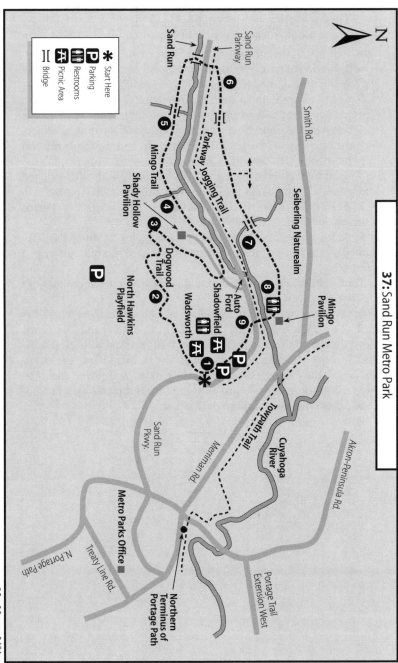

37: Sand Run Metro Park

© Gray & Company, Publishers

Run and Sand Run Pkwy. are below on the right. Cross a small brook flowing north to Sand Run, using a uniquely designed bridge.

5 After ascending and descending more hills, the trail reaches a bridge over another small stream (1.7 miles) and then crosses Sand Run itself, on another bridge, and Sand Run Pkwy. (2 miles). (Here you have the option of returning to the Wadsworth Area by walking east on the jogging trail marked with a green jogger sign.)

6 Continue uphill in an easterly direction, still on the Mingo Trail. Cross a footbridge and ascend another steep hill. Sand Run Pkwy. is now below on the right. Near the high point along the trail, a connector trail intersects to the left. This connector leads to the Fernwood Trail in Seiberling Naturealm (Ch. 36).

The terrain undulates through a stretch of forest with tall beech, red and white oak, and maple trees. Then the path descends steeply.

7 At 2.7 miles cross an old stone bridge built in the 1930s that spans a stream outlet from Seneca Pond.

8 Reach a junction with an entrance road going to Mingo Pavilion, named for the Mingo Indians who may have used this hilltop area as a campsite.

Turn right, taking the paved road downhill. Maintenance buildings are to the left (east).

9 Cross the bridge over Sand Run and immediately take the dirt trail on the right marked BT. Follow this path out to Sand Run Pkwy. Cross the road and enter the Dogwood Trail (marked with a leaf symbol), turning left and going east. Follow the Dogwood Trail parallel to and above the parkway to Shadowfield parking and picnic area. The wide dirt track leads to Wadsworth parking and picnic area just beyond Shadowfield to complete the loop. ∎

38 Gorge Metro Park and Riverfront Walk Cuyahoga Falls

Directions: From Cleveland take I-271 to Exit 18 (SR 8); south on SR 8 to exit for Broad Blvd. in Cuyahoga Falls; right on Broad for 1 block; left (south) on Front St. for several blocks; descend hill to traffic signal; right into Gorge Metro Park at next traffic light (park entrance is just before Cuyahoga River bridge).

From Akron take SR 8 north to exit for E. Cuyahoga Falls Ave.; left onto Gorge Blvd. to traffic light continue straight onto Front St.; cross Cuyahoga River bridge; park entrance on left at traffic light.

Parking & restrooms: Parking and restrooms are near the entrance.

Located in Cuyahoga Falls, 205-acre Gorge Metro Park contains some of the most beautiful and spectacular scenery in Summit County. The scenery alone is worth a visit, but there is another aspect of the gorge that makes it particularly intriguing. Here you can witness the power of the glaciers, in this case, the power to change the course of a river. Throughout Ohio glaciers altered the landscape and changed drainage patterns. The Cuyahoga's current course was shaped by the retreat of the last glaciers. The river flows south as it enters the park, then abruptly makes a sharp turn, flows west for a way, then heads north to merge into Lake Erie.

But what may seem sudden today results from thousands of years of geologic processes. The gorge was originally carved by a preglacial river. At the retreat of the last glacier, about 12,000 years ago, the river's south-flowing course was filled in and blocked by ice, then by sand and gravel dropping off the face of the melting glacier. The waters sought a new channel along this ridge of outwash, creating the U-shaped course we see today. The more recent Cuyahoga River is both excavating its way down into the ancient gorge and carving new valleys.

In this gorge, the river flows over a shale riverbed flanked by Sharon Conglomerate cliffs and ledges. Springs seep from the ledges, forming microclimates for ferns and mosses. Trees, including oaks, sourgums, tuliptrees, and birch, cling to the steep hillsides.

People have been enjoying this gorge for recreation since the 1880s. High Glens Park opened here in 1882 and offered both a thrilling roller- coaster and a dance hall. It closed in the 1920s. By then Northern Ohio Traction & Light Company (predecessor to Ohio Edison and FirstEnergy) had acquired part of the land for construction of a dam

and electric power plant. The dam was located near the site of a natural waterfall, the original "Cuyahoga Falls." That falls now lies beneath
the impoundment. In 1930, Northern Ohio Traction & Light donated
144 acres to the Akron Metropolitan Park District, thus forming the
core of the current park.

A notable feature of the park is Mary Campbell Cave, a huge rock
overhang that once sheltered Delaware Indians and a captive pioneer
girl brought here from Pennsylvania.

Some of the first industries in Summit County were started around
the natural waterfalls on the Cuyahoga River in what is now Cuyahoga
Falls. Here the early pioneers built water-powered mills. When steam,
and then later electricity, replaced water power, the river was no longer
the critical asset it had once been. Like many other American cities,
those in Summit County saw the river as little more than a repository
for its waste.

In the 1970s, Cuyahoga Falls—like many other medium-sized
cities—saw the success San Antonio had had in developing its riverfront and began to see the Cuyahoga River for the great natural asset it
truly is. Cuyahoga Falls planners began developing parks, an amphitheater, and riveredge boardwalks and encouraged walking by
eliminating the automobile from Front St. (as hikers will see in
Hike B). Riverfront Centre Boardwalk follows the Cuyahoga River upstream of Gorge Metro Park. Hike B explores the boardwalk and turns
around at the city dock north of the mall. From here Falls River Tours
takes visitors on narrated pontoon boat rides up the river (phone
330-971-8372 for information on fees and schedule). Plans call for
continuing the pedestrian-friendly design along the river by extending
and improving the trail from Gorge Metro Park all the way to Water
Works Park near the Munroe Falls border.

Hike A: **Gorge Trail**

Distance: 1.8 miles

Easy

Hiking time: 1.5 hours

Description: This trail in the Cuyahoga River gorge is wide and well marked
and involves climbing some hills and scrambling over rocks. Because of the
boulders, shoes with traction soles are recommended.

1 The upper segment of the Gorge Trail begins at the sign in the
northwest corner of the parking lot. Wayside exhibits along the path
help explain the natural and human history of the area. After entering
the trail, pass an ice-skating field (flooded in winter) on the left, and a
picnic area on the right. The trail soon passes a shelter on the left.

The shale rock along this portion of the trail belongs to the Cuya-

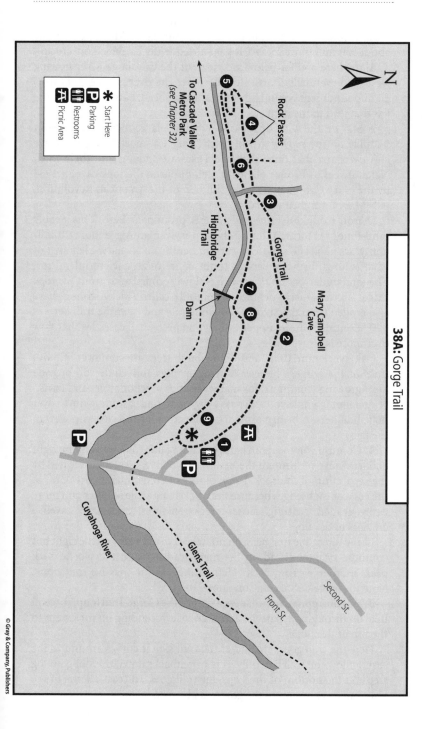

38A: Gorge Trail

N

To Cascade Valley
Metro Park
(see Chapter 32)

Rock Passes

Highbridge
Trail

Dam

Gorge Trail

Mary Campbell
Cave

Cuyahoga River

Glens Trail

Front St.

Second St.

★ Start Here
P Parking
Restrooms
Picnic Area

© Gray & Company, Publishers

hoga Formation (see Appendix A). It is composed of mud and silt layers laid down at the bottom of an ocean during the Mississippian Age about 350 million years ago. It has subsequently hardened into rock.

Along here and far below are views of the Cuyahoga River flowing west (and eventually north) to Lake Erie. The river is wide and forms an impoundment behind Edison Dam just ahead. Pass the steps on the left that lead to the dam.

2 Stay on the wide upper trail, passing a large rock wall. At about 0.2 mile on the right you will reach Mary Campbell Cave, a massive cliff overhang that once sheltered Delaware Indians and their chief, Netawatwees. A bronze plaque placed opposite the rock cave in 1934 by the Mary Campbell Society, Children of the American Revolution, tells Mary Campbell's story.

Sharon Conglomerate sandstone is prominent here. This pebbly sandstone was formed during the Pennsylvanian Age about 320 million years ago. The sand was carried here from a quartz-rich area of what is now northern Canada to the shore of an ancient inland sea. The sand underfoot on this trail has slowly eroded away from the rock ledges above. Quartz pebbles, commonly called "lucky stones," have also eroded from the Sharon Conglomerate and litter the trail here.

3 Continue on the upper trail, going past small cascades that flow over more layers of shale.

Oak, blackgum, tulip, and yellow birch trees are common on both sides of the gorge. The ever-flowing springs and sandy soil provide ideal growing conditions for many varieties of wildflowers and ferns.

At about 0.6 mile you will pass a high waterfall cascading down over huge boulders. A bridge provides a safe crossing and close-up view of the falls.

4 Continue on the main path, bypassing informal trails to the right and left. Next go through the first of two rock passes, clefts created by the separation of the rock. Large blocks of conglomerate break off at the edge of rock ledges because the underlying shale is softer and more easily eroded. Settling causes cracks, fissures, and large cavelike crevices to develop.

At the top of the first pass, do not take the rock steps on the right but continue straight ahead on the main trail to reach the second rock pass, another narrow, rocky cleft formed in the massive sandstone. Note the ledge of Sharon Conglomerate.

5 As you approach the far west part of the Gorge Trail loop, you will hike up through the pass, a narrow crevice, ascending on rock steps to the top of the slope.

Here the trail goes left, and at the trail sign it curves around to the east. Follow the trail carefully as it switchbacks down the slope on log steps. At the bottom of the steps, the trail goes left (east). Some of the river rapids common in the gorge can be seen below.

6 Continue along the trail to a bridge over a side stream. Below on the right, rapids appear in the river as the water leaves the dam.

7 Wooden fencing borders the trail as it reaches an overlook from which you can view the dam and river. Built in 1914, this dam was only used to generate electricity for a few years before a more efficient coal-fired generator plant was built on the river east of here (it closed in 1992).

8 Continue on the loop trail, staying on the lower level, nearest the river. (Steps to the left connect the lower level of the trail to the upper level.) Just below the picnic shelter, an accessible pier provides a safe place from which to fish.

9 The last portion of trail, from the fishing pier on, is asphalt-paved. Stay on this trail to reach the parking area. ∎

Hike B: Glens Trail and Riverfront Walk

Distance: 3.9 miles

Easy

Hiking time: 2.0 hours

Description: This hike begins on the well-marked Glens Trail along the Cuyahoga River, then climbs to Front St. and follows city streets for a few blocks to connect to the Riverfront Centre Boardwalk. The hike returns to the start of the boardwalk via the Riverfront Centre Mall, then retraces the rest of the route along city streets and the Glens Trail, back to the parking area.

10 Walk south through the parking lot to the exit and cross Front St. at the traffic light to begin the Glens Trail. The entry is located just south of the crosswalk. This trail is sandwiched between the Cuyahoga River and steep sandstone cliffs.

11 This scenic trail affords views high above the Cuyahoga River. Here the river's flow is slowed and impounded by the dam downstream. Directly across the river is the huge electric generating plant of the Ohio Edison Company, now closed. The large twin smokestacks remain from the period when electricity was produced by coal-fired steam generators.

Continue on the trail, following the west bank of the Cuyahoga River. Upstream from the power plant, on the east bank of the river, are the remains of several stone walls. Although the east bank of the river is now fairly inaccessible, the walls would suggest there was a time when there was more activity on that side of the river.

12 Near-vertical cliffs border the left side of the trail. At about 0.6 mile on the left is a huge rock overhang and just beyond, a sheer rock wall with a small spring (unsafe for drinking) flowing from its base. The spring provides enough moisture for liverworts, tiny ancient plants that depend on moist environments to thrive. Fossils of liverworts reveal to us that they have existed on earth for 400 million years. This quiet, shady trail is a delight in the heat of summer and harbors many wildflowers in the spring.

13 At the end of the trail, bear left and climb stone steps up the hill and out to Front St. near the American Legion Hall. Turn right (east) on Front St., walk 0.1 mile to Prospect St., and turn right again.

14 A wooden pedestrian observation platform offers a spectacular view of the Cuyahoga River. To the north are cascading falls and rapids, and to the south is a view into the narrowest part of the gorge. A century ago this gorge was crowded with mills and factories taking advantage of the water power.

From the platform, go back on Prospect to Front St., turn right, and walk north on Front St. to the Sheraton Suites hotel.

The hotel was designed to take advantage of the natural setting: the building hugs the edge of the gorge, and the restaurant and guest rooms overlook the cascades of the river. The hotel has earned a top rating among Sheratons nationwide.

At the north end of the hotel parking lot, go on the wooden boardwalk. The boardwalk begins at an outdoor bar (open Friday evenings in the summer). Descend the steps to walk under the Broad Blvd. bridge.

16 The boardwalk follows the river upstream, going up and down several sets of steps along the way, and passes the ruins of an old riverfront building. Here and there are tables and benches inviting a rest to view the ever-changing river. Pedestrians on Front St. may enter or exit the walk at several points. Reach a small riverfront amphitheater at Portage Trail.

17 Continue on the boardwalk until it ends, then follow the sidewalk past riverfront restaurants, offices, and condos. The restaurant on the right incorporates the remains of an old powerhouse, and has indoor and outdoor dining overlooking the river. The sidewalk ends at Cuyahoga Falls's North Pier Boardwalk, a city dock from which pontoon boat rides depart.

18 Retrace your steps back past the condos and watch on the right for a set of broad steps and a sign for Riverfront Centre Fountain. Climb the steps to the stone and marble fountain. You are now at the north end of Riverfront Centre Mall, a brick pedestrian mall lined with shops and other businesses. Turn left to walk south through the mall. Cuyahoga Falls hosts festivals, performances, and other public events here on the mall and at the amphitheater. Return to Sheraton Suites by continuing south, crossing Portage Trail and Broad Blvd. at street level, or return via the boardwalk by reentering it at one of the access stairways.

From the Sheraton Suites, retrace your steps to the American Legion Hall and the Glens Trail, back to the start of the hike. ■

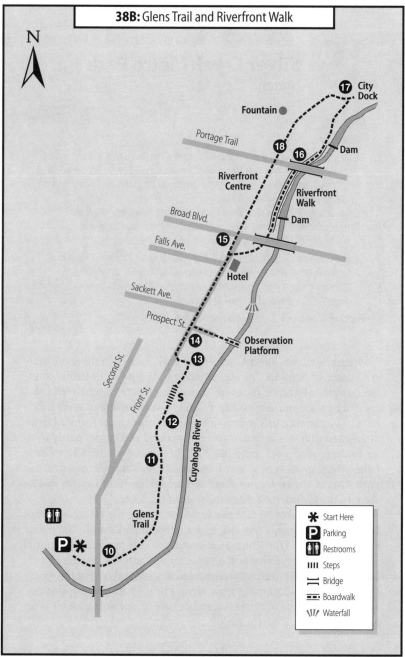

38B: Glens Trail and Riverfront Walk

N

City Dock 17

Fountain

Portage Trail

18 16 Dam

Riverfront Centre

Riverfront Walk

Broad Blvd.

Dam

Falls Ave.

15

Hotel

Sackett Ave.

Prospect St.

14 Observation Platform

Second St.

13

Front St.

S

12

Cuyahoga River

11

Glens Trail

10

	Start Here
P	Parking
	Restrooms
IIII	Steps
⊐⊏	Bridge
▭	Boardwalk
\\//	Waterfall

© Gray & Company, Publishers

39 Silver Creek Metro Park
Norton

Distance: 3.2 miles

Easy

Hiking time: 1.5 hours

Description: Two loop walks comprise this hike. The first is over flat and mildly rolling farmland and through wooded forests on the 2-mile Chippewa Trail. This trail passes an old barn, circles a small pond, and crosses Silver Creek and its tributaries several times.
Pheasant Run trail is reached midway and adds an additional 1.2-mile, nearly flat loop through fields and forests. Informational signs along the trails point out interesting tree species and other features.

Directions: From I-77 take Exit 136 (SR 21); south on SR 21 past I-76 and Norton to exit for SR 585 west; immediately exit to Hametown Rd.; left onto Hametown for 0.4 mile; left into the park; left at T intersection; cross dam for Silver Creek Lake; left into the Big Oak Area.

Parking & restrooms: At Big Oak Picnic Area.

Open since 1966, Silver Creek Metro Park, located in the southwestern corner of Summit County (adjacent to Wayne and Medina counties), covers 616 acres. Its major feature is 50-acre Silver Creek Lake, created by the damming of Silver Creek. Gathering many small tributaries along its way, this stream flows south through the former Harter family dairy farm. The water flows year round and comes partly from an underground coal mine on Wall Rd., northwest of Silver Creek Lake. Abandoned coal mines from the 1930s underlie most of this park. One of the largest northern red oaks in Summit County can be seen on the Chippewa Trail at the start of the hike.

A fully accessible bathhouse includes restrooms, changing areas, first aid and lifeguard stations, and a refreshments stand. The public swimming beach (for which a fee is charged) is open from Memorial Day to Labor Day. Parts of the surface and shoreline of Silver Creek Lake are restricted to allow undisturbed nesting and resting for waterfowl. Children's play areas, picnic areas, a bridle path, fishing, boating, swimming, wildlife observation, and cross-country skiing are all available at Silver Creek Metro Park.

1 Enter the Chippewa Trail (marked with a tomahawk symbol) at the west side of the parking lot. To the right (north) of the mulched trail there is a small pond. Behind the fence on the left is a huge north-

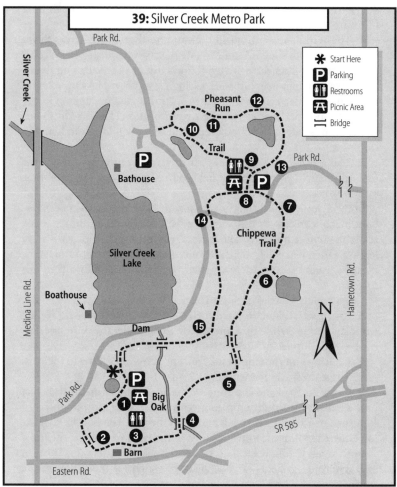

ern red oak. With a 20-foot circumference around its double trunk, its spreading limbs are supported by several steel cables. This grand old oak, estimated to be 150–200 years old, is considered one of the largest in Summit County. Its leaves, with between 7 and 11 pointed, toothed lobes, turn bright red in the autumn. This oak drops thousands of acorns in the fall, some of which sprout and propagate many smaller red oaks nearby. Continue ahead.

2 Cross a small footbridge and pass old farm buildings that once belonged to the Harter family dairy farm—two silos, a granary, and a shed. Part of the barn dates from the Civil War.

3 Enter a stand of young red pines. These trees were planted as seedlings by Girl Scouts of the Western Reserve Council between 1967 and 1983 in a series of Arbor Day events. Local scouts planted about

40,000 seedlings at various places in the park to initiate the beginning of future forests here.

4 The trail bends around to the east and then north. Cross Silver Creek on a footbridge (0.5-mile). Note the rusty, reddish-brown color of the water in the stream. When it flows out of the coal-mine shafts, the water is rich in iron but sterile. Moving south, it picks up oxygen, nutrients, and bacteria that produce an iron-oxide precipitate in the form of a powder that covers the stream bottom. These reddish deposits do not deter fish, amphibians, and other wildlife from living in the creek.

5 The mowed path continues across an open meadow toward the east. In the field you might see field sparrows, goldfinches, bluebirds, or butterflies.

Enter a young beech/oak/maple forest. Note the occasional shagbark hickory tree, with its distinctive bark composed of thin, narrow scales that curve outward. The leaves are 8 to 14 inches long with five leaflets. Often you will find hickory nuts scattered on the ground below this tree. In the spring, there are many varieties of wildflowers in this forest.

Cross two tributaries of Silver Creek.

6 Reach a trail junction and turn right (southeast) to visit a small woodland pond. White pine and spruce trees border the shoreline. Return to the Chippewa Trail.

7 Continue on the Chippewa Trail and cross a meadow to the park entry drive from Hametown Rd. (1.2 miles).

8 Cross the road and continue a very short distance on the trail. Just past a bench, turn right on a connector trail leading to the Pheasant Run Area parking lot. Turn left and go to the north end of the parking lot; enter the Pheasant Run Trail, just to the right of a picnic shelter.

9 Bear left to follow the loop trail in a clockwise direction. The trail begins through a field—a good place to watch for butterflies in the summer—and soon enters a woodland.

10 On the left is a small woodland pond (1.4 miles). Ponds of this type are important breeding habitat for amphibians, such as salamanders and wood frogs, and aquatic insects, such as dragonflies and damselflies. Just past the pond is a trail intersection. The trail to the left goes to the park road and bathhouse/swimming area. Continue straight ahead, staying on the Pheasant Run Trail.

11 The trail swings northeast, staying nearly level, leaves the forest, passes through scrub meadows and then through pines.

12 Here you reach a larger pond (1.7 miles), good habitat for "puddle ducks," such as mallards and wood ducks. These species feed on aquatic plants, seeds, and insects by dabbling and upending. Raccoons, deer, and other mammals visit the pond, and songbirds nest along the shores.

13 Continue on the trail through the scrub meadow, to the end of

the loop. Bear left and retrace your steps back through the parking lot to the connector trail. Turn right, walk a short way, then turn right again to get back onto the Chippewa Trail. The trail enters another forested section.

14 Next the path turns left (south) and re-crosses the park entry road (2.6 miles). Continue toward the dam and lake, enjoying a view across the field to the lake. Using binoculars, you might spot gulls, Canada geese, grebes, or mergansers on the lake. Red-tailed hawks prefer the open field. Notice the piles of boulders at the edge of the field: they are glacial erratics, gathered into piles by the farmer when this area was under cultivation.

15 The trail leads down below the dam and then crosses a bridge over the lake's outlet stream. Cross the last small footbridge over another of the rust-colored creeks to reach the Big Oak Picnic Area (3.2 miles). ■

I am monarch of all I survey
My right there is none to dispute.
            —Henry David Thoreau, *Walden*

40 Goodyear Heights Metro Park
Akron

Distance: 3.1 miles

Moderate

Hiking time: 1³/₄ hours

Description: The trails in Goodyear Heights Metro Park follow rolling hills through forests of pine, beech, maple, and tuliptrees. Alder Pond, an oasis in this urban park, offers wintertime ice-skating.

Directions: From I-76 (in Akron, after it splits from 1-77 on the east side of town), take Exit 27; follow signs to SR 91; north on SR 91 for ¹/₂ mile; left on Newton; park entrance on right.

Parking & restrooms: After entering the park, continue past first parking area on the right to second one straight ahead. Restrooms are here.

Located in Summit County south of Tallmadge, this 410-acre park opened in 1930 after Goodyear Tire & Rubber Co. and local farmer Gilbert Waltz each donated land for public recreation. During the Depression, work relief crews planted thousands of Scotch and white pines and tuliptrees, built a shelter at Alder Pond, and deepened the pond at its southern end. In the 1950s, Goodyear donated money for extensive park development that included a 37-acre playing field, a sledding hill, a much larger picnic shelter building, and other amenities.

Goodyear Heights Metro Park is frequently used by runners and local high school cross-country teams.

1 Start the hike at the northwest end of the parking area, going past the picnic tables on the right to an unmarked path. (Do not take the trails going east and north.) Follow the path northwest to Carver St. and continue west on Carver St. past Elko St. to another Metro Parks parking lot.

2 At the far end of this parking area enter the Alder Trail at the trail-head sign. At the first fork in the trail go straight ahead. At the second fork, bear left on the Alder Trail. Continue past the restrooms to Alder Pond.

3 Alder Pond, a popular place for ice-skating, is a tranquil spot at most any time of the year (0.4 mile).

Turn right (east) on the path nearest the pond.

4 At the next trail intersection, turn left (north) onto the Piney Woods Trail, a wide track marked with a pine tree symbol.

Cross a small stream.

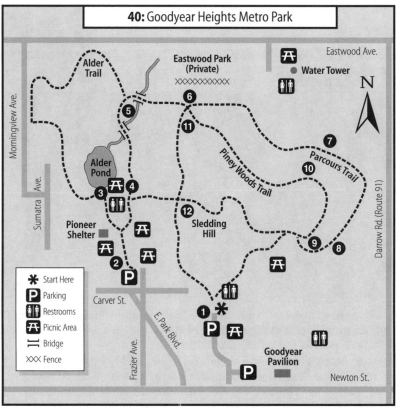

© Gray & Company, Publishers

5 Reach a trail intersection at 0.8 mile and turn right (east), staying on the Piney Woods Trail (the Alder Trail goes to the left). Cross the stream on another bridge. Continue uphill alongside a fence enclosing Eastwood Park, a privately owned pool and picnic park.

6 Reach a four-way trail intersection and turn left (east) on the Parcours Trail, marked with a jumping-jack symbol. Pass exercise stations 7, 8, 9, 10, and 11. The ball fields and water tower on the left are on Eastwood Ave.

7 Between exercise stations 11 and 12, a trail on the left loops around the water tower. (This optional 0.5-mile loop returns to the main trail just past station 13.)

Continue southeast past exercise stations 12–18 through a forest.

8 The path gradually bends southwest and crosses a wooden foot bridge at 1.8 miles. Continue past a path on the left.

Continue the walk uphill through a white pine forest. These tall trees are some of the small seedlings planted by relief workers during the 1930s soon after the park opened. After more than 60 years they

have grown to more than 70 feet tall. You can identify the eastern white pine by its bundle of five needles (W-H-I-T-E).

Pass exercise station 19.

9 Reach a trail junction (2 miles). Turn right (north) onto the Piney Woods Trail. Continue on this loop as it bends north then west.

10 Still on the Piney Woods Trail, follow the path through a beautiful forest of tall maple and beech trees to the four-way junction reached in Note #6. Eastwood Park is again ahead on the right (2.4 miles).

11 Turn left (southwest) at this next four-way trail junction to re-enter the Parcours Trail. Continue past exercise stations 7, 6, 5, and 4.

12 Reach another four-way trail junction and continue straight ahead (south) on the Parcours Trail. Just past exercise station 3 bear left uphill. Continue on the main trail as it winds uphill and downhill past stations 2 and 1. Pass a trail on the left (it goes to the sledding hill) and return to the parking area. ■

41 O'Neil Woods Metro Park & Schumacher Woods Bath

Distance: 6 miles (the Deer Run Trail is a 1.8-mile loop and the Buckeye Trail section is 4.2 miles round trip)

Strenuous

Hiking time: 3.5 hours (1 hour for the Deer Run Trail alone and 2.5 hours for the Buckeye Trail)

Description: This hike combines Deer Run Trail in O'Neil Woods Metro Park with a section of the Buckeye Trail in an adjacent area of Cuyahoga Valley National Park known as Schumacher Woods. Deer Run Trail is marked with a deer hoofprint symbol on trail signs. The Buckeye Trail intersects with Deer Run Trail just east of the O'Neil Woods parking lot. Blue blazes on trees mark the Buckeye Trail. Follow the blazes carefully, as many side paths wander through the Schumacher Woods area. Habitats along the route of the hike include mature mixed deciduous forest, pine woods, ravines, meadows, and creek valleys.

Directions: From Cleveland take I-271 to Exit 12 (SR 303); east on SR 303 to Peninsula; right (south) on Riverview Rd. at traffic light (just before crossing bridge over Cuyahoga River); continue past Everett Rd. and Indigo Lake; right (west) on Ira Rd.; left (southwest) on Martin Rd.; park entrance on left.

From Akron take Akron-Peninsula Rd. north; west on Bath Rd.; cross Cuyahoga River; bear right at intersection with Yellow Creek Rd. (stay on Bath); right on Shade Rd.; right on Martin Rd.; park entrance on right.

Parking & restrooms: Parking and restrooms are at the end of the entrance road.

O'Neil Woods Metro Park is a unit of Metro Parks, Serving Summit County. Located in Bath Township at the southern end of Cuyahoga Valley National Park (CVNP) and west of Hampton Hills Metro Park, this small, hilly, 295-acre park opened for public use in 1969. In 1968, M. Gerald O'Neil, the president of General Tire and Rubber Company, gave the park district permission to lease his family farm as a public park. The family later donated the farm outright, which led to the creation of the Metro Park. O'Neil, and his family had used the land for farming, horseback riding, and family gatherings since the 1930s. Their large white barn is visible from the trail at Bath Rd.

Deer Run is O'Neil Woods's only trail, a 1.8-mile loop. When taken in a clockwise direction, it descends a steep ridge, is joined by the Buckeye Trail (BT), follows the course of Yellow Creek a short distance, and then climbs back up out of the valley.

The blue-blazed BT then continues from the east end of the parking lot and gradually descends through Schumacher Woods to Ira Rd. The BT is identified by 2-by-6-inch rectangular blue tree blazes. This forest, through which the BT travels, was part of the pioneer-era farm of Conrad Botzum. The most recent owners, prior to acquisition by the National Park Service, were Sherman and Mary Schumacher, who enjoyed sharing the land with friends and visitors. The Schumachers owned another exceptional piece of property in Akron, which they donated to Metro Parks, Serving Summit County; known as Schumacher Valley, it is now part of Cascade Valley Park.

There are many varieties of trees, birds, and wildflowers both on the upper hilltop and in the stream valley; occasionally deer may be spotted here.

Of interest on the drive to the park is a nesting colony of great blue herons. These huge birds have built their nests in tall sycamore trees on the south side of Bath Rd., west of Akron-Peninsula Rd., near the Cuyahoga River. In April and May these four-foot-tall birds can be seen standing guard over their large nests made of sticks.

1 The trailhead for Deer Run Trail is at the east end of the parking area. This wide, well-marked trail soon enters the woods. Pass an intersection for the Buckeye Trail on the left and ascend an oak ridgetop. (This intersection is where the Buckeye Trail descends to Ira Rd. through Schumacher Woods on the second portion of this hike.) After about 0.4 mile the trail begins to descend the narrow ridge on steps.

2 The 180-foot drop continues steeply downhill on more steps and narrow switchback paths to yet another set of steps at the bottom of the ridge.

3 Cross Bath Rd. at 0.7 mile and note the large white O'Neil barn on the south side of the road. Arrive at Yellow Creek flowing east to the Cuyahoga River. The tall trees that thrive in this moist environment are cottonwoods, walnuts, sycamores, and willows. Many wildflowers, ferns, and bittersweet vines also grow here. Erosion occurs as the creek cuts into the loose, sandy soil.

4 Follow the trail west. Cross two wooden bridges over side streams as the trail leaves the creek at a point near the end of a field (1.2 miles).

5 Cross a tributary stream on a bridge and reach Bath Rd. again. Cross the road and begin ascending the hill. Partway uphill is a bench at which to pause and enjoy the tall oak/maple/beech forest. Continue ascending the steep hill and come to another welcoming bench before reaching the summit and parking lot.

6 Just before the end of the trail are old apple trees and a barn foundation. The blue blazes of the BT continue across the parking lot to its east end.

7 Reenter the Deer Run Trail, but this time (1.9 miles), take the left fork in the trail onto the well-marked, blue-blazed BT. You can often

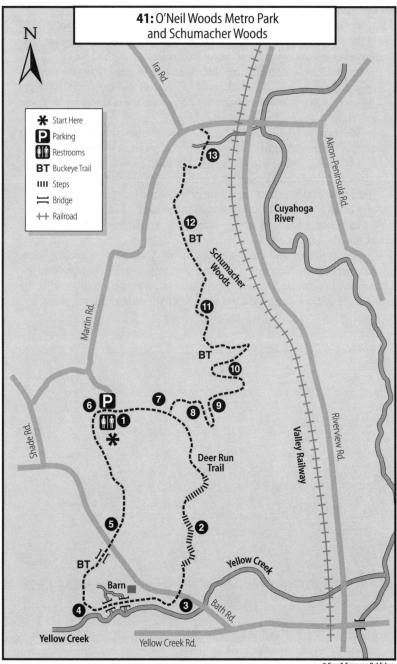

41: O'Neil Woods Metro Park and Schumacher Woods

N

* Start Here
P Parking
Restrooms
BT Buckeye Trail
IIII Steps
Bridge
++ Railroad

Ira Rd.

Akron-Peninsula Rd.

Cuyahoga River

13

12
BT

Schumacher Woods

11

BT
10

Martin Rd.

6 P 7
   1   8   9

*

Shade Rd.

Deer Run Trail

5

2

BT

Barn

4   3

Yellow Creek

Bath Rd.

Yellow Creek

Valley Railway

Riverview Rd.

Yellow Creek Rd.

© Gray & Company, Publishers

see bluebirds here, as the park provides them with nesting boxes in the meadow.

8 Enter the woods and reach a trail junction (2.0 miles). Follow the BT as it turns right (south), then continues east briefly. In spring, wildflowers bloom along the slopes of side valleys near the trail.

9 At 2.2 miles the BT turns left (north) and quickly makes another turn right (east). The BT makes use of some of the jeep trails that were maintained by the Schumachers. Other jeep trails intersect with the BT, so watch carefully for the blue blazes.

10 At about 2.8 miles the trail turns west, then north along a beech ridge. The historic Botzum Farm is far below in a clearing.

11 At 3.2 miles, the path enters a pine forest. Deer often move through the woods here and along the stream below. Coyotes have also been seen and heard in the Schumacher woods.

12 At 3.8 miles the BT descends the ridge.

13 Cross a creek on stones to reach the end of this section of the BT at Martin and Ira roads.

Turn around and return by retracing your steps through Schumacher Woods, following the BT in reverse. Cross the creek, ascend the hill, and continue following the blue blazes to the junction with the Deer Run Trail. Bear right to the O'Neil Woods parking lot. ■

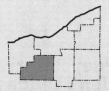

MEDINA COUNTY

The city of Medina sits near the very center of rural Medina County. Distinguishing the town is its restored public square. Medina, established in 1818, was built on the model of a New England village, with commercial businesses and government buildings surrounding a public square. After a devastating fire in 1870 destroyed most of the buildings on the square, they were rebuilt in the Victorian style. By the 1960s they had been changed and updated in various ways during various eras, leaving the town square looking patched together. As a result, the people of Medina formed the nonprofit Community Design Committee and launched a historic preservation/restoration effort that has resulted in one of the most attractive town squares in the state. In 1975 the square achieved the distinction of being listed in the National Register of Historic Places.

One of Medina's many town parks is 316-acre Reagan Park, located northeast of the city off Weymouth Rd. (SR 3). Among its recreational facilities are nature, fitness, and cross-country ski trails and an ice-skating rink.

For more information about Medina, call the Medina Area Chamber of Commerce: 330-723-8773 or the Medina County Convention and Visitors Bureau: 330-722-5502.

Medina County is home to one of Cleveland Metroparks's 14 reservations, Hinckley Reservation. A 90-acre lake in its midst, the ancient Whipp's and Worden's Ledges, and an annual celebration of the return of the buzzards (turkey vultures) contribute to Hinckley Reservation's popularity.

The Medina County Park District includes the following parks: Green Leaf, Hubbard Valley, Buckeye Woods, Letha House, Plum Creek, River Styx, Allardale, and Alderfer-Oenslager Wildlife Sanctuary, which includes Wolf Creek Environmental Center. York Rail Trail, northwest of Media, and Chippewa Rail Trail, south of Medina, will eventually be linked into one continuous multi-use trail. The park district is also restoring wetlands along Chippewa Lake, Ohio's largest natural inland lake, in the Chippewa Nature Preserve. The district continues to add acreage to Princess Ledges Nature Preserve and plans to open this area to the public in the future. Hidden Hollow Park is a special-use area available to organized groups for camping, hiking, and nature study. Information is available from Medina County Park District: 330-722-9364.

42 Hinckley Reservation: Worden's Ledges
Hinckley

Distance: 1-mile round trip

Easy

Hiking time: 1 hour

Description: The trail is not marked, but it can be followed with this description and map or by referring to the map posted on a garage adjacent to the Worden Heritage Homestead. The ledges are located directly under the hill below the homestead; the carvings are not difficult to find. Worden Heritage Homestead is managed by the Hinckley Historical Society and is usually open on Sunday afternoons in the summer (330-278-2154).

Directions: From Cleveland take I-271 to Exit 3 for SR 94 (North Royalton); right (north) on SR 94 (Ridge Rd.); right (east) on Ledge Rd.; pass Kellogg Rd. and Ledge Lake Pool to the Worden Heritage Homestead, about 1 mile ahead on left.

From Akron, take I-77 north to exit for SR 18; west on SR 18; north on SR 94; right (east) on Ledge Rd.; pass Kellogg Rd. and Ledge Lake Pool to the Worden Heritage Homestead, about 1 mile ahead on left.

Parking & restrooms: Very little parking is available at Worden Heritage Homestead, but a few cars can be parked along the side of the driveway. A restroom is available inside the museum, when open.

In 1851 Hiram Worden bought land in Medina County from the estate of Samuel Hinckley; it would later become Hinckley Reservation, one of 14 Cleveland Metroparks reservations (and the only one located outside Cuyahoga County). The Worden Heritage Homestead at 895 Ledge Rd. was built by Hiram Worden in 1862, the year his daughter Nettie was born, and was occupied by his farming family and their descendants until the 1980s. Nettie, who lived in the house all her life until her death in 1945, married her third husband, Noble Stuart (20 years her junior), in 1944. Noble and his son, George Stuart, continued to stay in the house until George's death in 1984, when Cleveland Metroparks acquired the home and Hinckley Historical Society became its manager.

Noble Stuart, a bricklayer, homebuilder, wanderer, and, most significantly, folk artist, began carving wood and wet concrete after his marriage to Nettie. He discovered huge sandstone ledges a half-mile beyond the Worden home and proceeded to carve figures and faces and other objects in the ledges over a period of several years. The carvings, which are gradually deteriorating, reflect aspects of Stuart's personal

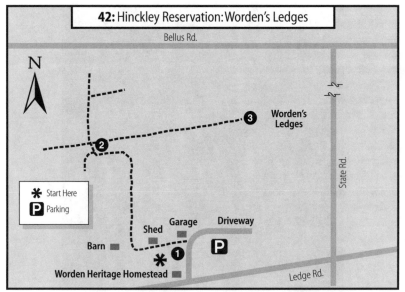

42: Hinckley Reservation: Worden's Ledges

Bellus Rd.

N

Worden's Ledges

State Rd.

✱ Start Here

P Parking

Garage   Driveway

Shed

Barn

P

Worden Heritage Homestead

Ledge Rd.

© Gray & Company, Publishers

life and his interest in history and range from a bust of his father-in-law to likenesses of George Washington and the Marquis de Lafayette.

Although Stuart was a skillful craftsman, authorities do not consider him a significant artist. He died in 1976 at the age of 94. When asked in 1948 why he did the carvings, he said he simply wanted to keep practicing stone carving and leave something that would last.

West of Worden Heritage Homestead on Ledge Rd. is popular Ledge Lake Pool and Recreation Area (216-351-6300). A small admission charge allows visitors to use the 80-by-100-foot pool, changing facilities, and picnic area. Seniors over 65 and children 5 and under are admitted free. It is open 10 A.M. to 8:30 P.M. Memorial Day to Labor Day.

Hinckley Reservation contains hiking trails, picnic areas, and an additional swimming area on Hinckley Lake that can be reached from Bellus Rd. Trail information is available from Cleveland Metroparks.

1 From the homestead, reach the trail to the ledges by going west parallel to Ledge Rd. (on your left) and past the sheds (on your right). Turn right (north) just before the barn and follow a farm lane past an abandoned gas well on the left. Soon the path curves around to the left and gently descends a small hill. The trail may be muddy, as it is also used by horses.

2 Near the foot of the slope ignore the minor trail going off to the left and turn right (east) immediately. Follow the trail until you see large Sharon Conglomerate sandstone ledges on the path directly ahead.

3 At the farthest set of rock outcroppings, you will see on the left an

eight-foot-long sphinx carved on top of a rock. This imposing creature seems to guard the entrance to the ledges area. Next is a large rock with "H. M. Worden 1851" carved on its face. On the northwest corner of this rock Stuart carved a bust of his father-in-law, to which he later added a cement beard when he noticed a photo of him sporting this adornment. "Nettie" is deeply incised in the next rock. A schooner can be seen high up on a ledge to the right. Farther along, also on a ledge to the right, are a cross and Bible intricately carved into the stone. Ty Cobb's face and name are on a north-facing outcropping, nearly obscured by moss.

Worden's Ledges were formed by the same ancient processes that shaped Whipp's Ledges (Ch. 45), located in another part of Hinckley Reservation. Other ledge formations can be found in Nelson Ledges State Park (Ch. 17), Chapin Forest Reservation (Ch. 8), and the Virginia Kendall area of Cuyahoga Valley National Park.

The rock forming these ledges is called Sharon Conglomerate sandstone because it is composed of sand and quartz. Embedded in it are white quartz pebbles that were washed downstream from a quartz-rich area of Canada. Pebbles mixed with sand and both eventually hardened to form the rock ledges we now see.

Return to Worden Heritage Homestead by retracing your steps in the reverse direction. ■

43 Hubbard Valley Park
Guilford Township

Distance: 1.3 miles

Easy

Hiking time: ½ hour

Description: This easy trail encircles Hubbard Valley Lake on a generally flat path. The first half of the hike allows enjoyable views of the water and its wildlife, and the last part, a pleasant walk through the woods.

Directions: From the north, take I-71 to Exit 218 (Medina/SR 18); west on SR 18 to Medina; south on SR 3 for about 6 miles; cross over I-71; left (east) on Blake Rd. (County Rd. 118) for 0.7 mile; right (south) on Hubbard Valley Rd. (Township Rd. 93) for 0.6 mile; park entrance on right.

From the south, take I-71 to Exit 209; east on SR 224/I-76 to Exit 2 (SR 3); north on SR 3; east on Blake Rd. (County Rd. 118) for 0.7 mile; right (south) on Hubbard Valley Rd. (Township Rd. 93) for 0.6 mile; park entrance on right.

Parking & restrooms: Park in the parking area just inside the entrance; restrooms are located here.

Hubbard Valley Park is one of Medina County Park District's parks and is dominated by an 18-acre fishing lake. This small, scenic park, located in the southern part of the county near Chippewa Lake, offers picnic shelters, a boat launching area, an observation overlook, a playground, and a hiking trail that surrounds Hubbard Valley Lake. Fishing for several different species is permitted from the shore or in a rowboat. Information about Hubbard Valley Park can be obtained from Medina County Park District, 330-722-9364.

1 Enter the paved All-Purpose Trail at the southwest end of the parking area near the kiosk, walking clockwise around the large lake. Lakeside Picnic Shelter is on the left.

Ahead is a sweeping view of the water. Often various kinds of waterfowl congregate here in large numbers, especially during migration seasons.

2 Continue on the paved trail past the boat launch facility, then up the slope. Go past the playground to the second mowed path, where there is a stone with a plaque on it. Follow this path across the dam. From the hill above are clear views of the lake. The trail is bordered in the fall by purple asters and yellow goldenrods. Butterflies often flit around these abundant wildflowers.

3 At the far end of the dam the trail turns right (north) through the woods, then bends left.

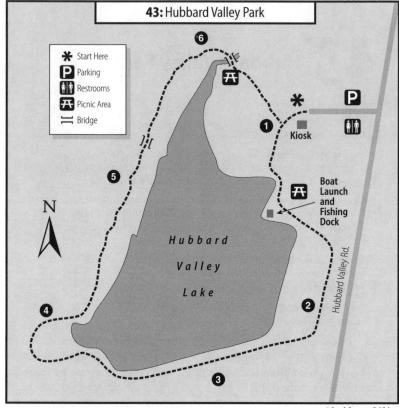

© Gray & Company, Publishers

4 The trail goes north through a meadow, then reenters the woods. Hubbard Valley Lake is to the right. The pleasant path winds through maples, beeches, and tuliptrees. On the left, an old farm fence lines the pathway.

5 At 0.8 mile pass a park bench on the right overlooking the lake. Cross a wooden bridge as the trail veers away from the water.

6 The path bends south at 1.2 miles, then bears left to cross another bridge.

Exit from the trail at a picnic shelter, and cross the lawn to the parking area to complete the loop. ■

44 Plum Creek Park
Brunswick Hills Township

Distance: 1.4 miles

Easy

Hiking time: ³/₄ hour

Description: This easy hike follows fairly flat terrain on a wide trail. Although Plum Creek itself is east of the park (and east of Plum Creek Pkwy.), several other smaller creeks in the park are crossed on wooden bridges.

Directions: From I-71 take Exit 222 (Medina/SR 3); turn to follow SR 3 south but take immediate right (west) on Hamilton Rd. for 0.8 mile; right (north) on Plum Creek Pkwy. for about 1 mile; left on S. Park Dr.; park close to the restrooms and shelter. N. Park Dr. is 100 yards north.

Parking & restrooms: Restrooms are located at both paved parking areas.

Plum Creek Park is located on Plum Creek Pkwy. off Hamilton Rd. in the northern part of Medina County. This pleasant park, part of which was once a landfill, is a good example of land reclamation. Available here are two fishing ponds, a nature trail, a demonstration wildlife planting, picnic tables, and reservable shelters. Acquisition of 74 additional acres of land west of the developed area brings this park's total land area to 191 acres.

Information about Plum Creek Park is available from Medina County Park District, 330-722-9364.

1 Enter the Nature Trail at the sign at the end of a paved path leaving from the south parking area. Walk straight ahead, following the green arrow sign. This is a new-growth forest consisting predominantly of young maple trees. Wildflowers also abound in this environment.

At 0.2 mile the trail bends to the north, goes down steps, and crosses a brook on a bridge. After another 0.1 mile, you will pass a deep ravine on the left, then descend a small set of steps.

2 Cross a boardwalk and bear left (north) to cross another wooden bridge. A bench at the top of a gentle rise invites a pause to contemplate this peaceful woods.

The trail now heads west above the ravine on the left, then northwest.

3 At a trail junction (0.45 mile), stay to the right on the main trail. The path bends north, then west.

4 At another trail junction, stay to the right. Descend some steps, cross a small bridge, and ascend the next set of steps.

5 The trail heads east, then southeast. At 0.6 mile, descend a small

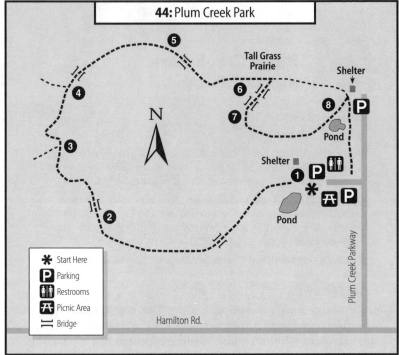

44: Plum Creek Park

Tall Grass
Prairie

Shelter

5

4

N

6

8

P

7

3

Pond

Shelter ■

1

P

2

Pond

Plum Creek Parkway

✳ Start Here
P Parking
🚻 Restrooms
⛱ Picnic Area
〕〔 Bridge

Hamilton Rd.

© Gray & Company, Publishers

hill to cross another bridge. The path now heads south. In the spring there are many beautiful wildflowers along here.

6 (0.7 mile) Reach a small circular demonstration planting. Turn right (southwest) on the main trail. (Ahead is a mowed, grassy path that leads to an enclosed, all-weather picnic shelter.)

7 Continue westward on the main Nature Trail. Cross a small bridge and hike through a tall beech forest. Other tall trees here include the cucumber magnolia and tuliptree. Cross another bridge over a stream.

8 At 1 mile the trail heads east and crosses an open meadow. Head to the left (east) at this meadow and pass a pond on the right. Dogwood trees bloom along here in the springtime.

Bear right to pass the small shelter. Continue on the path a few steps (east) to a parking lot.

Turn right (south) on N. Park Dr. for about 100 yards. Turn right (west) onto a trail, then immediately south over a boardwalk to reach the south parking lot. ■

45 Hinckley Reservation: Whipp's Ledges Hinckley

Distance: 5 miles

Strenuous

Hiking time: 2½ hours

Description: This hike, partly on the blue-blazed Buckeye Trail along Hinckley Lake, goes to Whipp's Ledges and returns mostly on a gravel trail along both sides of the lake to complete a loop. There is one steep hill to climb.

Directions: From I-271 take Exit 3 for Ridge Rd. (SR 94, Remson Corners); north on Ridge Rd.; right (east) on Hinckley Hills Rd. (SR 606); right (east) on Bellus Rd.; right (south) on West Dr. into reservation for 0.75 mile to sign for Boat House/Johnson's Picnic Area.

Parking & restrooms: Drive past the Boat House and go to Johnson's Picnic Area. Park in the second parking area, where the road dead-ends.

Hinckley Reservation, a Cleveland Metropark, surrounds 90-acre Hinckley Lake, into which the east branch of the Rocky River flows. The river was dammed in 1926 to form this beautiful lake. Hinckley, located in Medina County, is the only Cleveland Metroparks reservation outside Cuyahoga County. In it are Whipp's Ledges and Worden's Ledges (Ch. 42).

Hinckley is well known for its celebration (on the Sunday following March 15) of the annual migratory return of the buzzards (turkey vultures) from the south. The buzzards find the open fields, rocky ledges and cliffs, and abundant food an ideal habitat for nesting. In the spring and summer they can be seen soaring on the rising warm-air thermals created by the open fields.

1 Start the hike at Johnson's Picnic Area by finding the blue-blazed Buckeye Trail (BT). Access the BT by following the All-Purpose Trail across a bridge. Watch for the BT heading north on the uphill gravel path. The blue blazes are on the tall trees. The creek will be below on the left. Hinckley Lake comes into view along this route.

2 Turn left on State Rd. at about 0.7 mile and continue on the road across a sturdy pedestrian/bicycle bridge over the East Branch of the Rocky River.

3 Cross State Rd. and turn right onto Whipp's Ledges Rd., which leads to a picnic area. Immediately to the right the BT turns east from the road alongside a small creek, a tributary of the Rocky River.

4 The BT continues through a wet area, then goes into the woods and uphill.

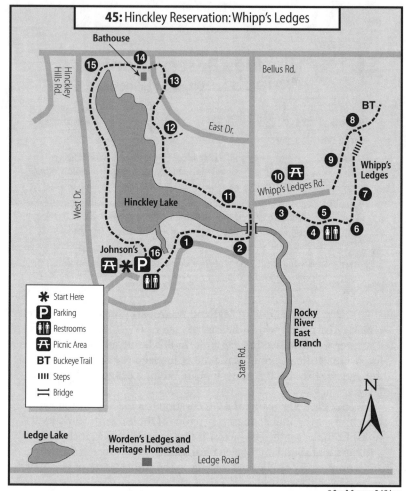

45: Hinckley Reservation: Whipp's Ledges

Bathouse

Hinckley Hills Rd.

Bellus Rd.

BT

East Dr.

Whipp's Ledges

West Dr.

Hinckley Lake

Whipp's Ledges Rd.

Johnson's

Rocky River East Branch

State Rd.

Start Here
P Parking
Restrooms
Picnic Area
BT Buckeye Trail
IIII Steps
Bridge

Ledge Lake

Worden's Ledges and Heritage Homestead

Ledge Road

N

© Gray & Company, Publishers

5 At 1.2 miles reach a stone restroom at Whipp's Ledges picnic and parking area. The BT turns right, then continues straight ahead uphill.

6 Still following BT blue blazes, start a very steep uphill climb to the foot of the moss-covered ledges. The BT turns left directly under these striking sandstone cliffs, which are estimated to be 320 million years old. They are composed of outcrops of Sharon Conglomerate, the pebbly sandstone formed during the Pennsylvanian Age. These magnificent rock formations rise about 350 feet above the level of Hinckley Lake. The small, shiny, rounded quartz pebbles that you see embedded in the sandstone are often called "lucky stones." These pebbles originated in a quartz-rich section of Canada and were carried here by streams of water, then rolled along the shores of a great inland sea that covered the land that is now Ohio. The sandstone hardened and formed these Sharon Conglomerate ledges, which are quite resistant to erosion.

7 Hike past small fissures and huge boulders, still following BT blazes. At 1.5 miles climb a flight of stone steps between two ledges. Because the rocks (of the Cuyahoga Formation) underlying these ledges are much softer than the sandstone, massive blocks of Sharon Conglomerate often break off the cliffs, causing cracks, fissures, and large cavelike crevices to develop, as seen here.

8 Hike along the top of the ledges to a trail intersection. Turn left (leaving the BT at this point) and carefully descend. There are several paths down; watch for the fourth, which is easiest.

9 Reach the trail under the ledges again and bear right onto a path that descends to Whipp's Ledges Picnic Area (2 miles).

10 At the picnic area walk down Whipp's Ledges Rd. to State Rd. Go directly across State Rd. and onto the gravel path marked with a blue sign depicting a great blue heron. This path goes north alongside Hinckley Lake.

11 There are fine views of the lake along this well-maintained path.

12 At 3.5 miles, continue straight ahead past an intersection with another trail joining from the right. Follow the path as it curves upward to East Dr.

13 Cross East Dr. and bear left, now following the paved All-Purpose Trail as it leads along the road to Bellus Rd. (3.75 miles).

14 Recross East Dr. to continue on the All-Purpose Trail past the swimming area, bathhouse, and spillway on the left. A purple sign with a jogger marks this trail.

15 After a short distance, leave the All-Purpose Trail to turn left (south) at the top of the spillway and follow a dirt trail downhill to the lake. This trail is again marked by a great blue heron sign.

16 Continue along this lakeside trail to the boat launch area and return to Johnson's Picnic Area. ■

46 Historic Medina

Distance: 2.25 miles

Easy

Walking Time: 1½ to 2 hours

Description: This walk is all on sidewalks except for one short section. It begins with the historic Public Square business district of Medina, then visits nearby tree-lined neighborhood streets with homes dating from the mid-1800s to the early 1900s.

Directions: From Cleveland, take I-71 south to Exit 218 (SR 18); west on SR 18 for 3.4 miles to Medina; follow SR 18 carefully approaching downtown Medina—it jogs right, then left, just before Public Square.

From Akron, take I-77 to Exit 137B (SR 18); west on SR 18 for 10.3 miles to Medina, watching carefully for SR 18 when it makes a jog just before reaching Public Square.

Parking and Restrooms: Park in the free municipal lot on W. Liberty St., just west of the square. There is a three-hour limit in this lot. An alternative is to park in the long-term lot located on S. Court St., one block south of the square. There are public restrooms in the library located immediately southeast of the square.

The story of how Medina came to be illustrates the typical way in which frontier Ohio was settled. Following the Revolutionary War, several states that had claims on lands in the Northwest Territory—the unsettled land west of Pennsylvania—ceded those claims to Congress. In recognition of claims by Connecticut, Congress allowed the state to retain a "reservation" for its future needs. The area, which became known as the Western Reserve or Connecticut Western Reserve, consisted of lands lying between Lake Erie and the 41st parallel, and extending 120 miles west of the Pennsylvania border. To facilitate settlement in this frontier territory, Connecticut sold most of the Reserve to a group of land speculators known as the Connecticut Land Company, which in turn sold off pieces of the "Ohio Country" to interested buyers.

Elijah Boardman of New Milford, Connecticut, acquired his piece of Ohio in this manner and sent Rufus Ferris and Captain Austin Badger to the frontier to survey and sell lots for a new town. Boardman reserved 237 acres of land for the town and set aside a little over two acres for a public square. Many families from Connecticut followed the surveyors, establishing what would become Medina. In the first few years the settlement was called Mecca, the birthplace of Mohammed and a name often used to denote a place of one's dreams. But when it came

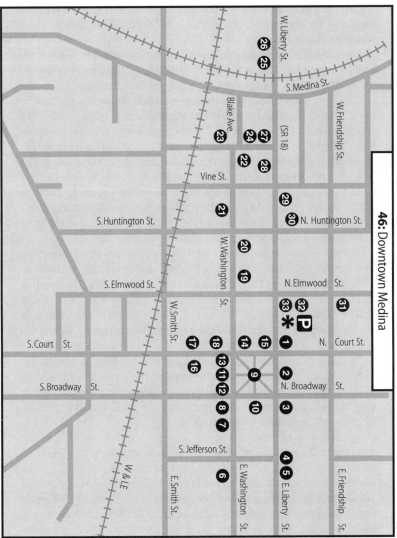

© Gray & Company, Publishers

time to incorporate the town, it was discovered that another town in Ohio was already named Mecca. The town founders then chose another Arabian name, "Medina," after the place where Mohammed's tomb is located.

The town of Medina has served as the county seat since 1835. During its first hundred years, the county around it was mostly rural, and the town developed the governmental and business services needed by the surrounding agricultural community. Many of these were established around the town square as planned. However the town fathers had failed to fund a fire department, and when a fire started in a building on the square in 1870, the results were devastating. Almost all the buildings on the square were destroyed. Among those that survived was the courthouse.

Undaunted, civic leaders and businessmen immediately began to rebuild the town square in the Victorian style of the time. But by the mid–20th century, the square would face another challenge. Highways and the move to suburbs were leaving many downtowns neglected. In the late 1960s the citizens of Medina noticed that the square needed a serious facelift. Their concern led to the establishment of the Community Design Committee (CDC), a nonprofit organization dedicated to restoring and protecting the architectural heritage of the community. The city administration was encouraged by its efforts and led the way by restoring the fire station on the south side of the square. In 1975 the public square area was listed in the National Register of Historic Places as the Medina Public Square Historic District. It is now one of the most photographed and celebrated squares in the Midwest.

The CDC's work continues, influencing restoration of properties throughout the town. This hike will show you the results of those efforts, beginning with the Public Square Historic District and ending with a visit to the Medina County Historical Society in the beautiful Queen Anne–style John Smart house. Allow enough time on this hike to enjoy some refreshment and shopping at the interesting downtown establishments. You could also schedule your visit to coincide with one of Medina's celebrations, such as the Ice Festival in February or the Parade & Muster of fire engines in September. For more information on Medina, call the Medina County Historical Society at 330-722-1341 or visit the Medina Chamber of Commerce at 145 N. Court St.; 330-723-8773; www.medinaohchamber.com.

1 From the parking lot, turn left and walk east along W. Liberty St. to the corner of W. Liberty and Court streets. The building on the northwest corner is known as the Barnard Block and dates to around 1871. The first building to occupy this site (and the first building on the square) was a double log cabin built in 1818 by Captain Austin Badger. Badger, from New York State, was a surveyor who came to the area to work with Rufus Ferris, surveying and selling lots for landowner Elijah Boardman. The first floor of the cabin served as a tavern and community house, and the second housed a court.

2 Cross Court St. and walk along the north side of the Medina Public Square. This string of buildings dates to the turn of the 20th century. The historic name of the building at 119 is the Spitzer building; it once housed the Savings Deposit Bank. The front is constructed of pressed brick with Berea Sandstone trim. Next to it is the I.O.O.F. building, home to the Medina Morningstar Lodge 26 of the Independent Order of Odd Fellows. At the corner of Liberty St. and North Broadway is a building that was originally the Princess Theatre.

3 Cross Broadway St. to the Meridian Stone, located on the northeast corner of E. Liberty St. and Broadway St. The Meridian Stone is dated 1832 and marks the exact longitude, latitude, and altitude of the site. The United Church of Christ, on the same corner, dates to around 1880. Continue walking east.

4 The Old Town Graveyard served as the town's burial ground until 1884. The newer cemetery is Spring Grove Cemetery, located just three blocks farther east.

5 Next to the Old Town Graveyard is St. Paul's Episcopal Church, built in 1884. The church is constructed of sandstone in a Gothic Revival style, with double-arched stained-glass windows. It is listed in the National Register of Historic Places.

6 Across from the cemetery is S. Jefferson St. Walk south one block on S. Jefferson St., to E. Washington St. Cross E. Washington St. to the southeast corner of the intersection. The Blake-McDowell House is the first house west of the intersection, at 314 E. Washington. Built in 1840, it was the home of one of Medina's most notable citizens, Harrison Gray Blake. Blake was born in 1819 in Vermont and was tragically orphaned at a young age. His surrogate father, Jesse Rhoades, brought the young Blake with him to Ohio in 1830. Blake was a bright and enterprising young boy who managed to read and study during the years that he helped Rhoades clear land near Guilford, in Columbiana County.

When he was 17, Blake moved to Medina to take a job as a clerk in a general store. Within a few years he became partner and then sole proprietor, while studying law at the same time. By 1859 he had established the law firm of Blake and Woodward and was well on his way to becoming a distinguished leader in Medina and the state. During his relatively short life of 57 years, he was mayor of Medina; served in both the Ohio House of Representatives and Senate; served in the U.S. Congress during the difficult years of the Civil War; and, after leaving Congress, founded the Phoenix Bank. H. G. Blake was a strong supporter of abolition, and his home served as a stop on the Underground Railroad. While in Washington, D.C., he earned the respect and friendship of President Abraham Lincoln.

7 Now turn back toward the Public Square and go west on E. Washington St., crossing S. Jefferson St. At 226 E. Washington St. is the Curtice-Phillips home, dating back to 1875. This home is in the Italianate style and has a double, grilled front door.

8 Continue west to the corner of E. Washington and S. Broadway streets. The Medina County District Library, named the Franklin Sylvester Library, sits on the corner. The first library in Medina County was the Medina Circulating Library Society, formed in 1877. It was housed in local businesses and financed through members' dues and donations. In 1904 Franklin Sylvester, a local businessman and cattleman, donated $10,000 to be used to build a library. Architect Frank

Gruninger of Warren, Pennsylvania, designed the library in the Carnegie style. The library was dedicated in 1907 and opened with 2,000 volumes. By 1958 its collection had grown considerably, so an addition was built, adding stacks and a reading room. A larger addition was completed in 1975, more than doubling the size of the library and adding new features, including a meeting room. The library is open daily and is an excellent place in which to delve into the rich history of the town.

9 Cross now to the heart of the town, Medina's Public Square. The tree-shaded square hosts many of the town's public activities, including the Ice Festival in February. It also provides the best vantage point for viewing the beautifully restored buildings facing the square. Again, note that most of the buildings on the square date to the late 1800s and early 1900s, as many of the earlier buildings were destroyed in the 1870 fire. Streetlights around the square are replicas of the original cast-iron fixtures dating to 1921.

In the center of the square is the bandstand, also known as the Gazebo. It was built in 1975 to replicate a bandstand seen in historic photos of the square. Because the specifications of the original could not be determined, this newer version was designed to duplicate exactly one found in Bellville, Ohio, dating to 1879. It is the location of summer band concerts and ice-cream socials.

10 Walk toward the east side of the square to get a view of the courthouse buildings: the historic 1841 courthouse on the corner of Broadway and Liberty streets and the 1969 courthouse to its right. The historic courthouse, like many buildings its age, began as a smaller structure and was added to over the years. Tucked within the current building is the original structure built in 1841: a rectangular, two-story Greek Revival–style building, originally topped with a cupola, in turn topped by a gilt ball.

Renovations in 1873 added rooms on each side in front and changed the look to Victorian-style by adding a mansard roof. Other changes and additions followed. A 1973 restoration brought the courthouse closer to its 1873 appearance. The main construction materials are native limestone and brick. Some notable details of the building are the fish-scale shingles on the roof, the dormer windows, clock tower, cast-iron and pressed-tin decorations, and Corinthian columns. The courthouse was one of the few buildings spared in the 1870 fire.

To the right of the historic courthouse is the newer Federal Revival courthouse, dedicated in 1969. To the right of the courthouse buildings is the Gensemer building. This 1873 structure began its life as a physician's home and office, then served as the Gensemer Funeral Home. In 1971 the First Federal Savings and Loan restored the building, showcasing its fine Italianate architecture.

11 Now walk along the south side of the square to view the buildings on Washington St. The Town Hall and Engine House (1878) stands out, with its bright-red brick, black-and-white trim, and gold lettering. The renovation of the historic downtown began here with the firehouse. It was the first building to be restored following the recommendations of the Community Design Committee, and led the way for the eventual restoration of the entire Public Square district. Funds from the city, the CDC, and the Letha House Foundation all contributed to the restoration. The work included replacing a missing bell tower. The Medina City Archive Commission is in the process of creating a museum and visitor center in the engine house. In accordance with bond agreements, the city must keep the engine house as a fire station until 2007. In compliance with this provision, the station now houses three historic fire trucks: an operable 1940s fire truck, a 1918 LaFrance Fire Engine, and a horse-drawn fire vehicle dating to the early 1900s.

12 To the left of the firehouse is the Gazette building. Charles D. Neil, owner and editor of the *Medina Gazette*, built this Romanesque-style building in 1895. Note the second-story bay windows on the east façade as well as on the side facing the square.

13 The buildings to the right of the firehouse also date from the 1870s to 1880. Note the broken pediment arch in the cornice of the Reinhardt building. The Phoenix Block, prominent on the corner of Washington and Court streets, has played a central role in Medina's history. After the devastating fire of 1870, civic leader H. G. Blake immediately began organizing the rebuilding effort as well as working to reopen his own business, the aptly named Old Phoenix Bank. Blake kept his bank going by temporarily using an office in the courthouse. He went on to rebuild the bank, including stores, offices, and a theater in the new building.

14 Move now to the west side of the square to see the fine set of restored storefronts facing Court St. On the way, note the plaque and the millstones brought here from the Bagdad Mill, which was located northeast of town. On the western edge of the square, halfway up the block, is the Cooley Fountain, a drinking fountain donated to the townspeople in 1907 by Reverend Lathrop Cooley, a gentleman quite involved in the temperance movement. The inscriptions on the fountain help explain the message implicit in the gift.

Now look across Court St. to view the historic downtown buildings. Starting from the left, the first building is the Albro Block (1875), which housed a pharmacy for nearly 100 years. The long two-story brick Union Block a couple doors up was originally divided into three storefronts. Renovations removed a 20th-century façade to reveal the handsome second-story windows.

A bronze plaque on the fourth building, at 23 Public Square, marks the site where A. I. Root began manufacturing beehives in 1869, leading to the successful business still operating today just west of downtown and visited later in this hike.

A historic cast-iron clock sits in front of the buildings, about half-way up the block. It too was restored thanks to the combined efforts of the city, the CDC, and the Letha House Foundation.

15 Note the two most northerly buildings on this block. The second from the corner is the only brownstone on the square and is decorated with intricate detailing around the windows and between the floors. The corner building, built between 1818 and 1821, was originally used as a courthouse for the new village. It and the courthouse across the square were two of the few structures that survived the 1870 downtown fire. It was the village's first public building and has served many purposes over the years. Champion Creek, just south of downtown, supplied stones for the structure.

16 Turn back south and leave the square, crossing Washington St. Walk south on Court St. The 19th-century buildings on both sides of the street housed many of the businesses important to the county seat and today house shops and businesses important to today's culture. The third building on the east side, at 250 S. Court St., dates to around 1870 and was once the Brenner Hotel. Ephriam Brenner owned a successful harness and saddle shop located across the street. At the end of the block, cross to the west side of Court St.

17 At the edge of the city parking lot is a diminutive building that represents an interesting historic element of Medina. It was associated with the Cleveland, Berea, & Medina Railway, part of the Cleveland, Southwestern, and Columbus interurban line, and was moved here from its original location. Interurbans were electric-traction rail lines that flourished throughout Ohio from 1895 to the 1920s. At the height of their development and use, they formed spider webs of systems around all the major cities in Ohio and played a major role in connecting rural areas to market cities, and the cities to leisure spots in the country, such as the beach communities along Lake Erie. At the height of the interurban era, according to transportation historian H. Roger Grant, Ohio had far more electric track in use than any other state.

Many of the interurban lines enticed riders by including amusement parks as a destination on the line. This was true of the so-called "Green Line" that came through the center of Medina. It often carried Clevelanders and others on their way to a day's outing at Chippewa Lake Park, less than five miles south of Medina. The interurban tracks extended down the center of W. Liberty St., then turned down Court St., along the Public Square.

18 Continue north along S. Court St. The eight side-by-side buildings here all date to the 1870s. Some of them have especially interesting details or construction. The first, the Lamb Building at 241 S. Court St., has a cast-iron storefront. The Mechanics Block next to it includes two storefronts. Brenner's harness and saddle shop was here, as well as A. Griesinger's shoe store. The two storefronts are linked by the second-story windows and the cornice, the top horizontal molding.

The northernmost building, on the corner at 201 Court St., is the Miller-Chamberlin Block. The original cast-iron columns seen today were uncovered and restored during the 1970s restoration.

19 Turn left (west) on W. Washington St. and leave the Public Square Historic District. The hike now travels along side streets to get a taste of the residential character of historic Medina. The houses passed will illustrate how the style of architecture changed, from the simple style of the earliest homes to the more elaborate styles of the Victorian era. Many of the sidewalks retain sections of the original sandstone pavement, some with ripple marks from when the sand was being deposited in shallow sea water.

Cross S. Elmwood St. At 211 W. Washington St., on the north side of the street, is the Rickard House, which dates to around 1854. The architecture of this house is typical of the style followed by early settlers of the Western Reserve.

20 At 231 W. Washington St. is the Dr. Ormsby House, a home dating to around 1860. During the years of the antislavery movement, it was one of several houses in Medina that sheltered escaped slaves on their journey north to freedom.

21 Continue west on W. Washington St., past homes of varying styles. Cross S. Huntington St. At 310 W. Washington St. is an Eastlake-style home that was built in 1891. The name "Eastlake" refers to Charles Eastlake, an English furniture designer who became popular in the late 1800s. Elements of his furniture design were used in architecture as well, associating his name with the style.

At 326 W. Washington St. is a home that dates to around 1843.
Cross Vine St.

22 On the north side of the street, at 421 and 431 W. Washington St., are sister homes—matching homes built for sisters Helen and Elizabeth Blake, daughters of city father H. G. Blake. The two sisters married brothers, O. H. McDowell and Robert M. McDowell. Robert was president of H. G. Blake's Old Phoenix Bank. These two handsome homes were built in 1875 in the Italianate style popular at the time. They exhibit fine examples of some of the features of Italianate style: low-pitched roofs with overhanging eaves, small, narrow windows with rounded crowns, double-grilled front doors, and small entry porches off to the side. Note also the double brackets in the cornices just below the roofs of both houses.

23 Cross Prospect St. R. M. McDowell, who owned one of the "sister" homes, built the Queen Anne–style house at 205 S. Prospect in 1890. This large house, sitting as it does back from the street and surrounded by lawn, certainly commands attention, with an aspect worthy of a bank president. The imposing three-story home has a wood-and-stone turret, a second-floor enclosed sleeping porch, and a showy stained-glass window. The rounded third-floor dormer window is quite unusual. An attached, drive-through porch, called a porte cochere, was used in the horse-and-buggy days.

The house to the left (south) of the Queen Anne was also built by R. M. McDowell. It dates to an earlier time, which is evident from its Greek Revival style, typical of the earlier Western Reserve homes.

24 Just north of the McDowell house, across Blake Ave., is the Munson House. Although it appears quite "in place," this house was saved from demolition and moved from 231 E. Washington St. to this location, 141 S. Prospect St. In 1887 Albert Munson, then newly elected probate judge for Medina County, had the home built on E. Washington St., just around the corner from the courthouse. In 1956 the home was bequeathed to the Medina County Historical Society and housed the organization until it moved to its present location on N. Elmwood Ave. (see Note #31).

The Munson House is home to two important Medina organizations. The Community Design Committee (CDC) is responsible for spearheading and continuing the restoration and protection of the city's architecture. It also maintains a resource center and library in the Munson House, open to anyone needing guidance in historic preservation. The Medina Summit Land Conservancy preserves and protects open space and natural areas in Medina and Summit counties. Together the two organizations work to preserve the town and country heritage of Medina County. The Munson House can be visited by appointment; call the CDC at 330-725-7516.

From the Munson House, go west one block on Blake Ave., then turn right on S. Medina St. and walk another block to W. Liberty St. (SR 18/57). Turn left (west), cross the railroad tracks, and go past the Medina railroad depot.

25 Reach the long two-story brick buildings of the A.I. Root Company, Medina's landmark manufacturer. The firm has been manufacturing beekeeping supplies and promoting the art and science of beekeeping at this location for over 100 years. The company is equally well known for its beeswax candles, which it began manufacturing in the 1930s.

Amos Ives Root, the founder of the company, was born in a log cabin two miles north of Medina in 1839. He had poor health as a child, but his mother encouraged his inquisitive mind. As a young man, he established a jewelry-making business on Medina's town square. One day, while working at the business, he noticed a swarm of honeybees alighting on his windowsill, a moment that led to his life-long fascination with the intriguing creatures. By 1869 he was manufacturing and selling a new type of beehive. After the devastating 1870 fire on the square, Root began to build a new factory at this W. Liberty St. location next to the railroad tracks and expanded the business to include other beekeeping supplies and honey. In response to inquiries from around the country, he also began publishing a circular that became *Bee Culture, The Magazine of American Beekeeping*, the premier guide for beekeepers. Candles were not originally one of Root's products. A. I.'s son, Huber H. Root, added beeswax altar candles to the product line in response to a need expressed by one of his friends, a local priest. Later the company began manufacturing scented and colored candles as well.

A. I. Root was always inventive and forward-looking. He believed in the value of the railroad in its infancy and made good use of it; he used a windmill generator to recharge his electric car. He was friends with the Wright brothers and published the first account of their historic flight in his beekeeping magazine in 1905.

The A.I. Root Company has weathered many storms over its long history. It was founded during a financially bleak time in the nation's history, and the candle making was launched during the Great Depression. The company's resiliency and resourcefulness have earned it the honor of induction into CWRU's Weatherhead School of Management Family Business Hall of Fame. The current president of the company is John A. Root, a fourth-generation Root. The retail store is located here in the West Liberty Commons and is open daily (330-723-4359). Offices are located in the A. I. Root building on the north side of W. Liberty St. Note the decorative bee and beehives molded into the eastern façade of the building.

26 Continue west on W. Liberty St. to reach the A. I. and E. R. Root Homestead, located at 662 W. Liberty St. A. I. Root built this brick home in 1879 in the Queen Anne style. The home is listed in the National Register of Historic Places. Because members of the Root family owned or occupied many of the other houses near the factory, this area came to be known as "Rootville."

27 Turn back east and retrace your steps past the A.I. Root Company and across the railroad tracks. Continue east one block on W. Liberty St. At 504 W. Liberty St. is a Queen Anne–style home. C. M. Spitzer, another prominent Medina citizen, built this home in 1890. Note that the original carriage house sits just behind the home, at 137 S. Prospect St.

28 Cross Prospect St. A Gothic Revival–style church is at 416 W. Liberty St.

29 At Vine St., cross to the north side of W. Liberty and continue going east. The second house in the next block, at 329 W. Liberty St., is the Sargent house, the only brick Greek Revival house in Medina. It dates to 1854.

30 Turn left and go north on Huntington St. The first house on the left is the Alcott house, built in 1846. Its style is Greek Revival, with a Victorian porch. It was built by Phineas C. Alcott and was visited by Louisa May Alcott.

31 Reach W. Friendship St. and cross to the north side. Turn right (east) and go one block to N. Elmwood St. Cross N. Elmwood to the home of the Medina County Historical Society at 206 N. Elmwood St. The historical society acquired this home in 1985 and renovated it entirely, including rebuilding the porches and having it painted in historically accurate colors.

The 14-room home was built in 1886 by Medina businessman John Smart. It is a handsome example of the Queen Anne style of architecture, with many interesting features, including triangular windows in the gables, a double-story stained-glass window on the north side, and two porches on the south side connected by a walk-through window/door.

The home serves as office and museum for the historical society. The office is open Tuesday and Thursday; the museum is open the first Sunday afternoon of each month, March to December.

Note the square of sidewalk at the northwest corner of this intersection, in front of the Smart house. The sandstone paving shows pronounced ripple marks.

32 Cross W. Friendship St. and go south on Elmwood St., past the Medina City Hall. Just south of the city hall is the Masonic Temple. This four-story building was designed by Akron architects Ridley and Glazier in the Neoclassical style, with a temple-like front and Ionic columns. It was completed in 1925 and has been nominated for inclusion in the National Register of Historic Places.

33 Turn left on W. Liberty St. At 139 W. Liberty St. is the Medina Theater, a movie theater that was added onto the Masonic Temple in 1937. This theater was a popular spot for many years.

Just past the theater, turn left into the parking lot where this hike began. ■

47 Allardale
Granger Township

Distance: 2 miles

Walking time: 1 ½ hours

Description: A great vista is one of the many attributes of this hike through a well-tended farm that is now a public park. The hike follows marked trails and unmarked farm lanes through both open and forested sections of the rolling farmland, with a couple steep climbs.

Directions: From Cleveland, take I-77 south to Exit 143 (Wheatley Rd.); right (west) on Wheatley; left (south) on Brecksville Rd. for 1.3 miles; right (west) on Everett Rd. for 3 miles; left (south) on Medina Line Rd. At the first stop sign, turn right (west) onto Remson Rd. for 0.5 miles ; entrance on right.

From Akron, take I-77 to Exit 137B (SR 18); west on SR 18 for 2 miles; right (north) on Medina Line Rd. for 3.5 miles; left (west) on Remson Rd. for 0.5 miles; entrance on right.

Parking & restrooms: Parking on north side of Remson Rd. Restrooms and drinking fountain at the edge of parking area.

Allardale is one of the newer units in the Medina County Park District and also carries the distinction of being one of the most scenic. The park is named after Stanley and Esther Allard, who donated their 126-acre farm to the park district in 1992. Five years later the park district enlarged the park area when they purchased 212 acres of the former Firestone Estate, located immediately east of the Allard farm. Allardale was opened to the public in 1997.

What makes this park so special is that it is a living testament to the Allards' love for and stewardship of their land and their generosity in sharing it. And it especially attests to Stan Allard's devotion to trees. The farm has a long history of good conservation practices. Stan Allard convinced his father to try soil-saving farming techniques, such as contour planting. Then, inspired by a trip to Louis Bromfield's Malabar Farm, he also began planting trees on the steep slopes of the farm. Allard's diligence and care in planting over 100,000 trees makes Allardale one of the finest examples of reforestation in Ohio; it earned him the Ohio Forest Stewardship Award in 1991. The hiking trails now pass many of these tree plantings, each identified by species and date of planting. This is a park to return to again and again over the years, to get to know the trees and see how their growth changes the nature of the farm.

There are good reasons to visit this park at any time of year, but it is especially enjoyable in the spring when the wildflowers are in bloom and in autumn when the views of fall color are spectacular. Visitors enjoy sledding and cross-country skiing in the winter. The park has picnic tables near the parking lot, as well as a reservable picnic shelter. There are three hiking trails: the accessible, asphalt-paved Inner Loop, the unpaved Outer Loop, and the Wildflower Path. The park district's plans to extend the trail system in the future include adding equestrian trails in the eastern part of the park, where the Bath Pony Club currently holds trail rides. The park district also hopes to enlarge the park by acquiring additional acreage on the northwest side of Allardale. For more information about Allardale, call the Medina County Park District: 330-722-9464.

1 Begin the hike at the trail kiosk next to the parking area. Paving tiles with tree-leaf imprints are both decorative and informative for this "tribute to trees" hike. Turn right (east) onto the Outer Loop Trail; follow the paved path downhill and onto a mowed path. The trail swings to the north in this open creek valley and crosses a small tributary on a bridge. This tributary eventually joins the East Branch of the Rocky River in Hinckley Reservation, north of here.

2 Part of the slope on the right is being kept open as mowed grassland. Tall white pines cover the portion of the slope that has been reforested. Cross the creek on a bridge and continue following the mowed path alongside the creek. Tree plots of various species and ages are identified along the trail.

3 At the trail intersection go straight, crossing the creek again and entering the Wildflower Path. Here a beautifully designed path reaches into the heart of a rich, mixed woodland. A mature beech/maple forest spreads from the creek bottom up the slope to the right and onto the ridge above. The wildflower display is at its best in the spring, when the woodland wildflowers are in bloom. Many of the early species have very brief bloom times, between the time that the soil warms up and the trees leaf out.

A dam and sawmill were once located in this small valley. The sawmill supplied lumber for building the Allard home and barn.

4 After several hundred feet, bear to the right onto a small loop in the trail. Several sections of boardwalk carry the path through this low, wet area.

5 The hike now leaves the Wildflower Path for a side trip into the beech/maple forest. You will return to this point later. This part of the hike is not well marked but follows fairly obvious paths. From the Wildflower Path, leave the boardwalks and cross a small tributary, then bear right to follow the edge of this creek ravine upstream. This section may be muddy and slippery. Nonetheless, avoid the wider, more eroded path on the south side of the ravine, which is a steeper climb.

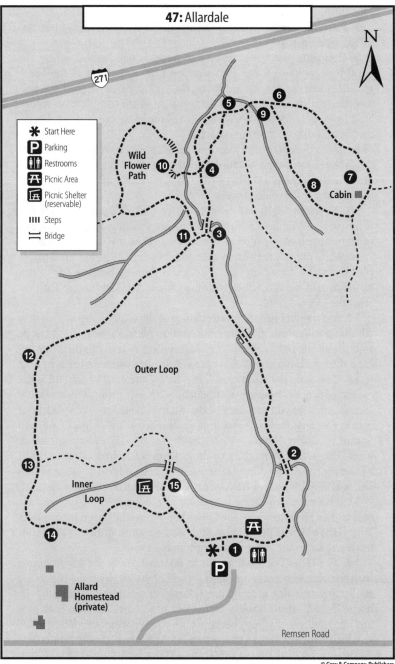

47: Allardale

Start Here
Parking
Restrooms
Picnic Area
Picnic Shelter (reservable)
Steps
Bridge

Wild Flower Path

Outer Loop

Inner Loop

Cabin

Allard Homestead (private)

Remsen Road

© Gray & Company, Publishers

6 At the top of this short climb, bear to the left to begin a short loop hike through the woods.

7 Here you reach an old cabin with an interesting past, as indicated by the sign nearby.

8 Continue past the cabin, watching for a path to the right. (The main trail goes south, out into an open field at the edge of the beech woods.) Turn right on the side path; the ravine will be on your left. Follow the path around to where you began (at #6) to complete the woodland loop. The mixed woods include oak, wild cherry, hickory, beech, maple, and other deciduous species.

9 Reach the end of the loop and turn left to retrace your steps back down the ravine to the Wildflower Path. Bear right (at #5) on the Wildflower Path at the point where you left it, and follow it as it swings left (south) along the main stream.

10 Now bear right and cross the stream on stepping stones. Continue on the Wildflower Path as it makes a winding ascent on a series of steps attractively edged in sandstone. At the top of this climb are some white pines. Reach an intersection beyond the pines; a red maple plot is nearby. Complete the Wildflower Path by bearing left at this junction and going back downhill to where the Wildflower Path rejoins the Outer Loop.

11 Turn right onto the continuation of the Outer Loop, which now climbs steadily through more reforestation plots. Partway up the slope a bench on the right provides a pleasant place to rest. On the slope behind the bench is a grand old sugar maple, the largest on the property.

12 Continue the steep climb. Just below the crest of the hill is the park's dedication boulder and bench, at an elevation of about 1,100 feet. From here you can survey the Allards' labor of love spread out below. The outstanding views to the east reach to the ridges of western Summit County. Those ridges divide the Rocky River watershed, where the farm is, from the Cuyahoga River watershed to the east. The hill below the dedication plaque has long been a favorite sledding hill and is also managed for field birds, including northern bobwhite.

13 Leave the dedication plaque and head south along the contour of the open slope to where the Outer Loop joins the paved Inner Loop. Turn right onto the Inner Loop, still heading south. Young oaks of uniform size cover the slope to the right in neat rows.

14 The Inner Loop swings to the east and passes the Allard home, with the barn and other outbuildings, all of which sit on the rise to the south. Stan Allard's grandparents, James and Sarah Allard, built the home in 1885 from lumber from the farm's woodlot. The barn was built in 1896, mostly from beech. Stan's parents were married in 1907, at which time the house was expanded into a two-family home. The Allards operated the farm mostly as a dairy farm until 1961. At that time Stan sold the cows and equipment and turned to producing hay for nearby horse farms.

Stan Allard recalls that the barn has withstood two severe storms: a summer storm with high winds in 1922 and a tornado in May of 1967. The tornado tore sheet metal off the roof, blew the door in, and shifted the barn a few inches, but the old barn otherwise rode out the storm. The machinery shed did not fare as well—it ended up upside down, but with the machinery unharmed

15 Continue on the paved path, down a slope toward the parking lot. Some interesting historical information about the farm is presented on a sign alongside the trail. A reservable picnic shelter is on the left, near the largest bitternut tree on the property. Just beyond the shelter, watch for an intersection where the Inner Loop turns left. Turn left here for a short side trip down to a V-shaped bridge in the deep shade of an evergreen grove. The shade creates a microclimate, cooling the air and the water in the creek. The trees provide food and shelter for animals such as red squirrels, who munch on pinecones like humans enjoying corn on the cob.

Return to the Outer Loop and turn left to return to the parking lot.

■

. . . my mind, set free by space and solitude and oiled by the body's easy rhythm, swings open and releases thoughts it has already formulated. Sometimes, when I have been straining too hard to impose order on an urgent press of ideas, it seems only as if my mind has slowly relaxed; and then, all at once, there is room for the ideas to fall into place in a meaningful pattern.

—Colin Fletcher, *The Complete Walker*

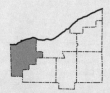

LORAIN COUNTY

Mostly rural, Lorain County extends along Lake Erie from the city of Avon Lake in the east to downtown Vermilion in the west, and continues south to Oberlin and Wellington. The county's east–west ridges, formed by ancient Lake Erie beaches, produced natural roadways for early settlers and facilitated subsequent development of the county.

Antique dealers abound in Lorain County; in Avon alone there are more than 100. Jamie's Flea Market in South Amherst is one of the largest in Ohio. Oberlin (Ch. 48) is a charming college town with an interesting history.

From its central headquarters at Carlisle Reservation, Lorain County Metro Parks manages more than 6,500 acres of green space, with 16 park units, including 11 reservations, a water park, a golf course, and the North Coast Inland Trail, a railtrail. This guide includes hikes in four of the reservations. Schoepfle Garden, a Lorain County Metro Park, is actually in Erie County (Ch. 56). An annual Pioneer Days Festival is held at Vermilion River Reservation in September. Yearly Halloween Walks and maple sugar programs are held at Carlisle Visitor Center. For information about programs and activities, call 800-526-7275 or visit www.loraincountymetroparks.com.

Findley State Park (440-647-4490) is in Wellington, and city parks in this county include Lakeview Park in Lorain and Cascade Park and Elywood Park in Elyria (Ch. 54).

More information about Lorain County is available from Lorain County Visitors Bureau: 800-334-1673; www.LCVB.org.

48 Oberlin

Distance: 3.75 miles

Easy

Walking time: 2 ½ hours

Description: This walk is entirely on sidewalks through the campus and town; it leads past college buildings, historical landmarks, and heritage homes and covers several square blocks of downtown Oberlin.

Directions: From Cleveland take I-480 west to Exit 1 for SR 10 (Oberlin/Norwalk); west on SR 10; west on SR 511 for 2.5 miles into Oberlin; left (south) on SR 58 (Main St.) in Oberlin for one block; left (east) on E. College St.; left (north) on Willard St.; right (east) into free parking lot.

From Akron take SR 18 west to Wellington; north on SR 58 for 8.6 miles to Oberlin; right (east) on E. College St.; left on Willard St.; right into free parking lot.

From Lorain go south on SR 58 (Leavitt Rd.) to Oberlin; left on E. College St., left on Willard; right into free parking lot.

Parking & restrooms: Park at free parking lot off Willard St. behind Oberlin Inn; restrooms are in any public building. Additional parking at the athletic complex at the north end of Woodland Ave. Parking in the business district is limited to 30 minutes or 2 hours, as posted.

Oberlin is a small, lovely, cosmopolitan town southwest of Cleveland, dominated by internationally known Oberlin College and Oberlin Conservatory of Music. Its population of 8,800 (including 2,900 students) cherishes the town's heritage and history and its many prized 19th-century homes and college buildings. A visitor to Oberlin immediately notices the brick-accented sidewalks, pots of plants hanging from lampposts, and the beautifully landscaped central green, Tappan Square, which create the impression of a quaint Victorian village. Yet Oberlin is a progressive community with a small but first-rate art museum, a modern hospital near the center of town, an excellent water treatment system, and a new continuing-care retirement community—Kendal at Oberlin—near downtown. An annual celebration of Oberlin's history, called Oberlin Heritage Days Festival, is held on Tappan Square each July.

Oberlin's history illustrates how the town and college have worked in partnership as a progressive community. When the town was founded in 1833, Oberlin opposed slavery as a violation of Christian principles. The village thus became a haven for abolitionists and runaway slaves. From about 1833 to the end of the Civil War, Oberlin was

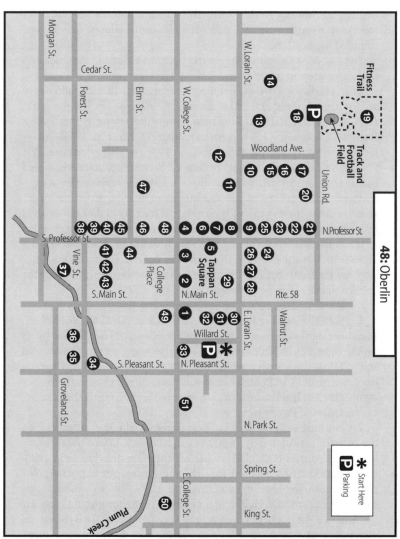

© Gray & Company, Publishers

one of the major stations (No. 99) on the Underground Railroad network that sheltered fugitives from the south. From here it was easy to transfer runaways to Lake Erie ports and waiting boats that took them to Canada and freedom. Many former slaves stayed in Oberlin, going into farming, business, or other types of employment, and raised their families here, leaving descendants who still live in Oberlin.

When the college opened, also in 1833, it admitted women, thus becoming the first coeducational college or university in the country. By 1835 it admitted African-American students, becoming one of the first colleges in America to do so. Oberlin was also active in crusades for temperance and women's suffrage. The Anti-Saloon League was founded here in 1893.

The 440-acre Oberlin campus has been called one of America's 35 best campuses, in Thomas A. Gaines's *The Campus as a Work of Art.* Oberlin graduates have earned more doctorates than the graduates of any other private liberal arts school in the nation. The college ranks high in scientific education. Three alumni have won Nobel Prizes: Robert Millikan, in 1923 (physics); Roger Sperry, in 1981 (medicine/physiology); and Stanley Cohen, in 1986 (medicine/physiology).

Oberlin calls itself the "City of Music," because concerts are offered by conservatory students and faculty almost every night of the week—and most are free. The outstanding quality of musical performance derives from the conservatory's high national ranking in the education of musicians at the undergraduate level. About 500 students are enrolled in the conservatory, including students who are pursuing double degrees from both the conservatory and the college. For more information, see the Chamber of Commerce website (www.oberlin.org) or the college website (www.oberlin.edu).

1 From the parking lot turn left and walk south along Willard St., then turn right (west) and walk along E. College St. The Oberlin Inn is on the right. It was built in 1954, and a large addition was constructed in 1969. It is the fourth hotel to be located at this spot. The first was a log cabin built in 1833 for pioneer travelers. On the lawn at the corner by the Oberlin Inn is a historical marker commemorating the first settler of Oberlin, Peter Pindar Pease.

2 Continue west on College St. and cross Main St. A memorial on the corner, surrounded by flags, was placed here to honor the memory of Charles Martin Hall. Hall graduated from Oberlin College in 1885, and the following year he discovered the process for extracting aluminum from the rock bauxite, making it possible to produce aluminum economically. Hall went on to found the Aluminum Company of America (ALCOA). Oberlin has recently been designated the eleventh "chemical landmark" in the country by the American Chemical Society in honor of Hall's discovery. Hall was also a philanthropist and became a generous benefactor of Oberlin College. Other tributes to his generosity include Hall Auditorium. His boyhood home is located at 64 E. College St.

A large old elm was at this site until the 1950s. It marked the spot where John J. Shipherd and Philo P. Stewart knelt in prayer in 1833, having located what they considered the perfect place for a new village and college. They named their proposed village and school Oberlin after a European pastor, John Frederick Oberlin.

3 Continue west along W. College St., along the south edge of Tappan Square. Thirteen-acre Tappan Square, with its many tall, mature

trees—about 300 trees of 58 different species—was named in honor of
Arthur Tappan, a wealthy New York businessman whose generous gifts
in 1835 ensured Oberlin's continued existence. His philanthropy was
contingent on the college admitting African-American students. Tappan Square is owned by the college but used by both Oberlin College
and the community. Festivals, concerts, and annual May commence-
ment exercises are held here.

The big round boulder near the southwest corner of Tappan Square,
on the lawn near W. College St., was put there by the Oberlin College
Class of 1898, who pried it out of Plum Creek. It is painted each year
by the graduating class (and by others expressing various messages, a
tradition started during the Vietnam War era). Just to the left of the
boulder is a tricolor beach tree, with lovely three-hued leaves.

4 The white building on the northwest corner with the lacy façade
is the King Building, the college's main classroom building. This beautiful 1964 building was designed by Minoru Yamasaki, who also designed the Conservatory of Music on the southeast corner. Warner
Center next to King houses the Department of Theater and Dance.

5 Turn right to walk north on N. Professor St. On your right, on the
west side of Tappan Square, is the 1903 Memorial Arch recognizing
Oberlin missionaries who were killed in the Chinese Boxer Rebellion
in 1900. A new plaque, written in both Chinese and English, was added
in 1994, in memory of Chinese civilians who lost their lives in the
violence.

6 Across the street is historic Peters Hall (1885), constructed, like
Baldwin and Talcott Halls, of rough-textured Ohio sandstone. This

complex structure was the college's main classroom building from the 1880s to the 1960s. It is the oldest building on the campus.

7 Cox Administration Building (1915) was designed by the well-known architect of the U.S. Supreme Court Building, Cass Gilbert, in an ornate Northern Italian Renaissance style. Gilbert designed several more of the college's buildings.

8 At the corner of Professor and W. Lorain streets is beautiful Finney Chapel, a 1908 design also by Cass Gilbert. Its 1,376-seat sanctuary is the site of many artist recitals, orchestral concerts, assemblies, and religious gatherings. The chapel was named in honor of Rev. Charles Grandison Finney, a prominent evangelist, antislavery advocate, and second president of Oberlin College.

9 Turn left (west) on W. Lorain St. On the northwest corner of Professor and W. Lorain is Severance Hall, housing the college's psychology department. Named for trustee Louis Henry Severance, it was built in 1900 and designed by Chicago architect Howard Van Doren Shaw.

10 To the west of Severance, on the corner of W. Lorain and Woodland Ave., is Kettering Hall (1961), housing the chemistry and biology departments and science library. Adjacent to it, visible from Woodland Ave., is the Roger Sperry Neuroscience Building, added in 1990. This addition was named after the 1981 Nobel Prize–winning scientist (a 1935 Oberlin graduate). The building was designed by Reed Axelrod to blend in with the older Kettering building and the brick dormitories at this end of the campus. A new science facility is located adjacent to and north of these buildings.

11 Wilder Hall (1911), on W. Lorain opposite Kettering, is the student union, a former men's dormitory. Most of Oberlin's student organizations have offices located here. In the basement are campus night spots—the Rathskeller (the "Rat") and Disco (the "Sco"). The main lounge and former residential library is now used as a performance space and multipurpose meeting room—"Wilder Main."

12 Behind and to the west of Wilder is Mudd Learning Center (1974), the college's central library, with over one million volumes.

Of the library's major collections, several are outstanding. The Violin Society of America/Goodkind Collection on the History and Construction of the Violin has been called the world's most important collection of information about the making, playing, and teaching of stringed instruments. The Antislavery Collection is one of this country's most historically significant assortment of pamphlets and books on slavery. The Collection on the History of the Book holds examples of bookmaking, binding, typography, and illustration from 1450 to the present. The Architecture Collection is almost a duplicate of Thomas Jefferson's architecture library.

13 Continue west on W. Lorain. On the right is Hales Gymnasium

(1939), housing Crane Pool (no longer in use), a six-lane bowling alley, and a favorite student hangout, Cat in the Cream Coffeehouse.

Oberlin's impressive athletic complex extends north from here to the Jesse Philips Physical Education Center (1971) and beyond.

14 To the west of Hales is the medical campus serving the entire community. Here is 100-bed Allen Memorial Hospital (1925) and the Oberlin Clinic.

Return to Woodland Ave. and walk north. Several of the small homes on the left are rented by students and faculty.

15 North of the new Science Center is Barrows Hall (1956), a large dormitory reserved entirely for first-year students. It was the set for a 1998 movie depicting college life, *The Edge of Seventeen.*

16 Next to it is Noah Hall, a neo-Georgian, coed dormitory built in 1932. Its high ceilings, chandeliers, wood paneling, and lounges with fireplaces create the feeling of an old English country home.

17 Zechiel House (1968) at the end of the block is a small men's residence occupied by many of the college's male athletes. It is just across from the Jesse Philips Physical Education Center.

18 On the left and extending for some distance are the buildings and grounds comprising the athletic complex. Inside huge Philips Gymnasium (1971) are an Olympic-sized pool, basketball, squash, racquetball, and tennis courts, and other facilities. Also located in the complex are field houses, an ice rink, the Savage football stadium, athletic fields, tennis courts, and a fitness trail. Students, faculty, staff, and townspeople all use these facilities.

19 The 1.25-mile fitness trail is a pleasant gravel path available to anyone for either running or walking. The trail was given to the college jointly by Southwood Corporation and the late Jim Fixx, a 1957 Oberlin College graduate who was a well-known marathon runner and author. The fitness trail begins at the southeast end of the football stadium, near Woodland Ave. and Union St. (If you wish to walk on this trail, parking is available in the lot at the southwest end of the football stadium.)

20 Turn right (east) on Union St. Langston Hall (1963), named for John Mercer Langston, Oberlin's most famous 19th-century black graduate, is on the right.

21 Turn right (south) on N. Professor St. On the right is Walter Bailey House (1968), also known as "French House," for French-speaking students. Two graduate assistants from France and a French faculty member also live here. All take their meals in a French-speaking, private dining room in Stevenson Hall.

22 East Hall (1964), next on the right, is unique in that the third floor is designated as a "quiet hall."

23 Next to East Hall is Barnard Hall (1968), a small residence for upperclass students.

24 Across from Barnard is Stevenson Hall, the college's main dining hall. It also houses a computer lab and career services center. Built in 1991, it was designed by architect Charles Gwathmey.

25 South of Barnard is Wright Laboratory of Physics (1942), named for Wilbur and Orville Wright. Their sister, Katherine Wright Haskell (an Oberlin College graduate), donated funds for the construction of the building in her brothers' names.

26 On the corner of N. Professor and W. Lorain streets is the Carnegie Building, built in 1908 as the library and now housing the admissions office for the College of Arts and Sciences.

27 Turn left (east) on W. Lorain. Bosworth Hall (1931), containing Fairchild Chapel, is another of Cass Gilbert's Mediterranean-style architectural designs. Behind Bosworth is Asia House/Quadrangle, also designed by Gilbert in 1931. The 60 coed students who live in Asia House share a common interest in Asian culture. Look for the relief sculptures that adorn the columns on walkways connecting Bosworth Hall with Asia House. This complex formerly served as Oberlin's Graduate School of Theology. Return to W. Lorain and continue walking east.

28 First Church, at the corner of N. Main St. and W. Lorain St., was built of red brick in 1844 in Greek Revival style. It has been well preserved both inside and out. It served as an early meeting place for all town gatherings and was the center of community life in Oberlin for many years. Mark Twain spoke here. First Church was once the largest structure west of the Allegheny Mountains. It is the only substantial building remaining from the original Oberlin colony. First Church and the Little Red Schoolhouse are the oldest buildings in Oberlin.

Turn right (south) on Main St.

29 Tappan Square's unusual Clark Bandstand (1987), designed by Oberlin College graduate Julian Smith, was constructed to be handicapped accessible (before this became common practice) and resembles a large Asian festival wagon. The bandstand is named for its benefactor, A.C. "Kenny" Clark, a businessman and member of the Oberlin College Class of 1948. Return to the corner of Lorain and Main and cross to the east side.

30 On the southeast corner of E. Lorain and N. Main streets is Allen Memorial Art Museum, designed by Cass Gilbert in 1917, with a modern extension designed by Robert Venturi added in 1976. This museum contains one of the finest collections of art on a college or university campus in this country. The 14,000-object collection ranges from ancient Egypt to contemporary America. Its particular strengths are in 17th-century Dutch and Flemish paintings, 19th- and 20th-century European art, contemporary American art, and Japanese woodblock prints. On the grounds around the building are a number of museum sculptures. The museum is open Tuesday–Saturday 10 A.M.–5.P.M., and

Sunday 1–5 P.M. (closed Mondays and major holidays). Admission is free (440-775-8665).

31 Adjacent to the museum is the Women's Gateway monument. It commemorates the admission of women to Oberlin College in 1833, making Oberlin the country's first coeducational college.

32 Under a gorgeous weeping beech tree is the Bacon Arbor, dedicated to Carl Bacon and his wife, who provided the plantings around Hall Auditorium. Hall Auditorium, named for Charles Martin Hall, is the home of Oberlin Opera Theater and venue for other theatrical and dance performances. Hall had the auditorium built in loving memory of his mother, Sophronia Brooks Hall. Architect Wallace Harrison's design for the curved-concrete structure was the focus of much controversy when the auditorium opened in 1953. Harrison had designed the United Nations building in New York a few years earlier.

33 Continue past the Oberlin Inn, then turn left (east) on E. College St. past the parking lot, to 64 E. College St. The restored 1853 Charles Martin Hall House, now a college faculty residence, formerly the boyhood home of the college's most generous benefactor. Hall, working in a woodshed behind his house in 1886 (a year after his graduation from Oberlin College), discovered the electrolytic process for extracting aluminum from bauxite ore, essential in making aluminum, a common material with many uses.

34 Turn right (south) on S. Pleasant St. and cross Plum Creek. Plum Creek joins the West Branch of the Black River four miles east of here in Carlisle Reservation (a Lorain County Metro Park) (Ch. 51). Turn right onto a paved walkway along Plum Creek to reach Martin Luther King, Jr. Memorial Park. This three-part tribute to African-Americans was created by the town's parks and recreation department with outside assistance, and dedicated in 1987. The first memorial, a tall, incised-brick portrait of Martin Luther King Jr., was designed by Paul B. Arnold, an Emeritus Art Professor. King visited Oberlin many times and was awarded an honorary Doctorate of Humane Letters degree in 1965.

Continue west on the walkway. The second memorial is a photographic monument honoring the Oberlin-Wellington Rescuers. In 1858, fugitive slave John Price, who came from Kentucky to Oberlin, was seized by slave-catchers and driven to the town of Wellington. A group of abolitionists then marched on Wellington, rescued and protected him by returning him to Oberlin, then helped him gain his freedom in Canada. This event was significant in inflaming antislavery sentiments nationwide leading up to the Civil War. The third monument commemorates three Oberlin men (John A. Copeland, Shields Green, and Lewis Sheridan Leary) who were killed in John Brown's 1859 raid on Harpers Ferry, another important event leading up to the war. This 1860 cenotaph, originally located in Westwood Cemetery, was moved here in 1971. (For more information on African-American history, the Lorain County Visitors Bureau offers an "African American Heritage Tour" leaflet guide. Call the bureau at 440-245-5282 or 800-334-1673, or visit the Oberlin Library.)

35 The white frame house set back from the road is the 1847 Wack-Dietz House at 43 E. Vine St. It is the former home of Chauncey Wack, a tavern keeper and prominent Democrat who was a witness in the trial of the Oberlin-Wellington Rescuers.

36 The small two-story brick house at 33 E. Vine St. is the former home of Wilson Bruce Evans. It was built in 1856 for Evans, a free black carpenter and cabinet maker from North Carolina. Evans, his brother Henry Evans, and Lewis Sheridan Leary, their brother-in-law, were arrested in the Oberlin-Wellington Slave Rescue. Evans is said to have opened his home to fugitive slaves and made it a stop on the Underground Railroad. The house is owned by an Evans descendant and is not open to the public. Continue west on Vine St. and cross Main St.

37 On the southwest corner of Vine and S. Main streets is Wright Park (dedicated in 1932), honoring Clarence J. Wright, a grocer whose first store once stood on this corner.

Across Plum Creek is the Soldier's Monument honoring 96 Civil War casualties of both town and college, and those killed in the Spanish-American War of 1898, World War I, World War II, the Korean War, and the war in Vietnam.

Continue walking west on Vine St. to Professor St. Here are several college residences for students with special interests. Turn right, walk north.

38 Facing the end of W. Vine St. is Max Kade House (German House), home to German-speaking students.

39 Harvey House (1968), adjacent to Kade, is for Spanish-speaking students (Spanish House).

Price (Third World House) is located to the rear of Harvey. This student residence functions as a political and cultural community and an arena for critical analysis and discussion.

40 At 68 S. Professor is the 1894 Lewis House, the Religious Life Center. Located here is the Office of Chaplains, which oversees the student-volunteer Community Outreach Program that serves 50 agencies throughout Lorain County annually.

41 On the east side of the street at 73 S. Professor are three historic buildings maintained by the Oberlin Historical and Improvement Organization (O.H.I.O.). Turn right on a brick walkway to reach this Oberlin Heritage Center. Jewett House (1883) was once the home of Frank Fanning Jewett, an Oberlin College chemistry professor who taught chemistry to Charles Martin Hall. Both the house and barn are in the National Register of Historic Places. The house and other buildings are open to the public for tours by calling 440-774-1700.

42 Down the walkway is the 1837 Little Red Schoolhouse, the first school for Oberlin children. It was originally built near First Church and later used as a residence on S. Main St. The schoolhouse was restored in 1958 and moved here in 1968. Third-graders use the building each June when they study Oberlin's history.

43 Another historic building is the James Monroe House, an Italianate brick building constructed in 1866 and moved here in 1960. This home belonged first to General Giles Shurtleff, Oberlin's leading Civil War hero. James Monroe, an abolitionist and classics professor at the college, lived in it after 1870 with his wife, Julia Finney Monroe, the daughter of Rev. Charles Finney, Oberlin's great religious leader. Return on the brick walkway to the sidewalk and turn north on S. Professor St.

44 Next on Professor is the prestigious Oberlin Conservatory of Music, this country's first conservatory when it opened in 1865. For most people, just hearing the word "Oberlin" conjures up thoughts of music. Rev. Charles Grandison Finney, an amateur cellist, was instrumental in starting the conservatory, and Charles Martin Hall, a piano student, provided funding and established America's first music professorship at the college. Other firsts in the country for the conservatory included: the first full-time chair in music history and appreciation (1892); the first four-year degree program in public school music (1921); the introduction of the Suzuki method of string pedagogy (1958); establishment of a pioneer program in electronic music (1969); and creation of the first arts exchange program between the former U.S.S.R. and the U.S. with the American Soviet Youth Orchestra, consisting of 100 students from both countries.

The conservatory building is one of the most unusual on campus. It was designed in 1964 by Minoru Yamasaki, the architect of the World Trade Center towers, tragically erased from the New York City skyline in the terrorist attack of September 11, 2001. The conservatory contains three distinct sections, each with a different function: Bibbins Hall, used primarily for teaching, contains classrooms, studios, a chamber music hall, and offices; the Central Unit contains two performance halls, Warner Concert Hall and Kulas Recital Hall, and an extensive music library, rehearsal rooms, and a lounge; the third section in the complex is Robertson Hall, containing individual practice rooms, each with its own grand piano and window overlooking the campus.

45 Fairchild House (1950) at Elm St. and S. Professor is another residence hall. Turn left (west) on Elm. St.

46 At 30 S. Professor, opposite the Conservatory of Music, is historic Baldwin Cottage, home of the Women's Collective, a community of women who share an interest in feminist issues. This lovely old building was originally built as a dormitory in 1885.

47 The Adam Joseph Lewis Center for Environmental Studies (2000) is one of the most advanced examples of sustainable design in America and the first academic building of its kind in the world. More than 350 Oberlin College students participated in the planning and building of this center. In addition to many other features, the center produces more energy than it uses, purifies and reuses wastewater on site, and uses no toxic materials.

Turn around and return to S. Professor St. Turn left to continue north on S. Professor St.

48 At W. College St. and Professor is Talcott Hall (1887), another architecturally distinguished residence hall. Its stone construction is Romanesque in style.

The Underground Railroad Monument in front of Talcott was designed and installed by students to commemorate the historical events that took place here during the mid-19th century. Oberlin was one of the first small towns in America to promise freedom to all who came within its borders.

Turn right at W. College St. and walk east, crossing S. Main St. once again.

49 The Oberlin Chamber of Commerce at 7 N. Main St. (inside the Oberlin Inn) has helpful information and brochures for your further exploration of Oberlin (800-962-3754). The Chamber is open Monday through Friday 9 a.m. to 5 p.m

Continue east on E. College St., going past Willard St. and across S. Pleasant St. Go two more blocks, crossing N. Park St. and Spring St.

50 The Langston House at 207 E. College St., built in 1856, was the home of John Mercer Langston, an ardent abolitionist and civil rights leader. Langston, who was born into slavery, graduated from Oberlin and went on to have a distinguished career in law, breaking many barriers: he was Ohio's first black attorney, the first black to practice law before the U.S. Supreme Court, the first black to be elected to any office in the United States, and the first black Congressman from Virginia.

51 Cross to the north side of E. College St. and turn left, heading back west. The Oberlin Seniors Center at 90 E. College St. (between N. Park St. and N. Pleasant St.) houses the Underground Railroad Quilt. Residents of Oberlin created this 24-square quilt to portray Oberlin's significant role in the antislavery movement. During weekdays visitors may step inside to view the quilt. Continue west on E. College St., across N. Pleasant St., to end at the parking lot on Willard St. where the hike began. ■

49 Black River Reservation
Elyria

Distance: 3.5 miles end to end or 7 miles round-trip (includes side loops)

Easy

Walking time: 1 ½ hours one-way or 3 hours round-trip

Description: The flat, 12-foot-wide Bridgeway Trail is asphalt paved. Information panels along its length describe the history and natural features of the Black River valley. Mile markers along the path make it a favorite for hikers and joggers. Two loop trails offer interesting side visits—one to a big cottonwood, one of the largest trees in Lorain County, and another to a tall waterfall.

Directions: From I-90 take Exit 148 in Sheffield (SR 254); west on SR 254 (Detroit Rd.) for about 1 mile; right (north) on E. River/Gulf Rd. for 1.8 miles; left (west) on E. 31 St.; cross bridge over Black River; park entrance on left (marked Day's Dam).

From Lorain take SR 57 (E. 28 St.) east; south on Grove Ave. (still SR 57) for 0.25 mile; left (east) on E.31 St. for 0.7 mile; entrance on right.

Parking & restrooms: Located at both Day's Dam and Bur Oak picnic and parking areas.

The Bridgeway Trail is in Black River Reservation, one of 16 units that make up Lorain County Metro Parks. The reservation's 833 acres along the Black River include scenic bottomlands, forests, meadows, and wetlands. Together they provide a lush green corridor within Lorain and Elyria. The park's most outstanding natural feature, the Black River itself, continues to carve through Cleveland Shale bedrock, forming impressive dark cliffs.

The three-mile hike/bike trail extends from Day's Dam picnic area in Lorain to Bur Oak picnic area in Elyria and provides access into the park for hikers, bicyclists, and people using wheelchairs or strollers. A free electric tram at the Day's Dam end takes visitors who otherwise would be unable to negotiate the trail into the valley. (Contact the park for scheduling information.) Midway along the trail, a 1,000-foot bridge spans the Black River, crossing it twice and providing views of both the river and the treetops.

The name "Day's Dam" derives from the early history of this part of the Black River valley. In the 1800s the Day family established a mill at this site. They constructed a dam across the river to provide the water power for the mill wheel. The area retains the family name though the dam and mill are no longer evident.

NOTE: Because this hike is on a north–south linear trail with a substantial round-trip distance, you may optionally park a second car at Bur Oak picnic area at the south end of the reservation to end this hike after 3 miles. To reach the reservation's south end from SR 254 west, follow the directions above to the Sheffield Fire Department intersection at SR 254 (Detroit Rd.) and E. River/Gulf Rd. Turn south onto Gulf Rd. Almost immediately (about 500 feet) turn right onto Ford Rd. and follow it downhill about a half-mile to the Bur Oak park entrance on the right.

The reservation is open daily 8 A.M. to dusk unless otherwise posted. There are restrooms, picnic shelters, parking, and trail information signs at both the Day's Dam and Bur Oak picnic areas. Information about all of the Lorain County Metro Parks is available at the website www.loraincountymetroparks.com, or by phoning 800-526-7275.

1 Begin the walk at Day's Dam, at the overlook above the Black River. From this high viewpoint you can see into the deep valley that you will soon be entering. Go south on the asphalt-paved walkway that now descends through black Cleveland Shale (see Appendix A). This layer of shale was formed about 360 million years ago when the land that is now Ohio was covered by a warm, deep, stagnant inland sea. Thick extensive deposits of mud accumulated on the sea floor and eventually solidified; the sea drained away, the land dried, and the hardened mud became shale. Carbonized plant fragments and numerous fish fossils have been found in Cleveland Shale. Note how this soft rock breaks up into thin, sharp-edged, slatelike fragments. Although it appears gray on the surface, the typical black color of this shale is revealed when it is broken in half. Here and there are brownish-red pieces that have been changed by weathering; occasionally marcasite or pyrite ("fool's gold") can be found in this shale. Cleveland Shale is visible in cliffs along rivers in eastern Erie County, northern Lorain County, and parts of Cuyahoga County.

2 At 0.3 mile on the left, a 0.1-mile woodchip-lined path, the Cottonwood Trail, leads to one of the largest trees in the area. At a fork in this trail, bear left to cross a small bridge to the huge cottonwood, surrounded by a viewing deck. The exact age of this tree is unknown. Return on the Cottonwood Trail to the paved Bridgeway Trail.

3 To the right, along the base of a shale cliff, is a former channel of the Black River. Sometime during the past 200 years, probably during a large flood, the river "straightened itself out." It jumped two meanders and established a straighter course. Now just a small stream flows through the old channel and under the trail to reach the present Black River. At the half-mile marker a fenced area on the left marks a good place to view the river.

4 Go off the main trail to follow another woodchip trail on the right (southwest), the Waterfall Trail. This path leads to a 25-foot-high

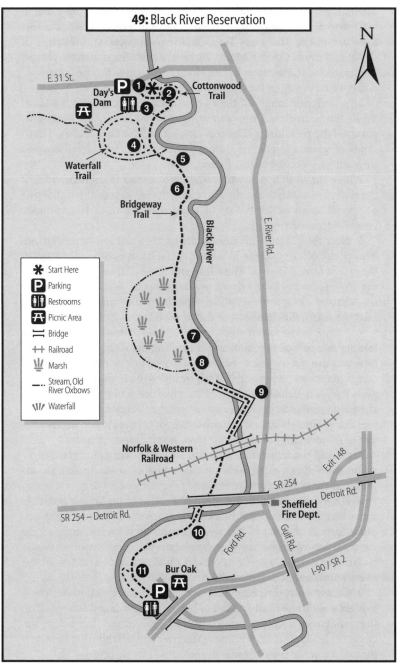

49: Black River Reservation

N

E. 31 St.

Day's Dam

Cottonwood Trail

Waterfall Trail

Bridgeway Trail

Black River

E. River Rd.

Start Here
Parking
Restrooms
Picnic Area
Bridge
Railroad
Marsh
Stream, Old River Oxbows
Waterfall

Norfolk & Western Railroad

Exit 148

SR 254

Detroit Rd.

Sheffield Fire Dept.

SR 254 – Detroit Rd.

Ford Rd.

Gulf Rd.

I-90 / SR 2

Bur Oak

© Gray & Company, Publishers

waterfall dropping over a Cleveland Shale cliff just below E. 36th St. The falls drops into the older river channel, now marked by a line of mature trees. This half-mile trail continues along the old river channel to return to the Bridgeway Trail. On the right (west) in the center of this loop Lorain County Metro Parks has established a small prairie, dominated in the summer by big bluestem, a native prairie grass.

Continue south on the Bridgeway Trail.

5 Scattered throughout the river valley are large granite boulders. While the bedrock in Ohio is mostly sandstone, shale, and limestone, granite-type rock forms the bedrock north of the Great Lakes. Thousands of years ago glaciers dumped the big gray boulders here and throughout glaciated parts of Ohio.

Where the trail dips down, it again crosses the former meander of the river. Just south of the dip and along the left side of the trail is one of several small wetlands that lie parallel to the trail. They provide good wildlife viewing areas.

6 Near the 1.0-mile marker on the right (west) is a large wetland. This pond, offering a fine habitat for wildlife, is another remnant of the river's former course. The Cleveland Shale cliff on the edge of the marsh was also cut by the river's previous course. Turtles and frogs use this wetland along with songbirds. In spring and summer you might hear the sweet, flutelike song of the wood thrush.

7 By the information sign "Once Upon a Forest" is a short trail leading to a fenced overlook and trail along the river. From the overlook you can get a glimpse of the 1,000-foot bridge carrying the trail across the river and beyond it, a tall trestle of the Lorain and West Virginia Railroad. Below the overlook the river drops over a series of small shale ledges. These tiny ledges are where the Cleveland Shale has broken along joints (long cracks) within the rock. These joints are also visible in the dry cliff bordering the river, just below the fence.

Return to the main trail. At the 1.5-mile marker is the tram turnaround as well as a small shelter, picnic tables, seasonal drinking fountain, and Porta-Potty.

8 Here you stand at the southern end of one of the largest and most active wetlands within the Black River watershed. This wetland, another former channel of the river, extends about a half-mile to the west. An information panel explains the many benefits of wetlands. Great blue herons, wood ducks, and muskrats are just a few of the many animals that use this habitat.

9 Cross two spectacular steel bridges over the Black River. These bridges were strategically placed to bypass the Cleveland Shale cliff on the right (west) and to provide beautiful views of the river below. Because the bridges are 25 feet above the river and neighboring land, you look down at the tops of some of the trees growing below.

Cleveland Shale, a Devonian-Age rock, contains few fossils but is famous for its giant armored fish fossil, *Dunkleosteus*, found in Cuya-

hoga County. (This huge fossil is on exhibit at the Cleveland Museum of Natural History.)

Follow the trail under the railroad trestle and the SR 254 bridge.

10 Cross a third bridge at the 2-mile marker and enjoy more views of the river, which flows north to Lake Erie. An information panel relates the story of one of the earliest written accounts of the Black River region.

11 At the 2.5-mile marker, a paved side trail loops over to the river and then leads back to the Bur Oak picnic and parking area and the 3-mile marker.

At this point, end the hike if a second car is parked here or return on the Bridgeway Trail to the start of the walk at Day's Dam.

50 Vermilion River Reservation
Vermilion

Directions: From I-90/SR 2, follow SR 2 west to exit for Vermilion/Sunnyside roads; left (south), cross over SR 2; right (west) on Jerusalem Rd. left (south) on Vermilion Rd. for 1¹/₂ miles; right on N. Ridge Rd.; go downhill, pass Bacon Woods entrance on right, cross bridge over Vermilion River; immediate left into park entrance.

From Lorain take US 6 west; south on Baumhart 2.7 miles; right (west) on N. Ridge Rd. until road seems to dead-end; right (north) for 0.3 mile; pass Vermilion Rd. and drive downhill; pass Bacon Woods entrance on right, cross bridge over Vermilion River; immediate left into park entrance.

From I-90 (Ohio Turnpike) take exit 135 (Baumhart Rd.); north on Baumhart for1.8 miles ; left (west) onto N. Ridge Rd. for 1.8 miles (road seems to dead-end); right (north) for 0.3 mile past Vermilion Rd. on right; enter park by continuing downhill; pass Bacon Woods entrance on right, cross bridge over Vermilion River; immediate left into park entrance.

One of the most frequently visited parks in Lorain County is 1,026-acre Vermilion River Reservation. It consists of two areas: Bacon Woods to the northwest and Mill Hollow to the southeast. The park is located alongside the Vermilion River, south of SR 2 in Brownhelm Township and about four miles south of the city of Vermilion. The park's outstanding feature is its spectacular 90-foot-high shale cliff, composed of layers of rock estimated to be 360 million years old. It has taken thousands of years of erosion to carve out the valley and expose this ancient rock. Also contributing to the park's popularity is its colorful past, when it was known as Mill Hollow. In its heyday in the 1860s, the hollow supported a busy mill town with many homes and commercial buildings.

In July 1817, Benjamin Bacon and other early settlers from New England established homes and built a sawmill, gristmill, and millrace at the neck of a wide bend in the Vermilion River. A church, school, and post office were soon added, and then a tannery, ashery, and blacksmith's shop. They called their settlement Brownhelm Mills; it later became known as Mill Hollow.

Benjamin Bacon's Greek Revival home (1845) and 114 acres of land were given to Lorain County Metro Parks in 1957 by Dorothy Bacon Demuth. Now fully restored with period furnishings, the Benjamin Bacon Museum is open to the public for tours (call for times). It is listed in the National Register of Historic Places. The phone number at Vermilion River Reservation is 440-967-7310. For information on Lorain County Metro Parks, phone 440-458-7275. The website is www.lorain-countymetroparks.com.

Annual events at this reservation are the Pioneer Days Festival, on the weekend after Labor Day, and the Keel Haulers Canoe Race, on the last Sunday in March. This race starts eight miles upriver in Birmingham and ends in Mill Hollow.

Hike A: Southeast Section

> **Easy**
>
> **Distance:** 0.8 mile
> **Hiking time:** Less than one hour
> **Description:** This hike, on flat trails, provides views of high Cleveland Shale cliffs, a waterfowl pond, and traces of the old mill sites along the river.
> **Parking and Restrooms:** Park near the Bacon Museum. Restrooms and information are located in the Carriage Barn behind the museum.

1 Start at the Carriage Barn for information about activities and programs in this and other Lorain County Metro Parks. This post-and-beam structure was built in 1996.

If the Benjamin Bacon Museum is open, it is worthwhile to take a tour. Modeled on New England architecture of the time, the central portion of this 2½-story house was built in 1845; a wing and summer kitchen were added later. The mill room off the main entry served as Mr. Bacon's office, where he bought timber, wheat, corn, and oats and sold flour, horse feed, and lumber. This room also was a social center and courtroom—Bacon was a justice of the peace for Brownhelm Mills. Other downstairs rooms are a parlor, bedroom, dining room, and kitchen; upstairs there are four bedrooms. The summer kitchen wing to the north served as woodshed, milkhouse, and washhouse.

2 From the parking area walk north toward the river's edge and the Cleveland Shale cliff. The path winds through the grassy embankment and in and out of the trees along the river's edge. Sometimes it is possible to walk along the beach by the river's edge, if the water is low.

The almost-vertical Cleveland Shale cliff has been carved by the Vermilion River over many millennia. It took 100 million years for the sediments that comprise these rocks to accumulate at the bottom of an ancient ocean floor during the Devonian Age (see Appendix A), and only about 12,000 years for erosion to carve this valley and expose the rock.

The lower two-thirds of this 90-foot-high cliff is composed of thin layers of dark, slatelike Cleveland Shale. The upper third of this cliff is Bedford Formation, which, from bottom to top, consists of a thin layer of grayish shale, then a protruding layer of sandstone, then a thick layer of soft, grayish-red shale. The sandstone is composed of fine sand and silt particles strongly cemented together to form very hard rock. The reddish-hued shale tints the cliff reddish-orange when it washes down in a rainstorm. (This shale is thought to have caused early inhabitants to name the river Vermilion, French for reddish-orange.) Glacial deposits and soil form the cliff's top layer.

Several interesting and unusual types of rocks can be found along the edge of the river. "Turtle Rocks" are concretions (called septaria by geologists) that have fallen out of the Cleveland Shale layers; they are about two inches in diameter and resemble rusty-brown turtle shells with prominent veins.

"Fool's gold," composed of the minerals pyrite and marcasite, may also be found as small nodules protruding from slabs of Cleveland Shale. At the base of the shale is a thin limestone layer. The limestone sometimes reveals whitish-gray pieces of rock that resemble a series of large fossil teeth. These are not teeth, nor are they fossils. The appearance is due to a structural pattern in the rock, called "cone-in-cone," that results from the way the limestone crystallized.

Also occasionally found along the river's edge are iron concretions of various shapes, siltstones, and "flow-stones." The flow-stones are contorted, twisted, and folded hunks of rock. They were formed when a force, such as an earthquake or weight from additional sediment, caused partly solidified sediments to shift. Eventually these soft materials hardened into rock, keeping their contorted shapes. These rocks have fallen down from the Bedford Formation in the top portion of the cliff.

3 Continue along the mowed grass. Note the various colors in the cliff: white, black, gray, red, and yellowish-brown. Some of these tints are a result of the reddish shale running down, some from soil washing down, and others from iron and sulphur compounds exposed to air and erosion. Plants have started growing on the talus slope created by an accumulation of fallen rocks. Springs emerge from the shale at various points, allowing moss and algae to grow. In winter, especially in January, these springs freeze into spectacular icicle formations and ice falls along the cliff faces.

4 Walk toward the pond, then take the boardwalk/observation deck across it. Any of several varieties of waterfowl may be enjoying the pond. Cross the grass to the left of the shelter and head down toward the river.

5 Near the water's edge (visible when the water level is low) is shale that is bluish, very soft, and easily broken. This 360-million-year-old Chagrin Shale lies beneath the Cleveland Shale and is the oldest exposed rock in Northeast Ohio (see Appendix A).

6 Head toward the picnic shelter to find the path between the shelter and the millrace. At this site, a mill dam was constructed to raise the

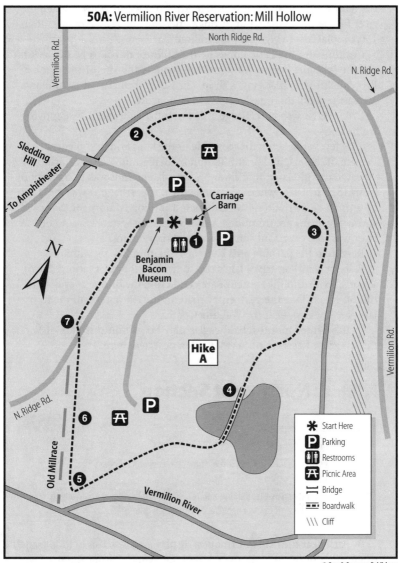

50A: Vermilion River Reservation: Mill Hollow

North Ridge Rd.

Vermilion Rd.

N. Ridge Rd.

Sledding Hill

To Amphitheater

N

Carriage Barn

Benjamin Bacon Museum

Hike A

N. Ridge Rd.

Old Millrace

Vermilion River

Vermilion Rd.

✳	Start Here
P	Parking
🚻	Restrooms
🛋	Picnic Area
⊨	Bridge
▦	Boardwalk
\\\	Cliff

© Gray & Company, Publishers

level of the river, thus enabling water to enter the millrace. This path leads to a wooden walkway/observation deck overlooking the old millrace and a more recent dam.

The millrace was built in 1825 and cut across the horseshoe bend of the Vermilion River. The race diverted water north to supply power to a sawmill and gristmill on N. Ridge Rd.

At the wooden walkway is a concrete dam that blocks the millrace;

the dam was built to keep N. Ridge Rd. from washing away when the river flooded. The road, put through after the mill ceased operation in 1900, replaced a bridge over the millrace.

Continue on the path alongside the millrace north to N. Ridge Rd. On the left, just before you cross the road, is the site of the original Brownhelm Mills blacksmith shop. The site of the original sawmill was across the road, on the west side of N. Ridge Rd.

CAUTION: Cross N. Ridge Rd. carefully, as there is fast-moving traffic here.

7 A few yards down the west side of the road and into the woods is the site of the original gristmill built by Benjamin Bacon for grinding wheat, oats, and corn into flour and meal. The mill was in operation from 1820 to 1876, when it burned down. A year later it was replaced by a three-story building with the latest milling equipment that used steam power to accommodate times when the water was low or the river was iced over. Only an old foundation remains.

Return to the parking area past the Benjamin Bacon Museum.

A short walk (or drive) takes you to trails in the reservation's Bacon Woods. Exit from the museum area and cross the bridge over the Vermilion River. Take the park entry road on the left and continue to the last parking area, near the Walking Center.

In the winter months, bald eagles may be seen in this part of Vermilion River Reservation, as they often nest near here.

Hike B: Northwest Section

Distance: 3.5 miles

Easy

Hiking time: 2 hours

Description: This hike follows three connected trails, all relatively flat, in the floodplain of the Vermilion River.

Parking and Restrooms: Parking and restrooms are located at the Walking Center at the end of the Bacon Woods entrance drive.

8 Park near the trail information display area. A series of loop trails offers the option of a short or long hike. After visiting the displays, begin the walk on the Bacon Woods Trail.

There are *two* entrances to the Bacon Woods Trail. Take the trail to the northeast, the trail entrance that is closest to the cliff on the right. NOTE: Waterproof boots are recommended here, especially in spring and late fall.

9 Continue on the Bacon Woods Trail, a wide crushed-limestone path. Considerable damage was done to the trees along this trail by a tornado in 1992 that opened up the woods to more light and sun. The

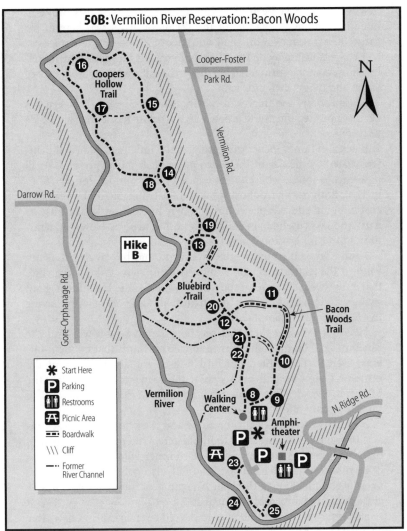

50B: Vermilion River Reservation: Bacon Woods

wet ground here results from frequent flooding on the river plain and poor drainage of the clay soil. This moist environment supports beech and maple trees, some of which were uprooted or had their tops twisted and snapped off in the tornado. Other trees that grow here are the sycamore (with its mottled white, green, and brown bark), black walnut, Ohio buckeye, box elder, tulip, and American elm. Spring wildflowers are especially abundant along this trail.

10 Stay to the right (east) on the Bacon Woods Trail where the sycamore tree goes off to the left. Cross a wooden boardwalk. These new walkways have been placed over swampy land that is prone to flooding. The main channel of the Vermilion River was here in the early 1800s. It is now more than a quarter of a mile west of here.

11 Spicebush may be found along here. It is recognized by its yellow flowers in the spring, red berries in the fall, and spicy fragrance of leaves and twigs when crushed.

Sensitive fern also thrives in this moist environment. This fern has nearly opposite pinnae and grows with a separate fertile stalk alongside its fronds.

Black and honey locust trees grow abundantly here and can be differentiated by the size of their seed pods: black locust pods are small (2–4 inches long), while honey locust pods are much longer (8–16 inches). Both trees have short spines on the trunk and limbs. Black locust is an introduced species brought here by early settlers because its hard wood was useful in making fence posts and poles. Now it is an important tree for erosion control.

Poison ivy is plentiful in this woodland and has twined itself up some of the locust trees with a thick, twisting stem. Other large vines that grow well here are grape vines (which sometimes form giant swings) and Virginia creeper (distinguished from poison ivy by having five leaflets rather than three).

12 After crossing the short second boardwalk you will find the Bluebird Trail on the right, named for the bluebirds that frequent this area, even in the winter. Bluebird houses are situated around the meadow. Follow the path a few steps to the open meadow, then take the branch to the left. This open area used to be a farm field where, until the 1970s, corn and soybeans grew.

Birding is excellent in this meadow and river floodplain. Black locust trees have gained a strong foothold here. Wild roses, cow parsnips, blackberry bushes, and a variety of summer wildflowers enjoy the open sunshine and rich soil. Ground nut, also called wild bean, is especially abundant along this trail. The pungent fragrance of its flower clusters is quite noticeable in August.

Side trails on the left lead over to the old river channel. A new river channel farther west was created during a huge flood in 1969. The old channel still carries water when the river is high but is often dry, with only a scattering of water holes.

13 As the trail turns right, a narrow fisherman's trail leads to the left along the river. Continue on the Bluebird Trail, and after 150 feet turn left (north) on the Bluebird Connector Trail that leads into the woods.

14 Where the trail divides, bear right (north) on the Coopers Hollow Trail, a 1.1-mile loop. You will later return to this point via the trail on the left. Thirty feet off the trail, in the woods to the right, is a structure built of five wooden poles in V formation capped with a metal shield. This contraption is left over from days when telephone poles

crossed the valley. It protected the telephone pole downriver by diverting ice chunks and debris being propelled downstream by floodwaters. Ice can do major damage—scars on the upstream sides of the trees nearby show where water-propelled ice jams have scraped off portions of their bark.

15 Here a road used to cross the valley, connecting Cooper-Foster Park Rd. on the east ridge of the valley with Darrow/Gore-Orphanage Rd. on the west ridge. The grassy path visible to the left is the approximate location of the old road. Continue walking north.

16 Here you again reach the Vermilion River and the midpoint of the hike. The many deer tracks show where deer access the river.

17 The sandstone block foundations seen here supported a bridge for the road crossing the valley.

18 Arriving at the trail split, go right (south), on the Bluebird Connector Trail and meet the Bluebird Trail.

19 Bear left (east) on the Bluebird Trail. A boardwalk crosses a muddy area, possibly an old river channel. One hundred feet beyond the end of the boardwalk, two trails go off to the right. Keep on the main trail.

20 Meet the end of the loop and leave the Bluebird Trail by turning left on the short connector, then bear right (south) to enter the woods on another section of the Bacon Woods Trail.

Thriving here, on both sides of the trail, is ostrich fern, reaching 5 feet in height. Note the smaller fertile frond, which is stiff and woody, surrounded by the much taller sterile, leafy fronds. The fertile fronds remain all winter after the leafy fronds have been killed; they release their spores the following spring, a feature unique to this particular fern. Most other ferns release their spores the same season that they are produced.

21 Turn left (east) on the Sycamore Trail (a short connector trail) for 100 feet to see an old, hollow, but still living, sycamore tree. Names and dates have been carved on the tree's south side but are nearly obliterated by the tree's growth rings around the scar.

22 Retrace your steps to the Bacon Woods Trail and turn left (south) to walk parallel to the old Vermilion River channel (on the right). Continue south on the path, passing trees twisted and cracked off by the 1992 tornado, to return to the Walking Center.

Continue south on the road past picnic shelter #4.

23 Turn right onto the wide, grassy trail located between picnic shelter #4 and a pond. Follow this trail westward a short distance to a trail along the river, identified by old blue blazes on the trees. Notice in the woods to the west and north there are trees exhibiting ice scars. Some trees show evidence of three episodes of ice damage, each scar partly healed before the next one was formed. A fungus can enter such wounds, causing rot that can eventually kill the tree. Turn left (south) along the river.

24 In the spring the wildflowers are beautiful along this riverside path. Virginia bluebell, jack-in-the-pulpit, nodding trillium, true Solomon's seal, and false Solomon's seal are some of the spring flowers. Trees along this trail include cottonwood, sycamore, hackberry, white ash, walnut, Ohio buckeye, and willows. Side trails lead to fishing spots along the river.

25 Near the end of the trail, follow a side path to the right (south), to the stone beach of the river, and a good view of the Cleveland Shale cliff. At the base of the cliff, during low water, the light-gray Chagrin Shale can also be seen. Hemlock trees grow on the cool, damp, north-facing cliff and slopes across the river. Seepage of water from the layers of shale forms spectacular ice falls and giant icicles in January. Return to the trail. Bear right and uphill to the grassy area just south of the small pond. The pond was created in 1962 during construction of the first roads into the park.

After reaching the pond, turn left (north) and head back to the parking area near the Walking Center or return to the Benjamin Bacon Museum. ■

51 Carlisle Reservation
LaGrange

Distance: 5.3 miles

Hiking time: 2 3/4 hours

Description: The trails in the reservation are flat or gently rolling. The most interesting landscape feature of Carlisle Reservation is the West Branch of the Black River and several creeks that feed it. This hike consists of three loop hikes—a short loop north of the Visitor Center and two longer loops near the equestrian center to the west of the Visitor Center, plus 1.5 miles of linear trail connecting the two areas.

Directions: From Cleveland take I-480 west to Exit 1 (SR 10/Oberlin); west on US 20/SR 10 for 8 miles to exit for SR 301 (LaGrange Rd.); south on SR 301 about 0.5 mile; right on Nickel Plate-Diagonal Rd. for about 1.5 miles; park entrance on right.

From Sheffield, Elyria, and Lorain's east side, take SR 301 south; right just past US 20/SR 10 on Nickel Plate-Diagonal Rd. for about 1.5 miles; park entrance on right.

From center of Lorain take SR 57 south, bypassing Elyria; right (south) on US 20/SR 10; right on Nickel Plate-Diagonal Rd. for about 1.5 miles; park entrance on right.

From Lorain's west side, take SR 58 south; left (east) on Russia Rd. to end; left on Oberlin-Elyria Rd. for about 0.3 mile; right (south) onto LaGrange Rd. (SR 301) for 2 miles; right on Nickel Plate-Diagonal Rd. for about 1.5 miles; park entrance on right.

From Akron take I-76/US 224 west to Lodi; north on SR 83 to Belden; left (west) on SR 303 for 7 miles past LaGrange; right (north) on Nickel Plate Rd. (becomes Nickel Plate-Diagonal Rd.); park entrance on left.

Parking & restrooms: At the Carlisle Visitor Center.

Lorain County's Carlisle Reservation is located south of Elyria and east of Oberlin. The West Branch of the Black River courses west to east through Carlisle's 1,720 acres of wooded forests, meadows, and lowlands. Approximately nine miles of hiking and bridle trails are maintained in the park. Five miles of the nine have been improved with a crushed-limestone surface; four miles have a natural soil base. There is also a grass-surfaced trail to and around some of the wetland areas. The hikes listed in this chapter are all on the improved trails, including some horse trails. Cross-country skiing is also popular on Carlisle Reservation trails, as well as in nearby Forest Hills Golf Center. When hiking in winter, please don't walk in the ski tracks. Carlisle Reservation is open daily 8 A.M. to dusk unless otherwise posted.

The park has a beautiful visitor and administrative center with a large wildlife observation area, nature exhibits, a children's nature room, seasonal displays, and a nature store. Here park naturalists provide maps, programs, guided hikes, and information about all of Lorain County's parks. The center is open daily 8 A.M.–4:30 P.M. at 12882 Diagonal Rd., LaGrange (800-526-7275).

On the west side of the visitor center is the Raptor Center, home for injured raptors such as owls, hawks, or eagles, that are unable to be released back into the wild. South of the parking lot is the Sugar Shack and displays illustrating the process for making maple syrup.

The Duck Pond picnic area northeast of Carlisle Visitor Center includes two ponds, a shelter, restrooms, and an accessible fishing dock. Trails from the duck ponds lead to a seven-acre constructed wetlands where the bird-watching is particularly good. This wet meadow/marsh and the restored wetlands near the equestrian center have become two of the most favored features in the reservation.

The equestrian center is located west of the visitor center, accessed via Nickel Plate-Diagonal Rd., and is open to people owning their own horses. Although designed primarily for horseback riders, the equestrian trails (a 1.6-mile north loop and a 1.2-mile south loop) are eminently suitable for hiking. Hikers should yield to horses by stepping off the trail and allowing them to pass.

The West Branch of the Black River and tributaries including Plum Creek and Meadow Creek contain water whose dark color is caused by mud and silt dissolved in it from constantly eroding stream banks. Floodwaters rush through these tributaries in the spring. Meander beds, which are dry the rest of the year, show where the high water flows. The West Branch cuts across a preglacial river valley that once was 192 feet deep and almost a mile wide in places. When glaciers pushed across this area, they filled in the old valley with mud, silt, and sand as they melted. The West Branch of the Black River has cut a valley about 35 to 55 feet deep into the glacial deposits. The river continues to gouge out glacial debris today. Glacial boulders, left here as "calling cards" when the glaciers melted, are scattered throughout the fields and valleys.

The first inhabitants of this area lived here about 4,000 years ago, as revealed by spear points and flint scrapers that have been found in cultivated fields. Most of the Indian settlements were on higher ground away from the river's floodplain, as were those of later inhabitants. However, farmers chose this area for settlement because of the fertile soil. They cleared timber (black walnut, cherry, and chestnut trees), built lumber mills and homes, and used the fields for pastures. Occasionally the stumps of these trees can be seen off the trail. Today the land is returning to its original forested condition.

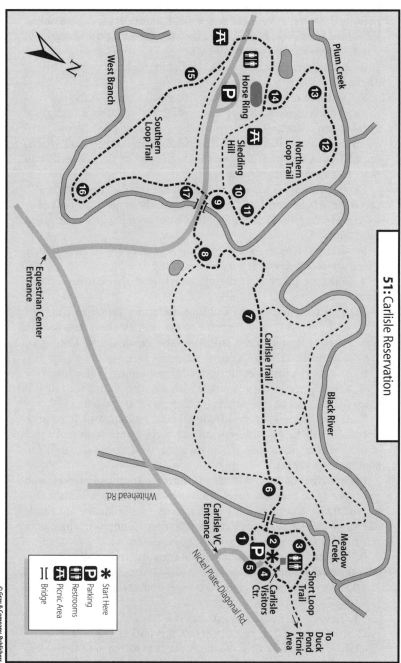

51: Carlisle Reservation

© Gray & Company, Publishers

1 Begin the hike at the south end of the parking lot. Enter the 0.4-mile Short Loop Trail, a handicapped-accessible trail. Follow the path heading downhill to your right. The small, meandering stream on the left is Meadow Creek, a tributary of the West Branch of the Black River; it is flowing north toward the river.

2 Stay on the Short Loop Trail, passing the trail junction and bridge on the left.

3 Continue northwest. At a trail intersection, stay to the right. As the trail curves around to the east, notice a 10-to 20-foot-high ridge ahead of you. Although it appears to be a manmade dike, it was actually formed by natural erosion. The ridge separates two small valleys. Spring floods and rains have eroded both sides of the hill so that all that remains is this narrow ridge.

Circle around the loop to now head southeast. This path is also called the "Halloween Trail," because it is traditionally used for a Halloween evening hike, when the path is lined with goblins, ghosts, and pumpkins.

Pass a set of steps on the left. The trail now gradually ascends a slope. Pass the Deer Trail, which goes off to the left.

4 Continue on the main trail, which leads back to the visitor center.

5 Cross the parking area south of the visitor center to enter the same trail (Note #1), and continue to the trail junction described in Note #2. Now turn left here, cross onto the Visitor Center Connector (yellow signs) and the bridge over Meadow Creek.

6 A wetland is just over the bridge. You now join the Meadow Loop Trail, a wide, improved trail marked with red signs, which you will follow westward. Avoid several side trails to the right and left.

7 At the power line, the Meadow Loop Trail curves left (south). Soon you will follow alongside an old barbed-wire farm fence that marks the edge of the woods above a steep bank. Continue south and southwest on the trail.

8 Bear right onto the Meadow Connector Trail, also marked with red signs. (The Meadow Loop Trail turns off to the left as an unimproved trail.) A pond and the central maintenance facility are visible ahead, on the left. Continue on the Meadow Connector, which goes downhill to the road leading to the equestrian center.

9 Turn right on the trail alongside the road and cross the bridge over the river.

10 Take an immediate right turn to get to the Northern Loop horse trail.

11 The Northern Loop horse trail is a 1.6-mile loop trail, marked with brown signs. Turn right (east) on this trail to follow it counterclockwise. Remember to step off to the side of the trail if you encounter a horse and rider. This trail offers scenic views of the West Branch of the Black River.

12 The trail enters the forest above the river. Note the unusual sycamore tree on the right, with its bifurcated trunk exposed by constant erosion of the soil along the riverbank. The path now circles around to the west to the confluence of Plum Creek with the West Branch.

13 Continue alongside Plum Creek—this is the same creek that flows through the town of Oberlin three miles upstream from here (Ch. 48).

14 Reach a trail junction and turn right, passing between the Horse Ring and a large fishing pond. Continue on the trail past restrooms and a picnic and parking area. Cross the road, bear left, and come to a trail junction.

15 Turn right (southeast) onto the Southern Loop horse trail (marked with yellow). Continue across a meadow and alongside the West Branch, hiking this loop counterclockwise.

16 The path enters the forest above another bend in the West Branch and then circles north.

17 At the approach to the entrance road, go off the loop trail and follow a short, grassy path to reach the road.

Once on the road, turn right and cross the bridge. Reenter the Meadow Connector Trail going eastward. Retrace your route back to the Carlisle Visitor Center. It is 1.5 miles back, following red signs for the Meadow Connector and Meadow Loop, yellow for the Visitor Center Connector, and white for the Short Loop Trail. ∎

52 Findley State Park
Wellington

Distance: 4.3 miles

Moderate

Hiking time: $2^1/_2$ hours

Description: This hike follows trails that are generally flat, but includes two very short, steep hills near the beginning. A wide variety of trees and pretty views of Findley Lake make this a very enjoyable hike in almost any season. The walk follows a loop around the lake on various trails, beginning and ending on a short section of the Buckeye Trail. It crosses the north end of the lake on an earthen dam.

Directions: From I-480 take exit for SR 10 (Oberlin); west on SR 10 west for 15 miles; left (south) on SR 58 (Oberlin Rd.) for about 9 miles; park entrance on left, 2 miles past Wellington.

From I-76/US 224, go west to Lodi; north on SR 83 to Chatham; left (west) on SR 162 to Huntington; right (north) on SR 58 for 2.4 miles; park entrance on right.

Parking & restrooms: After entering the park, turn right onto Park Rd. #3 and follow it around to the camp check-in building. Pass the building and turn left; park in the parking area south of the check-in building. Restrooms are in the small building just north of the nature center, by the road.

Findley State Park, located near Wellington, is a 903-acre tract of forested land surrounding 93-acre Findley Lake. It offers hiking, camping, boating, migratory bird hunting, fishing, swimming, and picnicking. Get information from the park office at 25381 SR 58 S., Wellington (440-647-5749; www.ohiostateparks.org).

The park, named for Judge Guy Findley, a local conservationist, offers nearly 10 miles of hiking trails, including a portion of the blue-blazed Buckeye Trail. Judge Findley purchased this land in 1936 and donated it to Ohio as a perpetual state forest for timber production and experimental foresting. The Division of Forestry then supervised the planting of nearly half a million trees, with much assistance from the Civilian Conservation Corps. In 1950 the forest was transferred to Ohio's Division of Parks and Recreation to be maintained as a state park. Between 1954 and 1956, a dam was built across Wellington Creek, creating Findley Lake, and further development led to the present public recreation area. The park's beautiful forest, consisting mainly of white and red oak, red maple, white ash, black cherry, red and white pine, and American beech trees, is a regrowth secondary for-

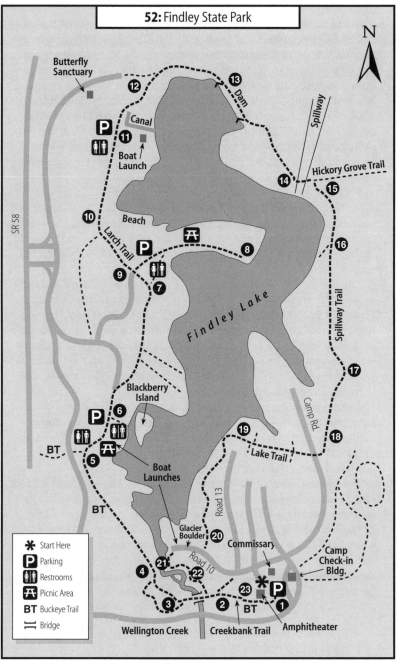

52: Findley State Park

N

Butterfly Sanctuary

12

13

Dam

Spillway

P

11

Canal

Boat Launch

Hickory Grove Trail

14

15

10

Beach

Larch Trail

P

8

16

9

7

Findley Lake

Spillway Trail

17

Blackberry Island

P

6

Camp Rd

18

19

BT

5

Lake Trail

Boat Launches

BT

Road 13

Glacier Boulder

20

Commissary

Camp Check-in Bldg.

21

Road 10

4

22

23

2

BT

1

3

Wellington Creek   Creekbank Trail   Amphitheater

Start Here
Parking
Restrooms
Picnic Area
BT Buckeye Trail
Bridge

SR 58

© Gray & Company, Publishers

est on abandoned dairy farmland. The forest floor nourishes an abundance of spring wildflowers.

In the northwest part of the park, visible from park road #9, is the Duke's Skipper Butterfly Sanctuary. In 1981 the Ohio Department of Natural Resources designated this approximately 30-foot-square area as a sanctuary to protect this extremely rare butterfly. The small, plain, brown butterfly, about 1½ inches long, emerges in July. The caterpillars feed at night on sedges, wetland plants that resemble tall blades of grass. The butterfly and its habitat are of interest to scientists not only because the Duke's Skipper is so rare, but also because the distribution of its small colonies is a mystery. It is theorized that the species made its way north after the last glacial retreat, inhabiting sedge meadows on the way. Collecting this species is strictly prohibited.

There are many other, and more colorful, butterflies to enjoy watching in the park, including swallowtails, monarchs, blues, buckeyes, frittillaries, and mourning cloaks. Mourning cloak butterflies, brownish with yellow wing margins, are among the first to emerge in the early spring: the adults overwinter under loose bark then float about on the earliest warm days.

The principal bedrocks underlying Findley State Park are Bedford Shale and Berea Sandstone, formed over 300 million years ago. In most places in Ohio, the Berea Sandstone is only 10 to 40 feet thick, but just north of here, in South Amherst, the sandstone is more than 200 feet thick. The South Amherst sandstone quarries are the largest and deepest in the world. The bedrock in Findley State Park is buried under a thick layer of glacial till. In wet seasons, the trails are often muddy, due to the high clay content of the soil.

Although this section of Lorain County was settled slowly, by the early 1800s New Englanders had begun to develop the present town of Wellington. Dairy farming and cheese production were the dominant industries of the area, and Lorain County became known as one of the greatest cheese-producing locations in the nation.

The present town of Wellington still reflects a New England influence. Many of its buildings are listed in the National Register of Historic Places, including the ornate 1885 town hall in the center of town. At the Herrick Memorial Library, on E. Herrick Ave. near Main St., is a large collection of Archibald Willard paintings and other items of historical interest. Willard, a Wellington native, painted the classic Revolutionary War image called *The Spirit of '76*. Information about the painter is also preserved in the Spirit of '76 Museum at 201 N. Main St., just north of Herrick Ave. (open free of charge on Saturdays and Sundays 2:30–5 P.M. April through October. Phone: 440-647-4567).

1 Enter the Buckeye Trail at the edge of the woods west of the parking lot and south of the nature center. The trail entrance is near the Naturalist Activity Center. The Buckeye Trail is blazed with 2-by-6-

inch light-blue rectangles painted on trees. Follow the blue blazes west past the camp amphitheater on the right.

2 At 0.3 mile the trail meets an old logging road. Turn left (west) here onto this wide path. Cross a bridge over Wellington Creek, which flows into Findley Lake at this point. Metal bird boxes standing in the water are nesting sites for wood ducks. Cross another small wooden bridge over a side creek. Maple, ash, and pawpaw trees thrive in this habitat.

3 At 0.4 mile the trail bends to the right (north) to go up a steep hill and, farther on, a ravine.

Option: an alternate trail on the left called the Buckeye Branch, marked with white tree blazes, goes around these two steep sections, then rejoins the Buckeye Trail in 0.2 miles.

4 Continue north on the Buckeye Trail through a pine forest. There red pines were planted in the 1950s to reforest former farmland. After descending to the lowlands, note evidence of beaver activity along here: sharp-pointed tree stumps. The beavers' ever-growing incisor teeth maintain a sharp edge that ensures their ability to down small trees for eating and for construction of dams and large domed lodges. Aspen, willow, and birch trees are their favorite foods.

5 At 0.8 mile reach Picnic Pines picnic area. (Here the BT veers off to the left and continues its journey westward.) Continue straight ahead (north), heading to the right of the wooden restroom building, then cross a footbridge to a large parking lot for the Boat Ramp picnic area. Walk through the parking and picnic area toward its north end.

6 At the far end of the picnic area, bear right to a dirt path heading northeast. (A side trail leads to the right down the slope for a view of Blackberry Island. This is the only island in Findley Lake.) Continue on the Larch Trail, by the sign "Larch Trail, to Picnic Point Area." Pass two side trails on the right that lead down to the lake.

7 At 1.2 miles turn right on a park road leading to Picnic Point Peninsula. Here there are picnic tables, a picnic shelter, and a restroom building. Pass a circular grove of white pines.

8 Continue out onto the peninsula for beautiful views of the water in all directions. The peninsula is popular with fishermen for shore fishing and ice fishing. Along the edge of the lake there may be large freshwater snails. Attractive bigtooth aspen and pine trees have been planted here.

9 Return to the parking area and turn right to enter the Larch Trail at the southwest end of the parking lot. This trail goes northwest and is marked by a sign, "Larch Trail, to Swimming, Beach." In 600 feet the Black Locust Trail joins on the left. Black locust trees, common in much of this rural area of Ohio, produce sweet-smelling flowers in May.

10 At 1.8 miles (about 200 feet north of the junction with the Black Locust Trail), an unmarked trail goes off to the right. This is where the beach concession stand was located until 1971. All that remains is a set of wooden steps, now overgrown. Continue north on the Larch Trail. Emerge from the woods into a grassy area, which is the swimming beach area. Continue north across the grass and onto the paved path by the concession and restroom building. Larch trees, among the pines, are growing along the path just south of the building. American larches, also known as tamaracks, have short needles in dense clusters along their branches, and tiny cones. In the autumn the larches stand out from the other trees when their needles turn a soft, burnished gold color. The larches, unlike other conifers, drop their needles and remain bare throughout the winter. Continue north on the path, then turn right, descend a small hill, then bear left onto a gravel path heading north parallel to the boat launch canal and rental area.

11 Continue north into the woods, at a sign marked "Larch Trail to Dam Area." In 75 feet, keep left where a side trail goes right. In another 75 feet, keep left where an older section of Larch Trail leads back to the picnic area.

12 At 2.1 miles, the Larch Trail ends at a gravel path to the earthen dam. Turn right (east) to cross the dam. (The trail to the left leads to a parking area, and about 0.1 mile down park road #9 is the Duke's Skipper Butterfly Sanctuary.)

13 The concrete structure visible in the water near the dam is a floodgate; the gate is periodically opened to allow the lake to be lowered. This operation permits removal of silt and allows park staff to make repairs to the beach or other shoreline facilities. The deepest part of the lake, at 25 feet, is here at the north end.

14 Arrive at the spillway, at the end of the dam. During times of high water this grassy spillway acts as an emergency escape for excess water to exit the lake. The water flows over the spillway dam, into Wellington Creek, and on to the West Branch of the Black River. There is often standing water in parts of the spillway in spring. Continue on the path through the spillway and up the hill on the opposite side.

15 Turn right onto the Spillway Trail, a former utility right-of-way, which parallels the east shore of Findley Lake. The trail heading east is the Hickory Grove Trail.

16 After the trail makes a jog to the right, a short side trail leads to a lakeside bench from which you can enjoy views of the lake and the peninsula. Return to the Spillway Trail and continue south. In 200 feet you reach the 3-mile mark.

17 Continue on the trail to the left, where a side trail goes right, and rejoins this trail a little farther ahead.

18 The Spillway Trail ends at park road #3, by campsite #88. Turn left on the road and walk to campsite #112. To the rear of this campsite is the trailhead for the Lake Trail. Follow the Lake Trail west into the woods. Cross a steep valley, then pass park road #13, visible on the left.

19 Where the Lake Trail turns left, a side trail continues west for a view of the lake. Continue on the Lake Trail as it descends.

20 The Lake Trail ends at park road #10. Turn right and walk along the road 200 feet to see a giant granite boulder in the park's maintenance area. This boulder "calling card" was left here by the retreating glaciers about 12,000 years ago. It was originally pushed here from what is now Canada, along with many other boulders, all polished and rounded by the weight and motion of the giant ice sheet. Glacial boulders of all sizes, most of them smaller than this, can be found scattered throughout Northeast Ohio, wherever the glaciers visited.

21 The road ends at the concrete Camp Boat Ramp. Large lake snails can be seen adhering to the side of the ramp, in the water, and also along the shore.

22 The Creekbank Trail starts by the trail sign to the south, across the grass. It heads into the woods and connects to the Buckeye Trail. The Creekbank Trail is a good trail to use to finish the hike but is usually too wet. If this is the case, the alternative route is to take park road #10 back east, uphill, to the parking lot, about 0.5 mile from the Camp Boat Ramp.

23 Arrive back at the parking lot. ■

53 French Creek Reservation
Sheffield Village

Distance: 2.5 miles (3.1 miles with additional loop hike)

Moderate

Hiking time: 1¼ hours or 1¾ hours

Description: This hike follows trails over moderately undulating terrain over-looking French Creek, Fish Creek, and Sugar Creek. The trails, which are color coded, go through woods, past former fields that are now being reforested, past outcrops of ancient Cleveland Shale and by remnants of supports for a railroad bridge that crossed the property years ago.

Directions: From I-90 take Exit 151 for SR 611 (Lorain-Avon Rd.); west on SR 611 (Colorado Ave.) for 2½ miles; pass SR 301; nature center entrance on left.

Parking & restrooms: At the nature center.

Beautiful French Creek Reservation, one of Lorain County Metro Parks's developed public recreation areas, is located on SR 611 in Sheffield, just east of Lorain. Its 428 forested acres include a nature center, two picnic shelters and a playground, and five miles of hiking and cross-country skiing trails. Fish Creek and Sugar Creek run through the park to join larger French Creek, which flows westward to eventually join the Black River on its way to Lake Erie. These park streams furnish a rich environment for wildlife and vegetation and provide the area with scenic wetlands, ravines, and exposed rock formations.

Captain Jabez Burrell was the first settler to own land, which he purchased from the Connecticut Land Company in 1815. He cleared the land for farming in 1816, and his descendants continued farming the land until the 1940s. They did not clear the ravine slopes where the land was too steep to farm, making it possible to find several trees over 200 years old still growing on the sides of the valley. Eleanor Burrell, the last descendent to live in the Burrell house, died in 2001, and the homestead is now managed by Lorain County Metroparks. There are plans to restore the homestead to its 1800s appearance.

French Creek Nature Center, built in 1990, continues the ongoing development of this park, which was acquired in 1964. This fine center offers nature exhibits, a gift shop, library, program hall, classrooms, and a wildlife observation area. A periodical called *The Arrowhead* describes the many nature activities, programs, and guided hikes offered by the park. The building is open daily from 8 A.M. until dusk. The reservation is open daily 8 A.M. to 9:30 P.M. unless otherwise posted.

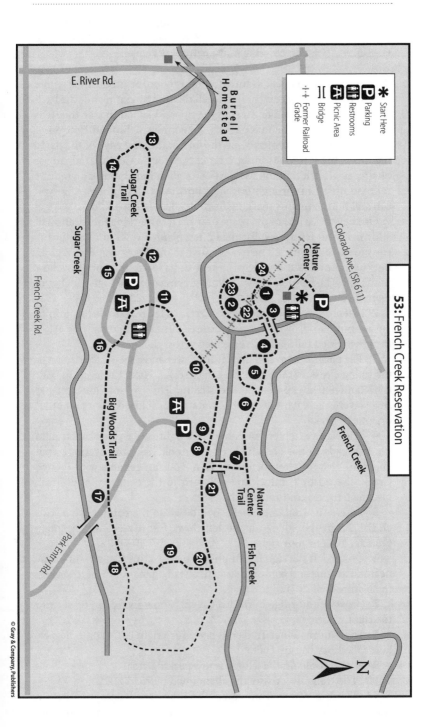

53: French Creek Reservation

Information about any of the Lorain County Metro Parks may be obtained from the park office, 12882 Diagonal Rd., LaGrange (800-526-7275; www.loraincountymetroparks.com).

1 If the French Creek Nature Center is open, begin the hike with a visit to this excellent center, then reach the trail by exiting out the back door and proceeding a few feet to the steps. Turn left to take the steps down to the creek, then pick up the hike midway through Note #4. If you do not visit the center, begin the hike at the west edge of the parking lot, at the information sign. Enter the Nature Center Trail, an asphalt-paved path that follows part of an abandoned railroad grade. A railroad once ran through this area, northwest to southeast, and you can still find remnants marking its route. Bear left at a Y fork.

On the left is a line of old osage orange trees marking the location of a former farm fence row. Farmers often planted rows of these thorny trees to serve as fences. The tree is native to the Arkansas/Texas region, but can now be found widely in the east. Its leaves turn bright yellow in the fall. The fruit is a heavy, yellow-green ball, three to five inches in diameter, which oozes a milky juice when squeezed.

2 A fenced overlook of French Creek valley marks the location of an old railroad bridge that once crossed the creek and valley, part of the abandoned railroad that extended across the property.

3 The path goes toward the nature center and a set of steps down to the valley. Cross a bridge over French Creek and note the layers of dark Cleveland Shale exposed by the stream. This 360-million-year-old shale layer is very dark because it contains carbonized plant and other organic material.

4 The Nature Center Trail now bears right, and a short side trail to the left leads to the French Creek Overlook. Take the overlook trail about 100 feet to a wooden deck. Here you can get a view of French Creek, shaded by hemlock trees. Return to the Nature Center Trail, bearing left, and continue south.

5 Where the trail circles left, look down to the confluence of two creeks. From the valley on the left flows Fish Creek, which enters French Creek to your right.

6 On the left is a sign for an unimproved Nature Center Trail connector. Pass this and continue straight ahead, then bear right to stay on the Nature Center Trail.

7 Cross a footbridge over Fish Creek. A boardwalk can be seen to the right.

8 The Nature Center Trail ends here. Turn right (west) onto the yellow-coded Big Woods Trail.

9 A boardwalk on the left leads to a parking area.

10 The trail now crosses the abandoned railroad grade.

11 The Big Woods Trail enters the Pine Tree Picnic Area near a reservation trail map sign. Here the hike temporarily leaves the Big

Woods Trail and continues on the 0.6-mile red-coded Sugar Creek Trail loop, accessed by walking up the road to the right for 500 feet to the Sugar Creek Trail post on the right.

If you choose to skip the Sugar Creek Trail loop and instead continue on the Big Woods Trail, go straight ahead across the road. Cross the picnic area on a paved path between the restroom and picnic shelter. Turn left to leave the picnic area. At the Big Woods Trail sign, you will rejoin the hike at #16.

The pine trees in the picnic area were planted around 1950 in former farm fields. Near the shelter is a Norway maple, called the Freedom Tree, that was planted in 1973 by Girl Scouts. Beside it are two granite markers honoring servicemen who died in the Vietnam War.

12 At the red-coded Sugar Creek Trail sign, turn right into the woods. The trail winds through woods overlooking French Creek.

13 As the trail circles south, Sugar Creek is visible.

14 A large granite boulder to the right of the trail is one of many that were left here thousands of years ago when the last glacier receded.

15 The Sugar Creek Trail ends here. Continue the hike by turning right and go along the road for about 550 feet.

16 At the trail sign, turn right onto the Big Woods Trail. Here the trail follows part of an old farm lane that was formerly used by the Burrells. The lane connected their home on Sheffield-Elyria Rd. (now E. River Rd.) with the farm fields to the east. The 1825 Burrell family home is listed in the National Register of Historic Places and is open for tours and special programs by prior arrangement. The house was one of the first brick homes to be built in Lorain County, and the homestead included a maple sugar operation. This part of the Big

Woods Trail is especially scenic in the autumn when the yellow-gold leaves of the sugar maples illuminate the path.

17 The trail crosses the road that connects the Pine Tree Picnic Area with Sheffield-French Creek Rd. This park road was built on the abandoned railroad right-of-way.

18 A trail on the right is an orange-coded section of the Big Woods Trail. This unimproved section forms a loop to the east, meeting up with the yellow-coded section at #20. You have the option of taking this extra loop for an even longer hike. To continue on the improved, yellow-coded trail, bear left, as it swings to the north.

19 This section of trail, heading north, is the dividing line between former farm fields to the left and woods to the right. The much smaller trees, compared to those in the wood lot, indicate where the fields were.

20 Turn left (west) on the Big Woods Trail where the orange-coded section joins in from the right.

21 Arrive at the trail intersection with the blue-coded Nature Center Trail, where you were earlier. Turn right and follow the trail into the valley, cross the bridge over Fish Creek, and continue on the limestone path. Cross the bridge over French Creek.

22 Turn left on the Nature Center Trail. (The steps ahead lead back up to the center.)

23 On the left is a concrete structure that was part of the railroad bridge.

24 At this trail junction and the site of the osage orange trees, bear right to return to the Nature Center, or go straight ahead to return directly to the parking lot. ■

54 Elyria
Cascade Park and Elywood Park

Directions: From I-90/SR 2 take Exit 145A for Lorain-Elyria; south on SR 57 for
1.5 miles; pass I-80; left (east) on SR 57/113 for 0.4 mile to the tall, blue
Elyria water tower; right (south) on Furnace St. for 0.6 mile; left (east) into
Hillsdale Court; entrance at small Cascade Park sign.

From I-77 take I-80 (Ohio Turnpike) west to Exit 145 (Elyria); south on SR 57 for
0.7 mile; left (east) on SR 57/113 for 0.4 mile to the tall, blue Elyria water
tower; right (south) on Furnace St. for 0.6 mile; left (east) into Hillsdale
Court; entrance at small Cascade Park sign.

Cascade Park and Elywood Park are located in downtown Elyria on
opposite sides of the Black River, near the confluence of the river's East
and West Branches. The Elyria Parks and Recreation Department
(440-365-7101) maintains both parks, together totaling 135 acres. For
more information, see the city's website at www.ci.elyria.oh.us and
click on the Parks and Recreation listing.

Cascade Park, which celebrated its centennial in 1994, is in a deep
gorge with two 40-foot waterfalls. There are short hiking trails, a number of observation decks, and many other features of historic and natural interest, most of which have been given descriptive names. A one-
lane automobile ford across the Black River takes visitors to Elywood
Park on the river's east side, where there are more short trails. Both
parks offer picnic areas, playgrounds, and fishing in the Black River.
Swimming in the river is prohibited.

Both parks are open all year; however during hazardous weather the
steep access roads are closed. The automobile ford is open only when
the water level of the river is low, usually in the summer and fall. An alternate route to Elywood Park is suggested in Hike B. The best time to
view the waterfalls in Cascade Park is springtime, when the volume of
water is greatest.

Cascade Park's greatest attractions are its rock cliffs, waterfalls, and
tumbles of rocks and ledges. The dominant rock in Cascade Park is
Berea Sandstone, a hard, resistant stone forming the impressive cliffs
and gigantic fallen blocks of rock along the paths and in the river. Large
quantities of this sandstone were mined out of quarries in Berea, Ohio,
known as the "grindstone capital of the world." This very hard rock has
been quarried in many places within 25 miles of Elyria, the best known
being South Amherst, where a 225-foot layer is still being quarried.

The sandstone was formed in ancient times when the Mississippian sea covered this region. Rivers dropped sandy sediments in the sea, forming deltas. Visible on the surfaces of some of the sandstone is a pattern called "cross-bedding," in which the layers of hardened sediment are at a steep angle. Cross-bedding indicates that waves from different directions washed the sand into position, similar to wind blowing sand onto the slope of a dune. When the sand hardened into sandstone, it retained the wave-washed pattern.

Underneath the Berea Sandstone is the reddish-brown Bedford Shale, which is very weak, crumbly, and easily eroded. The shale comes from silt and mud deposits that were on the bottom of the ancient sea. Where the hard Berea Sandstone has been undercut by erosion of the softer underlying shale, shelter caves have formed. Where water flows over the two rock layers, waterfalls are formed. The two waterfalls in Cascade Park were formed in this way.

A small section of dark-gray Cleveland Shale lies under the Bedford Shale. It is visible in a creek bank in Elywood Park. In addition to the sandstone and shale bedrock in the parks, there are also glacial deposits and erratics—rounded boulders of granite, gneiss, and quartzite dragged here by the glaciers, then left behind as the glaciers melted. These boulders are composed of rock not normally found in Ohio. The highest point in Cascade Park, Camel's Back, is topped by a layer of glacial till, which is unconsolidated soil composed of sand, clay, gravel, and boulders.

Cascade Park and, to a lesser extent, Elywood Park are unique in Northeast Ohio as city parks located in the midst of very extensive geological surroundings. While Cascade Park shows signs of wear from over 100 years of heavy use and visitation, it also shows recent care and attention from local supporters. Two volunteer groups have developed to support the city in planning parks and improving trails.

The Friends of Cascade Park is a small group that has helped develop a master plan for Cascade and Elywood Park improvements as part of a larger citywide effort called "Envision Elyria." Another volunteer group, Cascade Park Association, has raised funds and provided labor and materials to build the extensive observation decks, boardwalks, and other trail improvements found in Hike A. Volunteers working with the Elyria Rotary Club did much of this work.

The first edition of *Beyond Cleveland on Foot* included in Hike C a trail connecting the East and West Falls. Since that edition, a number of changes have occurred. The most exciting is that the city has begun to implement the portion of the citywide plan that will connect downtown to the Cascade Park via recreation trails. In the spring of 2003, the first phase of this project was completed when a series of bridges, boardwalks, and new observation decks at the East Falls were opened to the public. Future plans call for rebuilding the trail connecting the East and West Falls and installing a bridge below the West Falls to create the final link to Cascade Park. In this edition, Hike C explores the new decks and boardwalks and a rebuilt observation deck with an excellent view of the East Falls.

The three hikes in this chapter total less than three miles and can be completed in two to three hours, taking time to enjoy the many interesting stops and views along the way.

Hike A: West Falls

Distance: 1.2 miles

Easy

Hiking Time: 1 hour

Description: This is a loop hike along unpaved paths, wooden walkways, solid rock, and abandoned park road. The trail leads to the West Falls and several historic and natural features of the park, with names such as Bear's Den, Ancient Waterfall, and Camel's Back.

Parking & Restrooms: Park at the foot of the entrance hill in the first parking area on the left, just past the stop sign. Restrooms are near the trailhead, to the south.

1 Start the hike at the wooden observation deck overlooking the Black River. Two long branches of this river join in Cascade Park, just upstream of here. Just before joining, each branch cascades over a massive rock ledge; the twin waterfalls have long been a major attraction for area visitors. From the confluence of the two branches, the Black River flows generally north for 16 miles, emptying into Lake Erie at Lorain. The Black River, like many of Ohio's urban rivers, has suffered from pollution, but due to the concentrated efforts of government and volunteers, it has now made considerable progress toward full health. Parks protect much of the river between Elyria and Lorain and provide access to its rugged and beautiful wooded valley.

A trail sign on the deck points southwest for the West Falls Observation Deck Loop Trail. A trail insignia of waterfalls and deck marks the route. Leaving the deck, follow the unpaved path into the woods.

2 Where a wooden footbridge crosses a small wetland to the left, continue straight ahead and uphill to a flat area at the base of a 45-foot-high cliff of Berea Sandstone.

3 At the base of the cliff a portion of a concrete foundation is all that is left of the Bear's Den. Here a fenced-in bear cage and shed housed a black bear during the summer months from 1920 to the early 1970s. Over the years four different bears were kept here, an attraction that became popular with summertime visitors. Sophie, the last bear, died of old age in 1985. It is also believed that Native Americans may have used this spot for shelter hundreds of years ago. Excavations conducted at this site in 1916 uncovered ash-laden campfire soil. In 1876 explorers had found flints, pottery, and implements.

At the top of the cliff, known as Ancient Waterfall, there was a waterfall about two million years ago. The hike reaches this spot later on. The large semicircular amphitheater to the right, lined by bedrock, was carved by the ancient falls. The Black River's course has since changed, and the force of erosion has essentially moved the falls upstream to its current location at West Falls.

4 Return to the wooden footbridge in #2, cross the bridge, and after 100 feet turn right and follow a set of steps carved into the rock. These steps are worn from over 100 years of foot traffic on the trails. Look up to the top of the large rock, on the left, where a set of steps has been chiseled into the rock. It may seem like an odd location for a set of steps, but it once was a lookout area. There used to be a wooden bridge connecting the top of that rock with the top of the rock to the right. Continue on the path among the rocks.

5 Where a trail leads down to the left, continue on the trail uphill, to the right. A trail marker is on the face of a gigantic boulder on the left side of the trail.

6 On the cliff face to the upper right is Oyster Rock. A depression in the rock shows a pattern resembling an oyster shell.

7 Follow the wooden boardwalk to a deck with an excellent view of the confluence of the East and West Branches of the Black River. In total, the Black River drains 469 square miles and includes parts of Medina, Ashland, Huron, Cuyahoga, and Lorain counties. (The hike in Black River Reservation, Ch. 49, goes along another scenic stretch of the river downstream from here and includes more natural history information on the river valley.) In the early 1900s a road crossed the river here, from the confluence to West Falls. You can still see the foundation stones of the road on the opposite side of the river. There also was a swing pedestrian bridge across the river connecting the peninsula between the two river branches to the old quarry area just ahead.

Continue on the boardwalk and descend 15 steps.

8 Pass by a cliff. Erosion is turning it into a shelter cave. Watch your footing—the trail is slippery when wet as the eroding shale returns to mud.

9 Continue on the trail through Old Quarry. During the 1880s this quarry provided Berea Sandstone for local building purposes. You can see on the ledge, above the vertical grooves in the rock, where dynamite was placed to blast the large sandstone blocks from the sides of the quarry. An area of rusty-looking water on the ground is what is left of an iron-rich spring. Years ago the water was drinkable and considered therapeutic, though this is not advised today.

Continue west through the quarry.

10 Where the trail bears left, follow it to a wooden deck and descend the flight of 28 steps to the Old Auto Trail. Just to the left, 100 feet downhill, is where the old road forded the West Branch of the Black River. The flood of 1969 destroyed the ford. During low water it

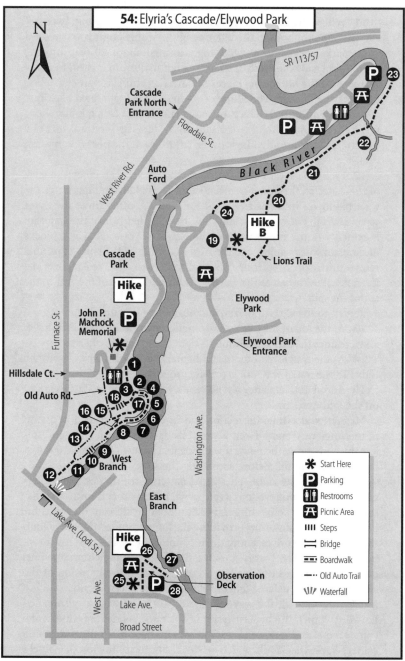

© Gray & Company, Publishers

is still visible, but too slippery to walk across. On this side of the river the old road is now used as a trail. Follow this trail uphill.

11 Where the Old Auto Trail begins to curve to the right, two narrow dirt side trails go to the left, downhill. At this point you can see a large, dark "rock" about 3 feet high, located about 20 feet into the woods alongside the old road. This is a remnant from an iron foundry that was on the hill above. Pieces of dark slag and glassy, rocky debris lie along the hillside. The foundry, dating to 1832, operated blast furnaces to produce steel (hence the name Furnace St., which is just above this hill). The Auto Road was originally a route used to transport raw materials to the foundry. Bear to the left to reach the next observation deck.

12 From the West Falls Observation Deck you can enjoy the view of the waterfall dropping over a 40-foot ledge. During high water the waterfall forms into one single torrent, while at other times the water separates into two streams. The wide arc on either side of the waterfall is evidence of the size of the falls thousands of years ago. Large blocks of sandstone have fallen into the river as a result of the falls's continual retreat upstream. The bridge above the falls carries Lake Ave. over the river. What is known as Big Cave is visible at the base of the cliff to the left of the falls.

Return to the Old Auto Trail and bear left, going uphill.

13 At the top of the hill a set of wooden steps leads up to Phillip Ct. and a residential area. Continue straight ahead on the old road.

14 As the trail levels out, the Old Quarry is visible below and to the right. To the left of the trail is private property.

15 About 100 feet after a fence ends, follow a side trail to the right off the Old Auto Trail.

16 Arrive at a trail intersection and fenced area. You are now on top of the Ancient Waterfall and Natural Bridge area. Turn right and follow the path along the fence toward a gated area where steps carved in bedrock lead uphill. Before ascending the steps, note the large sandstone block on the right. The pitted pattern on the rock surface has been formed by honeycomb weathering. In this process rainwater dissolves the weaker cementing minerals more quickly than the less soluble silica sand grains, thus providing the honeycombed texture. Climb the steps; just before reaching the top, notice to the left the large overhanging rock ledge. This is known as Shelf Rock. Fences from previous decades are located outside the present fence. Natural erosion of the cliffs necessitates placing fences farther "inland" periodically.

17 Continue all the way to the top to Camel's Back (also called Lookout Point), the highest point in the park. Its name is due to the color, shape, and texture of the hill, which resembles the humps on a camel's back. Glacial till, which erodes easily, forms the top of Camel's Back. From here you can see downtown Elyria, one-half mile away, with the First Merit building being prominent.

Retrace your way back down the stone steps to the fenced area atop the Ancient Waterfall and Natural Bridge.

18 At the end of the chain-link fence on the right, follow the wooden steps that descend the cliff face of the Ancient Waterfall. Go down 12 steps to an observation deck. Then turn right and continue down 34 more steps next to the cliff face to the trail and follow it among fallen sandstone blocks. The cliff on the right is called the Natural Bridge because a large horizontal crack separates it from the rock below. The trail along the base of the cliff is a cool and welcome relief in summer. After arriving at Bear's Den, beneath the overhang of the Ancient Waterfall, walk down the slope to the left and return to the starting point.

Before returning to your car you may wish to visit the Hillside Memorial garden just south of the playground. On a sandstone boulder is a memorial plaque to Elyria Parks superintendent John P. Machock for his 42 years with the Elyria Park System.

Hike B: **Elywood Park**

Distance: 1.2 miles   Easy

Hiking Time: 1 hour

Description: Hike B is an out-and-back trail with a small loop, in Elywood Park. It is mostly level, on woodland trails along the Black River.

Directions: Follow the directions for reaching Cascade Park, then drive north on the park road 0.3 mile to the automobile ford; right on the one-lane ford and cross to the east side of the river. (If the ford is closed, leave Cascade Park at the north entrance road (see map) and exit onto Floradale St., then turn right on W. River Rd.; right on SR 113/57 for 0.7 mile; right on Gulf Rd. for 0.6 mile; right (west) on Columbus St. for 0.6 mile; right (north) on Washington Ave. for several hundred feet; left into Elywood Park.)

Parking & Restrooms: Park in one of the parking areas on the east side of the one-way clockwise loop park road. Restrooms are nearby, in the picnic area.

19 Begin the hike at the sign by the edge of the woods marked "Lions Trail," on a trail developed and maintained by the Elyria Lions Club. Head east into the woods; the route is marked by red paint blazes on trees.

20 Arrive at a trail intersection after passing through a large bed of myrtle. Turn right onto the path known as Indian Trail, a 0.3-mile trail along the banks of the Black River. Cross a rocky stream; the trail continues paralleling the river.

21 Across the river is the playground and picnic area near the north end of Cascade Park.

NOTE: The trail beyond this point is sometimes washed out and muddy, making it hazardous to venture farther. The shale rock here has eroded, crumbled, and reverted to a very slippery mud. If passable, continue on to the end.

22 A footbridge crosses a side stream. During times of low water, a small section of the dark-gray-to-black Cleveland Shale is visible in the bedrock where the stream enters the Black River. This shale is the oldest rock exposed in Cascade and Elywood parks.

23 A little farther on the trail peters out at some fallen trees and steep valley walls. Ahead the river makes a big bend to the left. Retrace your steps along the river to the intersection at #20. At the trail junction, bear right and continue on Indian Trail. Cross a wooden footbridge and continue, paralleling the river.

24 Emerge from the woods by a sign for the Indian Trail. Seventy feet ahead is the park road. Return to the parking area by going left and uphill along the road.

Hike C: East Falls

Distance: 0.25 mile

Easy

Hiking Time: ½ hour

Description: A short walk to an observation deck in Cascade Park brings you close to the double-decker waterfall on the East Branch of the Black River.

Directions: The entrance to this part of Cascade Park is next to the Elyria Police Station on Lake Ave. From Elywood Park, right (south) on Washington Ave. for 0.5 mile; right (west) just past railroad overpass into narrow one-way alley; right at end of alley on Lake Ave. for about 0.1 mile; right into city of Elyria parking lot.

From Cascade Park, exit at Hillsdale Court; left on Furnace St. for three blocks; left on Lake Ave. for 0.2 mile; street bends to right and becomes West Ave.; continue on West for 0.1 mile; left on Lake Ave. just before railroad overpass for 0.1 mile; road bends to the right; left into driveway for police station; immediate right into city parking lot.

Parking & Restrooms: Park in the city lot. There are no restrooms at this end of Cascade Park.

25 The trailhead for this short trail is 200 feet north of the city of Elyria parking lot. At the start of the trail there is an entrance plaza made from recycled Belgium Block and millstones. This is the location of one of the historic automobile entrances into Cascade Park, before a flood in 1969 damaged the road and ford across the river. Now the road serves as the Old Auto Trail. Follow this trail downhill.

26 The East Falls observation deck, originally built in 1989 by the Friends of Cascade Park, provides excellent views of the 40-foot falls of the East Branch of the Black River. This is a double-level falls. The

upper level is actually a dam and spillway created in the 1800s to provide power for mills. Mill ruins are visible to the right of the falls. Leave
the Old Auto Trail and observation deck and follow a side trail southeast from the observation deck through the woods, toward the falls.

27 Just before reaching the ruins of a power plant to the right of the
falls, notice a large concave cliff face on the right. It is a "reflecting
rock" that echoes the sound of the falls back to the listener. Water diverted by the dam and spillway above the falls powered turbines in the
plant, generating electricity for mills, streetcars, and downtown Elyria
buildings from the late 1800s to the early 1900s. The power plant was
dismantled during World War II to obtain steel for the war effort. Also,
as early as 1840, gristmills were built near the falls to take advantage of
the water power.

Retrace your steps back to the observation deck. The Old Auto Trail
to the north used to curve around a point of land at the river's confluence and cross the west branch of the Black River. The road also served
as the first part of a trail between East and West Falls. The trail is impassable at this time, but the city plans to repair and reopen it in the future.

28 From the rebuilt observation deck, return uphill to the Entry
Plaza. Now follow the boardwalk toward the falls. Where a series of
stairs leads to the right and back to the street level, turn left to follow
the deck, now elevated above the Black River. Soon you come to two
observation decks from which to experience the falls at a more personal level. Continuing on the boardwalk will take you to another
Entry Plaza, this one on Lake Avenue. From there you can return along
the sidewalk to the parking lot. Otherwise, retrace your steps along the
river-carved gorge to return to your car. ■

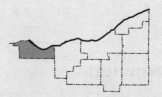

ERIE COUNTY

Erie County is bisected by two major east–west highways: SR 2 and I-80. One of its major cities, Vermilion, lies in both Lorain and Erie Counties. Downtown Vermilion, however, is entirely in Erie County.

The county seat, Sandusky, is one gateway port to the Lake Erie Islands (Kelleys Island is in Erie County, but North, Middle, and South Bass Islands are in Ottawa County). Numerous ferries transport people and cars to and from the islands (see Ch. 58).

Erie MetroParks manages ten parks and recreation areas. Information about the MetroParks, and a quarterly publication, *The Leaflet*, are available from Erie MetroParks Administrative Office: 419-625-7783; their website is: www.eriemetroparks.org.

Six of Ohio's state nature preserves are in Erie County, and all are open to the public. North Pond, on Kelleys Island, includes a boardwalk leading to an elevated wildlife observation tower overlooking a natural pond with abundant bird life. Also on Kelleys Island is the North Shore Alvar State Nature Preserve, protecting the unique and rare features of the limestone ledges bordering Lake Erie. Information is available from the Ohio Division of Natural Areas and Preserves, Old Woman Creek State Nature Preserve: 419-433-4919; www.dnr.state.oh.us/odnr/dnap/.

Schoepfle Garden (Ch. 56), though located in Erie County, is maintained and managed by Lorain County Metro Parks. The historical walk in downtown Vermilion (Ch. 55) is west of the Lorain–Erie county line and therefore in Erie County.

Of further interest in Erie County are the Milan Historical Museum and Thomas Alva Edison's birthplace in Milan. The museum is at 10 Edison Dr. and is open February through December (hours vary seasonally). For information about the museum call 419-4499-2968 or see www.milanohio.com. For information about the Edison birthplace call 419-499-2135 or see www.tomedison.org.

More information about Erie County is available from Erie County Visitors Bureau: 800-255-3743, or online at www.buckeyenorth.com.

55 Vermilion

Distance: 2 miles

Walking time: 1½ to 2 hours

Easy

Description: This easy walk, entirely on sidewalks, begins and ends at the Inland Seas Maritime Museum. It takes the visitor past historic homes and shops in the Harbour Town 1837 Historic District.

Directions: From I-90/SR2 west, follow SR 2 after the split from I-90 for 12 miles; take exit for Wakeman-Vermilion; right (north) on SR 60 for 2 miles to Vermilion; continue on SR 60 (Main St.) past US 6 to end of Main St.

Parking & restrooms: On-street parking is available in front of the Inland Seas Maritime Museum, 480 Main St., and at Victory Park on SR 60 south of US 6. Restrooms are in the Inland Seas Maritime Museum. A public restroom in Exchange Park on US 6 just east of Main St. is open from Easter weekend to mid-November.

Founded in 1808 and incorporated in 1837, Vermilion reminds one of a small New England seaport. The town, home of the Inland Seas Maritime Museum, has restored many of its old homes and shops along the waterfront to re-create the quaint, historic Harbour Town 1837 district. Sailing, yacht racing, fishing, and tourism are principal summertime activities here.

Yearly events attract thousands of visitors to Vermilion. The Fish Festival is in mid-June. The Woollybear Festival is the last Sunday in September or the first Sunday in October. Its all-day events include a large parade and contests honoring a fuzzy caterpillar whose dark-brown and orange bands are thought to predict the severity of the coming winter. The Great Black-Backed Gull Greeting Party is the third Sunday in September at the Main St. beach. This Audubon Society event celebrates the arrival of these large birds from 1,500 miles away in Labrador. The gulls spend several weeks on the Lake Erie shore before continuing their migration south.

Vermilion is also known for its many gift shops, homemade chocolates, and nearby pick-your-own berry farms.

Vermilion was so named because of the reddish clay lining the banks of the river. Early settlers, who first came from New England in 1808–09, cleared the heavily forested land and built cabins and other structures. Many were given land by the state of Connecticut as payment for having lost their property in fires during the Revolutionary War. This part of the Connecticut Western Reserve was known as the "Firelands," and

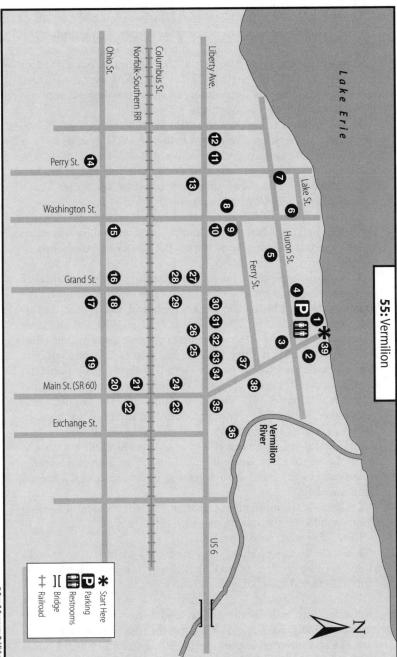

55: Vermilion

Lake Erie

Vermilion River

Lake St.

Huron St.

Ferry St.

Ohio St.
Norfolk-Southern RR
Columbus St.
Liberty Ave.

Perry St. 14
12
11
13
7
Washington St.
8
6
15
10 9
5
Grand St. 16
28 27
4
1
39
17 18
29
3
2
30
31 32
26
25
33 34
37
19
38
Main St. (SR 60) 20 21
24
35
22 23
Exchange St.
36

US 6

N

Start Here ✳
Parking P
Restrooms
Bridge][
Railroad ┼┼

© Gray & Company, Publishers

its settlers as "Firelanders." Actually, few of the direct beneficiaries themselves came to Vermilion; most sold their claims to others.

In 1841 the U. S. Corps of Engineers built two piers at the mouth of
the river, permitting large ships to use the harbor. This improvement
helped industries such as fishing, shipbuilding, importing, and ex-
porting (including quarry stone, timber, and iron products). Many
fine sailing and fishing vessels, and later steamboats, were constructed
in Vermilion during its shipbuilding boom. More than 50 ship captains built their homes here between 1830 and 1899.

More information is available from the Vermilion Chamber of Commerce, 5495 Liberty Ave., Vermilion (440-967-4477); Friends of Harbour Town, 5741 Liberty Ave., Vermilion (440-967-4262); Inland Seas
Maritime Museum (open daily 10 A.M. to 5 P.M.), 480 Main St., Vermilion (800-893-1485; www.inlandseas.org.); or the Ritter Public
Library, 5680 Liberty Ave., Vermilion (440-967-3798).

This walk through Vermilion takes you to over 40 historic houses
and public buildings. Many of the homes are private residences and are
noted as such in the text. Please respect the privacy of these homes.

1 Begin the walk at the Inland Seas Maritime Museum, which can
be visited now or at the end of the tour (admission is charged). The
museum, operated by the Great Lakes Historical Society, is in the former Frederick Wakefield House. It was built in 1909 and additions
were built in 1968 and 1997. Interesting maritime history of the Great
Lakes is presented here. On display are fine ship models, photographs,
artifacts, and memorabilia pertaining to lake shipping. Of particular
interest are a 1907 restored pilothouse from the freighter *Canopus* and
a 1992 replica of the 1877 Vermilion Lighthouse. The original lighthouse stood on the west pier of the Vermilion River but was dismantled in 1929 after being structurally damaged by ice. It was then re-
paired and moved to the east end of Lake Ontario, at the entrance to
the St. Lawrence River, where it remains today guarding ships in the
vicinity of Charity Shoal. Also of interest in the museum is a Fresnel
lighthouse lens.

2 Opposite the museum at 485 Main St. is the remodeled Captain
Thompson House (private residence), built in 1830.

Turn right (west) onto Huron St.

3 On the corner of Huron and Main (532 Main St.) is the Wells
Home (private residence), later named the Steamboat Hotel. It was
built in 1838 and enlarged with an 1865 addition.

4 The 1885 Captain J. C. Gilchrist House, on the right at 5644
Huron St., was built by the owner (and honorary captain) of the
largest fleet in the lakes. It is now listed in the National Register of Historic Places. Converted to the Lakeside Hotel around 1900, the house
is now a bed and breakfast.

5 The Captain Alva Bradley house (private residence) at 5679

Huron St. was constructed in 1848 in Greek Revival style. At that time, Bradley became captain of the *South America*, and later he initiated substantial shipbuilding in Vermilion. In the 1860s Capt. Bradley moved his shipbuilding business to Cleveland, because the deeper channel of the Cuyahoga River could accommodate the iron ships that were then being built. His company later became known as the American Ship Building Co. He was a good friend of Thomas Alva Edison of Milan, Ohio.

6 Turn right (north) to 520 Washington St. (private residence), another typical 1840 shipbuilder's home. Since being remodeled, this is one of several houses moved back from the lakefront because the shoreline eroded. Turn left (west) onto one-block-long Lake St. and then left (south) on Perry St. for one block. Many of these small old homes were once summer cottages. Turn left (east) on Huron St.

7 On the northeast corner of Perry and Huron (5750 Huron) is another early house built in the 1840s (private residence). Continue east on Huron St. for one block, then turn right (south) on Washington St.

8 At 598 Washington St. (private residence) is a home that was built in 1830 as an apothecary shop. It was remodeled about 1940. Originally located farther north, it was moved from the eroding shoreline.

Two houses south is the Jacob Abell House (private residence), at 624 Washington St., built in 1880. Abell was the local barber at the time. During remodeling in the 1990s, the current owners discovered that human hair was used in the original plaster walls.

9 On the southeast corner of Washington and Ferry streets, at the rear of Ritter Library, is a large boulder with the date "1784" and the name "S. Kenton" chiseled on it. Simon Kenton was an explorer and Indian fighter who laid claim to four square miles of land south of the Vermilion River mouth. Daniel Boone called Kenton "the bravest man I ever knew."

Kenton apparently hoped to establish a community here by carving his name on this rock, without filing any legal claims. He is generally considered to have been the first white man in this area. The boulder was found in 1937 on a farm a mile south of Vermilion; it now stands at this spot as a memorial to the first man to recognize Vermilion's potential for settlement. Continue south on Washington St.

10 On the corner of Washington and Liberty is the Ritter Public Library (1958), donated by George Ritter, a Toledo lawyer and philanthropist, to honor his parents, John and Louise Ritter. Containing a brightly decorated children's room with a play-sized replica of the sailing ship *Niagara*, the entire library was beautifully remodeled in 1994.

Turn right (west) on Liberty Ave. (US 6) and cross Perry St.

11 Captain Bell's house at 5760 Liberty was built in about 1870. It is currently an antique store.

12 Continue west on Liberty Ave. to 5780, the Old Pelton Hotel, one of the oldest homes still standing in Vermilion. The original house was built in 1832, but it has had several subsequent additions. It has been a nursing home and is currently a retail shop.

Return to Perry St. and cross at the signal to reach the southeast corner of the intersection.

13 The 1866 Italianate building at 5741 Liberty Ave. was the home of Frank Pelton. It is currently called Old Jib's Corner and is headquarters for the Friends of Harbour Town 1837, Inc. This local group was formed in the 1970s to promote preservation of Vermilion's nautical heritage and its historic buildings. Besides housing the friends group, the house is also used as an artisan's gallery, souvenir shop, and restaurant. "Old Jib" was Jib Snyder, a sailor, fisherman, and ferryboat operator during the town's early days.

Walk south along Perry St. and cross the railroad tracks to reach Ohio St. CAUTION: this is a very active railroad line.

14 On the southwest corner of Ohio and Perry streets, at 5753 Ohio St., is the 1870 Baxtine house (private residence). Note the ornate window and porch treatments.

Turn left (east) on Ohio St.

15 The Queen Anne house with triple-peaked roof at 5676 Ohio

St. (at the corner of Washington St.) is another ship captain's house (private residence). It was built in the 1880s by a Captain Weeks.

16 One of Vermilion's oldest churches is at 752 Grand St., on the corner of Ohio St. The Evangelical and Reformed Church (United Church of Christ) was organized in 1852 by German-speaking residents. Its first building was constructed in 1853 and the present building in 1869. A large religious education building was added in 1959.

17 At the intersection of Ohio and Grand streets are more captains' homes. The 1875 red brick at 5583 Ohio St. (private residence) is where Captain Gilchrist, Sr., resided. He was captain of the ship *W. H. Gilchrist*, which is frequently mentioned in shipping stories. The walls of this home are eight inches thick. Note the interesting Vermilion-kilned white brick window trim and the brackets under the eaves. This is one of Vermilion's few older brick buildings.

18 The 1857 home at 743 Grand St. belonged to Captain Phillip Minch, the owner of the ship *Western Reserve*, which sank in August 1892, taking the lives of many Vermilion residents.

Continue east on Ohio St.

19 At 5559 Ohio St. is the Burton House (private residence), built in 1848. Burton was an early postmaster. Turn left (north) onto Main St.

20 The Town Hall and Opera House on the corner at 736 Main St. has an interesting history. In 1883–84, when it opened, it became the center of activity in Vermilion. Costing $21,000, the hall contained a courtroom, council chambers, offices, a kitchen, a dining room, and a jail. The opera house on the second floor was the site of musicals, band concerts, minstrel and vaudeville acts, debates, lectures, medicine shows, high school commencements, and of, course, opera. The second floor, closed since 1940, still has the original stage, 450 seats, and its black velvet stage curtain.

21 Next to the Town Hall, at 728 Main St., is another church building—the former First Congregational Church, built in 1886 by the oldest church body in Vermilion. This congregation was first organized in 1818; in 1956 they built a new church on State St. The building here is now an antique shop and auction house.

22 Victory Park across the street is noted for its beautiful rose garden and gazebo. Concerts are held here every Sunday evening in the summer. A historic marker describes the settling of Vermilion and the area known as the Firelands.

23 Schwensen's Bakery (closed since 1994) at 681 Main St. was a well-known business in Vermilion for 101 years. Founded by a Danish family in 1893, it remained at the same site throughout its existence and was the oldest family business in town. The building now houses a retail store.

24 Englebry Dry Goods Store at 686 Main St. was another long-time business. The building at 672 Main St. was built in 1870, and the

Baumhart Building in 1916. A chocolate shop and other businesses now occupy these buildings.

Turn left (west) on Liberty Ave. (US 6).

25 This block is the heart of Vermilion's Harbour Town 1837 Historic District. Williams Law Offices at 5581 Liberty are located in a restored 1907 building (originally the Vermilion Banking Co.).

26 The Delker Dry Goods store, built about 1870 at 5591 Liberty St., became a theater in the early 1900s. It is currently a cafe and interior design shop.

Turn left (south) on Grand St.

27 The 1870 lighthouse keeper's house at 654 Grand St. (private residence) is now a business and residence.

28 Vermilion Hardware at 678 Grand St. was originally Sid Simon General Store (built about 1860) and represents another of the town's durable businesses. At one time wooden horse collars and baby coffins were sold here.

29 The building at 691 Grand St. was built about 1910. It housed the old library, then later a church, and then the Vermilion Police Station until May 1998. It is currently Pelican Cove, a retail shop. On certain days the shop offers "Picture yourself in jail without being incarcerated": visitors can go down to the old jail cells and take their pictures "in jail." Call ahead for details at 440-967-1180.

Return north to Liberty Ave., cross the street, then turn right to walk along the north side of Liberty.

30 Ednamae's Ice Cream Parlour and Cafe at 5598 Liberty Ave. is a favorite stop for visitors; the business is in an 1850s building that was formerly a funeral parlor.

31 The building at 5542 Liberty Ave., built in 1847, is considered the oldest downtown building. It is currently a retail shop. Throughout its long history it has been a doctor's office, drug store, grocery store, bicycle shop, dentist's office, pool hall, mayor's office, boutique, and The Harbour Store.

32 A barber shop has been in business at this location, 5532 Liberty Ave., since 1868. It is currently called the Captain's Chair.

33 The old Erie County Bank (now a real estate office at 5512 Liberty) was built in the 1890s. A later Erie County Banking Co. building is on the southwest corner of Liberty Ave. and Main St.

34 The building on the northwest corner of Liberty Ave. and Main St., at 5502 Liberty Ave., was built in this prime location in 1872. It has had many occupants over the years: the post office, a shoe shop, dry goods store, saloon, dentist's office, beauty shop, and offices. From 1920 to 1985 it was known as Hart's Drug Store, then Higgins Pharmacy until 1998, then Harbourtown Emporium. It is currently the Main Street Soda Fountain and Grill and still uses the old-fashioned soda fountain.

A Geological Survey marker here (near the sidewalk) indicates that Vermilion is 597 feet above sea level.

35 Cross Main St. to Exchange Park. Beginning in 1836 this area was part of Exchange Place, where the village farmers had built clapboard warehouses. Here farmers and other tradespeople could sell produce and wares. There was also a commission house for import and export transactions.

36 The Public Comfort Station is in a small red-brick building built around 1912. It was originally a public restroom, then Vermilion's jail, and later the Chamber of Commerce. The building was modernized in 1995.

Just 100 feet east of the restroom a path leads down to a small park on the Vermilion River. Here are benches, a playground, and picnic tables, all offering a pleasant rest stop and view of river traffic.

To the west (facing the river) are the Fisherman's Bend Condominiums, where Kishman Fish Co. was located from the 1880s until 1983. Between 1890 and 1945 there were six large fish companies along the Vermilion River with dozens of fishing boats harvesting the rich abundance of sturgeon, herring, pickerel, and perch from Lake Erie. The commercial fishing industry declined with the increasing pollution problems in Lake Erie, and the fisheries buildings have all been demolished. The catch is improving again as the lake's water quality improves, and sport fishing is a favorite activity for many residents and visitors to the area.

37 Return to Main St. and Liberty Ave. and go north on Main St. The old Hotel Wagner, at 628–630 Main St., was built in 1871 and has since been remodeled. It presently houses two businesses, the *Vermilion Photojournal* and a dental office. As a hotel it once provided lodging for many travelers and sailors cruising on lake vessels and, later on, for summer visitors arriving by train. The Lake Shore Electric Railway interurban brought many people to Vermilion from Cleveland and other towns until it ceased operating in 1938. (Its station was the building at 5475 Liberty Ave., now a bank.)

38 The Sail Loft Professional Building at 555 Main St., built in 1840, was originally part of an early shipbuilding yard. Chez François, a popular French restaurant, is in the lower level of this building.

Between the Sail Loft and the brick building (Water Co. at 537 Main St.) is another public park from which to view the boats passing up or down the river.

On the east side of the river are the Lagoons, lined with Cape Cod–style homes—white with dark roofs and shutters. Originally this land was a marsh along the eastern floodplain of the river. A wooden walkway crossed the marsh, connecting the high banks on the west side of the river with the high banks east of the river at Linwood Park. In 1929 Lewis Wells of Cleveland conceived the idea of converting the marsh into a series of lagoons. By 1930 four lagoons had been dug, forming navigable waterways connected to the river. The property was zoned as a residential area, and construction continued until the 1950s.

Just to the east of the Lagoons is Linwood Park. It began in 1883 as a religious community, with residences and recreation facilities clustered near a swimming beach. Today Linwood Park's privately owned cottages can be rented in the summer, and an entrance fee is charged to visit the community and use the beach. It is reached by car from Liberty Ave.

Continue north along Main St. toward Lake Erie.

39 At the end of Main St. near the museum is Main St. Beach, where the annual mid-September Great Black-Backed Gull Greeting Party is held on the observation deck. These majestic gulls migrate from their summer breeding ground in Labrador, up the St. Lawrence River to Lake Erie before flying farther south. They are very large birds with black backs and a wing spread of up to 5½ feet.

On the sandy beach you may note some small black patches in the sand. This is not oil but the mineral magnetite, a pure, magnetic, naturally occurring iron ore. When picked up, it feels like sand, though it is much heavier than ordinary sand. The black iron grains of this sand can actually be separated from the quartz and feldspar grains with a magnet. The light pinkish-purple mineral grains are garnet—not, however, gem quality. This black sand, with or without garnet, is found on the beaches of western Lake Erie, Kelleys Island, and South Bass Island. ■

56 Schoepfle Garden
Birmingham

Directions: From I-90/SR 2 follow SR 2 west after split to exit for Baumhart Rd.;
left (south) on Baumhart for 4 miles (past I-80); right (west) on SR 113 for 4
miles to Birmingham; left (south) on Market St. (first road after crossing Vermilion River) for 160 feet; parking area on left.

From I-80 (the Ohio Turnpike) take Exit 135 for Baumhart Rd.; right (south) on
Baumhart for 1.4 miles; right (west) on SR 113 for 4 miles to Birmingham;
left (south) on Market St. (first road after crossing Vermilion River) for 160
feet; parking area on left.

Parking & restrooms: Park in the lot off Market St. Restrooms are in the Visitor
Center located adjacent to the parking area.

Schoepfle (pronounced Sheff-lee) Garden is located in Birmingham
in eastern Erie County and is a unit of Lorain County Metro Parks. It
was created by Otto B. Schoepfle on land that once belonged to his
grandfather. Schoepfle (1910–1992) was a businessman and former
chairman of the Lorain County Publishing Co. He devoted much of
his life to creating his garden in a unique natural setting of woodlands,
ponds, sun, and shade—all within the residential area of Birmingham.

The garden, located alongside the Vermilion River, contains special
collections of trees, shrubs, and perennials, all of which are labeled
with both common and scientific names. The diverse and colorful garden reflects Schoepfle's travels around the world to study and learn
about horticultural collections in other lands and climates. In 1969,
after major plantings were made, Schoepfle donated his acreage to
Lorain County Metro Parks, thus opening the garden to all visitors.
Lorain County Metro Parks now provides education to visitors and
maintains and preserves the park in its natural beauty.

The 20 acres of horticultural gardens are located in a larger 70-acre
preserve that includes natural woodlands, ponds, and the river valley,
providing the opportunity for three different walks and options combining them, depending on your interests and time available: the Garden Tour, River Walk, and Interpretive Area. Schoepfle Garden Metro
Park is open daily, 8 A.M. to 8 P.M. in the summer and 8 A.M. to 5 P.M.
in the winter. Admission is free. The Visitor Center is open Wednesday
through Sunday, 10 A.M. to 4:30 P.M. during the summer and Saturday
and Sunday 10 A.M. to 4:30 P.M. during the winter. For more information or to arrange tours for 12 or more people, call the Visitor Center

at 440-965-7237. Picnic tables are located near the parking area, north of the Visitor Center. Pets are not permitted on the grounds.

Begin the walks at the Visitor Center, an 1840s house reconstructed in 1999. If the center is open, you can pick up a trail guide, enjoy a short video about Otto Schoepfle and his gardens, rent a portable audio tour of the garden, and browse the Nature Nook Gift Shop.

Hike A: Garden Tour

Easy

Distance: 0.6 mile loop

Walking time: 45 minutes

Description: The terrain is flat through the 20 acres of gardens, which can be viewed from grassy paths. They contain special collections of trees, shrubs, perennials, and annuals. The gardens can be visited any time of the year, with seasonal highlights as follows:

January: topiaries and specimen evergreens

February: snowdrops and other small bulbs

March: small bulbs, early spring perennials, wildflowers

April: magnolias, forsythia, flowering quince, daffodils, tulips, spring perennials, and wildflowers

May: flowering trees and shrubs including native dogwood in the valley, crabapples, viburnams, rhododendrons, and lilacs; perennials and wildflowers

June: Washington thorn, laburnum, Chinese dogwood, roses, perennials

July: lily-of-the-valley tree, hydrangea, many perennials, including daylilies and astilbe

August: perennials including hostas, magic lilies; annuals, especially dahlias and cannas, lilies, hardy passion flower; native wildflowers along the River Valley Trail

September: annuals and perennials including hardy begonia, grasses, and wildflowers

October: ornamental grasses, witch hazel, hardy cyclamen

November/December: American holly and Chinese bittersweet

An audio tour on portable CD player can be rented at the Visitor Center. The tour has 26 display-area stops; each stop has a numbered, photographic identification sign as well. Our tour follows the same general direction as the audio tour.

1 From the Visitor Center, follow the wide paved walkway west to the garden, and begin the tour with the Schoepfle Home on the right. This farmhouse was built in the 1840s and purchased by Otto Schoepfle's grandparents in 1882. Otto spent much time visiting here

as a youngster. In 1836 he purchased the house and renovated parts of it; the newest section is the east wing, added in the 1960s.

2 Here you enter the formal garden: in the European style, the long, grassy path is bordered by tightly sheared evergreen and broadleaf hedges. The broadleaf hedge is made of closely planted beech trees. The European beeches forming the hedge are about the same age as the 60-foot-tall beeches growing in other areas of the property. Beyond the hedges are a series of separate garden areas. From his travels throughout the world, Otto Schoepfle brought back many ideas for garden design. The mixed borders are next, to the left, followed by the "Holly harem." The holly, like a number of other species, has male flowers and female flowers on separate trees. Here there is one male American holly surrounded by 15 female hollies. The male flowers supply the pollen, while the female trees produce the berries.

3 Evergreen bushes and trees have been trained and trimmed into ornamental shapes in the topiary garden. This is an art that has been around since ancient times. This topiary garden includes the "schlag" (the German word for whipped-cream topping), created by Otto Schoepfle as a living souvenir of the dessert he enjoyed eating while visiting Austria. Its appearance is especially appealing on a winter's day after new-fallen snow. Other topiaries include a dog sitting in a chair, chickens, and a terrier. The terrier, found near the ornamental grasses, is one of the youngest topiaries, trained since 1985.

4 On the left, near the south end of the evergreen hedge, is a large dawn redwood tree (*Metasequoia*). A deciduous conifer, it bears cones but drops its needles in winter, unlike evergreen conifers, which bear cones and keep their winter greenery. The dawn redwood is often called a "living fossil," because 80-million-year-old fossils of this species have been found and it was believed to be extinct. However, in 1941 dawn redwoods were discovered growing in a remote part of China. Since then, they have been widely planted as ornamentals. This specimen was planted in the 1950s, as a three-foot seedling. Another deciduous conifer in Schoepfle Garden is the bald cypress, found near the south path leading down to the river.

5 On the left (east) is a ginkgo tree, identified by its fan-shaped leaf. (Schoepfle Garden has chosen the ginkgo leaf as a symbol in its publications.)

This tree, too, is considered a "living fossil;" some of its fossilized remains have been found to be 200 million years old. The ginkgo is considered to be the world's oldest living species, because it survives unchanged from its original form. Like American holly, a ginko tree is either male or female. This particular ginkgo is a female, whose unpleasant-smelling fruits ripen in August.

6 On the right is a collection of modern roses, followed by ornamental grasses, then "old garden" roses. (A nameplate indicates the rose's year of introduction.) Rose breeding began in China about 2,500 years ago. In the mid-1800s, modern rose breeding began in France, and hybridization of tea roses started in 1868.

Schoepfle's "old garden" roses include a species that has been propagated since 1581. In general, old-fashioned roses (those grown before the hybridization of tea roses in 1868) have a loose, open form and a single bloom period. They also are more resistant to disease and cold than modern roses.

Under the wellstone at the west side of the garden is where Otto Schoepfle's beloved poodle, Stacey, is buried.

7 To the left of the old-fashioned roses is the Daylily Trail. In 1970 over 60 different varieties of daylilies were planted. The collection changes with time, as species hybridize. The daylilies are at their height of bloom in July and August.

Next to the daylilies is a paperbark maple. Paper-thin pieces of its reddish-brown exfoliating bark roll into fringed curls and expose the smooth cinnamon-colored inner bark. Schoepfle enjoyed raising these from seeds; others are found near the back pond.

8 On the right, near the edge of the "old garden" roses, is a twin-trunked cedar of Lebanon tree. According to Biblical tradition, this is the tree used by King Solomon to build his great temple. This one is the only survivor out of ten trees planted in 1969; harsh winters killed the others. Schoepfle was about to remove this one, also thought to be dead, when he noticed signs of life at its base. The shoots developed into two trunks.

9 Continue south to a collection of conifers: pine, hemlock, spruce, and fir. Here are two bald cypress trees.

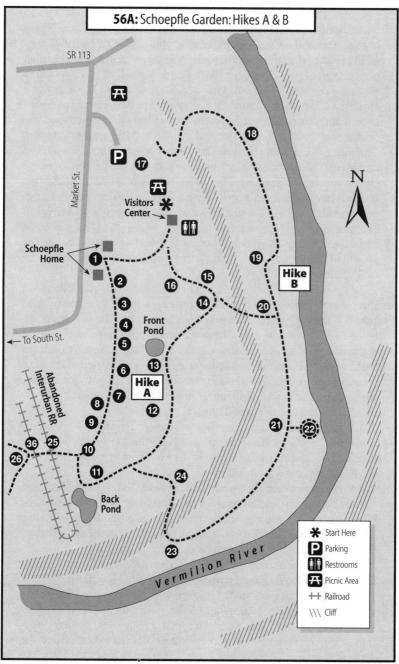

56A: Schoepfle Garden: Hikes A & B

SR 113

Market St.

P

Visitors
Center

Schoepfle
Home

To South St.

Abandoned
Interurban RR

Front
Pond

Hike
A

Hike
B

Back
Pond

N

Vermilion River

* Start Here
P Parking
Restrooms
Picnic Area
++ Railroad
\\\ Cliff

© Gray & Company, Publishers

10 Here the garden tour intersects with the trail into the Interpretive Area. Most of the plants in the 50-acre woodland are native and occur naturally. Schoepfle augmented these with plantings of osage orange trees and a few exotic and native bulbs (Hike C, Note #25).

11 Bear to the left: near the south edge of the horticultural garden is a spring-fed pond known as Back Pond. A patch of bamboo grows on the upper bank. This pond has been here since the 1800s. It was a familiar and welcome landmark that greeted passengers on the Green Line segment of the electric interurban railway as they crossed the bridge over the Vermilion River and approached Birmingham station. The interurban connected Lake Erie shore towns from Cleveland to Sandusky. The sandstone-block bridge abutment can be seen along the cliff southwest of the pond. The bridge was dismantled in 1929 when train service was discontinued. In the winter in the days before refrigeration, this pond was a source of ice for Birmingham. Blocks were cut and stored in sawdust in ice-houses. As a youngster, Otto Schoepfle considered it a good year if there was enough ice remaining on the Fourth of July to make ice-cream. Turn to walk north now, passing the trail on the right.

12 In 1991 Otto Schoepfle began planting these rhododendron shrubs in the shade of a grove of Scots pines. In 1961 he had planted 1,000 of these pines in what was once an orchard. He originally intended to harvest them as Christmas trees, but then chose to leave them as part of his garden. The trees provided shade, protection from harsh winter winds, and acid soil created by pine needles, making ideal growing conditions for rhododendrons. These bloom for several weeks during May and early June. Other older rhododendrons are located at the edge of the mixed borders (#2).

13 Front Pond was dug in 1961 to provide irrigation for the new Scots pine seedlings and other plants. Near the southeast corner is a tricolor beech tree, whose name is derived from the leaves, each of which has three shades of color.

14 Here you reach the turnoff for the River Valley Trail. This short trail leads down to and along the Vermilion River and ends near Back Pond. From there you can connect with the hike into the Interpretive Area. The River Valley Trail is especially enjoyable in the spring when the abundant wildflowers are in bloom. (See Hikes B and C.)

15 Near the intersection with the River Valley Trail is Schoepfle's planting of native dogwood trees. They are in full bloom in early May.

16 Walking back toward the beginning of the tour, you come to the shade garden. Hostas, astilbes, and ferns make up much of the collection. The stone wall to the west was constructed in 1991 from foundation stones of demolished local buildings. On the other side of the stone wall is an archway of lilac bushes, planted before World War II.

Bear to the right to return to the Schoepfle Garden Visitor Center.

Hike B: **River Walk** (includes River Valley Trail)

Distance: 0.6 mile, end to end

Easy

Walking time: 30 minutes

Description: Paths leading down to the Vermilion River are on a gentle slope, while the walk along the river is on level terrain.

17 Begin the hike at the picnic area north of the parking lot. The trail leads downhill and into the woods. At the bottom of the hill, bear right and follow this trail along the river.

18 The trail passes through some sandstone foundation structures that are all that remain of the former Birmingham gristmill, built in 1817. A dam constructed of timber and rocks spanned the river here.

19. The trail emerges from the woods into the open grassy area of the dogwood meadow.

20 The River Valley Trail comes in from the right (see #14). Continue straight ahead on the River Valley Trail.

21 Turn left on a side trail leading to the Vermilion River.

22. The elevation of the river here is 690 feet above sea level. The river flows north and enters Lake Erie in Vermilion, 8 miles away. Visible from this viewing area are outcrops of rock forming the cliff on the far side of the river. The dark cliff to the right is of Cleveland Shale, the same type of rock seen in many cliffs along rivers in Lorain County and eastern Erie County. The lighter-colored cliff directly across the river is composed of Berea Sandstone. It is the same type of rock, though of poorer quality, as that quarried from the deep quarries in South Amherst east of here.

Return to the main trail.

23 The trail turns sharply to the right and uphill toward the formal gardens.

24 Just before emerging onto the grassy area of the gardens, notice two bald cypress trees to the right of the path. These are deciduous conifers, losing their needles in winter, as does the dawn redwood.

From here, return through the gardens to the Visitor Center (about 0.2 miles) or bear left to continue on to Hike C.

Hike C: Interpretive Area

> **Distance:** 1.0 mile loop   **Easy**
>
> **Walking time:** 30 minutes
>
> **Description:** Trails lead through 50 acres of undeveloped woodland called the Interpretive Area, with views of the Vermilion River from cliff tops 50 feet above the valley. In contrast to the managed and manicured gardens, this woodland consists mostly of native trees and wildflowers.

25 Begin the hike at the south end of the gardens, near Back Pond. The trail heads southwest into the woods, crossing the embankment of the interurban railway that operated here until 1929.

26 Where the trail splits, bear to the left. From here you can see the Vermilion River valley below.

27 On the right is a row of osage orange trees. It was customary in the past to plant these trees in hedgerows and shelterbelts, or as property lines between farm fields. The thorny twigs were a barrier to animals.

28 A large white pine grows to the right of the trail. Sycamore trees can be seen across the valley, distinguished by their whitish bark.

29 Continue ahead, bearing left. A side trail to the right offers the option to shortcut the loop.

30 Another trail to the right offers another chance to shortcut. Continue straight ahead. Some of the trees throughout the woods along this trail include wild black cherry, American beech, Ohio buckeye, box elder, oak, and maple. Spring wildflowers include bloodroot, Mayapple, jack-in-the-pulpit, and violets.

31 Where the trail splits, bear right. The trail to the left leads to a lookout with some good views of the valley and some side trails that lead to the grassy area behind the Birmingham Community Center. The main trail soon swings north.

32 A narrow trail leads to the right, off the wider, grassy trail. Follow this winding trail. If you miss the trail and end up in the cemetery, you have gone too far and need to retrace your steps.

33 This is the "Don't Get Lost Here" junction. Two trails cross each other. Follow the trail to the extreme left.

34 Continue straight ahead, bearing right. Another trail branches off to the left.

35 The trail passes through the fencerow of osage orange trees.

36 Bear left to end the loop hike. Return to the Visitor Center through the formal garden or along the River Valley Trail. ■

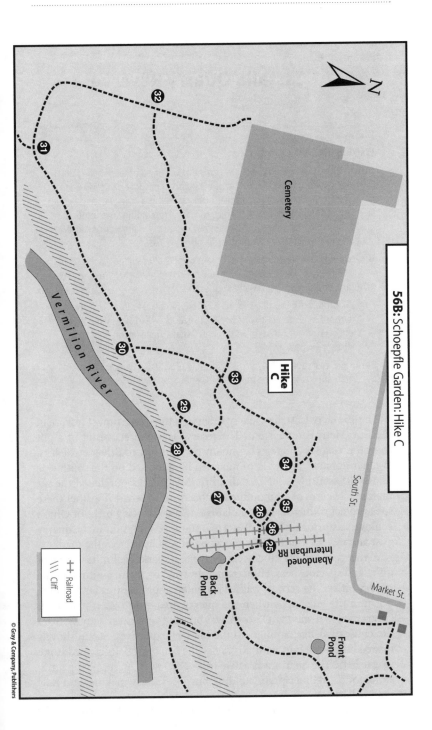

56B: Schoepfle Garden: Hike C

Hike C

Cemetery

Vermilion River

Railroad
Cliff

Back Pond

Front Pond

Abandoned Interurban RR

South St.

Market St.

© Gray & Company, Publishers

57 Castalia Quarry Reserve
Castalia

Distance: 3.5 miles

Moderate

Walking time: 2 hours

Description: This hike visits both the rim and floor of a limestone quarry and a small section of woodland north of the quarry. It provides an up-close look at the geologic history of Northwest Ohio as well as a chance to see special plant communities. Most of the hike is on level ground, however caution is advised due to the sheer cliffs formed by the quarry walls. From an observation tower you can see across the lake plain to Lake Erie.

Directions: From Cleveland, take I-90; west on SR 2 after split to exit for SR 101 (Castalia); left (south) on SR 101 for 4.6 miles through Castalia; trailhead on right about 1 mile past Castalia.

From Akron, take I-77 north; west on I-80 (Ohio Turnpike) to Exit 135 (Baumhart Rd.); north on Baumhart; west on SR 2 to exit for SR 101 (Castalia); left (south) on SR 101 for 4.6 miles through Castalia; trailhead on right about 1 mile past Castalia.

Parking & restrooms: Park on the north side of SR 101. Restrooms (without water) are located on the trail, near the entrance.

The 152-acre Castalia Quarry Reserve is the westernmost reserve in the Erie MetroParks system. The reserve is the direct result of a gift from the Wagner Quarries Company of Sandusky to Erie MetroParks. Wagner donated 110 acres of quarried land located on the south side of SR 101, southwest of Castalia. Erie MetroParks purchased the remaining 42 acres of land on the north side of the road. Together these sites protect numerous native plants and a fascinating piece of Ohio's geologic history. Erie MetroParks maintains several trails in the quarry area and two shorter trails in the wooded wetland across the road.

A visit to the quarry today can be quite remarkable for its feeling of quiet and spaciousness. Humans are dwarfed by the magnitude of the quarry pit and its vertical walls. This quiet emptiness was far from the norm in the late 1800s when the quarry operation was at its height. Quarry #5, as it was then known, was buzzing with noisy activity, from the crack of sledgehammers to the blast of explosives. Steam shovels loaded limestone into railroad cars, while conveyor belts carried stone to crushers. The quarry was active from 1879 to 1929, supplying limestone for shoreline riprap, building purposes, glass-making, and railroad ballast.

Many people have seen or traveled on stone from this quarry without realizing it, for in 1954 the Wagner Quarries Company restarted work at Quarry #5 to supply stone for the Ohio Turnpike. The stone also was used to construct other state highways and the foundations of the Sandusky Bay Bridge. The quarry was closed for good in 1965 after the highways projects were completed.

After the quarrying ceased, this area began to naturally revegetate. Apparently the seeds of many wildflowers had lain dormant in the soils, and once the quarrying ceased, these seeds sprang to life. Biological surveys have identified about 240 native plant species growing here now. Piles of crushed limestone and other features of the quarry have created unique habitats where several rare and threatened plant species live. Several of these are especially striking or unusual. Blazing star, a summer plant, has purple flowers and grows to three feet tall. Bluets are very small plants of spring and early summer. Though each individual flower is only about half an inch wide, masses of these flowers create a pale-blue haze on the floor of the quarry.

It is enjoyable to look for some of the other inhabitants of the quarry, such as birds and butterflies. Bluebirds are there year round, turkey vultures and hawks can be seen soaring overhead, and shorebirds feed along shallow wetlands. Other things to look for along the walk are fossils in the limestone and equipment remnants from the quarrying days. An additional reward on this hike is the view from the observation platform on the quarry rim.

Castalia Quarry Reserve is situated on terrain known as karst topography. Karst refers to areas of porous limestone, typically with caves. There is little surface drainage in such areas; most streams run underground. The term "blue hole" refers to a type of pondlike spring that occurs when the underground water comes to the surface. Such a blue hole was enjoyed by many young Ohioans who visited here with their parents in the 1950s. Though that private blue hole is now closed to the public, you can visit other blue holes in areas owned by the Ohio Department of Natural Resources. The nearest is located at the Castalia Fish Hatchery just north of Castalia. Reach the hatchery by going north on SR 269, then east on Heywood Rd. and east on Homegardner Rd. The hatchery is open daily, Monday through Friday, 8 A.M. to 3:30 P.M.

Another pond indicative of karst topography is the large one in the center of Castalia. Several artesian springs rise there and flow out of the pond as Cold Creek. The pond and creek do not freeze in winter and remain cold and clear throughout the summer. Visitors come to see the many ducks that gather on these ice-free waters throughout winter.

Castalia Quarry Reserve is open daily from 8 A.M. to dusk, year round. Because of the exposed nature of the quarry, it is best to avoid visiting during extreme weather. At all times, stay on marked trails and away from the edges of the quarry walls. There is a small picnic area at the reserve, but no drinking water. A permit is required for bicycle use. For more information about this reserve and other Erie MetroParks, call the park district: 419-625-7783 or visit www.eriemetroparks.org.

1 Begin the hike by crossing SR 101 and entering the trail at the trail sign. Climb gently to the level of the quarry rim and the first intersection. Continue straight, following the Quarry Rim Trail. A "Scenic Overlook" sign points the way. The trail goes east, following a shaded quarry road. Remnants from quarrying are scattered along the trail. One of the earliest wildflowers to bloom along the trail here in spring is round-lobed hepatica. The small plants produce delicate flowers in pink, blue, or white, and the three-lobed leaves remain year round. In less than half a mile the trail makes a U-turn to head southwest. The quarry can be seen on the right.

2 At 0.75 mile reach an intersection and bear left on the short path leading to the Wagner Quarries Company Observation Platform. This unique wooden structure consists of ramps leading up to the main observation area. From the observation platform, the quarry lies to the west and Lake Erie to the north. On a clear day you can see Perry's Victory and International Peace Memorial on South Bass Island. Other features on the horizon are the Sandusky Bay Bridge and the steeple of St. Paul's Church in Danbury. The northern section of the reserve, north of SR 101, and wetlands in the Resthaven Wildlife Area can also be seen. Personal binoculars or the public scope on the platform help bring these and other features into view. Return to the main trail and turn left to continue on the Quarry Rim Trail.

3 The trail goes directly south along the quarry to the southernmost point, then turns west, then north, staying along the quarry rim. After the turn to the north, views open to the opposite side of the immense quarry, and two levels of the quarry are revealed. The southern end of the quarry was not mined as deeply as the rest of it, and the trail now drops to the same elevation as the upper level of quarry. Water has risen to the surface here, creating a fair-sized pond. In summer you can often see goldfish in the pond, and dragonflies darting about above the water.

4 Continue straight north as the trail reaches the western rim of the deeper part of the quarry. In places, dogwood shrubs line the path, noticeable by their red twigs and white berries. Birds feed on the berries. Aspens are also numerous along this part of the quarry road. Aspens are known as pioneer species, because they are among the species that grow first in disturbed, barren, or cleared areas. They grow rapidly and are short-lived, making way for other tree species.

Continue on the Quarry Rim Trail as it winds along the western edge of the quarry, then swings back east.

5 Pass the restrooms and picnic grove. At the trail intersection turn right to reach the quarry floor via the Dolomite Trail. Dolomite is a

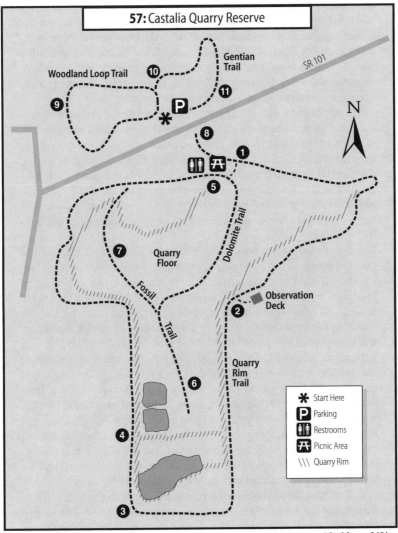

57: Castalia Quarry Reserve

Gentian Trail

Woodland Loop Trail

SR 101

N

Quarry Floor

Dolomite Trail

Fossil Trail

Observation Deck

Quarry Rim Trail

✳ Start Here
🅿 Parking
🚻 Restrooms
⛱ Picnic Area
\\\ Quarry Rim

© Gray & Company, Publishers

porous rock that began as limestone and is almost pure calcium-magnesium carbonate. It is found in the lower parts of Columbus Limestone deposits. The limestone was formed millions of years ago when a shallow saltwater sea covered most of what is now Ohio, and it preserves fossils of sea creatures such as horn coral, crinoids, and brachiopods.

6 Explore the quarry floor by following the Dolomite and Fossil Trails. Two small ponds lie at the base of the limestone cliffs at the southern end of the lower level. At times large numbers of killdeer can be seen in this lower level of the quarry, and many nest here. Killdeer are shorebirds that nest out in the open, often on bare ground. They will often choose pebbly sites, even gravel parking lots, where the stones help camouflage their buff-colored, dark-spotted eggs. Be especially cautious when walking the quarry floor during spring nesting season. The adult killdeer will try to distract intruders and draw them away from the nest by using the broken-wing display, fluttering away from the nest while dragging one wing as if injured.

The exposed rock of the quarry warms quickly and creates a microclimate. On sunny, cool days, the quarry is comparatively warmer than the surrounding countryside, and it warms more quickly in the spring. Insects therefore hatch out earlier, and they in turn attract migrating songbirds. One of the more interesting insects of the quarry is the cicada killer, a black-and-yellow wasp that preys on cicadas. Female cicada killers build tunnel nests in the ground in which they place captured cicadas for the wasp larvae to feed on. The cicada killer is Ohio's largest wasp.

7 After visiting the pond area, turn back north to an intersection near the center of the quarry. Imagine what it must have been like during the early days of quarrying. Quarry workers broke the stone by blasting it with explosives, then steam shovels lifted the rock into small railroad cars. Steam engines then pushed the cars up to the rim, where crushing machines broke the stone into smaller pieces. Finished stone was transported by railroad to shipping ports at Sandusky and Huron.

Bear left to leave the quarry floor. This path leads past old quarrying remnants and up an easy grade to the Quarry Rim Trail. Turn right and retrace your steps past the picnic area to the next trail junction. Turn left (at #5), then left again (at #1), to reach the trail entrance at SR 101.

8 Cross SR 101 and return to the parking area. To continue the hike, enter the Woodland Loop Trail on the western edge of the parking lot. This short trail can be very muddy, even totally under water (and buzzing with mosquitoes), in wet seasons. In that case, skip the Woodland Loop Trail and pick up the hike at Note #10.

9 The Woodland Loop Trail is in sharp contrast to the quarry. Here there is ample shade and moisture for woodland species of birds and insects. The swampy nature of this section of trail resembles that of Resthaven Wildlife Area to the north, and together these protected lands provide an extensive, contiguous corridor for wildlife. Follow the Woodland Loop as it circles west, north, and back east toward the parking lot.

10 At the parking lot, join the Gentian Trail, which follows the edge of the woods along the north and east sides of the parking lot. The path is mowed, but not well marked. Less than a half-mile long, it is surprisingly rich in wildlife: several rare species of wildflowers flourish here, as well as numerous butterflies, some also quite rare. Special species of wildflowers to look for are the fringed gentian and nodding ladies' tresses, both of which bloom in the late summer and fall.

Fringed gentians have four-lobed, violet-blue flowers that are 1½ to 2 inches long and fringed. Nodding ladies' tresses are in the Orchis family and, as is typical of orchids, have only basal leaves, and their flowers are all on one spike. The tiny white flowers come off the spike horizontally or nodding slightly. The plant overall is only 4 to 24 inches high.

A wide variety of butterflies can be found here, as well as a couple of very rare species, such as the tiny Henry's elfin. Each species of butterfly requires a specific plant food for its larvae and a nectar-producing plant for the adults to feed on. Along this trail the forest trees provide larval food, and the field flowers provide the adults with nectar, ideal conditions for butterflies to flourish. Redbud trees, here at the northernmost edge of their range, are one of the nearby trees providing food for some of the butterflies, including Henry's elfin.

11 Continue on the Gentian Trail as it now swings south toward SR 101. Along this part of the path you can find more wildflowers, especially late-summer species such as asters and goldenrods. There are over two dozen different species of goldenrods in the eastern United States, and even more species of asters. One of the goldenrods growing here is the Ohio goldenrod. It likes wet meadows and has yellow flowers arranged in a flat-topped flower cluster, different from the more familiar type of goldenrod where the flowers are arranged along curved stems.

Bear west to end this hike at the parking lot. ■

58 Kelleys Island

Directions to Kelleys Island: Transportation to Kelleys Island includes ferry-boat, airplane, commercial speed boat, and private boat. These directions are for driving to the ferryboat dock and taking your car to Kelleys Island. You can also leave your car on the mainland, then walk about the island, take your bicycle, or rent a golf cart or bicycle from rental services near the ferry dock on the island. Two ferry lines leave from Marblehead Peninsula. Neuman Boat Line, Inc. operates mid-March through November (800-876-1907) and docks 0.8 mile west of downtown. Kelleys Island Ferry Boat Lines, Inc. operates year round, weather permitting (888-225-4325), and docks 0.6 mile east of downtown, at the Seaway Marina. Reservations are recommended for Sundays and holidays. Island Express Boat Lines in Sandusky offers passenger-only service to the downtown dock on Kelleys Island (800-854-8121). Also, Griffing Flying Service has air service to Kelleys Island Municipal Airport from Sandusky and Port Clinton. For more information phone 800-368-3743.

From Cleveland, go west on I-90/SR 2; follow SR 2 after split from I-90 toward Sandusky and Toledo; at far end of Sandusky Bay Bridge, take exit for SR 269 (Marblehead); north on SR 269; right (east) on SR 163 toward Marblehead for 5.3 miles; left (north) on Frances St. to Neuman Boat Line parking. For Kelleys Island Ferry Boat Line, continue 0.2 mile on SR 163. From either dock the trip is 4 miles and takes 20 minutes.

Kelleys Island, one of the largest freshwater islands in the U.S. at approximately 4 square miles (2,800 acres), is listed in the National Register of Historic Places. Located in the western basin of Lake Erie, Kelleys Island is 4 miles north of Marblehead and 12 miles north of Sandusky. A permanent year-round population of 200 people is joined by thousands of visitors on summer weekends.

In late prehistoric times, Kelleys Island was used as a hunting ground by American Indians. Archeological studies here have found village sites, burial mounds, and many other points of interest. At Inscription Rock State Memorial on the south shore of Kelleys Island there are pictographs on a large limestone boulder, most likely carved by Indians during the 1600s.

A man named Cunningham was believed to have been the first white man to inhabit the island, between 1800 and 1812. It became the property of the Connecticut Land Co. in 1817 and was divided into 13 lots given to stockholders in that state. Settlement of Cunningham Is-

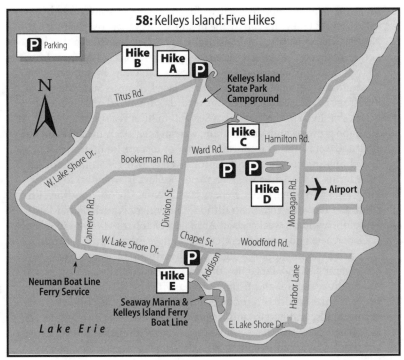

58: Kelleys Island: Five Hikes

P Parking

N

Hike B
Hike A
P
Kelleys Island
State Park
Campground

Titus Rd.

W. Lake Shore Dr.

Hike C
Hamilton Rd.

Bookerman Rd.
Ward Rd.

P   P

Hike D
Airport

Cameron Rd.

Division St.

Monagan Rd.

W. Lake Shore Dr.
Chapel St.
Woodford Rd.

P
Addison

Neuman Boat Line
Ferry Service

Hike E

Harbor Lane

Seaway Marina &
Kelleys Island Ferry
Boat Line

E. Lake Shore Dr.

Lake Erie

© Gray & Company, Publishers

land (or Island No. 6, as it was then called) began in 1833 when Datus and Irad Kelley purchased the land for $1.50 an acre and then gave their name to the island. They and their descendants developed the island's industries, including quarrying, grape growing, and fishing. An impressive three-story mansion, built in the 1860s by Addison Kelley for his father Datus Kelley, sits on a spacious shorefront lot in the center of town.

Limestone quarrying was once the most important industry on Kelleys Island. The bedrock of the island is composed of valuable Columbus Limestone, which contains an exceptionally pure form of calcite. Pure limestone is used in agriculture, in cement manufacturing, as an aggregate in concrete, and perhaps most importantly, as a metallurgical flux to remove impurities from iron ore during smelting. So much limestone was being mined here in the early 1900s that the island was mostly one big quarry. Although some quarrying continues today, most of the limestone has been removed.

One of the remaining chunks of limestone has been preserved because it reveals the power of the glaciers that shaped the land long ago. Glacial Grooves State Memorial is internationally known as the world's largest and most spectacular display of grooves cut by glaciers. Although it is difficult to imagine the force and impact of the glaciers, which moved imperceptibly slowly and over thousands of years, the monument here helps bring it to life. The gouges were carved into solid rock 18,000 years ago by the great ice sheet that covered much of North America during the Pleistocene Age. The glaciers, over the long period of their advancing and retreating, scoured away anywhere from 10 to 60 inches of the top layers of limestone in Ohio. Besides showing these effects of glacial movement, the Glacial Grooves State Memorial limestone also reveals a marvelous record of fossilized marine inverte-brates that lived in the Devonian Sea 360 million years ago.

Grape growing and wine making were at their peak around the year 1900 and were another important source of income for many residents. The climate of the island, with a prolonged growing season and nearly six months of frost-free weather, makes Kelleys Island ideal for grow-ing grapes and other fruits. Kelleys Island Wine Co. on Woodford Rd. continues the wine-making tradition. The winery is open daily, May to September, and on weekends in April and October (419-746-2537).

Fishermen and vacationers crowd Kelleys Island in the summer. Lake Erie's waters support walleye, perch, catfish, smallmouth bass and other game fish. Boaters enjoy the waters around the island for pleas-ure boating, sailing, and fishing. Along with the handful of other is-lands in Lake Erie, it also provides important habitat for birds such as herons, gulls, and egrets, and its marshes provide spawning grounds for certain fish. The island offers many opportunities for pleasurable walking and wildlife watching, as well as great sunsets and scenery.

The Cleveland Museum of Natural History owns 116 acres of the is-land, including some prime wetlands. Monarch butterflies feed on milkweed and blanket the East Quarry area in September as they rest on their yearly migration to their mountain refuges northwest of Mex-ico City. Monarchs return to Kelleys Island in late May.

Kelleys Island State Park occupies 676 acres of land on the north end of the island. The park has 129 campsites, including a few yurts. Near the campground is a small, sandy, public beach with changing booths and latrines. Picnic tables, grills, a boat launch, and a fishing area are all open to the public. For information call 419-746-2546 in season and 419-797-4530 in the off-season. The website for Ohio state parks is www.dnr.state.oh.us/parks.

There are two state nature preserves on Kelleys Island: North Shore Alvar and North Pond. Both are visited in the hikes in this chapter. More information about these sites is found on the Ohio Department of Natural Resources website and at www.kelleysisland.ws/.

Kelleys Island is well situated as a rest stop for flocks of birds mi-grating across Lake Erie in the spring and fall. The 17 miles of shore-line and many acres of protected and diverse habitat provide food and shelter for many species, making the island a popular spot for bird-watching. Bird-watching information is available by calling the Erie County Visitors Bureau at 800-255-3743 or visit their website at

www.buckeyenorth.com; click on Birdwatching. Another contact for birders is the Kelleys Island Audubon Society, at 419-746-2258 or 440-461-1084.

In mid-May a Lilac Walk is open to the public. Call the Kelleys Island Chamber of Commerce to verify dates. The ¼-mile loop walk is through a grove of lilacs. The trailhead is on the south side of Ward Rd., ⅓ mile east of Division St. A sign indicates its location, in season.

Visitor information is available at the Kelleys Island Chamber of Commerce, 130 Division St., Kelleys Island (419-746-2360), or online at www.kelleysisland.com. The office is open Memorial Day to Labor Day, 10 A.M. to 5 P.M.

The hikes on Kelleys Island range from the north end to the south end, but since the island is only about 2 miles from top to bottom, they are all relatively close to each other. Total mileage is less than six miles, with the hikes ranging from 0.25 to 2 miles, so they could all be hiked in one long day or a weekend. The hikes in the north end are at the Glacial Grooves State Memorial, Kelleys Island State Park, and the North Alvar State Nature Preserve. Closer to the middle of the island are North Pond State Nature Preserve and the East Quarry Trail (part of the state park). The southernmost walk is through the downtown of Kelleys Island and includes Inscription Rock State Memorial. Please note that pets are not permitted in state nature preserves.

Hike A: Glacial Grooves State Memorial

Distance: 1/4 mile

Easy

Hiking time: 1/2 hour

Description: A large area of grooved limestone is situated behind a protective fence at the northwest end of the island. The hike circles the rock on a paved path that includes short sets of steps. Ten plaques offer information on the geology and history of the area. A one-page leaflet has more information on the rock and fossils keyed to lettered stops on the trail. Pick up the leaflet at the Chamber of Commerce or the state park office.

Directions to reach the hike: Follow Division St. (located off Lake Shore Dr., midway between the two ferry docks) to north end of island. About 50 feet past Titus Rd., turn left into the small parking lot for Glacial Grooves State Memorial.

Parking & restrooms: If lot is full, use additional parking at end of park road leading to boat-launch lot and swimming beach. Access this lot downhill on one-way park road at end of Titus Rd. Restrooms at beach parking lot.

Glacial Grooves State Memorial encompasses 3.5 acres and has been administered by the state of Ohio since 1932. These spectacular grooves were created about 18,000 years ago by the Wisconsinan Glacier, which advanced from the highlands of Labrador, Canada, to this part of Ohio over a period of 5,000 years. As the mile-thick glacier advanced, the weight of ice above sculpted these grooves in the limestone bedrock. The grooves are in the bed of a 400-foot-long trough. They reveal a wealth of fossilized marine invertebrates.

NOTE: Please only *observe* the fossils. *Collection of fossils here is strictly forbidden. Contact the state park office for information on obtaining permits for collecting fossils from North Quarry and East Quarry.*

Just north of, and parallel to, Titus Rd. is a ledge of rock 3 to 7 feet high. It is the ancient shoreline of a smaller island. The slow retreat of the glaciers left much meltwater behind. About 3,000 years ago the lake level was 25 feet higher than it is now. Two islands existed where there is now one. The smaller island was a circular piece of land that is now occupied by the glacial grooves, the large parking lot, and North Quarry. The larger island was to the south. The shoreline of that island is visible as a ledge going roughly east–west, just north of Ward Rd. Division St. crosses the old shoreline as does the trail in North Pond State Nature Preserve. The area between the two islands was a shallow waterway and is now a fertile valley known as Sweet Valley.

There are two geological features visible at Glacial Grooves State Memorial. On the surface are the glacial grooves, with origins around 35,000 years ago. The other is the bedrock and its fossils, which formed about 360 million years ago. Geologically, the bedrock and fossils are ten thousand times older than the grooves.

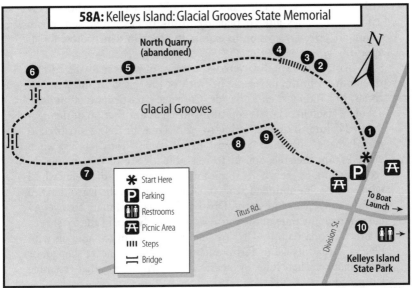

58A: Kelleys Island: Glacial Grooves State Memorial

North Quarry (abandoned)

Glacial Grooves

Start Here
P Parking
Restrooms
Picnic Area
IIII Steps
Bridge

Titus Rd.

Division St.

To Boat Launch →

Kelleys Island State Park

© Gray & Company, Publishers

The bedrock here, Columbus Limestone, has many of the fossils commonly seen in this rock, which ranges south through Columbus to southern Ohio. The limestone along the walkway was formed from mud and shell remains of marine animals deposited at the bottom of the warm, shallow sea that covered Ohio during the Devonian Age 360 million years ago. It was also during the Devonian Age that fishes first appeared in the world's seas. The shelled creatures and the early fishes had no backbones. Over time, the shells of the marine creatures and the limy mud compacted and cemented together to form limestone. Corals, brachiopods, pelecypods (clam shells), gastropods (snails), cephalopods, and portions of crinoids (sea lilies) are the most abundant fossils found in the limestone at the site of the grooves. They are visible on the surface of the rock as glacially polished cross-sections.

1 Begin the walk by the sign at the northwest corner of the parking lot. This gives the history of the grooves and the glacier that formed them. Written accounts claim that the grooves were discovered in the mid-1800s. They are considered the most famous glacial grooves in the world due to their size and easy access by visitors.

2 An information plaque describes the Wisconsin Glacier, an immense ice sheet that visited what is now Ohio 25,000 years ago. It is thought that the glacier moved out of present-day Labrador, Canada, at a rate of one or two inches a day, which gives new meaning to the phrase "glacial speed"! When the grooves were being gouged out, the glacier was about a mile high. Imagining that much ice helps one to understand the force exerted by the creeping glaciers.

3 The fossils seen in this rock are crinoidea (sea lilies), whose decay left small, round, scattered, platelike fossils. It may have taken several thousand years for erosion to expose the rock in which these fossils appear.

4 Geologists have discovered 47 species of ancient fossilized marine animals in the limestone bedrock of this park. At this stop are corals, brachiopods, and criasids. Corals are particularly abundant. Tabulate (tablelike) corals appear fossilized as a collection of flat, segmented columns; rugose (wrinkled) corals may be found fossilized as round shells with internal divisions or septa; "horn" corals, when viewed from the side, appear to resemble a cone or cornucopia. In cross-section, as seen here, it appears as a one-inch-diameter wheel with spokes. The abundance of corals indicates that the Devonian Sea was shallow, clear, and warm. Obviously, a major climate change occurred from the time of the warm sea to the advance of the ice sheet.

Brachiopoda (lamp shells) are one-inch fossils of sea animals with bivalve shells in various forms such as fan-shaped, heart-shaped, or wing-shaped. Their folds or creases form vertical lines that resemble lampshades.

The tortuous winding of some of the smaller glacial grooves (as explained at this stop) may be due to preglacial or subglacial stream flow.

5 The rock in the glacial grooves appears as dark and light layers or strata. Crinoid (sea lily) fragments make up the dark strata; the light strata are composed of fossil fragments compacted together and forming a fine, powdery, limy material called "fossil hash."

The rock underfoot contains corals, gastropoda (snails), and cephalopoda—all typical fossilized Devonian Sea animals. Snails often left a cast of their coiled shape rather than the shell itself.

Cephalopoda (nautiloids and ammonoids) grew shells divided into many compartments or chambers. Fossilized cephalopoda show the external lines of the many chambers. Examples of modern cephalopods are squid and the chambered nautilus.

6 This stop presents a view of the abandoned North Quarry, which operated from 1833 to 1900. Although even larger grooves were destroyed during the quarrying, these in the state memorial were preserved with the halt of the mining. Up until 1971, only 35 feet of the grooves were exposed. It was then decided to have workers remove a hill of soil, glacial debris, and quarry rubble to expose the expanse of rock that visitors see today. It was fortunate that limestone quarry operations ceased when they did, providing this unusual opportunity to study life as it existed in this area millions of years ago. (Hike B visits North Quarry.)

7 The glacial grooves, deepest at this point, inspire respect for the awesome size and depth of the massive ice that carved them. The last glacier retreated permanently about 12,000 years ago.

8 At this stop the grooves below you are deep and straight. But trapped in the mile-high ice were granitelike boulders that, as they were pushed forward, acted as giant grinding and abrading machines. Evidence of different-sized granite rocks frozen into the bottom of the ice is revealed by the smaller winding grooves and striations in the softer limestone.

Fossils seen in this location include crinoids (sea lilies), solitary rugose coral, colonial tabulate coral, and brachiopoda.

It is a wonder that these sea organisms, millions of years old, have been uncovered by a glacial process that, relatively speaking, is of such recent origin.

9 The exhibit here gives information on the location of other glacial grooves and striations. Some of these can be seen at the North Shore Alvar State Nature Preserve on Hike B and along the beginning of the East Quarry Trail on Hike D.

Descend the steps just ahead to return to the parking lot.

10 Across the street, by the boat launch road is an old oven. Built about 1875, it was one of two in the area used for baking bread for the quarry workers. In the vicinity were several buildings including a large two-story dormitory for quarry workers and a general store.

Some information in Hike 58A was adapted from *A Glacial Grooves Fossil Walk on Kelleys Island* by L. M. Bowe and C. E. Herdendorf. ■

Hike B: **North Shore Loop Trail**
and North Shore Alvar State Nature Preserve

Easy

Distance: 1.5 miles

Hiking time: ³/₄ hour

Description: This hike follows part of an abandoned quarry road, then makes a loop through the woods and along the rocky limestone ledge of the north shore of Kelleys Island, where there are good views of other islands and Lake Erie. The Kelleys Island Audubon Society has prepared a one-page leaflet with information on quarry features and plants found here, keyed to numbered markers along the trail. Pick up the leaflet at the Chamber of Commerce or the state park office.

Directions: Follow Division St. (located off Lake Shore Dr., midway between the two ferry docks) to north end of island; right at end of street on Titus Rd.; follow one-way boat-launch road downhill and counterclockwise to reach a large parking lot.

Parking & restrooms: Restrooms at swimming beach parking lot, located off same one-way road, before boat-launch lot.

This part of the north shore of Kelleys Island is protected as a preserve, the North Shore Alvar State Nature Preserve. Here rare plants grow in a harsh environment on a glacially scoured limestone "prairie."

Also of interest along the route are leftovers from quarrying days. Poison ivy grows abundantly along the trail, so be especially cautious.

1 The entrance to North Shore Loop Trail begins in the large parking lot used by boaters and fishermen. Enter the trail at trail marker #1, west of the parking lot and 400 feet north of Glacial Grooves State Memorial, at the edge of North Quarry.

The first stop provides a view of abandoned North Quarry, where John Clemmons started quarrying limestone in 1830. This was the second quarry to open on Kelleys Island, and operations continued here until about 1900. The stone was of such superior quality that it was used throughout Ohio, Michigan, and the eastern U.S. The first American lock at Sault St. Marie contains this limestone, as does the Cedar Point breakwall and many buildings and bridges in Cleveland. Continue north on the trail.

2 At a trail intersection, turn left. Just ahead and on the right, now covered by bushes, is an old rusty flatbed truck. Where the trail meets a quarry road, turn left again, onto the road.

3 This loader was built in 1888 and used to fill rail cars with crushed stone to be taken to the dock or lime kilns. At one time Kelleys Island Lime and Transport Co. had 16 kilns operating and produced 1,500 barrels of lime per day. Continue ahead, going over or around a vehicle barrier.

4 Leave the quarry road and bear right (northwest) onto a narrow trail.

5 This large manmade hill is a spoil bank built to provide workers with access to the stone crusher located in the building next to the loader. The hill is made of fine pieces of stone, a by-product of the stone-crushing process.

Bypass the side trail to the north going up over the spoil bank.

6 Bear right (north) at the next trail intersection. (The trail to the left passes stone building foundations of homes used by quarry workers.)

7 At 0.5 mile reach the shoreline of Lake Erie. Follow the side trail to the right, to the shoreline. This limestone bedrock between the woods and the water is part of the two-acre North Shore Alvar State Nature Preserve. An alvar is a flat expanse of nearly barren limestone that has been scraped and gouged by glaciers and has little plant life due to the effects of waves, wind, and ice. One definition is "a limestone prairie surrounded by water." The word "alvar" is from a Swedish word for similar landforms found on islands off the coast of Sweden near the Baltic Sea. Only certain plants can tolerate this harsh environment, and some are very rare. Some of the plants growing on the North Shore Alvar are northern bog violet, balsam squaw-weed, columbine, Kalm's lobelia, and Pringle's aster. There are also mosses and a lichen called showy orange lichen. The alvar extends for about 0.25 mile along the

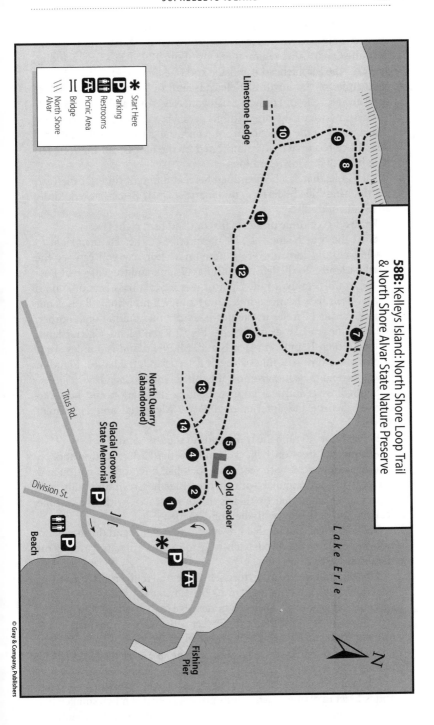

58B: Kelleys Island: North Shore Loop Trail
& North Shore Alvar State Nature Preserve

Lake Erie

N

Fishing Pier

Beach

Division St.

Titus Rd.

Glacial Grooves
State Memorial

North Quarry
(abandoned)

Limestone Ledge

Old Loader

Legend
- ✳ Start Here
- 🅿 Parking
- 🚻 Restrooms
- ⛲ Picnic Area
-][Bridge
- \\\ North Shore Alvar

© Gray & Company, Publishers

shore, sandwiched between the North Shore Trail and the lake. It can be reached by several side trails branching off the North Shore Trail.

In the Great Lakes region there are about 120 alvar sites, including some on the Marblehead Peninsula and one on Canada's Pelee Island, eight miles to the north of Kelleys Island. In North America, large-sized alvars are found only in Michigan, New York, and Ontario.

This limestone ledge also exhibits parallel scratches called striations, which attest to the direction from which the glaciers traveled, northeast. More recent activity is indicated by the blocks of limestone left here from quarrying operations.

Lake gulls that can be identified here, at different times of the year, are the Ring-billed, Herring, Bonaparte's, Great Black-backed, Little, and Glaucous gulls.

Return to continue on the main trail and turn right (west).

8 At the fourth side trail, at interpretive marker #6, turn right to reach a clifftop lookout. From here on a clear day you can see the nearby islands. To the left is South Bass Island and the village of Put-in-Bay, 6 miles away; to the right of it is Middle Bass Island, 7 miles away. North Bass Island, 8 miles away and behind Middle Bass, is not visible. About 11 miles to the north, across the international border, are the Chicken Islands of Canada: Big Chicken Island, Chick Island, Little Chicken Island, and Hen Island. Middle Island is 5 miles away, and just north of it, 8 miles away, is Pelee Island, the largest island in Lake Erie and the southernmost inhabited land of Canada.

South Bass Island is a popular boating destination and home to Perry's Victory and International Peace Memorial and Heineman Winery.

9 At about 1.0 mile the trail bends to the left (south).

Among the trees on Kelleys Island are the Eastern cottonwood, a fast-growing species with seeds that look like tiny fluffs of cotton and leaves that are triangular with marginal teeth. Green and white ash trees can be identified by their compound leaves, with five to nine leaflets, and dark bark with diamond-shaped ridges.

Red and sugar maples that grow here are second- and third-generation trees. Maple was used extensively to fuel steamboats traveling on the Great Lakes.

10 At a trail intersection, turn left. (The trail to the right leads to an abandoned quarry building. On its brick front is printed, barely discernably, "explosives.") The high stone ledge to the right of the trail and parallel to the trail for the next 450 feet is the edge of the quarry. It is also part of an ancient shoreline, from when the level of Lake Erie was about 610 feet, 3,000 years ago. The present lake level at Kelleys Island is about 575 feet.

11 Ohio's state tree, the Ohio buckeye, usually grows to 40 feet tall and is 2 feet in diameter when fully grown. Here it is much smaller, because it is growing in thin soil over limestone bedrock. It is identified

by its compound leaves in groups of five and the spiny capsules that surround the shiny buckeye seed. (In contrast, the yellow buckeye, which also has leaves in groups of five, is slightly larger, and its seed capsule is smooth rather than spiny.)

12 The foundations is this area once supported buildings occupied by quarry workers who came from Italy, Germany, and other European countries to work in the pits.

Continue straight ahead where other side trails go off to the right and left.

13 Eastern red cedar is a juniper that commonly grows in poor soil and is abundant on Kelleys Island, thriving in the limestone soil. This tree has round or four-sided branchlets covered by closely overlapping, dark-green scales. Its round, quarter-inch-long cones are green at first, then blue, and are covered with a gray, waxy substance. This slow-growing tree may live for 300 years.

14 The trail meets a quarry road. Bear left and continue on the quarry road, reaching the intersection near the start of the trail, at the loader. Continue straight ahead and retrace your steps to the start of the trail. ■

Hike C: North Pond State Nature Preserve

Distance: 1 mile

Hiking time: ½ hour

Description: The nature preserve is a 36-acre sanctuary consisting of forest, marsh, and natural pond. A hiking trail leads from its access at Ward Rd. north along dirt and gravel paths and boardwalk to the pond. There are informative plaques along the way describing the nature of the area.

Directions: Follow Division St. (located off Lake Shore Dr., midway between the two ferry docks) toward the north end of the island for about 1 mile; right (east) on Ward Rd. for 0.5 mile to parking lot.

Parking and restroom: The parking lot is on the south side of the road. No restrooms. To reach the start of the trail, walk west along Ward Rd. and cross to the north side at the sign for the nature preserve.

The pond at North Pond State Nature Preserve is a "lake embayment," referring to the pond's water levels rising and falling with the water level of Lake Erie. The pond has characteristics of both marsh and estuary. Periodically its water level is high enough for it to be connected to Lake Erie by a small, temporary channel. North Pond is also fed by runoff from the island. When the water level is high enough, huge carp can be seen in the shallow channel, swimming into the pond from the lake.

Part of the trail is a boardwalk winding through forest and swamp. It is constructed of recycled plastic lumber and natural wood. Plaques placed along its 1,700 feet credit companies that donated materials.

1 Begin the hike at the information display describing Kelleys Island and the preserve. Trees growing in the immediate area include juniper (eastern red cedar), sumac, hackberry, blue ash, redbud, red maple, and slippery elm. Wildflowers include nodding wild onions and herb robert.

Head north along the trail. Private property on the right is a 4-H camp.

2 The trail descends a rocky slope. About 3,000 years ago, there were two islands where now there is one. This east–west ledge was the shoreline of the larger island. The smaller island was north of here. A shallow channel of water separated the two islands. The channel subsequently filled in and is now a fertile valley (though with very shallow soil), known as Sweet Valley. The trail drops down into this valley, from an elevation of 620 feet at the trailhead to 575 feet at North Pond.

The tallest trees here are Eastern cottonwoods, which eagles find

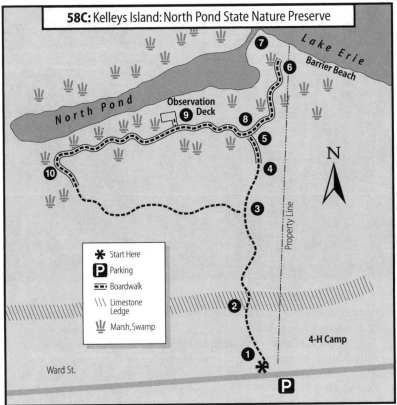

58C: Kelleys Island: North Pond State Nature Preserve

Lake Erie

Barrier Beach

North Pond

Observation Deck

★ Start Here
P Parking
▬▬ Boardwalk
\\\ Limestone Ledge
Ⱳ Marsh, Swamp

Property Line

4-H Camp

Ward St.

N

© Gray & Company, Publishers

suitable for nest sites. Loss of habitat and pesticide poisoning from the 1950s to the 1970s nearly extirpated bald eagles in Ohio. The numbers of bald eagles successfully nesting along Lake Erie shores have been steadily increasing in recent years in response to pollution controls, especially the banning of DDT, and other conservation measures.

One of the showier wildflowers on Kelleys Island is the orange-flowered trumpet creeper, which attracts hummingbirds and insects. It is a rather aggressive vine and can climb quite high into trees. Another vine doing very well here is poison ivy, identified by its "leaves of three." Many bird species relish the berries, but even a slight touch of any part of the plant to human skin causes an itchy rash for most people. Plants that have similar-looking leaves are the box elder tree and the fragrant sumac shrub.

3 A sign at this trail intersection describes the work of the Ohio Department of Natural Resources, including the Division of Natural Areas and Preserves, and tells the difference between nature preserves and state parks. Continue straight ahead on the trail, going north.

4 The boardwalk that begins here elevates the trail above a low-lying, frequently wet area. Volunteers and state employees cooperated in building the boardwalk.

5 A kiosk here gives more detailed information on North Pond State Nature Preserve and pictures a number of the more common birds, reptiles, amphibians, and plants. There are two distinct habitats here in the preserve—the plants and animals of the pond area differ from those found on the barrier beach. Bear to the right on the boardwalk to reach the barrier beach.

6 This beach is the physical barrier separating the pond embayment from Lake Erie. A channel cutting through the beach allows the lake and pond to connect at certain water levels. The channel opens and closes depending on the lake level, rainfall, and waves. Beach dunes, such as those found here, are now rare in Ohio due to development and heavy recreational use. On this barrier beach the rare dune plants are protected.

The beach to the left is part of Kelleys Island State Park. When walking the beach, take care not to disturb the beach plants. Watch the beach area for shorebirds, such as killdeer and ruddy turnstones, being especially cautious during nesting season. Always avoid beach areas if there are active nests.

7 Down the beach 350 feet is the small channel that connects Lake Erie and the North Pond. Water snakes, beneficial in the chain of life on the beach, are often found here.

Return along the beach to the boardwalk.

8 At the kiosk, turn right to continue on the trail. On the right is an exceptionally large Eastern cottonwood tree.

9 Climb the steps to the observation deck on the right. This is an excellent place from which to observe the plant communities and birds. Which plants flourish in the pond depends partly on the water level: when the water is high, water lilies emerge from the center of the pond; when the pond is dry, swamp rose mallow grows. Other wild-flowers in the area include smart weed with its small pink spikes, wild blue iris blooming in May along the boardwalk, and cardinal flower, blooming in late summer. Birds include indigo buntings, warblers, Eastern kingbirds, herons, and red-winged blackbirds.

10 The trail curves to the south and the boardwalk ends. Continue to the start of the loop and turn right to reach the trailhead.

The Lilac Walk is 700 feet west of here, from a trail off the south side of Ward Rd. It is open only when the lilacs are in bloom, around early May. ■

Hike D: East Quarry Trail

Distance: 2 miles   Easy

Hiking Time: ³/₄ hour

Description: The East Quarry Trail system, located near the center of the island, is part of Kelleys Island State Park. The trail follows the rim of a quarry for 0.5 mile, then makes a 1-mile clockwise loop to the south through the woods, returning on the same quarry rim trail. Bicyclists also use the East Quarry Trail.

Directions: Follow Division St. (located off Lake Shore Dr., midway between the two ferry docks) toward the north end of the island for about 1 mile; right (east) on Ward Rd. for 0.7 mile.

Parking and restrooms: The small parking lot is on the south side of the road, across from the 4-H camp. No restrooms. This trail is only 0.2 mile east of the trailhead for North Pond State Nature Preserve.

The East Quarry Trail and the quarry itself are rich in fossils. Al-though the trail does not go down into the quarry, you may wish to de-scend one of the easier access routes to spend some time looking at the fossils, including corals, brachiopods, gastropods, and crinoids. Col-lecting fossils is prohibited without a written permit from the Ohio Department of Natural Resources (ODNR). For a permit, write to ODNR, Division of Parks and Recreation, 1952 Belcher Dr., Bldg. C-3, Columbus, OH 43224, or contact the Kelleys Island State Park office located in the campground on the north shore of the island.

The area known as East Quarry was part of a much larger quarry that extended west past Division St. and Bookerman Rd., almost to the western shore of the island. The East Quarry section extends from Di-vision St. to Monagan Rd. The Kelleys Island Lime and Transport

Company quarried this area from 1933 to 1940. Most of the limestone was used as flux for the steel-making process. Some of the old narrow-gauge railroad tracks still lie in Horseshoe Lake and on the quarry floor in the western end, left over from the days when quarried material was hauled west under the Division St. bridge.

Among the interesting attractions along the East Quarry Trail are Horseshoe Lake, with limestone rocks edging it, fossils embedded in rocks underfoot, glacial striations on the surface of the limestone bedrock, Lakeside daisies (which bloom in May), some old fence lines of typical island construction, and an interesting variety of trees. There are 13 numbered signposts along the trail, keyed to information printed in a one-page leaflet available from the state park office. Please be aware that there are many informal paths here, some of which criss-cross the main trail.

1 Enter the trail on either side of the barrier. Head southeast on a wide path. Horseshoe Lake is just ahead. Stay on the quarry rim trail, a wide path going clockwise around the lake. Here you see large slabs of quarried limestone at the edge of the lake. Narrow grooves in the bedrock, called striations, were made by the scraping, gouging action of the glaciers.

2 Among the wetlands on Kelleys Island is the marsh located east of Horseshoe Lake. Wetlands such as this provide important habitat for plants that have adapted to life in saturated soil, including some rare and endangered species. Some of the birds that frequent the wetland are red-winged blackbirds, common yellowthroats, and marsh wrens, all of which nest in or near the marsh plants.

In some places along the rim trail, the very rare Lakeside daisy grows in the thin soil on top of the nearly barren limestone. The Lakeside daisy is considered the rarest of more than 200 plants currently listed as endangered in Ohio. Its bright yellow flower blooms in May. Each basal rosette of leaves produces a single stalk up to a foot tall, topped with a solitary flower. As part of a restoration/transplantation project in 1989, plants and seeds were brought to the East Quarry from a colony of the daisies growing on the Marblehead Peninsula.

3 Horseshoe Lake is a rapidly aging lake that is smaller than it was originally. Nutrients have found their way into the once-clear water, so plant, fish, and aquatic life is beginning to thrive. Many smallmouth bass live in the lake as well as other species of fish. The lake provides food for great blue herons, egrets, gulls, fox, and raccoon. Human fishermen enjoy the lake as well, with the proper license. Swimming is prohibited.

4 At 0.5 mile bear left off the main trail, then immediately right onto a grassy trail going southwest.

Black cherry trees, which in other environments eventually grow to 50–60 feet tall and, 1–3 feet in diameter, and may live 150–200 years,

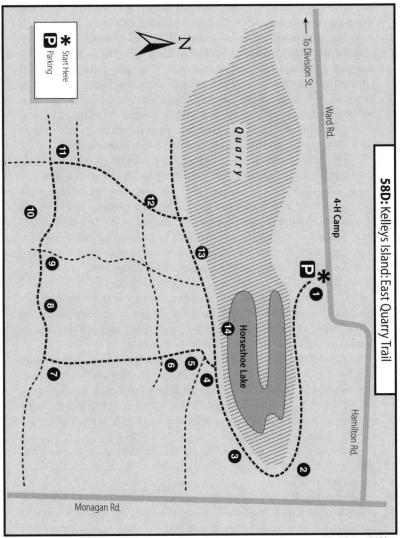

Start Here

P Parking

N

Quarry

To Division St.

Ward Rd.

4-H Camp

58D: Kelleys Island: East Quarry Trail

P *

Horseshoe Lake

Hamilton Rd.

Monagan Rd.

© Gray & Company, Publishers

cannot reach their full size here because of the thin topsoil on Kelleys Island. The black cherry's oval leaves are 2–6 inches long and have finely toothed margins. The bark of these young cherries is smooth, dark reddish-brown or black. The bark of more mature cherry trees resembles burnt potato chips. The wood of the cherry is prized for furniture making.

5 Pass the trail on the left. Growing nearby are hackberry trees. Hackberry trees grow best in rich soil but are also commonly found on limestone outcrops. Certain varieties are used as ornamentals and are capable of living under adverse moisture and soil conditions. Hackberry bark is characteristically grayish brown with corky ridges and warts. Its ovate leaves are 2–4 inches long with toothed margins.

6 The American basswood tree produces valuable white, straight-grained lumber. It is also valued as a soil improver because its deciduous leaves contain calcium, magnesium, nitrogen, phosphorus, and potassium. The leaves are heart-shaped and very large—5–6 inches long and 3–4 inches wide. The small honey-flavored flowers and fruit are attached to a leafy bract 5–6 inches long. Its dark-gray bark is ridged and furrowed and was used by Iroquois Indians to make rope.

Cross an east-west side trail (0.6 mile) and continue south.

7 The osage-orange tree, originally a southern species, has been grown extensively for fencerows and hedges. The thorny spikes and dense growth make a good barricade. Its ovate deciduous leaves are 3–5 inches long with smooth margins. This tree can achieve a height of 50–60 feet and bears large, round (3–5 inches in diameter), inedible fruit. The wood of the osage-orange tree is characteristically bright orange and yields a yellow dye when soaked in hot water. Since it is used to make archers' bows, the tree is often called "bowwood."

Just past Sign No. 7, turn right at a "T" junction.

8 Continue ahead. The Chinkapin oak is a small tree found on dry limestone outcrops. Its 4-to-9-inch-long leaves have sharp teeth and fine white hairs on the undersides. Its small, ovate acorns are brown to black, and its bark is ash gray, rough, and flaky.

9 Signpost #9 marks the former site of a fence-line marker. Only parts of the marker remain. The method of fencing on Kelleys Island was dictated by the shallow soil above limestone bedrock, which prevented the driving-in of fence posts. Islanders filled barrels with rocks to hold the posts, then strung wire from post to post to form an enclosure or delineate property lines.

Continue west on the trail. Pass a trail on the right, another old quarry road. Here Eastern red cedar grows abundantly in the poor limestone soil.

10 On the left is an Eastern hop hornbeam, *Ostrya virginiana*, which is often called "ironwood" because its wood is heavy and tough. The bark has a shredded appearance, with broken, shaggy plates that curve away from the trunk. Its birchlike leaves are three to five inches long and have double-toothed margins. The Eastern hop hornbeam produces two-inch-long catkins and clustered seed pods with flattened, leafy bladders containing seeds. Common names for trees can be confusing. *Carpinus caroliniana*, a tree with similar leaves, is also called "ironwood," as well as "American hornbeam." It's also called "muscle wood" because of the muscle-like appearance of its smooth, blue-gray, sinewy bark. Both trees are found throughout Ohio and most of the eastern states.

11 Turn right (north) at the four-way intersection (1.2 miles). The crisscrossing trails in this park are former quarry trails and are used by hikers, maintenance personnel, and wildlife. They also serve as fire breaks for the quarry area.

12 On the left is the fast-growing honey locust tree, growing well in limestone soil. This tree is distinguished by thorny spines, compound leaves, and 7-to-18-inch-long brown seedpods. The flattened and twisted seedpod contains a sweetish pulp. Cattle, deer, rabbits, and squirrels all eat these fruits. In rich soil, this tree can reach 75–80 feet.

The trail meets the quarry rim. Turn right (east) to walk above the old East Quarry.

13 Here again you may see 360-million-year-old Devonian Sea fossils embedded in the limestone rock underfoot on the trail. Scattered around this area are corals, crinoids (sea lilies), brachiopods (lamp shells), gastropods (snails), cephalopods (nautiloids and ammonoids), and pelecypods (clams or bivalves). Brachiopods and corals are most common.

14 A bench is provided for sitting and enjoying the view of Horseshoe Lake. Continue on the path past the junction in Note #4. Follow the perimeter trail to the beginning of the hike and the parking area. ■

Hike E: Downtown Walk and Inscription State Memorial

Distance: 1.1 miles

Easy

Hiking Time: $1/2$ hour

Description: This walk is a clockwise loop on sidewalks around a downtown block of Kelleys Island. A short walk from the street to Inscription Rock is on a gentle, grassy incline.

Directions: In the business section at the south shore of Kelleys Island.

Parking and restrooms: Park on Division St. or W. Lake Shore Dr., just west of Division St. There is also parking at the municipal park on Addison Rd., or a little farther away, at Seaway Marina, 0.2 mile east of Inscription Rock. Public restrooms are at Seaway Marina, the municipal park, and Portside Marina.

Gift shops, restaurants, and other tourist services cluster around the compact downtown area. Private residences line Lake Shore Dr. and side streets. Just a few of the many points of interest in downtown Kelleys Island are listed here.

Most of the historic homes facing Lake Erie are privately owned and not open to the public, while some provide accommodations. A book, *Kelleys Island, a Tour Guide,* prepared by the Kelleys Island Historical Association, gives the history and provides details about many of the homes and buildings. Chamber of Commerce publications also list points of interest, shops, services, and lodging options.

The Downtown Walk can be started from any of the parking locations. It is described here starting from the parking area in the municipal park on Addison Rd. From the lot, cross the road and walk right (south) on the sidewalk toward Lake Erie.

1 The Kelley Mansion at 211 E. Lake Shore Dr. is privately owned but is sometimes open to the public for tours, for a fee. Kelley Mansion is a three-story limestone rock home with a widow's walk, built in the 1860s by Addison Kelley, co-founder of Kelleys Island, for his father, Datus Kelley. Inside is a freestanding spiral staircase, handsome woodwork, and rose-colored, cut-crystal windows. Displayed inside is a collection of letters and photos from presidents and dignitaries and a small museum with articles pertaining to the home's residents.

The Civil War–style architecture of Kelley Mansion is similar to that of several other homes on the island's south shore. It is thought that homes built around the time of the Civil War were constructed by confederate prisoners held captive on nearby Johnson's Island in Sandusky Bay. Walk west across Addison Rd., then cross to the lake side of Lake Shore Dr.

2 Inscription Rock State Memorial is by the lake, off the south end of Addison Rd. It is believed that sometime between 1200 and 1600 A.D., Native American inhabitants of the area inscribed the pictographs seen on this flat-topped limestone rock. The rock, measuring 32 feet by 21 feet, contains drawings that resemble humans, birds, and other animals. In 1850 U.S. army officer Captain Seth Eastman measured and drew a copy of the rock's figures. One of the figures is a person with headdress, smoking a pipe. Many years of weathering have all but obliterated the original drawings on the rock, but a plaque was made from the Eastman drawing to show what the original might have looked like. In 1969, the Ohio Historical Society erected a shelter to help protect the plaque and rock. Although no one knows for sure what purpose the drawings served, a widely accepted theory is that the rock was used as a "message stone." People passing through would leave pictorial messages that conveyed how the fishing and hunting had been, where they traveled from, or where they were headed.

Cross the street to the sidewalk along the north side of E. Lake Shore Rd. and go west.

3 Himmelein House, at 129 E. Lake Shore Dr., is a three-story white frame house with dark-blue shutters. This handsome home facing the lake has been a private residence since 1920. The original section was built about 1859 by Johann Himmelein as a private residence. By 1870 it was being used as a hotel. By 1890, two wings and a third story were added, and it resembled the structure we see today.

Continue west on the sidewalk.

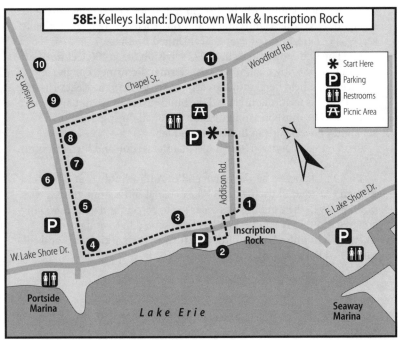

58E: Kelleys Island: Downtown Walk & Inscription Rock

Woodford Rd.

Chapel St.

Division St.

Addison Rd.

E. Lake Shore Dr.

W. Lake Shore Dr.

Inscription Rock

Portside Marina

Lake Erie

Seaway Marina

✱ Start Here
P Parking
🚻 Restrooms
🛆 Picnic Area

N

© Gray & Company, Publishers

4 At the corner of Division St. and Lake Shore Rd. is the heart of downtown Kelleys Island. The public park at the corner is Memorial Park.

Turn right and walk along Division St.

5 At 130 Division St. is the Kelleys Island Chamber of Commerce. Tourist information is available inside during business hours, and outside in the racks on the porch.

6 At 135 Division St., across the street and a short distance north from the Chamber of Commerce, is the South Side School, now a private residence. It was built in 1853 and closed in 1901 when the Estes School opened at the corner of Division St. and Ward Rd. Elementary students were taught on the first floor, while 7th- and 8th-graders were on the second.

7 The Godfrey Schock House, at 140 Division St., is also a private residence. This home is built entirely of local stone. Godfrey Schock was a stonemason who came to Kelleys Island from Germany in 1918. He built many stone structures on the island and on the mainland, including the war memorial in Memorial Park, five houses, the kitchen and dormitory buildings at the Kelley Mansion, and two churches, one in Marblehead and one in Detroit. He also built the house just to the south of his own, in 1937.

8 On the southeast corner of Division St. and Chapel St. is the water tower, visible from miles around.

9 The Zion United Methodist Church is located on the northeast corner of Division St. and Chapel St. Constructed in 1893, it originally served a congregation of Evangelical United Brethen.

10 The Old Stone Church, at 222 Division St., is 400 feet north. It was built in 1867 by members of the German Reformed congregation. Services were held here until the early 1900s. In 1985 the Kelleys Island Historical Association purchased the building for its headquarters and museum. The museum and gift shop are open during the tourist season, and on weekends in the spring and fall.

Return to the Division St./Chapel St. intersection and turn east onto Chapel St.

11 On Chapel St., at the north end of Addison Rd., is St. Michael's Roman Catholic Church. In 1863 the original "little stone church" was built. By 1915 the building was enlarged to accommodate the growing congregation. In recent years it has been served by visiting priests.

Turn right onto Addison Rd. to return to the parking area and the municipal park. ■

I believe a leaf of grass is no less than the journey-work of the stars.

—Walt Whitman, Leaves of Grass

APPENDIX A

Generalized Geological Column for Northeast Ohio

Age	Rock Unit	Section	Years before the Present
Quaternary	Glacial Deposits		20,000 or less
Pennsylvanian	Sharon Conglomerate		320 Million
Mississippian (Cuyahoga Formation)	Meadville Member		350 Million
Mississippian (Cuyahoga Formation)	Strongsville Member		350 Million
Mississippian (Cuyahoga Formation)	Sharpsville Member		350 Million
Mississippian (Cuyahoga Formation)	Orangeville Member		350 Million
Devonian	Berea Sandstone		360 Million
Devonian	Bedford Formation	Euclid Bluestone	360 Million
Devonian	Cleveland Shale		360 Million
Devonian	Chagrin Shale		360 Million

Legend: conglomerate, siltstone, crossbedding, sandstone, red shale, black shale, gray shale

Source: Joseph Hannibal, Cleveland Museum of Natural History, 1996

Acknowledgments

Second Edition

We owe a debt of gratitude to Karen Fuller and the rest of the staff at Gray & Company for their support and patience in working with us throughout this revised and updated edition.

Like many successful outings in the woods, this too was a group effort. We would like to thank our volunteer hike reviewers. We not only enjoyed working with our friends again, but also were pleased to make new hiking acquaintances in the process. Larry and Sophia Morton rehiked all of the Medina County hikes and recommended additions for that county. Carl and JoAnn Bochmann covered Geauga County. Kim Norley (and family) provided assistance with some of the Lake County hikes and helped with suggested map changes. Glenn Harper and Carole Endres checked out hikes on Kelleys Island and gathered research material. Lynn Schreiber and Warren Davis rehiked many of the hikes in Summit County. Rodger Judson pitched in at the last minute on a few trails in Lake and Portage Counties. And last, but far from least, Flora Burkholder was invaluable. She rehiked and rewrote all the hikes in Lorain and Erie Counties as well as providing information and making suggestions on some of the new areas in both counties (more, unfortunately than we had room for). Her thoroughness and expertise, especially on the geology of Northeast Ohio, are evident in the hikes of those two counties.

Of course, no acknowledgments page in a book such as this would be complete without thanking the professionals who plan, design, construct, and maintain the excellent parks, nature preserves, historical areas, and memorials that make this part of Ohio an outstanding place to live and work. In particular we would like to thank those who met with us and provided information on their districts: Erie MetroParks's director, Jonathan Granville; Portage County Park District's director, Christine Craycroft; and Nelson Ledges State Park's assistant manager Norman Swann.

We also wish to thank the many individuals who supplied us with information and enthusiasm for the places visited in the six new chapters. For historical information for the Medina town hike, we are indebted to Janet Senkar and the Community Design Committee of Medina; for help with the Allardale chapter, we thank Richard E. Heaton, ASLA, landscape architect with the Medina County Park District. We are grateful to Lois VerDeen, naturalist and program supervisor with Erie MetroParks, for her invaluable information and insights regarding Castalia Quarry Reserve. For the Kent chapter, we thank the late James F. Caccamo, former executive director of the Kent Historical Society for historical background on the town, and Cathy Ricks of the environmental education division, Kent Parks and Recreation, for supplying information on Riveredge Park and the historic Kent Jail. We are grateful to Doris Cook, tour director for Geauga County Historical Society's Century Village, for information and support on the Burton hike, as well as for leading us to Gerald Rouge, who supplied material produced by the Tuesday Club that formed the basis of our hike in Burton. Doris also led us to Donna Keeler, tour guide, and Lee Stone, Burton Chamber of Commerce, who both shared more information about Burton. We thank Ann Dewald, director of the Indian Museum of Lake County, Ohio, for information on the museum and Native American history used in the Painesville hike. And finally, we are deeply grateful to our good friend Glenn Harper, Preservation Services Manager, Ohio Historic Preservation Office, Ohio Historical Society, who helped us with information on properties listed in the National Register of Historic Places as well as insights into architectural history and styles in Ohio.

—Rob & Peg Bobel

First Edition

First and foremost I wish to acknowledge the special contributions to *Beyond Cleveland On Foot* by my late husband and co-author of *Cleveland On Foot*, Harry M. Cameron. His help was there whenever I needed it. He walked the trails with me, reviewed chapters after they were written, and supported me in every way. His expert knowledge of the intricacies of word processing was invaluable. I could not have written this book without him.

I am also indebted to many people who helped us put together *Beyond Cleveland On Foot*, but especially:

Flora Burkholder, who supplied the bulk of information for walks and hikes in Lorain and Erie Counties. I am especially indebted to Flora because she prepared detailed maps, trail descriptions, and geological and historical information, and then hiked and re-hiked most of the trails in Lorain and Erie Counties with me. She also reviewed the chapters describing hikes in these counties to ensure their accuracy.

Charles Briggs, who reviewed chapters describing hikes in Metro Parks Serving Summit County and walked several trails with me.

Thomas Vince, who reviewed the chapter on Hudson Village for historical accuracy.

Jack Gieck, who provided substantial information and suggestions for, and carefully reviewed, the chapter on Cascade Locks.

Bruce Norton, for his review of the Cascade Locks chapter.

Jennifer Maurer and Edith McNally, who supplied information about Cascade Locks.

Diane Chesnut and Roze Smith, who reviewed the chapter on Vermilion for historical accuracy.

Geoffrey Blodgett, Danforth Professor of History, Oberlin College, who reviewed the walk in Oberlin and supplied valuable textual suggestions.

Ran Taylor, for his review of the Oberlin chapter.

William Gray, for guiding me through Portage Lakes State Park.

Jim Sprague, for the information on Schumacher Woods.

Patricia Morse, Naturalist, Lake Metroparks, who reviewed maps and chapters describing hikes in Lake Metroparks.

Doreen Brennan, Public Relations, Lake Metroparks, for supplying photographs, and to all the talented photographers in Lake County.

Walter Starcher, Director, Metro Parks Serving Summit County, for reviewing maps and chapters describing hikes in the Metro Parks.

John R. O'Meara, Director, Geauga Park District, who reviewed maps and chapters describing hikes in Geauga Park District.

Gary Gerrone, Naturalist Supervisor, who reviewed maps and chapters describing hikes in Lorain County Metro Parks.

Elinor Polster, who walked many of the trails with me and provided useful information from the hiker's viewpoint.

Joseph T. Hannibal, Curator of Invertebrate Paleontology, Cleveland Museum of Natural History, who helped clarify geological information and supplied the chart in Appendix A.

Daniel T. Melcher, President of the Audubon Society of Greater Cleveland, who supplied substantial help with the chapter on the Aurora Sanctuary.

I also wish to acknowledge the contributions of staff members in all the county park districts who were helpful in supplying information and photographs.

Last, but not least, I wish to express my appreciation to fellow hikers in the Buckeye Trail Association, Cleveland Hiking Club, St. Paul's Walking Group, and others with whom I have spent many pleasant hours enjoying our great outdoors.

—Patience Cameron Hoskins

Photo Credits

Photos are courtesy of following:

Bibliography

Banks, P., and R. Feldmann, eds. *Guide to the Geology of Northeastern Ohio.* Cleveland, OH: Northern Ohio Geological Society, 1970.

Blodgett, Geoffrey. *Oberlin College Architecture: A Short History.* Oberlin, OH: Oberlin College, 1979.

Bowe, L. M. and Herdendorf, C.F. *A Glacial Grooves Fossil Walk on Kelleys Island.*

Brockman, C. Frank. *Trees of North America.* New York: Golden Press, 1968.

Carlson, E. *Minerals of Ohio.* Columbus, OH: Ohio Department. of Natural Resources, Division of Geological Survey, 1991.

Cuyahoga Valley Trails Council. *Trail Guide Handbook, Cuyahoga Valley National Recreation Area.* Akron, OH: Cuyahoga Valley Trails Council, 1991.

Ellis, William Donohue. *The Cuyahoga.* Dayton, OH: Landfall Press, 1966.

Field Guide to the Birds of North America. Washington, D.C.: National Geographic Society, 1983.

Folzenlogen, Robert. *Hiking Ohio: Scenic Trails of the Buckeye State.* Glendale, OH: Willow Press, 1990.

Friends of Harbour Town 1837, Vermilion, OH. Pamphlets and maps. Vermilion, OH: The Friends, n.d.

Geauga Park District. Maps and brochures. Geauga County, OH: Geauga Park District, n.d.

Gieck, Jack. Personal communication, August 1995.

———. *A Photo Album of Ohio's Canal Era, 1825–1913.* Kent, OH: Kent State University Press, 1988.

Grant, H. Roger. *Ohio on the Move: Transportation in the Buckeye State.* Athens, Ohio: Ohio University Press, 2000.

Grismer, Karl. *Akron and Summit County.* Akron, OH: Summit County Historical Society, 1952.

Haddad, Gladys. *Ohio's Western Reserve: A Regional Reader.* Kent, OH: Kent State University Press, 1988.

Hartman, Roy. "History of Carlisle" in *Lorain County Metro Parks Bulletin.* Lorain County, OH: Lorain County Metro Parks, 1980.

Hatcher, Harlan. *The Western Reserve.* Kent, OH: Kent State University Press, 1991.

Hoskins, Patience. *Cleveland On Foot, 3rd Edition.* Cleveland, OH: Gray & Company, Publishers, 1992–2002.

Hudson Library and Historical Society. Leaflets on Hudson History. Hudson, OH: Hudson Library and Historical Society, n.d.

Izant, Grace Goulder. *Hudson's Heritage.* Kent, OH: Kent State University Press, 1985.

Kelleys Island Chamber of Commerce. Brochure, maps. Kelleys Island, OH: Kelleys Island Chamber of Commerce, 1995.

Knepper, George W. *Ohio and Its People*. Kent, OH: Kent State University Press, 1989.

Lafferty, Michael B., ed. *Ohio's Natural Heritage*. Columbus, OH: Ohio Academy of Science, 1979.

Lake Metroparks. Maps and brochures. Lake County, OH: Lake Metroparks, 1988–93.

Linhardt, Becky. *Kelleys Island, An Island for All Seasons*. Kelleys Island, OH: Kelleys Cove, 1995.

Lorain County Metro Parks. Maps and brochures. Lorain County Metro Parks, 1994.

Lorain County Visitor's Bureau. "African-American Heritage Tour." Lorain, OH: Lorain County Visitor's Bureau, 1995.

Lupold, Harry F., and Gladys Haddad, eds. *Ohio's Western Reserve: A Regional Reader*. Kent, Ohio: Kent State University Press, 1988.

Medina County Park District. Maps and brochures. Medina County, OH: Medina County Park District, n.d.

Metro Parks, Serving Summit County. Mini-maps and brochures. Akron, OH: Metro Parks, 1992.

Newcomb, Lawrence. *Wildflower Guide*. Boston: Little, Brown, 1977.

Oberlin Area Chamber of Commerce. *Oberlin, a guide to the "Most Cosmopolitan Small Town in America."* Oberlin, OH: Oberlin Area Chamber of Commerce, n.d.

Oberlin College, Admissions Office. *Oberlin College of Arts and Sciences*. Oberlin College, Admissions Office, 1994.

———. *Oberlin Conservatory of Music*. Oberlin College, Admissions Office, 1994.

Ohio Department of Natural Resources. *A Glacial Grooves Fossil Walk on Kelleys Island*. Columbus, OH: Ohio Department of Natural Resources, n.d.

———. *Ohio's Trees*. Columbus, OH: Ohio Department of Natural Resources, 1990.

———. *Ohio's Natural Areas and Preserves: A Directory*. Columbus, OH: Ohio Department of Natural Resources, 1987.

Ramey, Ralph. *Fifty Hikes in Ohio*. Woodstock, VT: Countryman Press, 1990.

Rosche, L., ed. *Birds of the Cleveland Region*, 2nd ed. Cleveland, OH: Cleveland Museum of Natural History, 1988.

Szubski, Rosemary N., ed. *A Natural History of Lake County, Ohio*. Cleveland, OH: Cleveland Museum of Natural History, 1993.

Weber, Art. *Ohio State Parks, A Guide to Ohio's State Parks*. Saginaw, MI: Glovebox Guidebook Publishing, 1994.

Western Reserve Academy. *Reserve* [Catalog]. Hudson, OH: Western Reserve Academy, 1994.

Index

Cleveland Guides & Gifts
More good books from Gray & Company

Try one of these other great books about Cleveland ...

Cleveland On Foot / Self-guided walking tours through Greater Cleveland's neighborhoods, suburbs, and metroparks. *Patience Cameron Hoskins* / $14.95 softcover (each)

52 Romantic Outings in Greater Cleveland / Easy-to-follow "recipes" for romance—for a lunch hour, an evening, or a full day together. *Miriam Carey* / $13.95 softcover

Bed & Breakfast Getaways from Cleveland / 80 charming small inns perfect for an easy weekend or evening away from home. *Doris Larson* / $14.95 softcover

Cleveland Ethnic Eats / Details on hundreds of authentic ethnic restaurants and markets—taste the flavors of the world without leaving town! *Laura Taxel* / $13.95 softcover

One Tank Trips (Book 1)
More of Neil Zurcher's One Tank Trips (Book 2)
One Tank Trips Road Food (Book 3)
Hundreds of unusual nearby getaway ideas in three books by Northeast Ohio's favorite TV travel reporter. Each book features different attractions. *Neil Zurcher* / $13.95 softcover (each)

Ohio Oddities / This armchair guide describes the offbeat, way out, wacky, oddball, and otherwise curious roadside attractions of the Buckeye State. *Neil Zurcher* / $13.95 softcover

Cleveland Family Fun / Great ideas for places to go and things to do with kids of all ages. Written by parents, for parents. *Jennifer Stoffel* / $13.95 softcover

Cleveland Cemeteries / Meet Cleveland's most interesting "permanent" residents in these 61 outdoor history parks. *Vicki Blum Vigil* / $13.95 softcover

The View from Pluto / Terry Pluto's best newspaper columns about Northeast Ohio sports—Indians, Browns, Cavs, and more—from 1990–2002. $24.95 hardcover

Indians on the Game / Quotations from favorite Cleveland ballplayers give an insider's look at the game of baseball. *Wayne Stewart* / $9.95 softcover

Omar! / Cleveland Indians star shortstop Omar Vizquel retells his life story on and off the field in this candid baseball memoir. Includes 41 color photos. *with Bob Dyer* / $14.95 softcover

Cleveland Sports Trivia Quiz / Test your knowledge with these 500 brain-teasing questions and answers on all kinds of Cleveland sports. *Tim Long* / $6.95 softcover

On Being Brown / Thoughtful essays and interviews exploring what it means to be a true fan of the Cleveland Browns. *Scott Huler* / $18.95 hardcover, $10.95 softcover

Cleveland Golfer's Bible / All of Greater Cleveland's golf courses and driving ranges are described in this essential guide for any golfer. *John Tidyman* / $13.95 softcover

Golf Getaways from Cleveland / 50 great golf trips just a short car ride from home. Plan easy weekends, business meetings, reunions, other gatherings. *John Tidyman* / $14.95 softcover

Cleveland Fishing Guide / Best public fishing spots in Northeast Ohio, what kind of fish you'll find, and how to catch them. Directory of fishing resources. *John Barbo* / $13.95 softcover

Continued ...

Photo from *Cleveland: A Portrait of the City*, by Jonathan Wayne